KRISTI L. WILEY (B.S., Santa Clara University; M.A. and Ph.D., University of California at Berkeley) is a visiting lecturer at the University of California at Berkeley. She teaches courses on Indian religions and religion and ecology. Her area of specialization in Jainism is karma theory. She has published articles in *Approaches to Jaina Studies* (ed. N. K. Wagle and Olle Qvarnström), *Doctrines and Dialogues* (ed. Peter Flügel), *Essays in Jaina Philosophy and Religion* (ed. Piotr Balcerowicz), *Jainism and Early Buddhism* (ed. Olle Qvarnström), *Jainism and Ecology* (ed. Christopher Key Chapple), and *Philosophy East and West.* She is a member of the American Academy of Religion and the American Oriental Society.

THE A-TO-Z OF JAINISM

KRISTI L. WILEY

VISION BOOKS

www.visionbooksindia.com

www.visionbooksindia.com

(Authorised edition for sale in the
Indian sub-continent and South-East Asia.)

ISBN 10: 81-7094-690-5
ISBN 13: 978-81-7094-690-8

First Edition 2006
Reprinted 2014

Published in arrangement with
Scarecrow Press, Inc., U.S.A.
by
Vision Books Pvt. Ltd.
(Incorporating Orient Paperbacks & CARING imprints)
24 Feroze Gandhi Road, Lajpat Nagar 3
New Delhi 110024, India.
Phone: (+91-11) 2984 0821 / 22
e-mail: visionbooks@gmail.com

Printed at
Anand Sons
C 88, Ganesh Nagar, Pandav Nagar Complex
New Delhi 110 091, India.

To

John Cort and Paul Dundas

for their encouragement and support

Contents

Editor's Foreword

One would like to believe that the important thing about a religion is not its size but the contributions it has made in the past and continues to make at present. The Jains are a rather small community, numbering about three-and-a-half million, not even half a percent of the Indian population. But the values they have promoted are precious. Foremost among these is the duty to minimize harm not only to other human beings, but also to animals and plants, or indeed to oneself. The acceptance that no one view is always right and that every issue must be examined from different perspectives is understood today to be a form of intellectual non-harming or ahiṃsā. In order to minimize harm, one should voluntarily place limits on possessions and thus one should not waste or squander. These virtues are far from outmoded; rather, they lie at the root of many modern movements which they can enrich: nonviolence and peaceful resistance, conservation and environmentalism, charity and community service, and animal rights and vegetarianism. All of this makes Jainism significant not only for its members, but also for others.

As in other religious traditions, there have been periods of greatness, decline and renewal, and theological conflicts and factionalism leading to divisions within the mendicant and lay communities. The history and values, concepts and scriptures, eminent mendicant and lay leaders and scholars are all included in the dictionary section. There are also entries on significant places, institutions, and social or cultural factors. This is easier to grasp thanks to a comprehensive introduction and a chronology that covers the amazing span of over 2,500 years, making Jainism one of the oldest religions in this series. The bibliography, thanks to a recent spurt of scholarly interest, can provide many leads to further reading.

It is amazing how much more can be learned from a book of a few hundred pages as opposed to the few pages, or barely a few paragraphs, that are usually devoted to the topic in general encyclopedias. This shows the value of such a series. But *The A-to-Z of Jainism* is a very worthwhile work in its own right. It not only covers a lot of ground looking into crucial details that are often overlooked, but it presents countless complicated concepts in a sufficiently clear and concise manner so that they can be understood by newcomers and still appreciated by initiates. The author, Kristi L. Wiley, lectures on Indian religions at the University of California, Berkeley, with a specialization in Jainism. She has also published a number of articles and chapters on that subject. But there are always things one does not know and it is fortunate that the Jain scholars, unlike those in many other disciplines, actually cooperate and contribute to the collective wisdom. And Dr. Wiley has wisely benefited from this, just as we can benefit from her efforts.

Jon Woronoff
Series Editor

Preface

When I was invited to prepare this historical dictionary, I was pleased to hear that Scarecrow Press wanted to include a volume on Jainism in its Religions, Philosophies, and Movements series. In recent times there has been a growing international interest in this religious tradition, rooted in the principle of ahiṃsā, that has existed as an unbroken tradition on the Indian subcontinent for more than 2,500 years. I knew that such a volume would add to the growing research and literature on Jainism in English that has appeared since the 1990s. I am honored to have the opportunity to produce a work that incorporates all aspects of Jainism.

I was fortunate to have as guides two volumes in this series, *The A-to-Z of Buddhism*, by Charles S. Prebish (volume 1) and *The A-to-Z of Hinduism,* by Bruce M. Sullivan (volume 13). Both were valuable sources for deciding what entries to include in the dictionary and for the organization of the bibliography. I share their sentiments about this undertaking, that it is indeed a daunting task. As Prebish noted in his preface, "The dilemma one confronts squarely at the outset is the overwhelmig mass of material to be assembled and the enormously hard choices that must be made in determining just precisely what to include."

What has made this task a joy rather than a burden has been the support and encouragement of other scholars of Jainism, and I have viewed this as a collaborative project from the beginning. John Cort and Paul Dundas have always been there for me, from the time that we circulated lists of terms and wrestled with what to include and what to cut. It was my good fortune that the second edition of Paul Dundas's *The Jains* was published before my writing was complete. His work provided me with an up-to-date survey text on Jainism written from a historical perspective to use as a reference. John Cort had agreed to assist me with entries on which little was available outside of India. Whenever he received my many requests for help, he promptly sent me copies of relevant material from his vast collection. Because of his willingness to help, I was able to include a number of entries on Jain mendicants and Jain scholars in India who have made significant contributions to Jain scholarship but are not well-known in the West. He agreed to review the first draft of the manuscript and offered many excellent suggestions for improvement. Peter Flügel also has made an important contribution to this volume by providing me with material on the Sthānakavāsīs, Śvetāmbara Terāpanthīs, and A. M. Paṭel, and by sending me a copy of his "Democratic Trends in Jain Monasticism," to be published in *Doctrines and Dialogues: Studies in Jain History and Culture*. The population statistics for the Jain mendicant community are taken from this article. I would like to thank Nalini Balbir for sharing her knowledge with me on the Chedasūtras, Piotr Balcerowicz for a manuscript copy of *Essays in Jaina Philosophy and Religion*, Sin Fujinaga for material on Japanese scholars of Jainism, and Robert Zydenbos for current information on Digambara bhaṭṭārakas and maṭhas. I am most appreciative for the material that I received from Gyan Chand Biltiwala, Jaipur, on the biographies of several Digambara munis and on Digambara associations in India; and for the the biography of Hiralal Kapadia from Lalit Kumar and Jitendra B. Shah of the L. D. Institute of Indology, Ahmedabad. I would like to extend a special thanks to Padmanabh S. Jaini who patiently answered the many questions that I had for him over the course of my writing.

I also am grateful to those who assisted me in the technical aspects of producing this volume. Vinita Singh graciously volunteered her time for proofreading and reference checking. My husband, Jim Wiley, agreed to provide computer assistance, even though he was aware of a karmic incompatibility between myself and modern technology. He has calmly endured not only my moods from the ups and downs of writing, but also my frustrations with software glitches. He and Carlos Hueso produced the camera-ready layout and the map. Jim also worked wonders with Adobe Photoshop, making it possible to include a few of my photos in this volume. Finally, I would like to thank Jon Woronoff, series editor, Kim Tabor, acquisitions editor, and Nicole Carty, editorial assistant, at Scarecrow Press for their advice, assistance, and support for this project.

It is my hope that scholars who use this dictionary will find it useful for their research and teaching and that students will be inspired to investigate some aspect of Jainism in more depth.

Reader's Notes

PRONUNCIATION GUIDE

Most of the foreign language terms and names in this volume are in Sanskrit. Early Jain texts were written in a Prākrit language. Śvetāmbara texts were written in Ardhamāgadhī, and Digambara texts were written in Jain Śaurasenī. However, it is standard Jain practice to use Sanskrit for titles of the texts and for the terms found in them.

Scholars have established a system of transliteration for the 26 letters of the Latin alphabet to represent the 49 letters of Sanskrit that uses additional markings, called diacritical marks, to distinguish the letters from each other. The following guidelines are based on the pronunciation guide in Bruce M. Sullivan's *The A-to-Z of Hinduism,* volume 13 in this series.

1. Vowels and diphthongs

• a	is pronounced like	a in mica
• ā		a in ah
• i		i in pit
• ī		i in police
• u		u in full
• ū		u in rule
• e		e in grey
• o		o in tote
• ai		ai in aisle
• au		ow in how

Note: ai is pronounced like e in grey in modern north Indian languages, such as Hindi and Gujarati.

2. Consonants

(a) Consonants with dots under them are called retroflex or cerebral consonants (ṭ, ṭh, ḍ, ḍh, ṇ, ṣ). They are pronounced by placing the tip of the tongue on the roof the mouth at its highest point. The semivowels ṛ and ḷ sound like ri and li, so Ṛṣabha is pronounced like Rishabha.
(b) Aspirated consonants (kh, gh, ch, jh, ṭh, ḍh, th, dh, ph, bh) are sounded by expelling breath as the consonant is pronounced. Thus, th in artha sounds like art-house.
(c) Nasal consonants are of two types. The ñ sounds like the Spanish ñ. It follows the consonant j, forming the conjunct jñ. It can be pronounced in two ways: either prajñā like pragnyā or prajñā like prajnyā. The nasal ṅ sounds like sing. The nasal ṃ takes on the quality of the consonant that follows it, so Sāṃkhya sounds like Sāngkhya. However, the ṃ in saṃsāram is sounded with the lips closed and sounds like sumsāra.
(d) Indic languages have three sibilants. The ś sounds like sh, so Śvetāmbara is pronounced Shvetāmbara. Often in works that do not use diacritical marks h is added to the word, so it would appear as Shvetambara. The ṣ is also pronounced as sh with the tongue placed as described above in (a). The unmarked s sounds like the s in so.
(e) The consonant c has the sound of ch, so candra is pronounced chandra.
(f) At the beginning of a word or between vowels, the v sounds like a v in English, but combined with other consonants it takes on a sound halfway between v and w.
(g) Doubled consonants are both pronounced.
(h) Other consonants sound like their English equivalents.

SPELLING CONVENTIONS

The medial and final short a is pronounced in Prākrit and Sanskrit but generally is silent in Hindi and Gujarati, except when it follows a consonant cluster. Some authors spell these words as they are pronounced by speakers of these modern languages, for example, Tīrthaṅkar, not Tīrthaṅkara; Mahāvīr, not Mahāvīra; and Sthānakvāsī, not Sthānakavāsī. For purposes of standardization, in this dictionary most terms are written as they are pronounced in Sanskrit, retaining the medial and final short a. Thus, in this dictionary one finds Śvetāmbara Mūrtipūjaka Tapā Gaccha, while elsewhere one might find Śvetāmbar Mūrtipūjak Tapā Gacch. I have deviated from this general rule in several instances when the non-Sanskritic spelling has been adopted by the vast majority of scholars in contemporary writing. Therefore, I have used Jain, not Jaina; and Panth, not Pantha. For individuals who lived in more recent times and movements associated with them, I have usually followed the spellings in Paul Dundas's *The Jains*, second revised edition, 2002. Thus, in this dictionary one finds Tāraṇ Svāmī, not Tāraṇa Svāmī. In some instances in the entry headings, the medial a is offset with parentheses, especially in names that could be listed either way in various electronic library holdings. When I found authors in World Cat, I have used that spelling in the entry heading so that readers can locate holdings in academic libraries.

2. Variations in spelling also occur with Sanskrit words ending with "in," for example, Sthānakavāsin. This is the stem form of the word as listed in a Sanskrit dictionary, but many authors use the masculine nominative form (-vāsī). However, occasionally the neuter (-vāsi) may be found. In this dictionary, the -vāsī form is generally used.
3. Panth (path, way) is a term used for a group that follows the teachings of a religious leader (e.g., Tāraṇ Svāmī Panth, Terāpanth). In Sanskrit, the "in" ending is used for an individual who belongs to this group, (e.g., Terāpanthin). Thus, authors use Terāpanthī, although occasionally the neuter, Terāpanthi, is found. By extension, this word is commonly used for the group itself. Therefore, Terāpanth, Terāpanthī, or Terāpanthi may be found for the Śvetāmbara sectarian tradition started by Ācārya Bhikṣu. In this dictionary, the ī form is used for these sectarian traditions.
4. Within both the Śvetāmbara and Digambara sectarian traditions, there is a subsect called Terāpanthī. They are differentiated by writing Śvetāmbara Terāpanthī and Digambara Terāpanthī.
5. As mentioned in the pronunciation guide, ś sound like sh. In works that do not use diacritical marks, h often is added to the word, so Śvetāmbara would be written as Shvetambara. Because this dictionary uses diacritics, the term Śvetāmbara would follow the term sūtra. Likewise, c sounds like ch, so candra can be written as chandra. The ca form is used in this dictionary.
6. Diacritics are used for ancient place names and for modern city names that are dictionary entries. In descriptive writing, for modern names of other cities and states, English forms as printed on maps with no diacritical markings are used.
7. Diacritics for names of languages follow conventions in Bruce M. Sullivan's *The A-to-Z of Hinduism,* volume 13 in this series.
8. Italicization has been dropped for Sanskrit words. Titles of books are italicized.

MENDICANT NAMES AND POPULATION STATISTICS

1. In conversation, a mendicant is addressed in an honorific manner by prefacing his mendicant name and rank with the honorific term śrī (blessed) and appending the honorific -jī to his name, and then giving him the additional titles mahārāj sāhab, "Great King and Master." Therefore, Muni Jambūvijaya would be referred to as Muni Śrī Jambūvijayajī Mahārāj Sāhab, and his name may be written in this manner as well. For Digambara monks, the auspicious number 108 is often used, for example, Muni Śrī 108 Supārśvasāgarajī. As is commonly done in academic writing, in this dictionary these honorifics are omitted except when -jī has become part of a mendicant's name.

A number of the mendicants found in the dictionary belong to the Tapā Gaccha, the largest mendicant lineage in the Śvetāmbara Mūrtipūjaka (image-worshipping) sectarian tradition. At the time of initiation into this mendicant lineage, a man receives a new religious name. Part of the name is specific to him, and part indicates the branch of the Tapā Gaccha that he belongs to, either the Sāgara or the Vijaya branch, which is appended to his name. There are four ranks of male mendicants in the Tapā Gaccha: muni, paṁnyāsa, upādhyāya, and ācārya. Two of these ranks have an additional title (paṁnyāsa-gaṇi and ācārya-sūri) that is appended to the name. It can be written together or separately; thus, both Ācārya Buddhisāgarasūri and Ācārya Buddhisāgara Sūri are found. In this dictionary, the title is appended directly to the name.

3. In indexes in academic works, titles usually are not used for mendicants who lived in the earlier centuries but often are used for mendicants who lived more recently. I have included the title for mendicants in the entry headings beginning in the 11th century when the mendicant lineages in existence today began to be formed. The entry would appear as Buddhisāgarasūri, Ācārya.

4. The names of mendicants usually change if they receive a second initiation into a different sectarian tradition. For example, Muni Ānandavijaya of the Tapā Gaccha had first taken initiation in the Sthānakavāsī tradition as Ātmārāmjī. In some mendicant lineages, the name of a mendicant changes if he receives seniormost initiation as ācārya. For example, Muni Nathmal of the Śvetāmbara Terāpanthī tradition now is known as Ācārya Mahāprajña. In the Vijaya branch of the Tapā Gaccha, it is common to reverse the branch and personal names upon promotion to ācārya. For example, Muni Ānandavijaya became Ācārya Vijayānandasūri. In this dictionary, the entry is found under

Vijayānandasūri, Ācārya. However, elsewhere his name could be indexed as Ānandasūri, Ācārya Vijaya.

5. Titles for nuns vary according to sectarian tradition. Sādhvī is used for Śvetāmbara Mūrtipūjaka and Terāpanthī nuns, Sādhvī or Mahāsatī for Sthānakavāsīs nuns, and Āryikā for Digambara nuns.
6. The numbers of mendicants in each of the mendicant lineages are taken from an essay by Peter Flügel entitled "Democratic Trends in Jain Monasticism," to be published in *Doctrines and Dialogues: Studies in Jain History and Culture*. He bases his study on the annual Samagra Jaina Cāturmāsi Sūcī, which is produced and published by B. U. Jain. Peter has noted that he has counted only those ascetics who were listed individually and not B. U. Jain's considerably higher estimates, which may represent a more accurate picture.

ABBREVIATIONS

Dig. = Digambara
Pkt. = Prākrit
Skt. = Sanskrit
Śvet. = Śvetāmbara

GENERAL

Users of this volume should note that cross-references in each dictionary entry are printed in **boldface** type.

The Jain Scriptures

The Jain scriptures, which are known as the Āgama ("canon") or Siddhānta ("doctrine"), are divided into two main categories of texts. Aṅgas ("Limbs") form the body of scripture. According to tradition, knowledge contained in the Aṅgas is transmitted by a Tīrthaṅkara directly to his chief mendicant disciples (gaṇadharas), who systematize his teachings into the 12 Aṅgas. His gaṇadharas also compose texts called Pūrvas ("Ancient"), which are said to contain the first teachings of a Tīrthaṅkara. The other main category of texts is called Aṅgabāhya ("Outside the Aṅgas"). They are composed later by mendicant elders (sthaviras). These texts may be grouped into various subcategories, such as the Upāṅgas, Chedasūtras, Mūlasūtras, and Prakīrṇakasūtras. In historical times, the knowledge contained in the scriptures is based on the teaching of Mahāvīra, the 24th and final Tīrthaṅkara of this era.

The term canon is problematic because there is not a single authoritative list of texts accepted as sacred scripture by all of the sectarian traditions. In most discussions of the Jain scriptures, it is assumed that there is a fixed canon of 45 texts dating from the 5th century C.E. when a final redaction was made at the Council of Valabhī, in Saurashtra, under the leadership of Devarddhigaṇi Kṣamāśramaṇa. This set of texts is accepted by all Śvetāmbaras either in its original form (all 45 texts) by the Mūrtipūjakas, or in a modified form (32 texts) by the Sthānakavāsīs and Terāpanthīs. However, there is no record of the texts codified at the final redaction at Valabhī. Although the Aṅga and Upāṅga texts are uniform in the various listings, there is variation from list to list in the other categories of Aṅgabāhya texts (the Chedasūtras, Mūlasūtras, and Prakīrṇakasūtras) with respect to the subcategories of texts, the texts included in the subcategories, and the total number of texts. The earliest reference to the listing of the 45 texts that is considered normative today dates from the 13th century. None of these texts are accepted by Digambaras, who have questioned the authenticity of the recitations and redaction, which may have occurred in the absence of their mendicant leaders.

The term scripture is also problematic because there are different opinions regarding what should be considered as authoritative. For example, Ānandghan, a 16th-century devotional poet, maintained that the following were interrelated and thus authoritative: the basic scriptural texts (Āgama or sūtra), the four classical modes of commentary on these texts, and the interpretation of these as found in the doctrine and practice followed in an authoritative teacher lineage (paraṃparā).

ŚVETĀMBARA ĀGAMAS

The Śvetāmbara Āgamas are written in a vernacular Prākrit language called Ardhamāgadhī. Following common practice, titles are given in the Sanskritized forms with the Prākrit titles in parentheses.

I. Pūrvas ("Old Texts")

Fourteen "ancient" texts, all of which are extinct. Portions of the Pūrvas were incorporated into the 12th Aṅga, the *Dṛṣṭivāda*, which became extinct prior to the redaction of the canon.

II. Aṅgas ("Limbs")

1. *Ācārāṅga Sūtra* (*Āyāraṅga Sutta*). Mendicant conduct, obligatory mendicant vows, instructions on avoiding injury to minute life-forms, and on obtaining requisites of food, clothing, lodging, etc. Narrative of Mahāvīra's life.
2. *Sūtrakṛtāṅga* (*Sūyagaḍaṅga*). Refutation of heretical doctrines.
3. *Sthānāṅga* (*Ṭhāṇaṅga*). Numerical classification of subject matter from one through 10 (e.g., four types of mendicants, seven schisms, etc.).
4. *Samavāyāṅga* (*Samavāyaṅga*). Numerical classification of subject matter, a continuation of the third Aṅga (e.g., description of the 12 Aṅgas, names of the 24 Tīrthaṅkaras of this era).
5. *Vyākhāprajñapti* (*Viyāhapannatti*) or *Bhagavatī* (*Bhagavaī*). In questions asked by Indrabhūti Gautama and the answers of Mahāvīra, discussions of a wide variety of topics (e.g., soul [jīva], matter [pudgala], heavenly beings [devas], hell-beings [nārakis], etc.). Account of Mahāvīra's encounters with the Ājīvika teacher Makkhali Gosāla.

6. *Jñātṛdharmakathāḥ* (*Nāyādhammakahāo*). Religious narratives (dharma-kathā), including that of Mallī, the 19th Tīrthaṅkara of this era, who was female according to the Śvetāmbara tradition.
7. *Upāsakadaśāḥ* (*Uvāsagadasāo*). Lives of 10 exemplary laymen (upāsakas), including that of Ānanda.
8. *Antakṛddaśāḥ* (*Antagaḍadasāo*). Narratives of 10 mendicants who attained liberation through undergoing extreme austerities. Includes stories of Vāsudeva Kṛṣṇa, who according to Jain mythology was the cousin of Nemi, the 22nd Tīrthaṅkara of this era.
9. *Anuttaraupapātikadaśāḥ* (*Aṇuttarovavāiyadasāo*). Narratives of 10 mendicants who attained rebirth (upapāta) in the highest heavenly abodes, the anuttara heavens.
10. *Praśnavyākaraṇāni* (*Paṇhāvāgaraṇāiṃ*). Discussion of the five great vows of mendicants (mahāvratas).
11. *Vipākaśruta* (*Vivāgasuyaṃ*). Narratives of karma and the results (vipāka) of good and bad deeds performed in previous lives.
12. *Dṛṣṭivāda* (*Diṭṭhivāya*) (extinct). Thought to have contained sections of the Pūrva texts.

III. Aṅgabāhya ("Subsidiary Canon")

A. Upāṅgas (Uvaṅgas) ("Subsidiary to the Aṅgas"). These texts contain more detailed developments of points discussed in the Aṅgas and narratives addressed to the laity. Their ordering is in accordance with the theoretical association of each Upāṅga with one of the Aṅgas.

1. *Aupapātika Sūtra* (*Uvavāiya Sutta*). Reception of Mahāvīra by King Kūṇika when he stayed in a park outside the city of Campā. Narrative of non-Jain mendicants who fasted to death and attained rebirth in heavenly abodes.
2. *Rājapraśnīya* (*Rāyapaseṇaijja*). Narrative of King Pāesi (Prasenajit) of Seyaviyā, who questions Keśi, a disciple of Pārśvanātha, the 23rd Tīrthaṅkara of this era, about the nature of the soul.
3. *Jīvājīvābhigama* (*Jīvājīvābhigama*). Discussion of the categories of living (jīva) and non-living (ajīva).
4. *Prajñāpanā* (*Pannavaṇā*). Explanations of a variety of technical topics, including the soul (jīva), types of births (gati), bodies (śarīra), sexual feelings (vedas), passions (kaṣāyas), karma, and so forth. Written by a monk named Ārya Śyāma (ca. 79 B.C.E.), it is said to be based on portions of the extinct Pūrvas and *Dṛṣṭivāda*. It is similar in content to the *Ṣaṭkhaṇḍāgama* of the Digambaras.

5. *Sūryaprajñapti* (*Sūriyapannatti*). Movements of the sun. Contents are virtually identical with number 7 below.
6. *Jambūdvīpaprajñapti* (*Jambuddīvapannatti*). Cosmography of the island-continent of Jambūdvīpa, including our area of the universe, the continent of Bharata. Discussion of progressive (utsarpiṇī) and regressive (avasarpiṇī) cycles of time. Narratives of Ṛṣabha, the first Tīrthaṅkara of this era, and of his son Bharata.
7. *Candraprajñapti* (*Candapannatti*). Movements of the moon. Contents are virtually identical with number 5 above.
8. *Nirayāvalī* (*Nirayāvaliyāo*). Narratives of the 10 princes who were half brothers of King Śreṇika (Kunṇiya or Ajātaśatru) of Campā. They were killed in battle by their grandfather, King Ceḍaga of Vesāli, and were reborn in various hells.
9. *Kalpāvataṃsikāḥ* (*Kappāvaḍaṃsiāo*). Narratives of 10 sons of the above-mentioned princes who attained rebirth in various heavens after renouncing the household life.
10. *Puṣpikāḥ* (*Pupphiāo*). Narratives of 10 gods and goddesses who came to earth in their heavenly chariots (puṣpakas) to worship Mahāvīra.
11. *Puṣpacūlikāḥ* (*Pupphacūliāo*). Narratives similar to those in the *Puṣpikāh.*
12. *Vṛṣṇidaśāḥ* (*Vaṇhidasāo*). Narrative of the conversion of the 12 princes of the Vṛṣṇi dynasty by Nemi, the 22nd Tīrthaṅkara of this era, including Vāsudeva Kṛṣṇa.

B. Chedasūtras (Cheyasuttas). The word "cheda" is a technical term for a reduction in a mendicant's seniority for offenses committed. They contain rules of mendicant conduct and penances and atonements for transgressions.

1. *Ācāradaśāḥ Sūtra* (*Āyāradasāo Sutta*) or *Daśāśrutaskandha.* Compendium of rules for mendicants, including offenses against mendicant vows, acts of disrespect (āśātanā), qualifications of a mendicant leader (gaṇin), progressive stages of mendicant austerities (bhikṣu-pratimā), and progressive stages of lay restraint (upāsaka-pratimā). The eighth chapter, "Paryuṣaṇā-kalpa" or "Sāmācārī," contains rules (kalpa) of mendicant conduct for the four-month rainy season period. It takes the monk as the general standard and gives specific cases, when the need arises, for nuns. This chapter forms part of a separate work entitled the *Kalpa Sūtra* of Bhadrabāhu.

2. *Bṛhatkalpa* (*Bihākappa*). A short text on monastic law.
3. *Vyavahāra* (*Vavahāra*). Procedures and atonements for monks and nuns, especially on isolation from the monastic group (parihāra).
4. *Niśītha* (*Nisīha*). Title is a false Sanskritization, which may correspond to prohibition ("niṣedha"), or it may refer to a "place of study." Its 20 chapters list transgressions and their sanctions, including isolation from the mendicant group ranging from one to six months. The 20th chapter deals with the six-month isolation. Part of it is a reproduction of the beginning of the *Vyavahāra* to which additional punishments have been added.
5. *Mahāniśītha* (*Mahānisīha*). Rules of mendicant conduct and didactic narratives. References to goddesses and to magic spells (vidyās). It is written in Mahārāṣṭrī, rather than Ardhamāgadhī. Scholars believe this text is of a comparatively late date.
6. *Jītakalpa* (*Jīyakappa*). Atonements for breaches of mendicant conduct.

6a. *Pañcakalpa* (*Pañcakappa*) (extinct).

Note: 5, 6, and 6a are not included in Sthānakavāsī and Terāpanthī lists.

C. Mūlasūtras (Mūlasuttas). These may have been called "Root Texts" because they are to be studied by those who are at the beginning (mūla) of their monastic careers.

1. *Daśavaikālika Sūtra* (*Dasaveyāliya Sutta*). Ten lectures on topics associated with the mendicant life. It is said to have been composed by Ārya Śayyambhava (ca. 429 B.C.E.) for the instruction of his son Maṇaka. Contains a narrative of Rājīmati, the prospective bride of Prince Nemi.
2. *Uttarādhyayana* (*Uttarajjhayaṇa*). Thirty-six lectures on a wide variety of topics that are said to comprise the last sermon of Mahāvīra, the 24th Tīrthaṅkara of this era. Narrative of Rājīmati, the prospective bride of Prince Nemi. Dialogue between Keśi, a follower of Pārśvanātha, the 23rd Tīrthaṅkara, and Indrabhūti Gautama, a chief disciple (gaṇadhara), of Mahāvīra.
3. *Āvaśyaka* (*Āvassaya*). Discussion of the six obligatory duties (āvaśyakas) of a mendicant. Among Mūrtipūjakas, its verse commentary (niryukti) is considered part of the text. Sthānakavāsīs and Terāpanthīs have excluded the niryukti portions from their version of the *Āvaśyaka*.

4. *Piṇḍaniryukti* (*Piṇḍanijjutti*) and *Oghaniryukti* (*Ohanijjutti*) are usually grouped together. These verse texts describe rules for alms gathering and care of monastic implements, such as alms bowls.

4a. *Pākṣi* (*Pakkhi*). Verse liturgy of the 14-day confession for mendicants, the Pākṣi-Pratikramaṇa.

Note: 4 and 4a are not included in Sthānakavāsī and Terāpanthī lists.

D. Prakīrṇakasūtras (Paiṇṇasuttas) ("Miscellaneous Texts"). There is a great deal of variation in the texts in this category. The editors of the Jain Āgama Series have included 20 texts in their edition. None of these texts is included in Sthānakavāsī and Terāpanthī lists.

1. *Catuḥśaraṇa Sūtra* (*Causaraṇa Sutta*). The four refuges, namely, Arhats, Siddhas, Sādhus, and Dharma.
2. *Āturapratyākhyāna* (*Āurapaccakkāṇa*). Renunciation into mendicancy (i.e., taking the five mendicant vows or mahāvratas) at the approach of death.
3. *Bhaktaparijñā* (*Bhattaparinnā*). Renunciation of food at the approach of death.
4. *Saṃstāraka* (*Saṃthāraga*). Preparing the deathbed. Discussion of a mindful death.
5. *Taṇḍulavaicārika* (*Tandulaveyāliya*). "Contemplation on Rice," on subjects associated with the formation and nourishment of the body.
6. *Candravedhyaka* (*Caṅdāvijjhaya*). "Hitting the Mark," or maintaining consciousness at the time of death.
7. *Devendrastava* (*Devindatthaya*). Praise of the Jinas by the king of gods. Description of categories of heavenly beings (devas) and their abodes. Description of the sun, moon, planets, and stars.
8. *Gaṇividyā* (*Gaṇivijjā*). Discussion of prognostication (nimitta) or auspicious times for monastic activities.
9. *Mahāpratyākhyāna* (*Mahāpaccakkhāṇa*). Renunciation at the time of death.
10. *Vīrastava* (*Vīratthava*). Hymn of praise (sthava) to Mahāvīra.

E. Cūlikāsūtras (Cūliyāsuttas) ("Appendix Texts")

1. *Nandī Sūtra* (*Nandī Sutta*). Enumeration of 24 Tīrthaṅkaras and 11 gaṇadharas and a listing of elders (therāvalī). Discussion of a variety of topics, including the five types of knowledge. Summaries of material found in other canonical

texts. Its authorship is ascribed to Devavācaka or Devarddhi-gaṇi Kṣamāśramaṇa, the redactor of the Āgamas.

2. *Anuyogadvāra* (*Aṇuogaddārāiṃ*). Discussion of a variety of topics of Jain religion and philosophy and mendicant conduct. Summaries of material found in other canonical texts. Its authorship is ascribed to the Elder Ārya Rakṣita.

F. Other Texts. There are several early extra-canonical texts that have attained a status equivalent to the scriptural texts, including the *Ṛṣibhāṣitāni* (*Isibhāsiyāiṃ*) and the *Aṅgavidyā* (*Aṅgavijjā*).

DIGAMBARA ĀGAMAS OR SIDDHĀNTA

I. Pūrva, Aṅga, and Aṅgabāhya Texts

In Digambara sources, there are listings of the 14 Pūrvas and of the 12 Aṅgas that are identical with those in the Śvetāmbara Āgama. Some of the Aṅgabāhya texts also correspond with those in Śvetāmbara lists. However, Digambaras do not accept the authenticity of the extant Śvetāmbara canon, which apparently was codified in a series of recitations at councils where Digambara mendicant leaders were not present. Thus, Digambaras maintain that all of the Pūrva, Aṅga, and Aṅgabāhya texts were lost, possibly as early as the 2nd century C.E.

However, Digambaras believe that a few of their mendicant leaders (ācāryas) remembered those portions of the 12th Aṅga, the *Dṛṣṭivāda*, that contained material from the Pūrvas that dealt with karma theory. Dharasena (ca. 137 C.E.) taught what he remembered from this text to his disciples, Puṣpadanta and Bhūtabali, who wrote the *Ṣaṭkhaṇḍāgama* "Scripture in Six Parts." Shortly thereafter, another mendicant named Guṇabhadra wrote a second work on karma entitled *Kaṣāyaprābhṛta*. Both are written in a vernacular Prākrit language called Jain Śaurasenī.

II. Anuyoga ("Expositions") Texts

Most of the Digambara scripture is comprised of post-canonical works composed by various mendicant leaders, which are divided into four categories called Anuyogas ("Expositions"). This system of classification also is used by Śvetāmbaras for their later works. Important Digambara works from each category are listed below. All dates refer to the common era (C.E.)

A. Prathamānuyoga ("Primary Expositions"). Biographies of the *Tīrthaṅkaras* and famous mythological figures.
   1. *Padmapurāṇa* of Raviṣeṇa (7th century).
   2. *Ādipurāṇa* of Jinasena (8th century).
   3. *Harivaṃśapurāṇa* of Jinasena (8th century).
   4. *Uttarapurāṇa* of Guṇabhadra (9th century).

B. Karaṇānuyoga ("Expositions on Technical Matters"). Texts on cosmology, astronomy, karma, and mathematics.
   1. *Trilokaprajñapti* (*Tiloyapaṇṇattī*) of Yativṛṣabha (ca. 6th–7th centuries).
   2. *Dhavalā* and *Mahādhavalā* of Vīrasena, commentaries on the *Ṣaṭkhaṇḍāgama* (9th century).*
   3. *Jayadhavalā* of Vīrasena and Jinasena, commentary on the *Kaṣāyaprābhṛta* (9th century).*
   4. *Gommaṭasāra* and *Trilokasāra* of Nemicandra-Siddhāntacakravartī (11th century).

   *sometimes classified as Āgamas because of their association with the two Digambara Āgama texts, *Ṣaṭkhaṇḍāgama* and *Kaṣāyaprābhṛta*

C. Caraṇānuyoga ("Expositions on Conduct"). Texts on mendicant and lay conduct.
   1. *Mūlācāra* of Vaṭṭakera (ca. 2nd century).
   2. *Bhagavatī Ārādhanā* of Śivārya (ca. 2nd century).
   3. *Niyamasāra* of Kundakunda (ca. 2nd or 3rd century).*
   4. *Pravacanasāra* of Kundakunda (ca. 2nd or 3rd century).*
   5. *Samayasāra* of Kundakunda) (ca. 2nd or 3rd century).*
   6. *Ratnakaraṇḍa-Śrāvakācāra* of Samantabhadra (5th century).

   *sometimes classified as Dravyānuyoga texts

D. Dravyānuyoga ("Expositions on Substances"). Texts on philosophy and logic.
   1. *Tattvārthādhigama Sūtra/Tattvārtha Sūtra* of Umāsvāti/Umāsvāmī (ca. 2nd century).*
   2. *Pañcāstikāyasāra* of Kundakunda (ca. 2nd or 3rd century).
   3. *Nyāyāvatāra* and *Sanmatisūtra* of Siddhasena Divākara (5th century).*
   4. *Āptamīmāṃsā* of Samantabhadra (5th century).
   5. Various works by later authors, such as Akalaṅka (8th century) and Vidyānanda (9th century).

   *also accepted by Śvetāmbaras

Jain Sites in India

Chronology

Prior to the 8th century C.E. dating is often uncertain. Estimates may vary by as much as five centuries. When applicable, both traditional dating and the range of scholarly opinions on dating have been included. The person or event has usually been placed in the earliest century within the range of scholarly opinions.

The term Mūrtipūjaka ("image worshipping") was not used prior to the establishment of non-image-worshipping sectarian traditions in the Śvetāmbara community. However, I have used it as a term of reference beginning in the 11th century with the formation of mendicant lineages (gacchas) that comprise the Śvetāmbara Mūrtipūjaka mendicant community today.

PREHISTORIC PERIOD

Ṛṣabha, the first Tīrthaṅkara of this era, through Neminātha, the 22nd Tīrthaṅkara of this era.

10TH CENTURY–9TH CENTURY B.C.E.

Pārśvanātha, the 23rd Tīrthaṅkara of this era establishes his mendicant lineage. He is believed to have lived in Banaras 250 years prior to the time of Mahāvīra (traditional dating, ca. 950–850 B.C.E.).

6TH CENTURY B.C.E.

Vardhamāna Mahāvīra, the 24th and last Tīrthaṅkara of this era, establishes his mendicant lineage. He attains liberation (nirvāṇa) at the the age of 72 at Pāpā (modern Pāvāpurī, near Patna). Traditional dating varies: 599–527 B.C.E. (Śvet.), 582–510 (Dig.), 499–427 B.C.E. (Śvet. Hemacandra). In accordance with the revised later dating of the Buddha as proposed recently by some scholars, Mahāvīra's dates would be approximately 100 years after the earliest traditional dating.

Eleven chief disciples (gaṇadharas) of Mahāvīra compose the Pūrva and Aṅga texts based on the teachings of Mahāvīra.

Indrabhūti Gautama and Sudharman, chief disciples (gaṇadharas) of Mahāvīra, assume leadership of the mendicant community.

Gaṇadhara Indrabhūti Gautama attains omniscience hours after the death of Mahāvīra (traditional dating, 527 B.C.E.). Ceases leadership of mendicant community. Attains liberation 12 years later.

Beginning of the Vīra-nirvāṇa period, longest continuous era in Indian history (527 B.C.E.).

Gaṇadhara Sudharman, last chief disciple of Mahāvīra, leads the mendicant community for 12 years and teaches the sacred texts to Jambū. Attains omniscience and liberation 24 years after the death of Mahāvīra.

King Śreṇika (= Bimbisāra), contemporary of Mahāvīra, rules Magadha (modern Bihar) from Rājagṛha (540–490 B.C.E.).

Life of Siddhārtha Gautama, the historical Buddha, younger contemporary of Mahāvīra (563–483 B.C.E., scholarly dating varies).

5TH CENTURY B.C.E.

Jambū, first elder (sthavira) in the lineage of Mahāvīra, leads mendicant community for eight years. Attains omniscience and liberation 64 years after the death of Mahāvīra. Last person in this era to attain liberation. Jinakalpa mode of mendicancy comes to an end.

4TH CENTURY B.C.E.

Bhadrabāhu, seventh elder (sthavira) in the lineage established by Mahāvīra, the last person to have knowledge of all Pūrva and Aṅga texts. Died 175 years (Śvet.) or 162 years (Dig.) after the death of Mahāvīra (ca. 352 or 348 B.C.E.).

Sthūlabhadra, eighth elder (sthavira) in the lineage established by Mahāvīra, presides over the First Council at Pāṭaliputra where mendicants gathered to recite the sacred texts 160 years after the death of Mahāvīra (traditional dating, 367 B.C.E.). (Authenticity of recitation not accepted by Digambaras.)

Nanda dynasty rules Magadha (ca. 364–320 B.C.E.).

Candragupta Maurya rules from Pāṭaliputra in Magadha (ca. 320–293 B.C.E.). According to some Digambara accounts, Candragupta becomes a Jain monk, migrates to the south with Bhadrabāhu, and fasts to death at Śravaṇa Beḷgoḷa.

3RD CENTURY B.C.E.–3RD CENTURY C.E.

Inscriptions at Mathurā from the pre-Kuṣāṇa and Kuṣāṇa periods contain names of mendicant lineages that are listed in the Śvetāmbara *Kalpa Sūtra* of Bhadrabāhu (mid-2nd century B.C.E.–3rd century C.E.).

Monks on the pedestals of Tīrthaṅkara images at Mathurā from the pre-Kuṣāṇa and Kuṣāṇa periods are depicted covering their nudity with a half piece of cloth (ardhaphālaka) (2nd century B.C.E.–3rd century C.E.).

Aśoka Maurya rules from Pāṭaliputra in Magadha (268–233 B.C.E.).

Mauryan dynasty comes to an end with assassination of Bṛhadratha (185 B.C.E.).

Hāthīgumphā inscription at Udayagiri in Orissa (late 1st century B.C.E. or the early 1st century C.E.) mentions that King Khāravela of Kaliṅga invaded Magadha to recover a Tīrthaṅkara image carried off by an army of the Nanda dynasty (ca. 364–320 B.C.E.).

Dharasena, Digambara mendicant leader (ca. 137 C.E.), transmits knowledge of scriptures to Puṣpadanta and Bhūtabali, who write the *Ṣaṭkhaṇḍāgama* (traditional dating, 156 C.E.).

Guṇabhadra, Digambara mendicant leader, writes *Kaṣāyaprābhṛta* (traditional dating, 2nd century).

4TH CENTURY– 5TH CENTURY C.E.

Kundakunda, Digambara mendicant leader, writes a number of important works, including the *Pravacanasāra* and *Samayasāra* (ca. 4th–5th centuries, but dated as late as 8th century, traditional dating, 2nd–3rd centuries).

Umāsvāti/Umāsvāmī writes the *Tattavārtha Sūtra*, accepted by Śvetāmbaras and Digambaras (ca. 4th–5th centuries, dated as early as 2nd century).

Second Council convened at Mathurā under the leadership of Skandilasūri (300–343) for recitation of the sacred texts. Concurrently, there was a recitation at Valabhī under the leadership of Nāgārjuna. (Authenticity not accepted by Digambaras.)

Siddhasena Divākara, logician claimed by both Śvetāmbara and Digambara traditions, writes *Nyāyāvatāra* and *Sanmati-sūtra* (ca. 4th–5th centuries).

Earliest extant image of a Tīrthaṅkara wearing a lower garment found at Akota (near Baroda) (ca. 450); cognizances found on Tīrthaṅkara images.

Earliest extant mānastambha, Kahaon Pillar, Uttar Pradesh (460).

Third Council convened at Valabhī under the leadership of Devarddhigaṇi Kṣamāśramaṇa to resolve differences in the two previous recitations of the sacred texts. Compiled the final redaction of the extant canon in written form (456 or 466). (Authenticity not accepted by Digambaras.)

Drāviḍa (Dramila) Saṅgha, extinct Digambara mendicant lineage, founded at Madurai, Tamil Nadu, by Vajranandin (d. 469).

Kāṣṭhā Saṅgha, extinct Digambara mendicant lineage, established by Loha I (5th century) or by Kumārasena (7th century).

Samantabhadra, Digambara mendicant leader and logician, writes *Āptamīmāṃsā* and other works, including *Ratnakaraṇḍa*, the first Digambara work on lay conduct (ca. 5th century).

6TH CENTURY C.E.

Mānatuṅga, devotional poet, composes the *Bhaktāmara Stotra* accepted by Śvetāmbaras (44 verses) and Digambaras (48 verses) (second half of the 6th century).

Pūjyapāda, Digambara monk, writes *Sarvārthasiddhi* commentary on the *Tattvārtha Sūtra*.

Yogīndu, Digambara author who flourished sometime after Kundakunda and Puṣpadanta and prior to Hemacandra (6th–10th centuries), writes the *Paramātmaprakāśa* and *Yogasāra*.

Earliest inscription near Śravaṇa Beḷgoḷa (ca. 600) mentions previous migration of the community to the south under the leadership of Bhadrabāhu.

7TH CENTURY C.E.

Memorials erected at Śravaṇa Beḷgoḷa for mendicants who ended life by fasting until death (7th–10 centuries).

Haribhadra, Śvetāmbara mendicant leader and philosopher, writes a number of important works including *Ṣaḍdarśanasamuccaya*, *Yogabindu*, *Yogadṛṣṭisamuccaya*, and *Yogaśataka* (traditional dates of death 478 and 529; ca. 7th–8th centuries C.E.).

8TH CENTURY C.E.

Akalaṅka, Digambara logician, writes *Nyāyaviniścaya*, the *Rājavārtika* commentary on the *Tattvārtha Sūtra* (780), and the *Aṣṭaśatī* commentary on the *Āptamīmāṃsā*.

Destruction of Valabhī by Turkish invaders (782).

9TH CENTURY C.E.

Vīrasena, Digambara monk, completes the *Dhavalā* commentary on the *Ṣaṭkhaṇḍāgama* (816).

Jinasena (ca. 770–850), Digambara mendicant leader, writes the *Jayadhavalā* commentary on the *Kaṣāyaprābhṛta* (820) and the *Ādipurāṇa*, which is completed by his disciple Guṇabhadra.

Guṇabhadra, Digambara monk, writes the *Uttarapurāṇa* (completed 897).

Vidyānanda, Digambara monk, writes the *Ślokavārttika* commentary on the *Tattvārtha Sūtra*.

Śilāṅka, Śvetāmbara monk, writes Sanskrit commentaries on the first two Aṅgas (*Ācārāṅga Sūtra* and *Sūtrakṛtāṅga Sūtra*).

10TH CENTURY C.E.

Hariṣeṇa, Digambara monk, composes the *Bṛhatkathākośa*.

Gommaṭeśvara, colossal image of Bāhubali, erected at the Digambara pilgrimage site of Śravaṇa Beḷgoḷa by Cāmuṇḍarāya, minister to kings in the Gaṅga dynasty (981).

Memorials erected at Śravaṇa Beḷgoḷa for laity who ended life by fasting until death (10th–15th centuries).

Nemicandra, Digambara monk, writes *Gommaṭasāra* at the request of Cāmuṇḍarāya (late 10th, early 11th century).

11TH CENTURY C.E.

Earliest inscription at Mount Śatruñjaya on image of Puṇḍarīka (1007).

Abhayadevasūri, Śvetāmbara mendicant leader, writes Sanskrit commentaries on the remaining nine Aṅgas of the Śvetāmbara canon.

Hemacandra (1089–1172), Śvetāmbara mendicant leader, appointed court scholar and historian by Jayasiṃha Siddharāja of the Caulukya dynasty of Gujarat. Writes *Triṣaṣṭiśalākāpuruṣacaritra* and *Yogaśāstra*.

Kharatara Gaccha, Śvetāmbara Mūrtipūjaka mendicant lineage, founded either by Vardhamānasūri (d. 1031) or by his pupil Jineśvarasūri (fl. 1024).

Vimala Vasahī, Śvetāmbara temple dedicated to Ṛṣabha, erected at Mount Ābū by Vimala Śāh, a minister to Bhīma I of the Caulukya dynasty (1032).

12TH CENTURY C.E.

Ācārya Jinadattasūri (1075–1154), the first Dādāguru, becomes mendicant leader of the Śvetāmbara Mūrtipūjaka Kharatara Gaccha (1112).

Śvetāmbara temple dedicated to Neminātha erected at Mount Girnār by Sajjana, a minister to Jayasiṃha Siddharāja of Saurashtra (1128).

Śvetāmbara temple dedicated to Ṛṣabha erected at Mount Śatruñjaya by Vāgbhaṭa, a minister to Kumārapāla of the Caulukya dynasty (1154).

A(ñ)cala Gaccha, Śvetāmbara Mūrtipūjaka mendicant lineage, founded by Āryarakṣitasūri (1156).

Ācārya Jinacandrasūri (1140–1166), Śvetāmbara Mūrtipūjaka Kharatara Gaccha mendicant leader and the second Dādāguru, converts many followers to Jainism.

Śvetāmbara temple dedicated to Ajitanātha erected at Tāraṅgā by King Kumārapāla of the Caulukya dynasty (1164).

Āgamika Gaccha, Śvetāmbara Mūrtipūjaka mendicant lineage, founded by Śīlaguṇa and Devabhadra (1193).

13TH CENTURY C.E.

Growth of the institution of bhaṭṭārakas in the Digambara community.

Tapā Gaccha, Śvetāmbara Mūrtipūjaka mendicant lineage, founded by Ācārya Jagaccandrasūri (1228).

Lūṇa Vasahī, Śvetāmbara temple dedicated to Neminātha, erected at Mount Ābū by Tejaḥpāla, a minister to Bhīma II (1230).

Ācārya Devendrasūri (d. 1270), Śvetāmbara Mūrtipūjaka Tapā Gaccha mendicant leader, writes the *Karmagranthas*.

14TH CENTURY C.E.

Temples on Mount Śatruñjaya desecrated by Turkish invaders (1313).

Ācārya Jinakuśalasūri (1280–1332), Śvetāmbara Mūrtipūjaka Kharatara Gaccha mendicant leader and the third Dādāguru, revives Jainism in Sindh.

15TH CENTURY C.E.

Digambara temple at Mūḍbidrī, Tribhuvana-Tilaka-Cūḍāmaṇi Basadi (The Crest-Jewel of the Three Worlds Temple), erected (1429).

Śvetāmbara temple at Rāṇakpur, Dharṇā Vihāra, dedicated (1441).

Kaḍuā Gaccha, Śvetāmbara Mūrtipūjaka ascetic lineage, founded by Kaḍuā Śāh (1438–1507).

Loṅkā Śāh (15th century), Śvetāmbara layman, begins efforts to reform lax mendicant practices and discourages laity from financing temple construction and performing temple rituals (ca. 1451).

Loṅkā Gaccha, Śvetāmbara mendicant lineage that rejects image worship, founded by Muni Bhāṇa, the first disciple of Loṅka Śāh (ca. 1475). Soon thereafter, image worship was reaccepted.

16TH CENTURY C.E.

Tāraṇ Svāmī (1448–1515), Digambara layman who late in life takes vows of a naked monk, rejects image worship and the authority of bhaṭṭārakas. Followers establish the Tāraṇ Svāmī Panth in the Bundelkhand region of central India.

Pārśvacandra Gaccha, Śvetāmbara Mūrtipūjaka mendicant lineage, founded (1515).

Loṅkā Gaccha splits into separate branches and sublineages. Renaissance of image worship and lax mendicant practices especially among the quasi-mendicants (yatis) who did not take the five mendicant vows (mahāvratas) (last quarter of the 16th century).

Ācārya Hīravijayasūri (1527–1596), Śvetāmbara Mūrtipūjaka Tapā Gaccha mendicant leader, invited to the court of the Moghul emperor Akbar (1506–1605) at Agra. Persuades Akbar to ban the slaughter of animals on Paryuṣaṇa (1587–1590).

Ācārya Jinacandrasūri II (1537–1612), Śvetāmbara Mūrtipūjaka Kharatara Gaccha mendicant leader, persuades the Moghul emperor Akbar (1506–1605) to protect Jain temples from desecration (1591).

Banārsīdās (1586–1643), lay reformer and mystical poet associated with the Adhyātma Movement in Agra, writes *Ardhakathānaka* ("Half-a-Story").

17TH CENTURY C.E.

Muni Ānandghan (1603–1673), Śvetāmbara monk and mystical poet, composes hymns in praise of the 24 Tīrthaṅkaras.

Five reformers, Muni Jīvarāja (ca. mid-16th to mid-17th centuries), Muni Dharmasiṃha (1599–1671), Muni Lavajī (ca. 1609–1659), Muni Dharmadāsa (ca. 1645–1703, or 1717), and Muni Hara (17th century) split from branches of the Loṅkā Gaccha and the Ekal Pātrīya Panth (a lay movement of unknown origin) and found the principal Sthānakavāsī mendicant traditions, which still exist today. These mendicants and their lay followers rejected image worship. Mendicants permanently wear a mouth-cloth (muhpattī) and adhere to strict mendicant conduct with an itinerant lifestyle as described in the 32 Śvetāmbara scriptures acceptable to them.

Mahopādhyāya Yaśovijaya (1624–1688), Śvetāmbara Mūrtipūjaka Tapā Gaccha reformer, authors works on philosophy and logic, including *Jainatarkabhāṣa*, *Jñānabindu*, and *Nyāyāloka*, and a polemical work entitled *Adhyātmikamatakhaṇḍa* defending the Śvetāmbara view of the nature of an enlightened being and the ability of women to attain liberation.

Adhyātma movement flourishes in north Indian cities, including Agra, Banaras, Delhi, Lahore, and in towns near Jaipur (mid-17th to mid-18th centuries).

Digambara Terāpanthī tradition founded under the influence of the Adhyātma movement in the region of Jaipur, Rajasthan. They reject the authority of bhaṭṭārakas (mid-17th century).

Dyānatrāy (1676–1726), Digambara mystical poet associated with the Adhyātma movement in Agra and Delhi, composes liturgies and devotional poetry.

18TH CENTURY C.E.

Paṇḍit Ṭoḍarmal (fl. first half of the 18th century), leader of the Digambara Terāpanthī tradition in Jaipur, writes *Mokṣamārgaprakāśaka*.

Gumānīrām, son of Paṇḍit Ṭoḍarmal and leader of the Digambara Terāpanthī tradition in Jaipur, establishes the Gumān Panth (1770s).

Ācārya Bhikṣu (Muni Bhīkhanjī) (1726–1803) and four other monks separate from the Sthānakavāsīs over disagreement regarding merit-making activities (1760). Founder and first mendicant leader (ācārya) of the Śvetāmbara Terāpanthī tradition.

19TH CENTURY C.E.

Yatis and śrīpūjyas predominant in Śvetāmbara Mūrtipūjaka mendicant community.

Bhaṭṭārakas lead the Bīsapanthī Digambara community in north India and the undivided Digambara community in south India.

Ācārya Jaya (1803–1881) appointed fourth mendicant leader of the Śvetāmbara Terāpanthīs (1852). Writes rules of mendicant conduct used today and establishes the annual meeting of all mendicants (maryādā mahotsava) and the office of chief nun (sādhvī pramukhā).

Fully initiated mendicants (saṃvegī sādhus) of the Śvetāmbara Mūrtipūjakas and leaders of the lay community begin reform of lax mendicant practices (mid-19th century).

Śrīmad Rājacandra (1867–1901), mystic and reformer, composes works, including *Ātmasiddhi*, about the direct experience of the inner soul. Corresponds with Mohandās (Mahātmā) Gāndhī. Followers establish the Kavi Panth.

Vīrcand Rāghavjī Gāndhī (1864–1901) represents Jain community at World's Parliament of Religions in Chicago (1893).

Migrations of Jains to east and south Africa.

20TH CENTURY C.E.

Decline of bhaṭṭārakas in the Digambara community.

Revival of the tradition of naked monks (munis) in the Digambara community.

Decline of yatis in the Śvetāmbara Mūrtipūjaka mendicant community and disintegration of their mendicant orders headed by śrīpūjyas.

Śvetāmbara Mūrtipūjaka mendicant community grows from about two dozen fully initiated mendicants (saṃvegī sādhus) at the beginning of the 19th century to around 6,800 monks and nuns at the end of the 20th century.

Establishment of Jain lay community organizations, including the Bhāratavarṣīya Digambara Jain Mahāsabhā (1895), Jain Śvetāmbara Conference (1902), Akhil Bhāratavarṣīya Śvetāmbara Sthānakavāsī Jain Conference (1906), Terāpanth Sabhā (1913), and Akhil Bhāratavarṣīya Digambara Jaina Pariṣad (1923).

Establishment of Jain institutions of higher education, including Yaśovijaya Jain Pāṭhśālā, Banaras (Śvet., 1902); Syādvāda Jain Mahāvidyālaya, Banaras (Dig., 1905); Pārśvanātha Vidyāpīṭh, Banaras (Sthānakavāsī,

1937); Jain Vishva Bharati, Ladnun (Śvet. Terāpanthī, 1970).
Kānjī Svāmī (1889–1980), Sthānakavāsī monk, renounces his vows and becomes a Digambara layman (1934). Founds the neo-Digambara Kānjī Svāmī Panth at Songadh, Gujarat (1934).

Ācārya Tulsī (1914–1997) becomes ninth mendicant leader of the Śvetāmbara Terāpanthīs (1936).

Aṇuvrat movement begun by Śvetāmbara Terāpanthī Ācārya Tulsī (1949).

Centrally organized Śramaṇa Saṅgha of the Śvetāmbara Sthānakavāsīs established (1952).

Chitrabhanu travels to the United States (1971). Establishes Jain Meditation International Center in New York City.

Jain Samaj established in Leicester, U.K. (1973). Reconstituted as Jain Samaj Europe (1980).

Celebration of the 2,500th anniversary of Mahāvīra's nirvāṇa. Adoption of the Jain pratīka (symbol of the Jain faith) (1974).

Ācārya Sushil Kumar (1926–1994), Sthānakavāsī mendicant leader, travels to the United States (1975). Establishes Siddhachalam in Blairstown, New Jersey (1983).

Samaṇ/samaṇī, intermediate class of novice mendicants in the Śvetāmbara Terāpanthī tradition, established by Ācārya Tulsī (1980).

Federation of Jain Associations in North America (JAINA) established (1981).

Institute of Jainology (IoJ) established in London (1983).

Ācārya Mahāprajña becomes 10th mendicant leader of the Śvetāmbara Terāpanthīs (1994).

21ST CENTURY C.E.

Celebration of the 26th birth centenary year of Mahāvīra (2001–2002).

Introduction

BACKGROUND

Jain is the term used for a person who has faith in the teachings of the Jinas ("Spiritual Victors"). Jinas are human beings who have overcome all passions (kaṣāyas) and have attained enlightenment or omniscience (kevala-jñāna), who teach the truths they realized to others, and who attain liberation (mokṣa) from the cycle of rebirth (saṃsāra). At the core of these teachings is nonviolence (ahiṃsā), which has remained the guiding principle of Jain ethics and practices to this day. In comparison with other religious traditions of South Asia, Jains are few in number, comprising less than one percent of India's population. The Jain lay and mendicant communities, however, have maintained an unbroken presence in India for more than 2,500 years and have influenced its culture throughout this time.

As Jains migrated from the region of Magadha (modern Bihar), linguistic divisions took place, and by the beginning of the common era differences in mendicant practice had developed. The Jain community today is divided into two main sectarian traditions that arose around this time, which are named after the appearance of their mendicants. Śvetāmbaras are the followers of monks and nuns who are "white-clad." Digambaras are the followers of monks who practice nudity and thus are called "sky-clad." Beginning in the 15th century there were further divisions within the Jain community. A layman named Loṅkā Śāh convinced some Jains in Ahmedabad to abandon temple worship. This reform movement evolved into a subsect of mendicants and lay followers that today is known as Sthānakavāsī ("Hall-Dwellers"). In the 18th century, a few monks separated from the Sthānakavāsīs and founded a second Śvetāmbara non-image-worshipping subsect called Terāpanthī ("Path of Thirteen"). Śvetāmbaras who continued to worship the Jinas in iconic form became known as Mūrtipūjakas ("Image Worshippers"). Around this same time, several reform movements arose within the Digambara community. The leaders of these movements were inspired by the writings of the Digambara mystic Kundakunda. In the 16th century, the followers of a Digambara named

Tāraṇ Svāmī, who had rejected image worship, founded the Tāraṇ Svāmī Panth in the area of Madhya Pradesh. They emphasized the study and worship of texts authored by him. In Rajasthan in the 18th century, some members of the Digambara lay community questioned certain aspects of temple worship and the authority of ascetic clerics called bhaṭṭārakas. They formed a separate Digambara sectarian tradition headed by lay intellectuals (paṇḍits) that also is called Terāpanthī ("Path of Thirteen"). At this time, those who continued to follow the older traditions began to call themselves Bīsapanthī ("Path of Twenty"). The Digambara community in south India remained undivided and continued to follow the older traditions. In the 20th century, new movements arose based on the teachings of Śrīmad Rājacandra and Kānjī Svāmī. Except for the Śvetāmbara Terāpanthīs who are headed by one mendicant leader (ācārya), there is no central spokesperson for the various sectarian traditions.

BASIC TEACHINGS OF JAINISM

Doctrinal differences between Śvetāmbaras and Digambaras have focused on three key issues: the texts that contain the authoritative teachings of the Jinas, the interpretation of the mendicant vow of non-possession, and the question of whether or not a woman can attain spiritual liberation. However, the basic teachings of Jainism are accepted by all sectarian traditions. They are outlined in the *Tattvārtha Sūtra* ("That Which Is"), a text written by Umāsvāti/Umāsvāmī, a philosopher who probably lived in the 4th or 5th century C.E. As in other religious traditions that arose in South Asia, Jains believe that this life is just one in a series of lives in the cycle of birth and death (saṃsāra) and that it is possible to attain liberation (mokṣa or nirvāṇa) from this cycle. Umāsvāti opens his work with the statement that the path to liberation is a proper perception (samyak-darśana) or a proper view of reality, proper knowledge (samyak-jñāna), and proper conduct (samyak-cāritra). He then states that a proper view of reality entails belief in the category of truths (tattvas): (1) the sentient soul (jīva); (2) that which is insentient (ajīva); (3) influx (āsrava) of karma to the soul; (4) binding (siddha) of karma with the soul; (5) stopping the influx of karma to the soul (saṃsāra); (6) separation of karma from the soul (nirjarā); and (7) liberation (mokṣa). In later sources two additional tattvas are listed: (8) beneficial (puṇya) karmas and (9) harmful (papa) karmas, which Umāsvāti includes in the binding of karma. From beginningless time, there has been an infinite number of souls that have as their inherent nature infinite consciousness, infinite energy, and infinite bliss. However, in most souls these qualities are not realized to their fullest because they are negatively affected by karma. In Jainism karma is not a mental factor but an extremely subtle form of matter that is found everywhere in the occupied universe (loka-ākāśa). The insentient category includes all matter as well as space, time, and the principles of motion and rest. Outside of the occupied universe there is only infinite empty space. In Jainism there is no creator God because all substances (dravya) are beginningless, uncreated, and eternal as is the universe itself.

All substances, including the soul and the material universe, are multifaceted in nature. An omniscient being, who has infinite perception and knowledge, is able to simultaneously apprehend all possible aspects of an object. However, expression of this reality is difficult due to the inherent limitations of human language to discuss seemingly mutually contradictory terms. Jain philosophers have developed a system of formal argumentation to express this multifaceted, or non-one-sided, view of reality (anekānta-vāda) that uses the doctrine of qualified assertion (syādvāda) for different philosophical standpoints in a system of sevenfold predication (sapta-bhaṅgi-naya). In this way, one can argue, for instance, that the soul is permanent and unchanging from the perspective of a substance because it always has existed, will never cease to exist, will always have the qualities of knowledge and so forth, and will never change into another substance, such as insentient matter. However, from another perspective, the soul is constantly changing. For example, knowledge may constantly fluctuate from the effects of karmic matter on the soul. Therefore, one can say that the soul is both permanent and impermanent depending on one's perspective. From a Jain point of view, other religious traditions such as Hinduism, which is based on permanence, and Buddhism, which is based on impermanence, are not incorrect in their views but represent only a partial view of reality. This qualified acceptance of the views of others is seen by Jains today as an expression of the principle of non-harming (ahiṃsā).

The cause of bondage of a soul in saṃsāra is karmic matter, which is beginningless but not necessarily endless. Karma is attracted to the soul by activities of the body, speech, and mind. It is bound with the whenever these activities are conditioned by passions (kaṣāyas) in the form of attraction (rāga) or aversion (dveṣa). There are eight main varieties of karmic matter. Four are classified as destructive (ghātiyā) because they have a negative effect on the soul. They prevent the soul's realization of its innate capabilities of consciousness, energy, and bliss, and they are the cause of passions and improper conduct. The other four varieties of karma are classified as nondestructive (aghātiyā) because it is possible to attain proper perception, knowledge, and conduct even though these karmas are still bound with the soul. They are associated with various aspects of embodiment. They determine the type of body, its longevity, its social circumstances, and its experiences of pleasure and pain.

It is possible to bring the cycle of birth and death to an end by stopping the influx of new karma to the soul and removing all previously bound karma from the soul. Because the bondage of the soul is real and not an illusion associated with ignorance or delusion, Jains have tended to place more emphasis on physical means to remove karmic matter from the soul rather than on meditative practices. One's progress in the purification of the soul is measured in 14 stages called guṇasthānas that are envisioned as a ladder with 14 rungs (see appendix). One of the most crucial transitions is from the first stage, that of spiritual ignorance, to the fourth stage, that of a proper view of reality. A soul that attains the fourth stage may fall back again into spiritual ignorance, but it definitely will attain liberation in some future birth as a human being. A person may make further spiritual progress by formally taking the lay vows (fifth stage) or the mendicant vows (sixth stage). For those who have renounced the world, it is possible to attain higher stages of spiritual purity. By eliminating all destructive karmas from the soul a person attains omniscience (kevala-jñāna) and perfect conduct. Such a soul remains embodied until the karmas that cause its embodiment are exhausted and one's life span comes to an end. At that point, the soul is free from all karmic matter and it rises to the top of the universe, where it remains disembodied forever, experiencing its own infinite knowledge and bliss. Although all perfected souls that have attained liberation are worthy of worship and are called God or Supreme Soul, in Jainism there is no soul that has never been bound in the cycle of saṃsāra, nor is there a universal soul. Even in a liberated state, all souls remain individual and isolated from each other.

Time is subject to cycles in which living conditions gradually become better or worse. A complete cycle of time is divided into a progressive half (utsarpiṇī) and a regressive half (avasarpiṇī). Each half-cycle is divided into six time-stages, from extremely happy to extremely unhappy. The progressive and regressive half-cycles follow each other with no intervening period of demanifestation. In our location of the universe, during the third and fourth stages in each progressive and regressive half-cycle of time a series of 24 human beings are born who attain enlightenment or omniscience and perfect conduct through their own efforts. They preach the eternal truths of Jainism and establish a fourfold community of followers (tīrtha) of monks, nuns, laymen, and laywomen, showing them the path of salvation from the cycle of birth and death. In this current descending cycle of time, the first of these Jinas ("Spiritual Victors") or Tīrthaṅkaras

("Fordmakers") was Ṛṣabha. He was born at the end of the third stage. The 24th and final Tīrthaṅkara of this era was Mahāvīra. He was born at the end of the fourth stage. We are currently in the fifth stage of the descending half-cycle, which began approximately three years after the death of Mahāvīra and will last for a total of 21,000 years. It will not be possible to attain liberation here again until the third stage in the next ascending cycle arrives, some 84,000 years from now. However, it is believed that there are locations in the universe that are not subject to cyclical time where conditions always are appropriate for the birth of a Tīrthaṅkara. There always are Tīrthaṅkaras preaching there, and liberation is always possible for a human being who is born in one of these locations.

THE LIFE OF MAHĀVĪRA

The 24th Tīrthaṅkara-to-be was born to a warrior (Kṣatriya) family of the Jñātṛ clan living in the city of Kuṇḍagrāma, near modern Patna in Bihar. He was named Vardhamāna ("He Who Brings Prosperity") but is commonly known by the epithet Mahāvīra ("Great Hero"). Although he is often called the "founder" of Jainism, this is not the case. His parents were lay followers of the 23rd Tīrthaṅkara, Pārśva, who had lived in Banaras about 250 years earlier. It is said that Vardhamāna was disinterested in worldly matters, and he left the household life at age 30. He went to a garden outside the city where he removed his ornaments and his clothing and pulled out his hair in five handfuls. According to Digambaras, from this time onward he practiced total nudity. According to Śvetāmbaras, he put on a divine cloth (deva-dūṣya) given to him by the god Śakra (Indra), which he wore for 13 months until it was lost accidentally. These two versions of Mahāvīra's renunciation reflect a difference in interpretation of the mendicant vow of non-possession (aparigraha). The question of whether or not this vow requires that a mendicant renounce all clothing eventually led to the division of the Jain community into the two main sectarian traditions that still exist today.

Mahāvīra apparently did not join the monks who were followers of Pārśva but in isolation renounced all possessions and took a single vow of equanimity that encompassed all evil actions. After renunciation, Mahāvīra wandered for 12 years practicing severe austerities of lengthy fasts and bodily mortifications. He undoubtedly met others who had left the household life in their quest for salvation and were engaged in various types of austerities and meditational practices. In addition to those of the brahmanical tradition who were seeking direct knowledge of brahman, there were teachers and their followers collectively known as śramaṇas, or strivers, who did not believe in the authority of the Vedas or in the efficacy of vedic sacrifices. One of these was Siddhārtha Gautama, the historical Buddha, who was a younger contemporary of Mahāvīra. There is no evidence that Mahāvīra and Gautama the Buddha ever met nor is there any mention of the Buddhists in early Jain texts, but Gautama must have known of Mahāvīra. In a Buddhist text called the *Sāmaññaphala-sutta* ("Fruits of the Life of a Śramaṇa"), Ajātaśatru, the king of Magadha, tells the Buddha about six śramaṇa leaders, including the Nigaṇṭha Nātaputta (= Nirgrantha Jñātṛputra), which was the family name of Mahāvīra. He also mentions Makkhali Gosāla, who was the leader of the Ājīvikas. According to Śvetāmbara texts, prior to Mahāvīra's attaining omniscience Gosāla had been a disciple of Mahāvīra and the two of them spent six years together. Of the various śramaṇa movements that existed during Mahāvīra's time, only the Nirgranthas, who came to be known as Jains, survived as an unbroken tradition in India.

At the age of 42, in his 13th year of mendicant life, after fasting for two-and-a-half days, absorbed in meditation, Mahāvīra attained a complete understanding of the nature of the universe. Because he had through his own efforts uprooted all worldly desires, which are the immediate cause of bondage in the cycle of birth and death (saṃsāra), he would attain liberation at the end of his life. As is customary for Tīrthaṅkaras, he began preaching in a special assembly hall (samavasaraṇa). In this area of Magadha lived 11 Brahmins who, after hearing him preach, became his chief disciples (gaṇadharas). They composed the sacred texts based on his teachings and served as leaders for the mendicant community. Mahāvīra initiated his mendicant followers with the five great vows (mahāvratas) of non-harming (ahiṃsā), truthfulness, taking only what is given, celibacy, and non-possession. The principles underlying these vows are the basis of Jain ethical practices of both the lay and mendicant communities to this day.

Mahāvīra's mendicant community grew rapidly and soon they were joined by a group of women whom Mahāvīra initiated, appointing Candanā as their head. Mahāvīra attained nirvāṇa at the age of 72 at Pāvāpuri. By traditional Jain accounts, at the time of his death, the community had grown to 14,000 monks, 36,000 nuns, 159,000 laymen, and 318,000 laywomen.

According to Jain sources, Mahāvīra lived from 599 B.C.E. to 527 B.C.E. (most Śvet.) or 582 B.C.E. to 510 B.C.E. (Dig.). Since Mahāvīra was an elder contemporary of the historical Buddha and both lived during the reign of King Śreṇika (= Bimbisāra), scholarly opinions regarding his date vary in accordance with understandings about when the Buddha might have lived. Pārśva, the 23rd Tīrthaṅkara, lived 250 years earlier than Mahāvīra, around 950 B.C.E. to 850 B.C.E. It is not possible to establish that the remaining 22 Tīrthaṅkaras were historical figures.

THE JAIN COMMUNITY IN THE EARLY COMMON ERA

After the death of Sudharman, the leadership of the mendicant community passed to Mahāvīra's senior disciples (sthaviras) and their successors, and the community began to spread from the Magadha region to major population centers in the east and northwest and then into central and southern India. Like the Buddhists, the Jain community flourished with the support of the Nanda and Mauryan dynasties. However, after the fall of the Mauryan dynasty in 185 B.C.E., large-scale migrations of Jains and Buddhists took place and few Jains remained in the Magadha region. The migration of Jain monks and their lay followers followed the two major trade routes of ancient India. In the east, it went from Patna in Bihar to Orissa and south into Andra Pradesh, Karnataka, and Tamil Nadu. The earliest evidence for this migration is an inscription of King Kharavela, who ruled around 150 B.C.E. from Udayagiri, near the modern city of Bhuvaneshvara in Orissa. The western route paralleled the Ganges River and terminated in Mathurā, near modern Agra, on the Yamuna River. By the 2nd century C.E. Jains had moved farther west into Saurashtra (modern Gujarat) where a set of 20 rock-cut cells from this time have been found near Junagadh.

Mathurā was an important center for the Jain community at this time. A number of votive tablets and Tīrthaṅkara images have been recovered here from the pre-Kuṣāṇa and Kuṣāṇa periods (mid-2nd century B.C.E. through 3rd century C.E.). On them are inscriptions naming the lay donors in the Jain community who commissioned them at the urging of their mendicant teachers. Stūpa worship is depicted on these votive tablets, and there are references to the installation of Tīrthaṅkara images in temples. These findings are indicative of a well-established lay community that was closely associated with Jain mendicants, who encouraged the laity in their merit-making activities. This close interaction between mendicants and laity has remained characteristic of the Jain community in India to this day.

In the period after Mahāvīra's death, divisions arose within the Jain community regarding whether of not the mendicant vow of non-possession included renunciation of clothing. There also was a disagreement over which texts constituted the authentic teachings of Mahāvīra. Śvetāmbaras and Digambaras agree that oral transmission of the scriptural canon continued in an unbroken line from the time of Jambū, the elder who led the mendicant community after the death of Gaṇadhara Sudharman, until the time of Bhadrabāhu (ca. 300 B.C.E.), the fifth in the line of elders. At this time, there seems to have been a scattering of the mendicant community due to a severe famine in the Magadha region and knowledge of the texts gradually began to be lost. Accounts of what happened after this vary. According to Śvetāmbara sources, after the famine was over a congregation of mendicants gathered at Pāṭaliputra (now Patna) under the leadership of Sthūlabhadra to recite what each of them remembered of the scriptural canon, but Bhadrabāhu was not present at this recitation. Because of this council, they were able to preserve some of the sacred texts. In the 4th century C.E., two other recitations were held concurrently at Mathurā and at Valabhī in Saurashtra, an important Gupta center where many Jains had now settled. In the 5th century, a final council was held in Valabhī to resolve the differences in the earlier recitations. It is not known whether the scriptures, or Āgamas, were committed to writing prior to the final council, but this redaction was preserved on palm leaves. Digambara monks apparently were not present at the final council at Valabhī, and they do not believe that the extant Śvetāmbara canon contains the authentic teachings of Mahāvīra. According to them, a Digambara monk named Dharasena (ca. 137 C.E.), who was living near Valabhī, taught what he remembered of the sacred texts to two monks named Puṣpadanta and Bhūtabali, and they wrote the *Ṣaṭkhaṇḍāgama* based on this knowledge. Around the same time, another Digambara monk named Guṇabhadra wrote the *Kaṣāyaprābhṛta* based on his recollection of the sacred texts. Digambaras maintain that after this time knowledge of the sacred texts was lost. Thus, with the exception of a few texts like the *Tattvārtha Sūtra*, Śvetāmbaras and Digambaras have separate textual traditions.

The interpretation of the mendicant vow of non-possession (aparigraha) is associated with a difference in belief regarding the capacity of a woman to attain liberation from the cycle of death and rebirth. Digambaras believe that this vow entails the renunciation of all clothing. Women can become nuns (āryikās) in the Digambara tradition. However, because they are not permitted to practice nudity, they take the vow of non-possession in a modified form, and they do not have the same spiritual status as monks. Because liberation is possible only for those who take all five mendicant vows, Digambaras maintain that a woman cannot attain liberation in that life. She may, however, attain liberation in a future life if her soul is reborn in a male-gendered body. On the other hand, Śvetāmbaras do not consider mendicant clothing possessions that must be renounced. They are like implements, such as the whisk broom (rajoharaṇa or piñchī), which

Digambara mendicants also use, or alms bowls. Śvetāmbaras believe that both monks and nuns are capable of attaining liberation because they take identical mendicant vows.

It is not known when a split in the mendicant community and their lay followers might have taken place, but from archeological and inscriptional evidence, it seems to have occurred gradually, with the communities living separately sometime between the 2nd and 5th centuries C.E. Prior to the 5th century, all images of Tīrthaṅkaras are unclothed but beginning in the 5th century some are depicted wearing a lower garment. Over the next few centuries, this became the standard practice among Śvetāmbaras. Also, there is an inscription in south India from the late 5th century recording land grants that refers to Śvetāmbaras and Nirgranthas. This would indicate that by the 5th century in some parts of India Śvetāmbara and Digambara mendicants lived separately and their lay followers no longer worshipped the same images. Śvetāmbaras and Digambaras probably had begun to worship in separate temples, as is still the practice in India today.

MENDICANT PRACTICES

During the time of Mahāvīra, a monk could choose to live with a group of mendicants (sthavira-kalpa) or he could choose to live in isolation (jina-kalpa). Since this time, mendicants have been required to live in an organized mendicant lineage, called a gaccha (Śvet.) or a saṅgha (Dig.), under the supervision of a mendicant leader. This group is subdivided into smaller units, the most basic of which is a group of monks or nuns who travel together and who stay together during the four-month rainy season period (cāturmāsa). A person becomes a monk or nun by taking the five great vows (mahāvratas), which are designed to avoid harming and to subdue passions and attachments. The first of these is the vow of ahiṃsā, not to harm, to cause harm, or to approve of harm committed by others in thought, word, or deed. In accordance with this vow, mendicants are strict vegetarians and do not eat root crops. Because this vow includes all living beings, even those with just one sense, mendicants are prohibited from lighting a fire to cook food (since it would harm one-sensed fire-bodied beings) and from gathering vegetables or fruits themselves, since picking them harms plant life. Instead, mendicants accept food from Jain laity that has not been prepared specifically for them. To minimize harm, they do not use mechanical or animal conveyance. They walk barefoot, and they inspect the path as they walk. The second vow is to speak only the truth (satya) and the third not to take anything that is not freely given (asteya). The fourth vow of total celibacy (brahmacarya) avoids passions and attachments, and the fifth vow of non-possession (aparigraha) avoids attachment to objects. In taking initiation, a mendicant also agrees to observe the six obligatory daily rites (āvaśyakas). The first of these is the attainment of equanimity (sāmāyika) in which monks and nuns always remain mindful of their actions. The second, caturviṃśati-stava, is the veneration of the 24 Jinas through the recitation of a devotional hymn, and the third, vandana, is veneration of one's mendicant leader. The fourth, pratikramaṇa, is a rite of repentance for faults or infractions of one's vows. It is performed each morning and evening, with special rites every fortnight, every four months, and annually. The fifth, kāyotsarga, is a form of standing meditation, and the sixth, pratyākhyāna, is a statement of intention to perform austerities that cause the destruction of karma.

Throughout mendicant life monks and nuns have tried to prevent the influx of new karma through careful observation of their vows, and to destroy previously bound karma through acts of austerity (tapas), such as fasting. If their vows become difficult to observe due to terminal illness or old age, a monk or nun may choose to die voluntarily by undertaking a ritual fast ending in death (sallekhanā). Performed under the guidance of a preceptor, food and water are gradually reduced until they are eliminated altogether. By renouncing the attachment to the body and dying in a state of equanimity with no fear and no desire to cling to life, spiritual progress made in this life will not be compromised.

LAY PRACTICES

Although the life of a mendicant represents the ideal for the Jain community, the number of individuals who have adopted this austere life always has been quite small. While a mendicant's life is focused on the destruction of all karma, a householder's life is focused on well-being in this life and a good rebirth in the next. Varieties of karmic matter have been divided into two groups: beneficial (puṇya) karmas and harmful (papa) karmas. For mendicants who are focused on liberation, all karma is bad because their goal is to overcome all types of karmic bondage. However, a layperson strives to perform actions that bind beneficial varieties of karma that cause rebirth in circumstances conducive to spiritual progress, for example, as a human being. They try to avoid performing actions that bind bad varieties of karma that cause rebirth in undesirable states of existence, for example, as an inhabitant of the hellish realms, or as an animal, insect, or vegetable life.

It is recognized that the life of a householder must entail some degree of harm, because one must cook and engage in occupations. However, harm should be minimized whenever possible. Laypeople also are vegetarian but their dietary restrictions are less stringent than those of a mendicant. Most Jains fast on occasion, especially on the day of the annual rite of repentance, but it is usually women who undertake longer fasts and adhere to more restrictive diets. In addition to this, a layperson may choose to observe a more disciplined life that has been patterned after monastic practices. A number of manuals outlining lay discipline were composed by monks detailing the 11 stages of spiritual progress for a layperson, known as pratimās (see appendix). A person who has firm faith in the teachings of the Jinas may take 12 lay vows of restraint. These include the five minor vows (aṇuvratas) of non-harming, truthfulness, taking only what is freely given, sexual restraint, and non-possession. These vows are further enhanced by seven supplementary vows (guṇa-vratas and śikṣā-vratas) that entail specific restraints in diet, travel, accumulation of possessions, and so forth. In progressing on this path, there is a gradual withdrawal from the normal activities of household life until all connections with the family are renounced and a person begins living with a group of mendicants. At the end of life, a layperson may choose to take the vow of fasting until death (sallekhanā) as described above.

Supporting the Jaiṇ religion through veneration of those who are worthy of worship and through gifting to worthy recipients is one of the ways in which a layperson can bind karma associated with well-being and a good rebirth. This includes veneration of the Jinas, the veneration of Jain mendicants, and gifting to the mendicant community. For image-worshipping Jains, gifting also includes sponsoring various rituals, pilgrimages, the installation of images, and contributing to the construction and maintenance of temples and pilgrimage sites. Although mendicants venerate the Jinas through mental worship (bhāva pūjā), laypeople also may venerate the Jinas with material forms of worship (dravya pūjā) by making offerings to images in home shrines or in temples. Certain aspects of Jain temple worship differ from rituals in a Hindu temple where a ritual specialist performs the daily rites of worship and makes offerings to the consecrated image on behalf of the devotees. In most Jain temples in north India, laypeople perform all aspects of daily worship themselves. If they are in a state of ritual purity, both men and women may enter the inner sanctum and make offerings to the consecrated image. The image of the Jina on the altar is understood to represent the ultimate ideal, that of a human being who has overcome all passions and attachments and has attained liberation. A worshipper seeks to embody these qualities through meditative reflection during acts of worship. Like all souls that have attained liberation, the souls of the Jinas permanently reside at the apex of the universe in total isolation from all other souls. They do not interact with worshippers here on earth and they do not enter into the images. Therefore, there is no transaction or exchange between the liberated Jinas and those who worship them. Offerings made to the Jinas are symbolic of renunciation and are permanently given up. They are not returned to the worshipper as a sanctified substance (prasāda). Some Jains propitiate non-liberated deities, such as yakṣas and yakṣīs, who are attendants of the Jinas and protectors of their teachings. Because non-liberated deities are part of the world of saṃsāra, they are able to respond to the worldly concerns of those who worship them.

GROWTH OF THE JAIN COMMUNITY

It is likely that the differences between Śvetāmbaras and Digambaras were intensified by the concentration of the two groups in different regions of India during the period of growth. As mentioned above, Jains spread to Tamil areas of south India via the eastern route quite early. However, by 1000 C.E. Jains had declined significantly in this area. On the western route, Digambaras left Valabhī and moved to the coast of the Arabian Sea, and then into the Deccan and further south into southwestern India where they became a prosperous and influential community with royal patronage. In Karnataka a Digambara monk named Siṃhanandi reportedly was instrumental in the founding of the Gaṅga dynasty in the 3rd century C.E. For the following seven centuries, the Jain community benefited greatly from their close association with the Gaṅga kings. In 948 C.E., the Gaṅga general Cāmuṇḍarāya commissioned the famous image of Bāhubali at Śravaṇa Beḷgoḷa. The Rāṣṭrakūṭas ruled to the north of the Gaṅga kingdom from the 8th to the 12th century and some of their kings were followers of Jainism. It was during their reign that Jains constructed cave temples at Ellora. Ācārya Jinasena (ca. 770–850 C.E.), the author of the *Ādipurāṇa*, a legendary history of Jainism during the current cycle of time, was an advisor to Amoghavarṣa, who may have abdicated the throne to become his mendicant disciple. After the Gaṅga dynasty, the Hoysalas ruled Karnataka and they too were generous patrons of the Jain community. However, with the rise of the Vijayanagar empire in the 14th century, Jain influence came to an end in this region. The growing popularity of Hindu devotionalism in the south contributed to a decline in the Digambara community as many converted to Hinduism. Beginning in the 12th century, Jains also suffered from the rise of the Śrīvaiṣṇavas and the militancy of the Hindu Vīraśaiva movement. Although smaller in number, Digambaras remained in south-western India, especially in the coastal regions of Karnataka, where they became part of the agricultural community.

To the north in Gujarat, a ruler came to power in the 8th century who was sympathetic to the Śvetāmbaras. The wife of a deposed ruler had given birth to a son named Vanarāja. For a time, he was raised by a Śvetāmbara monk named Ācārya Śīlaguṇasūri. Later, he was given some land and in 746 C.E. established the city of Aṇahillavāḍa Paṭṭaṇa (= Patan). When he installed himself as king, his consecration was performed by Śīlaguṇasūri. Conditions remained favorable for the Jain community when the Caulukya or Solaṅkī dynasty came to power in the mid-10th century. Patan was on the trade route between the cites of north India and the ports of western India, and the Jain merchant community flourished there. Jain laymen served as government ministers, and Jain mendicants were spiritual and intellectual advisors at court. According to Śvetāmbara sources, a debate was held at the court of Jayasiṃha Siddharāja between the Śvetāmbara Devasūri and the Digambara Kumudacandra on the questions of mendicant nudity and the spiritual liberation of women. Kumudacandra was defeated and all Digambara mendicants were forced to leave Patan. The disappearance of virtually all Digambara Jains from Gujarat is often linked to this event. Jayasiṃha Siddharāja was succeeded by Kumārapāla, who had developed a close relationship with Ācārya Hemacandra, a court scholar and historian for Jayasiṃha. Kumārapāla, who is said to have become a Jain layman, financed the construction of Jain temples and manuscript libraries. In the following century, Vastupāla (d. 1240 C.E.) and Tejaḥpāla (d. 1248–1252 C.E.), wealthy merchants who served as government ministers and military generals to the Vāghelā dynasty, built a number of temples, including an ornate marble temple at Mount Ābū and a temple at Mount Girnār. They also led large pilgrimages to Mount Śatruñjaya and Mount Girnār. Śvetāmbara monks continued their influence at court under Muslim rule. Hīravijayasūri and Jinacandrasūri persuaded the Mughal emperors Akbar and Jahangir to ban the slaughter of animals on Jain festival days and to protect commercial interests of Jain merchants. Jain laymen served as ministers and advisors to Rajput kings of western and central India, and as merchants were important to the growing economy in this region.

REFORMS IN THE ŚVETĀMBARA MENDICANT COMMUNITY

In keeping with the vows of non-harming and non-possession, mendicants should lead an itinerant lifestyle except during the four-month rainy season period (cāturmāsa) when travel would unduly harm the numerous insects and minute forms of life that flourish then. Eventually, however, mendicants began to spend more time in one place and became more involved in performing various rituals for the lay community and in the installation of images. Those mendicants who lived a more affluent life and stayed permanently at temple complexes were called caityavāsīs ("temple-dwellers"). Those mendicants who led a more austere itinerant life were called vanavāsīs ("forest-dwellers"). Beginning in medieval times, these sedentary mendicants became known as yatis. These quasi-mendicants did not take the full mendicant vows and most did not perform all of the six obligatory daily rites (āvaśyakas). They could reside in one place, possess property, use money, sleep in beds, and so forth. They performed temple rituals for money and were expert in rituals with magical or tantric elements. Some served as administrators and clerics, managing the temples and their lands as well as the manuscript libraries. Their mendicant orders were headed by a person with the title of śrīpūjya. He carried out the functions of his office from the mendicant dwelling-hall (upāśraya) in which his lineage's traditional seat of power was located. Some śrīpūjyas amassed a great deal of wealth and were closely associated with the courts of Muslim and Rajput rulers.

In the 11th century, there were efforts to reform these "lax" mendicant practices and to reestablish orthodox modes of conduct. New mendicant lineages (gacchas) were formed as monks left their teachers because of disagreements over these issues. However, in the course of time, lax practices would often again become the norm, and a few mendicants would again leave to establish new "orthodox" lineages. In medieval times, there was a large number of gacchas, 84 according to traditional accounts. Only a few of these are still in existence today. One of these originated with a monk named Vardhamānasūri (d. 1031) who defeated a temple-dwelling monk in a debate in 1024 C.E. at the court of King Durlabha in Patan. The mendicant lineage established by him or by his disciple Jineśvarasūri (1023) was called the Kharatara Gaccha because of his sharp-witted debate. In the 12th and 13th centuries, the A(ñ)cala Gaccha was founded by Āryarakṣitasūri (1156) and the Āgamika Gaccha was founded by Śīlaguṇa and Devabhadra (1193). The largest of the image-worshipping (Mūrtipūjaka) mendicant lineages today, the Tapā Gaccha, was founded in Chitor (southern Rajasthan) by Jagaccandrasūri in 1228 C.E. However, in the following centuries, mendicants in all of these lineages began to adopt a sedentary lifestyle, even though there were ongoing efforts at reform.

Although reforms often came from within the mendicant community, on occasion members of the lay community were instrumental in initiating these changes. One such individual was Loṅkā Śāh, a copyist of Jain manuscripts in Ahmedabad, Gujarat. He noticed that the sedentary life of Śvetāmbara mendicants did not conform with the precepts outlined in the early texts. Around 1451 C.E. he began his efforts to reform mendicant conduct and to discourage the lay community from performing temple rituals. Although he himself never became a monk, several monks who had left the Tapā Gaccha and had become his followers founded the Loṅkā Gaccha around 1475. In the following centuries, however, lax mendicant conduct and support for temple worship soon reemerged. In the 17th century, four monks split from the Loṅkā Gaccha, and the mendicant lineages that they established evolved into the non-image-worshipping subsect called Sthānakavāsī. In the 18th century, a Sthānakavāsī monk named Muni Bhīkhanjī (Ācārya Bhikṣu) and four other monks split with their mendicant leader over mendicant conduct and the efficacy of meritorious actions of the lay community. They formed a second non-image-worshipping subsect called the Śvetāmbara Terāpantha.

REFORMS IN THE DIGAMBARA COMMUNITY

A sedentary lifestyle developed within the Digambara mendicant community as well. Digambara mendicants eventually began to stay permanently in monasteries located at temple complexes. These lineages were headed by a celibate cleric known as a bhaṭṭāraka, who wore orange-colored robes. Bhaṭṭārakas were usually associated with one caste of Jains. They managed temple complexes, performed rituals, adjudicated caste disputes, and represented their community at court. As the institution grew, a total of 36 pontifical centers, or thrones, were established throughout India. By the 13th or 14th century, because of pressure from Muslims, most Digambara monks wore clothing in public, and in the following centuries the ancient tradition of itinerant naked monks essentially died out.

Dissatisfaction arose within the Digambara community over the growing influence and wealth of the bhaṭṭārakas and over the emphasis that was being placed on temple rituals. Some Digambaras turned to the writings of the Kundakunda for inspiration, which described a direct mystical experience of the pure innate soul and which emphasized internal transformation rather than external rituals. The first of these reformers was a celibate layman from Madhya Pradesh named Tāraṇ Svāmī (1448–1515) who became a naked Digambara monk toward the end of his life. He criticized the institution of the bhaṭṭāraka and rejected all image worship. His followers in the Tāraṇ Svāmī Panth installed books containing his writings on altars in temples and worshipped them. From the mid-17th century to the mid-18th century, the Adhyātma movement flourished in Agra, Delhi, Banaras, and other cities of northern India. It grew out of discussion circles of laymen who met to study the texts of Kundakunda and others in the Digambara mystical tradition. Many of these circles attracted both Śvetāmbara and Digambara laymen, which was unusual given their sectarian rivalry and their separation by caste. They criticized the conduct of the Digambara bhaṭṭārakas and the Śvetāmbara yatis and the emphasis that was placed on rituals in both sectarian traditions. Banārsīdās (1586–1643), who was a leader of the Agra study circle, was one of the leaders of this movement and is considered by some to be its founder. The Adhyātma movement also spread to the area of Jaipur where the Digambara Terāpanthī tradition developed under its influence in the 18th century. Having rejected the authority of bhaṭṭārakas, lay intellectuals like Paṇḍit Ṭoḍarmal became leaders and provided the intellectual foundation for the growth of this community. In their temples, images of Tīrthaṅkaras are worshipped but not images of any non-liberated guardian deities, such as kṣetrapālas and yakṣas/yakṣīs.

REFORMS IN THE 20TH CENTURY

By the middle of the 19th century, most mendicants in the Śvetāmbara Mūrtipūjaka community were not fully initiated mendicants (saṃvegī sādhus) who observed the five great vows (mahāvratas) but were sedentary quasi-mendicants (yatis) who had taken lesser vows. It is estimated that there were only a few dozen saṃvegī sādhus with no mendicant leaders (ācāryas) among them. At this time, several monks in the Tapā Gaccha began efforts to reform the mendicant community. They included Paṅnyāsa Maṇivijayagaṇi (1796–1879) and one of his disciples named Muni Buddhivijaya (also known as Buṭerāyjī, 1807–1882). One of Buddhivijaya's disciples, Ātmārāmjī (also known as Ācārya Vijayānandasūri) was appointed to the position of ācārya in 1887 by leaders of the Mūrtipūjaka lay community. Both Buṭerāyjī and Ātmārāmjī were first Sthānakavāsī sādhus who, upon a study of the texts, became convinced of the correctness of image worship, and so took a second initiation as Mūrtipūjaka sādhus. Both of them were active in preaching against Sthānakavāsī iconoclasm and saw this as an integral part of their reforms. These two sādhus, along with several other activist mendicants, were successful in bringing about reforms in the Mūrtipūjaka mendicant and lay communities. Similar reform movements arose in the Sthānakavāsī mendicant community. As a result, there are only a handful of yatis remaining today and the community of fully initiated mendicants has grown substantially. As of 1999, there were approximately 11,000 Śvetāmbara mendicants (2,400 monks and 8,600 nuns).

At the beginning of the 20th century, there were some men in the Digambara community who had taken the most advanced lay vows of an ailaka, renouncing all possessions except for a loincloth. In the 19th century, there were a few solitary forest monks who practiced nudity but there were no longer any mendicant lineages with fully initiated naked monks (munis). In 1920, during an image-installation ceremony in Karnataka, one of these ailakas, Śāntisāgara (1873–1955), discarded his loincloth and pulled out his hair, thereby initiating himself in the presence of the Jain community gathered there. Although Śantisāgara often is credited with reestablishing the tradition of naked Digambara monks, there were two other men who took self-initiation early in the 20th century and also became mendicant leaders (ācāryas) and initiated followers. They are Ādisāgara (1868–1943), who lived in Maharashtra and became a muni in 1913, and Śāntisāgara Chāṇī (1888–1944), who lived in Rajasthan and became a muni in 1923. As of 1999, the Digambara mendicant community totaled around 1,000 (610 male renunciants, including munis, kṣullakas, and ailakas, and 350 female renunciants, including āryikās and kṣullikās). The number of fully initiated naked monks (munis) is not known. It has been estimated that in the 1970s there were approximately 65 munis and in the 1980s approximately 100 munis. With the growing number of munis in the 20th century and the reform movements that had begun in the 17th century in north India, the influence and power of bhaṭṭārakas (ascetic clerics) has declined. By the end of the 20th century, all bhaṭṭāraka seats of power in north India had become extinct. However, bhaṭṭārakas are still an important part of the Digambara community in south India, where five main seats remain occupied.

By the end of the 19th century, leaders of the lay community also had become active in addressing issues of religious and social concern and in initiating reforms. A number of lay associations were organized at this time along sectarian lines. Membership in many of them was exclusively of one caste, or was dominated by one caste, or was from one local area. However, there were several all-India associations that were formed to represent all Jains of one sectarian tradition throughout India, and an All-India Jain

Association that was open to all Jains. These all-India associations held large conferences every few years and communicated with their members through the publication of magazines and newspapers in English and in vernacular languages. They represented the Jain community in legal matters during British colonial rule and fostered a sense of Jain identity that transcended caste and local concerns. In the Śvetāmbara image-worshipping community, they were instrumental in the decline of the yatis and in placing the monasteries, temples, and manuscript libraries that were controlled by them under the supervision of lay trusts. Early in the 20th century, a number of Jain educational institutions were established for the religious and secular education of the community, and Banaras became an important center of intellectual activity for lay scholars educated there, especially within the Digambara community. Some of these scholars were influential in encouraging the publication of Jain texts.

In the 20th century, several new movements arose that have continued to attract followers. A Sthānakavāsī layman named Śrimad Rājacandra taught a mystical form of Jainism that focused on meditation and inner transformation. The movement that grew up around his teachings has attracted followers from both the Śvetāmbara and Digambara communities. A Sthānakavāsī monk named Kānjī Svāmī (1889–1980) was influenced by the writings of the Digambara mystic Kundakunda. In the 1930s, he renounced his monastic vows and declared that he was a Digambara layman. His followers established the Kānjī Svāmī Panth, a neo-Digambara sectarian tradition, that is centered in Gujarat and in Jaipur. In the 1960s, a non-Jain layman in Surat named Ambālāl Paṭel began teaching a syncretic blend of Jainism and Hinduism. The question of whether or not his teachings are part of Jainism remains a controversial issue.

The number of Jains living in India today is unknown. The Census of India figures for 1991 are the most recent that are available. Out of a population of 838 million, Jains constituted about 3.35 million, or about 0.4 percent of the total population. The largest numbers of Jains are found in the states of Gujarat (491,331), Karnataka (326,114), Madhya Pradesh (490,324), Maharashtra (965,840), and Rajasthan (562,806). The large number of Jains in Maharashtra includes a sizable population of Gujarati and Rajasthani Jains in Bombay. Rajasthan is the only state in which the Jain population has dropped since the census of 1981. Population statistics always have been unreliable because some Jains report that they are Hindu for census purposes. Therefore, the actual number of Jains is somewhat larger with some estimates as high as 5 million. There are no data for the number of lay Jains in the various sectarian traditions. However, it has been estimated that approximately one-third of Jains are Digambaras.

THE JAIN DIASPORA

In the late 19th century, Jains were part of the migration that took place from various parts of western India to Bombay. For centuries, Jains had moved in smaller numbers at the invitation of local rulers for the purpose of trade, and they had settled in other large metropolitan areas, such as Ahmedabad, Jaipur, Delhi, Calcutta, Madras, and Bangalore. It was at this time that large numbers of Jains, primarily Gujaratis from the Śvetāmbara Mūrtipūjaka community, began migrating to East Africa in search of business opportunities. Beginning in 1968 many East African Jains moved to Britain because of the political situation in Uganda during the rule of Idi Amin. Most Jains live in London, but a significant number have settled in Leicester, where a Jain temple was constructed in 1980. There are communities of Jains in Antwerp, Belgium, who are diamond traders, and in Kobe, Japan, who are pearl merchants. Jains also have emigrated to cities in Canada and Australia and in the Middle East to the Gulf oil states. With the liberalization of immigration laws in the United States in 1965, the number of Jains in North America increased rapidly. It is estimated that there are between 100,000 and 150,000 Jains living outside of India with approximately 30,000 living in Britain and Europe, 20,000 in Africa, 50,000 in North America, and 5,000 elsewhere in Asia.

There are several factors that distinguish the Jain diaspora communities from Jains living in India. It is impossible for a mendicant to observe the mendicant rules of conduct to their fullest extent and travel abroad. Therefore, the Jain diaspora community does not have close contact with the mendicants and it is almost exclusively a lay community. Recently, there have been several mendicants who have broken with tradition and traveled abroad. In 1971, a Śvetāmbara Mūrtipūjaka monk named Candraprabhasāgara (now known as Chitrabhanu) settled in New York. Chitrabhanu formally renounced his mendicant status and as a result he is now known to his followers as Gurudev. Muni Sushil Kumar (1926–1994), a Sthānakavāsī monk who came to the United States in 1975, did not renounce his mendicant status. Since this time, several other Sthānakavāsī mendicants have traveled abroad to visit the diaspora community. In the Śvetāmbara Terāpanthī community, a class of novice mendicants called samaṇ and samaṇī was established in 1981. Their vows permit them to travel abroad, and they have served an important role in the diaspora community. Digambara bhaṭṭārakas are permitted to travel by mechanical conveyance and therefore also travel abroad. Another factor that differentiates Jains living abroad from those living in India is their relatively small numbers in any one city, with a local population that may be composed of Jains from all sectarian traditions. Because of this, some Jain temples outside of India contain both Śvetāmbara and Digambara images, along with a meditation hall for Sthānakavāsīs, Śvetāmbara Terāpanthīs, and the followers of Śrīmad Rājacandra and Kānjī Svāmī. Most Jain temples in North America are shared by the entire community.

Jains in India and abroad have continued to address problems facing the industrialized world at the beginning of the 21st century. In accordance with their firm commitment to ahiṃsā, Jains have actively supported animal rights movements and vegetarianism, and some have promoted a vegan diet. Ecological concerns, such as global warming and deforestation, that cause harm to all living beings and to the earth itself are frequently discussed in Jain publications today. In 1990, Jains presented "The Jain Declaration on Nature" to Britain's Prince Philip, president of the World Wildlife Fund, to mark their entry into the WWF's Network on Conservation and Religion. Jains understand anekāntavāda, a non-one-sided view of reality, as an expression of ahiṃsā through tolerance of the views of others. In this regard, they have participated in interfaith activities, including an interfaith dialogue with the Vatican in 1995. The year 2001–2002 marked the 26th birth centenary year of Vardhamāna Mahāvīra, and a number of events celebrating his teachings of ahiṃsā and anekāntavāda were held throughout the world.

The Dictionary

– A –

ABHAVYA. A **soul** (**jīva**) that does not have the inherent capacity for attaining liberation (**mokṣa**) from the cycle of rebirth (**saṃsāra**) because it lacks the quality of **bhavyatva**. Such souls always remain in a state of delusion (mithyātva), or the first stage of spiritual purity (**guṇasthāna**). Nevertheless, they can attain rebirth in all four states of existence as heavenly beings (**devas**), hell-beings (**nārakis**), humans, and animals (**tiryañc**). *See also* BHAVYA.

ABHAYADEVASŪRI (11th century C.E.). Śvetāmbara mendicant leader who authored **commentaries** on nine **Aṅgas** of the Śvetāmbara canon (**Āgama**). He was born in Ujjain and was initiated in the Candra Kula, a prestigious **mendicant lineage** that the **Kharatara Gaccha** and **Tapā Gaccha** both incorporated into their mendicant lineages. He was appointed **ācārya** in 1063, some 40 years after the defeat of the temple-dwelling monks (**caityavāsī**) by **Jineśvarasūri** at Patan, Gujarat, in 1021 and the establishment of a new mendicant lineage based on mendicant conduct prescribed in the **scriptures**. According to tradition, a tutelary **goddess** appeared to Abhayadevasūri and told him he should compose new commentaries on the Aṅgas because all but those on the first two Aṅgas had disappeared at the time of a severe famine. When he expressed doubts about his ability to do such work, the goddess assured him that whenever he needed clarification, she would travel to the continent of **Mahāvideha** and consult with the **Tīrthaṅkara Sīmandhara Svāmī**, who was preaching there. Thus, his commentaries are understood to be inspired by direct knowledge from an omniscient Tīrthaṅkara. It is also believed that he suffered from a skin disease, possibly leprosy, which was cured when he discovered a lost **image** of **Pārśvanātha** at Cambay.

ABHIṢEKA. Rite of lustrating the **image** of a **Tīrthaṅkara** either with purified water or with one or more of the five nectars (pañca-amṛta). In **Digambara Bīsapanthī** temples in south India and in some Digambara Bīsapanthī temples in north India, this is performed daily by a Jain priest (**Jaina Brahmin**, **Upādhye**), although the substances offered may vary. The basic form is the milk abhiṣeka, in which the priest successively pours water, milk, water, yellow sandalwood water, and water over the image. In more elaborate rituals, the five nectars are offered. These may include (1) coconut juice, sugarcane juice, milk, yellow sandalwood water, and red sandalwood water, or (2) milk, curds, water, yellow sandalwood water, and red sandalwood water. Sometimes, a nine-pot or a 108-pot abhiṣekha may be performed. Occasionally, there is a 1,008-pot abhiṣekha of the image of **Bāhubali** at **Śravaṇa Beḷgoḷa**. Digambaras in north India generally use only water for lustration, even in the context of the more elaborate rituals. *See also* AṢṬAKA PŪJĀ; AṢṬAPRAKĀRĪ PŪJĀ; MASTAKĀBHIṢEKA; PŪJĀ; SNĀTRA PŪJĀ.

ĀBŪ. *See* MOUNT ĀBŪ.

ACALA GACCHA. *See* A(Ñ)CALA GACCHA.

ĀCĀRĀṄGA SŪTRA. "Book of Conduct." The first **Aṅga** in the **Śvetāmbara** scriptural canon (**Āgama**). It consists of two parts. Part one originally contained nine lectures but the seventh has been lost. The lectures discuss proper conduct (ācāra) for **mendicants**, which is based on the principle of non-harming (**ahiṃsā**). Proper methods of obtaining requisites, such as food, shelter, and clothing are discussed here, along with ways to avoid harming one-sensed beings (**ekendriya**) in the course of daily activities. It also contains the earliest narrative of the life of the 24th **Tīrthaṅkara**, **Mahāvīra**. On the basis of linguistic and metrical evidence, scholars believe that some of the oldest portions of the extant canon have been preserved in part one. Part two, which consists of four chapters called appendices, may have been a later addition to the text.

ĀCĀRYA. Literally, "teacher." Often translated as mendicant leader, ācārya is the title for the topmost leader of a group of **mendicants** who is appointed or elected to this position. An ācārya is empowered to initiate new mendicants (although initiation also may be given by any fully initiated **monk**, irrespective of rank in the **mendicant hierarchy**), to oversee a group of mendicants, to impose penances for infractions of the mendicant vows (**mahāvratas**), to interpret **scriptures**, and to appoint a successor.

At the time of installation, **Śvetāmbara Mūrtipūjaka** ācāryas are given a secret, sacred formula called the sūri-mantra, which is said to have been given by **Mahāvīra** to his chief disciples (**gaṇadharas**), including **Indrabhūti Gautama**. The title **sūri** ("learned man") is appended to the name of the ācārya. At the time of initiation, they may take a new name. Within the **Tapā Gaccha**, it is common to reverse the ācārya's given name and the branch name of his mendicant lineage (e.g., Muni Vallabha-vijaya becomes Ācārya Vijaya-vallabha-sūri).

In some **mendicant lineages**, especially among the Śvetāmbara Mūrtipūjakas, there may be several ācāryas in one **samudāya**. In this case, there is usually a chief teacher (gacchādipati) who presides over the other officials in the lineage, including subordinate ācāryas. Traditionally, only male mendicants have been appointed ācāryas. Recently, however, in one of the Sthānakavāsī lineages, a nun named **Candanā** was appointed ācārya.

ADHARMA-DRAVYA. The principle of rest. It is one of the substances (**dravyas**) that is non-material and non-sentient (arūpi-**ajīva**). *See also* DHARMA.

ADHIṢṬHĀYAKA DEVAS. Presiding deities of the **Śvetāmbara Mūrtipūjaka mendicant lineages (gacchas)**. They include Kālikā and Cakreśvarī for the **A(ñ)cala Gaccha**, **Ambikā** and **Bhairava** for the **Kharatara Gaccha**, Bāṭuk Bhairava for the Pārśvacandra Gaccha, and **Māṇibhadra Vīra** for the **Tapā Gaccha**. As non-liberated deities, they are able to intervene in worldly matters on behalf of their devotees.

ADHO-LOKA. Lower realm. In Jain cosmography, the portion of the occupied universe (**loka-ākāśa**) below the middle realm (**madhya-loka**) It consists of seven lands or hells (**narakas**), one below the other, composed of earth, which are named in accordance with their hues (prabhā): (1) Ratnaprabhā (gem-hued), (2) Śarakāprabhā (pebble-hued), (3) Vālukāprabhā (sand-hued), (4) Paṅkaprabhā (mud-hued), (5) Dhūmaprabhā (smoke-hued), (6)Tamaḥprabhā (dark), (7) Mahātamaḥprabhā (pitch-dark).

A **soul (jīva)** of a human being or a five-sensed animal may be born in the next life as a hell-being in one of these hells from the **karmic** effects of violent or cruel actions that they committed. The lower the hell, the more intense is the soul's suffering and the longer is the duration that the soul must spend in this state of existence. Because some beings are thought to be incapable of performing deeds of extreme cruelty, there are specific rules regarding the hell that one can be born into. The lowest possible rebirth in the seven hells is as follows: (1) five-sensed animals without the capacity to reason (first hell), (2) reptiles with legs, (3) birds, (4) land animals, such as lions, (5) snakes, (6) female humans, (7) male humans and aquatic animals, such as fish. The souls of other types of plants or animals (**tiryañc**) and the souls of heavenly beings (**devas**) cannot be reborn as hell-beings in their next life.

After their allotted life span here comes to an end, the souls of hell-beings are born again in the middle realm (madhya-loka) as either a five-sensed animal with the capacity to reason or as a human. If born as a human in their next life (and according to **Digambaras**, as a male), it is possible for those from the first four hells to attain liberation (mokṣa) and from the first three hells to become a **Tīrthaṅkara**. It is not possible for hell-beings to be reborn in their next life as a heavenly being nor can they be reborn again in their next life as a hell-being.

Certain demigods reside in the adho-loka. Because of misguided deeds in their previous lives, some asurakumāra devas (a class of **bhavanavāsī devas**) are predisposed to cause suffering, and they torture hell-beings living in the first three hells. Rākṣasas (a class of **vyantara devas**) reside in the upper portion of the first hell. Other bhavanavāsī devas reside between the earth and the first hell.

ADHYĀTMA MOVEMENT. A movement that flourished from the mid-17th century to the mid-18th century in north India. It grew out of discussion circles of Jain **laymen** in Agra and several other north Indian cities who met to study texts of the **Digambara** mystical tradition authored by **Kundakunda, Yogīndu**, and Rāmasiṃha Muni, and to compose their own religious poetry. Many of these circles attracted laymen of both the **Śvetāmbara** and Digambara traditions, which was unusual given their sectarian rivalry and their separation by **castes**. These laymen criticized the conduct of Digambara **bhaṭṭārakas** and Śvetāmbara **yatis** and the emphasis on rituals that were an important part of both traditions. They believed that emphasis should be placed on inner spiritual transformation. One should understand the knowledge of the difference (bhedavijñāna or bhedajñāna) between the immortal, pure **soul (ātman**) and everything else, including the soul's bondage with **karma**. Although they agreed with Digambaras regarding the spiritual liberation of **women (strī-mokṣa)** and the characteristics of the body of a **kevalin**, they maintained that **monks** should possess nothing and therefore should not carry their insignia of a peacock-feather whisk broom (**piñchī**) and gourd water pot (**kamaṇḍalu**).

Banārsīdās, who was a leader of the Agra study circle, was one of the leaders of this movement and is considered by some to be its founder. After the death of Banārsīdās in 1643, the movement continued under the leadership of Kauṅrpāl. He encouraged Hemrāj Pāṇḍe to write a critique of Śvetāmbara Jainism entitled *Sitapaṭa Caurāsī Bol* ("Eighty-Four Pronouncements on Śvetāmbaras") and to compose a Hindi paraphrase of Kundakunda's *Pravacanasāra*. The poet **Dyānatrāy** participated in Adhyātma discussion circles in Agra and Delhi. Other cities with Adhyātma circles included **Banaras**, Lahore, and Multan. The Adhyātma movement also spread to Kaman and to Sanganer, a town a few miles south of Jaipur, where the Digambara **Terāpanthī** tradition developed under its influence. Although **Nāthūrām Premī** has traced a straight-line development between the earlier Adhyātma movement and the Terāpanthī in the area of Jaipur, John Cort understands the Adhyātma movement to be a trans-sectarian circle of spiritual seekers rather than a sect with a clearly delineated social identity like the Terāpanthī. At the heart of the Adhyātma movement was philosophical contemplation rather than the creation of a distinct sectarian ritual culture, which characterized the Terāpanthī movement.

ĀDINĀTHA. The First Lord. An epithet for the **Ṛṣabha**, the first **Tīrthaṅkara** of this era.

ĀDIPURĀṆA. *See MAHĀPURĀṆA.*

ĀDISĀGARA, ĀCĀRYA (1868–1943). One of three mendicant leaders who revived the **Digambara** tradition of naked **monks** (**munis**) in the 20th century. Born in the village of Ankali, Maharashtra, he was named Śiva Gauḍā. After his parents died, he was responsible for his younger siblings and married against his wishes. In the course of time, he was initiated as a **kṣullaka** by **Bhaṭṭāraka** Jinappā and was given the name Ādisāgara. Three months later, he took the vows of an **ailaka** and began to study Jain texts. In 1913, at a **pilgrimage** site called Kunthalagiri, he initiated himself as a Digambara muni, pulling out his hair and discarding his loincloth. Named as **ācārya** by the local community, he initiated 32 monks, 40 **nuns**, and one kṣullaka in Maharashtra. *See also* ŚĀNTISĀGARA; ŚĀNTISĀGARA (CHĀṆĪ).

ĀGAMA. A term used for Jain sacred texts, which often is translated as "**scripture**" or "canon." Other collective terms for these texts include **Siddhānta** (Doctrine), Nigaṇṭha-pāvayāṇa (Sermons of the **Nirgranthas**), and Gaṇi-Piḍaga (Basket of the **Gaṇadharas**). According to tradition, the truths contained in the scripture are beginningless and uncreated. After attaining omniscience (**kevala-jñāna**), each **Tīrthaṅkara** perfectly understands these truths, and he communicates this knowledge to his chief disciples (gaṇadharas). Each gaṇadhara composes a set of verse texts (sūtras) based on his preachings, arranged as 14 **Pūrvas** and 12 **Aṅgas**. These texts are said to exist in the fourfold lineage (**tīrtha**) established by every Tīrthaṅkara. Because a gaṇadhara ceases his leadership activities after attaining omniscience, it is thought that the present canon is based on the recensions of **Mahāvīra**'s chief disciples who were the last to attain omniscience, **Indrabhūti Gautama** and **Sudharman**. Some time after this, various mendicant elders (**sthaviras**) composed a number of texts that form the subsidiary portion of the canon, the **Aṅgabāhya**. For some time, all of these texts were preserved orally, perhaps in keeping with the mendicant vow of non-harming (**ahiṃsā**) (by not writing on palm leaves) or of non-possession (**aparigraha**), or perhaps to restrict access to certain of these texts.

However, mendicant leaders became apprehensive about the loss of knowledge of their sacred texts. Several councils were convened for a recitation of these texts reportedly after a severe drought and famine caused the scattering of the mendicant community. The first council was held in Pāṭaliputra (now Patna) under the leadership of **Sthūlabhadra** 160 years after Mahāvīra's death (367 B.C.E.). After another famine, a second council was convened by Skandilasūri at **Mathurā** in 300 C.E. In this same year another recitation was organized by Nāgārjunasūri at Valabhī. It is not known when the canon was first committed to writing, but some have speculated that it was at these two councils. A final council was held to resolve the differences in these two recitations. It was organized by Devarddhigaṇi Kṣamāśramaṇa in Valabhī in either 453 or 466 C.E. After this council, copies of the authorized version of the Āgamas containing the first 11 Aṅgas, written in a vernacular Prākrit **language** called Ardhamāgadhī, were circulated. The 12th Aṅga, the *Dṛṣṭivāda*, previously had become extinct, perhaps as early as the first council. It is not known which of the Aṅgabāhya texts found in the normative listing today were codified at these councils. Scholars believe that some of these texts show evidence of later dates of redaction.

Digambaras do not accept the authenticity of the redaction of the canon from these councils, which apparently were held in the absence of their mendicant leaders. They maintain that all of the Aṅga and Aṅgabāhya texts have been lost, perhaps as early as the 2nd century C.E. (For a listing of the individual texts, see "The Jain Scriptures," pp. xix–xxvi.)

ĀGAMIKA GACCHA. A **Śvetāmbara Mūrtipūjaka mendicant lineage**, also known as the **Tristuti Gaccha**. It was founded in 1193 by two **ācāryas** named Śīlaguṇasūri and Devabhadrasūri, who had previously belonged to the **Pūrṇimā Gaccha**. Followers of this group did not worship protector deities (**kṣetrapālas**) or **Sarasvatī**, the **goddess** of learning (śrutadevatā). Because of this, they omitted three hymns (tristuti) to her from their ritual of confession (**pratikramaṇa**). The Āgamika Gaccha was concentrated in Rajasthan and the Kathiawar region of Gujarat. The latest reference to it is found in an inscription dated 1626 C.E. After the 17th century, this **gaccha** ceased any independent existence, and its monastic and lay followers were absorbed into other gacchas. There currently is a Śvetāmbara mendicant lineage called Tristuti Gaccha (also known as the Bṛhat Saudharma Tapā Gaccha) that follows the tristuti doctrine. However, it is unlikely that group is a remnant of the Āgamika Gaccha because of an important difference in their ritual calendars. The Āgamika Gaccha followed the Pūrṇimā Gaccha in performing pratikramaṇa on the full and new moon days. The contemporary Tristuti Gaccha follows the **Tapā Gaccha** in performing pratikramaṇa on the 14th of each fortnight.

AGRAGAṆYĀ. The title of a **nun** in the **Śvetāmbara Terāpanthī** tradition who is the leader of a small group of nuns that lives and travels together. Unlike a **guruṇī** in the Śvetāmbara **Mūrtipūjaka** mendicant community, she has no decision-making authority. Within her group, she is responsible for carrying out decisions made by the male mendicant leader (**ācārya**), which are usually communicated to her through the chief nun (**sādhvī pramukhā**). She relinquishes her leadership to the ācārya during the annual meeting of the mendicant community (**maryādā mahotsava**). The ācārya may name another nun to this position although she is usually reappointed. He also may reconstitute the members of her group. *See also* MENDICANT HIERARCHY.

ĀHĀRA-DĀNA. The ritual of giving food to a **Digambara mendicant**. Except when **fasting**, Digambara mendicants eat food and drink water just once a day in one house, observing total silence. Because they eat from the joined palms of their hands and have no alms bowls, they do not collect food for other mendicants in their group. They walk with the tips of the fingers of their right hand resting on top of their right shoulder, a gesture signifying that they will accept food. Mendicants sometimes make a silent resolution to accept food only if certain conditions are met. This is in keeping with the mendicant vow of non-harming (**ahiṃsā**) because they avoid the harm that would have been committed had they caused a **layperson** to prepare food specifically for them.

The ritual associated with feeding a mendicant may vary according to location and whether the mendicant is a **monk** (**muni**) or a **nun** (**āryikā**). In the case of a monk, laypeople stand outside their houses with auspicious objects and invite the muni to eat, assuring him that the food, water, and donors are pure. If the muni stops, the members of the household circumambulate him and escort him into the house. He sits on a wooden stool while his feet are washed. While he stands on a short wooden platform, laypeople place food in his cupped hands, which he eats after proper inspection. If he finds any impurity in the food, he stops eating and does not accept any more food that day. A nun does not stand while eating but sits on a wooden platform. In some regions, it is not customary to perform ceremonies of worship in front of an āryikā because she does not have the same status as a muni, who observes the mendicant vow of non-possession (**aparigraha**) in its totality by practicing **nudity**. Advanced laypeople who have renounced the household life and live with the mendicant community (**kṣullakas/kṣullikās** and **ailakas**) also eat once a day in the house of a layperson. *See also* GOCARĪ.

AHIṂSĀ. Non-harming or nonviolence. Ahiṃsā is the central moral tenet in Jainism and is the basis for the practices and vows for **mendicants** and **laypeople**. Jains today view the statement "nonviolence is the highest religious duty" (ahiṃsā paramo dharmaḥ) as an all-encompassing expression of the Jain faith. Non-harming is emphasized in the ***Ācārāṅga Sūtra***, the earliest **Śvetāmbara** text on mendicant conduct, which states that "all breathing, existing, living, sentient creatures should not be slain, nor treated with violence, nor abused, nor tormented, nor driven away. This is the pure, unchangeable, eternal law which the clever ones, who understand the world, have proclaimed" (1.4.1.1–2, as translated by **Jacobi**). In the ***Tattvārtha Sūtra***, violence (**hiṃsā**) is defined as taking away life by actions of the body, speech, or mind that are done out of carelessness (pramāda) and are influenced by passions (**kaṣāyas**). The ahiṃsā-vrata is the first of five mendicant vows (**mahāvratas**) and **lay vows** (**aṇuvratas**). In taking this vow, a person agrees (1) not to harm other living beings oneself with body, mind, or speech (kṛta); (2) not to cause harm to others (kārita); and (3) not to approve of harmful actions (anumodana).

A mendicant vows to refrain from harming all living beings, including human beings and life-forms with one to five senses (**tiryañc**), namely animals and insects, as well as vegetable life and other other one-sensed beings (**ekendriya**). To avoid harming one-sensed air-bodied beings, mendicants do not fan themselves and some do not use microphones. To avoid harming fire-bodied beings, they do not kindle or extinguish fires. To avoid harming water-bodied beings, they drink water that has been properly boiled, and they do not swim, wade, or use excessive water for personal hygiene. To avoid harming earth-bodied beings, they do not dig in the earth. Mendicants obtain food from laypeople because gathering and cooking food entails harm to plant life and fire-bodied beings. They travel by foot, inspecting the path in front of them, and avoid walking on greenery. They do not travel during the four-month rainy season period (**cāturmāsa**) when various life-forms abound.

In contrast, the life of laypeople is always associated with some degree of harm because in order to live they must prepare food and engage in an **occupation**. Laypeople who choose to take the lay vow of ahiṃsā agree not to harm living beings with two or more senses. Some curtail harmful activities through their choice of occupation. Others may decide to take additional lay vows of restraint, namely, one or more of the three supplementary vows (**guṇa-vratas**) and the four vows of spiritual discipline (**śikṣā-vratas**), which are designed to further minimize harm. Although most Jains do not formally take the vow of ahiṃsā, they recognize that harm should be minimized whenever possible and are advocates of a **vegetarian** diet.

AILAKA. The title of a **Digambara layman** who has attained the second level of the 11th stage of renunciation (**pratimā**). The etymology of this term is uncertain. It could be Prākrit for acelaka ("unclothed" or "partially clothed"). He usually has already taken the vows of a **kṣullaka**, and at the time of initiation (**dīkṣā**), he discards his outer garments and keeps only a loincloth. He lives with other male renunciants and is part of a **mendicant lineage**. He eats once a day in the home of a layperson, remaining seated, but eating from the cupped palms of his hands. He periodically plucks his hair and beard by hand. This is the highest stage of renunciation possible for a layman and is seen as preparatory for taking the mendicant vows (**mahāvratas**) of a full-fledged naked **muni**.

AJĪVA. The category of substances (**dravya**) that is non-sentient. It includes the non-sentient substance with form (rūpi-ajīva), namely, matter (**pudgala**), and non-sentient substances without form (arūpi-ajīva), namely, space (ākāśa), the principle of motion (**dharma**-dravya), the principle of rest (**adharma-dravya**), and according to some, time (kāla).

ĀJĪVIKAS. An ascetic religious tradition that emerged in the Ganges Valley prior to Buddhism that expounded a philosophy based on determinism. Although none of their texts has survived, the Ājīvikas are mentioned in inscriptions, and their philosophy and mendicant practices are described in Buddhist and Jain texts. The Ājīvikas maintained that fate (niyati) was the operating principle of the universe. The course that each **soul** follows in a long series of rebirths is determined strictly by fate, with the operative mechanism being **karma**, or the effect of past deeds on present and future circumstances. Human effort could not change this predetermined course of rebirths for better or worse, which is likened to the unwinding of a ball of string. However, liberation (**mokṣa**) would be attained eventually. Renunciation and ascetic practices are understood to be a direct result of fate, but they could not affect circumstances of rebirth or cause premature liberation from the cycle of death and rebirth (**saṃsāra**). Mendicants renounced all possessions, begged for food, undertook arduous **fasts** and other acts of bodily mortification, and often fasted to death. Their monks practiced total **nudity**.

Makkhali Gosāla was the mendicant leader of the Ājīvikas during the time of the **Buddha** and of **Mahāvīra**. According to accounts in the **Śvetāmbara** ***Bhagavatī Sūtra***, prior to Mahāvīra's attaining omniscience (**kevala-jñāna**), the two spent six years traveling together before disagreements caused them to separate. The Ājīvikas must have been a very influential community at this time because the Buddhists considered them to be their chief rivals. Their mendicant community continued to expand during the Mauryan period (ca. 3rd century B.C.E.) as evidenced by donations of land to them for cave monasteries. Although the Ājīvikas apparently had died out in north India by the Gupta period (4th century C.E.), they survived in south India until the 14th century.

AKALAṄKA (8th century C.E.). Digambara logician. According to traditional accounts of his life written several centuries after his death, Akalaṅka assumed the guise of a Buddhist monk and studied in a monastery in order to gain the knowledge needed to refute the arguments of the great Buddhist logicians of the time. Through his mastery and systematization of epistemology and logic found in earlier Jain texts, he was able to use sophisticated logical techniques to counter the arguments of the logician Dharmakīrti regarding fundamental Buddhist doctrines like impermanence, as well as logicians in the brahmanical schools of philosophy. His most important works include *Aṣṭaśatī*, a **commentary** on **Samantabhadra**'s *Āptamīmāṃsā*, and *Nyāyaviniścaya*, which discusses the subject of perception and refuted the brahmanical claim that the vedic scriptures are non-created. He also wrote an important commentary on the ***Tattvārtha Sūtra*** entitled *Rājavārttika*, which itself was commented upon in a lengthy work by the Digambara author Vidyānanda (9th century).

AKHIL BHĀRATAVARṢĪYA DIGAMBARA JAINA PARIṢAD. *See* ASSOCIATIONS OF JAINS IN INDIA.

AKHIL BHĀRATAVARṢĪYA ŚVETĀMBARA STHĀNAKAVĀSĪ JAIN CONFERENCE. *See* ASSOCIATIONS OF JAINS IN INDIA.

AKHIL BHĀRATĪYA TERĀPANTH MAHĀSABHĀ. *See* ASSOCIATIONS OF JAINS IN INDIA.

AKRAM VIJÑĀN MĀRG. *See* PAṬEL, AMBĀLĀL.

AKṢAYA-TṚTĪYĀ. Undying Third. **Festival** commemorating the first occasion in the current descending **cycle of time** (avasarpiṇī) when alms were given to a **mendicant**. It is celebrated on the third day of the bright half of Vaiśākha (April/May). According to tradition, **Ṛṣabha** did not eat for some 13-and-one-half months after renunciation because no one knew what food was appropriate to give to him. Finally, he was offered sugarcane juice by Prince Śreyāṃsa (his grandson, a son of **Bāhubali**), who recalled feeding a Jain **monk** in a previous life. The term "undying" refers to the great merit (**puṇya**) generated by this first act of religious gifting (**dāna**) in our era. This festival is celebrated by publicly honoring those who have observed a series of **fasts** over the course of the previous year (Varṣī-Tapas). For **Śvetāmbaras, Mount Śatruñjaya** is one of the most popular locations to celebrate this occasion. It is said all **women** who fast are helped by the **Yakṣī** Cakreśvarī whose **image** is installed in the main temple here. Another popular location for this celebration is Hastinapur, the legendary spot of Śreyāṃsa's gifting, where a temple with images of Ṛṣabha and Śreyāṃsa was consecrated in 1978. *See also* TAPAS.

ALL-INDIA JAIN ASSOCIATION. *See* ASSOCIATIONS OF JAINS IN INDIA.

ALSDORF, LUDWIG (1904–1978). Indologist and scholar of Prākrit **languages**. Born in Laufersweiler, Germany, he studied Indology at Heidelberg University with Heinrich Zimmer and at Hamburg with **Walther Schubring**. He received a Ph.D. in 1928 for his study of the Apabhraṃśa portions of the *Kumārapālapratibodha* of Somaprabha. He was reader in German and French at the University of Allahabad from 1930 to 1932. While in India, he photographed manuscripts of the *Harivaṃśapurāṇa* of Puṣpadanta (10th century C.E.). His text edition and German translation of this **Digambara** work (Hamburg, 1936) contains a detailed study of the genre of Jain **Universal History**. In examining parallels to the *Harivaṃśapurāṇa*, Alsdorf discovered that the *Vasudevahiṇḍi* of Saṅghadāsa Gaṇin was a Jain version of the lost *Bṛhatkathākośa* of Guṇāḍhya. His expertise in the Apabhraṃśa language and meter led to his publication of *Apabhraṃśa-Studien* (Leipzig, 1937). He wrote a series of articles on selected chapters of the ***Uttarādhyayana Sūtra*** and on Jain exegetical literature. Prior to his appointment to the chair of Indology at the University of Hamburg in 1950, Alsdorf taught in Berlin and Münster. In 1951, at the invitation of **Muni Puṇyavijaya**, he went to India to photograph palm-leaf manuscripts in the Jain **manuscript libraries** of Cambay, **Jaisalmer**, and Patan. A bibliography of his works has been published in *Ludwig Alsdorf and Indian Studies* (Delhi, 1990). His collected papers have been published in *Kleine Schriften* (Wiesbaden, 1974).

AMAR MUNI, UPĀDHYĀYA (1902–1992). Śvetāmbara Sthānakavāsī preceptor. He was initiated at the age of 11 and studied Jain philosophy and Buddhist and Vedic scriptures. He is known for his progressive interpretation of Jain **scriptures**. He rejected the prohibition against travel by mechanical conveyance, although he did not go abroad. He was the inspirational force behind the modern Veerayatan order, which was founded by Sādhvī **Candanā** in 1974. The **mendicant lineage** established by him, the Amarmuni Sampradāya, is the only group to have appointed a **nun** to the rank of **ācārya**. The status of this lineage is controversial among some Jains.

AMBIKĀ. A **goddess** who is the **yakṣī** of **Neminātha**. Around 500 C.E. she became associated with all 24 of the **Tīrthaṅkaras** as an attendant deity. Around 900 C.E. the yakṣīs began to be differentiated, and she became the attendant of Neminātha. Ambikā means "mother," and she may have been a goddess of childbirth and children. She often is depicted with her two sons. She is an important goddess for the **Śvetāmbara** Jains in Gujarat. She is the protector goddess at the **pilgrimage** site of **Mount Girnār**. In some **Digambara** texts, the yakṣī of Neminātha is named Ambikā, but in the *Trilokaprajñapti* she is known as **Kūṣmāṇḍinī**.

AMOLAK ṚṢI, ĀCĀRYA (1877–1936). Śvetāmbara Sthānakavāsī mendicant leader. Born in Medata in the Marwar region of Rajasthan, he was raised by his maternal uncle in Bhopal, Madhya Pradesh, because his father had taken initiation as the **mendicant** Kevala Ṛṣi. In 1887, he too was initiated in the Ṛṣi Sampradāya and was appointed **ācārya** in 1932. He translated the 32 **Āgamas** accepted by Sthānakavāsīs into Hindi. In addition to editing texts, he was the author of some 70 independent works.

ĀNANDA. A lay disciple of **Mahāvīra**. He is considered an exemplar of lay conduct. His life story is recounted in the *Upāsakadaśāḥ*, one of the **Śvetāmbara Āgamas**. Ānanda was a prosperous businessman living in Vāṇijagrāma, the capital of the Licchavi country. After listening to Mahāvīra's preaching, he took the 12 **lay vows** of restraint, and his wife did likewise. They carefully observed their vows and gave generously to Jain **mendicants**. After 14 years, Ānanda found that he could not remain in the household and observe these vows in their totality, so he went to live in a community fasting hall. For five-and-a-half years, he undertook severe **fasts** and progressed through the 11 stages of renunciation for a layman (**pratimās**). Because his body had become weak, he decided to observe the religious death through fasting (**sallekhanā**). At this time, he gained supernatural vision (avadhi-jñāna) of such an extent that one of Mahāvīra's **gaṇadharas**, **Indrabhūti Gautama**, doubted that a **layperson** could have attained such powers. After a month of fasting, Ānanda died and was reborn as a heavenly being (**deva**) in the first heaven. His next birth will be as a human in **Mahāvideha**, where he will attain liberation (**mokṣa**).

ĀNANDA ṚṢI, ĀCĀRYA (1901–1992). Śvetāmbara Sthānakavāsī mendicant leader. He was born in Ahmadnagar, Maharashtra, and was named Nemicand Devicand Gugaliya. In 1913, Ratna Ṛṣi initiated him as Ānanda Ṛṣi in the Ṛṣi Sampradāya. In 1926, he was appointed successor-designate (yuvācārya) and, in 1942, at Ahmadnagar he was appointed **ācārya**. In 1949, when five **sampradāyas** decided to merge into one group, Ānanda Ṛṣi was elected ācārya of this group of some 300 **mendicants**. When the centrally organized **Śramaṇa Saṅgha** was formed in 1952, he resigned his position as ācārya and was appointed chief secretary of this **saṅgha**. After becoming ācārya of the Śramaṇa Saṅgha in 1958, he initiated a large number of disciples into this **mendicant lineage**.

ĀNAND(A)GHAN(A), MUNI (1603–1673). Śvetāmbara monk and mystical poet. The place of his birth and his name are unknown, but scholars have speculated that he may have been from Gujarat and that he was a Śvetāmbara **Mūrtipūjaka** monk, most likely in the **Tapā Gaccha**. At initiation, he was given the name Lābhānanda, but he wrote under the name of Ānandghan. His two works are composed in old Gujarati mixed with Rajasthani and Brajbhasha. *Ānandaghana Caubīsī* contains hymns of praise (**stavan**) to the 24 **Tīrthaṅkaras**, although hymns to the last two, **Pārśvanātha** and **Mahāvīra**, may not have been composed by him. *Ānandaghana Bahottarī* contains some 72 verses written in the style of the poet-saints Kabīr, Mīrā, Sūrdās, and Tulsīdās. His hymns contain expressions of devotion (bhakti), including the sentiments of love (sṛṅgāra) and separation from the beloved (viraha), as well as expressions of mystical spirituality. His works influenced **Mahopādhyāya Yaśovijaya**, who wrote *Śatapadi* in praise of him. Although he has been identified with a poet-saint who lived in Vṛndāvan (also called Ghanānanda) and one who lived in the village of Nanda, it is now generally accepted that there were three poet-saints who wrote under the name Ānandaghana.

ĀNANDASŪRI, ĀCĀRYA SĀGARA. *See* SĀGARĀNANDASŪRI, ĀCĀRYA.

ĀNANDASŪRI, ĀCĀRYA VIJAYA. *See* VIJAYĀNANDASŪRI, ĀCĀRYA.

ANARTHA-DAṆḌA-VRATA. One of three specialized vows of restraint of a **layperson (guṇa-vratas)**. It entails refraining from unwholesome activities that serve no useful purpose. These include harmful brooding (e.g., contemplating harm to others or to oneself), purposeless activities (e.g., gambling, cutting trees, or digging in the ground for fun), furnishing means of destruction (e.g., distributing poisons or weapons), and giving advice that leads others to cause harm (e.g., encouraging warfare or helping hunters to find animals). **Digambara** texts also include listening to stories that increase one's tendencies toward lust or violence (**hiṃsā**). *See also* VRATA.

A(Ñ)CALA GACCHA. A **Śvetāmbara Mūrtipūjaka mendicant lineage.** It was founded by a **monk** named Āryarakṣitasūri (1079–1169/1179 C.E.), who was from Dantani, a village in Rajasthan near **Mount Ābū**. He separated from the **Pūrṇimā Gaccha** in 1112 C.E. over a disagreement about mendicant praxis. This group has been known by three names. It is thought that Āryarakṣita named the group Vidhi Pakṣa, "The Party [that follows proper] Ritual." According to tradition, the name Acala, "Steady," was given to this group by King Siddharāja when Āryarakṣita stood firm and kept his word. The name Añcala is associated with the unique practice of their **laypeople** using the border (añcala) of their garments, rather than the usual mouth cloth, in performing certain ritual acts. The name Acala is preferred by members of this group.

Some ritual practices of the Acala Gaccha differ from other Śvetāmbara Mūrtipūjaka **gacchas**. Their lay followers perform the traditional eightfold worship (**aṣṭaprakārī pūjā**) in a modified form. They do not offer lamps or solid foods such as fruits and nuts to images of **Tīrthaṅkaras**, nor do they perform evening worship in **temples**. Laypeople are prohibited from using mendicant implements, namely, the mouth cloth (**muhpattī**), whisk broom (**rajoharaṇa**), and the symbol of the guru (**sthāpanācārya**), when performing ritual acts in the context of the obligatory duties (**āvaśyakas**) and during the observance of **poṣadha**. There is a slight variation in the wording of their version of the **Namaskāra Mantra**, which concludes with verses honoring their tutelary deity, the **Yakṣī** Cakreśvarī.

Today, this is the second largest Mūrtipūjaka gaccha. The mendicant community is centrally organized and is headed by a monk with the title gacchādhipati. Since 1993 this position has been held by Ācārya Guṇodayasāgarasūri (born 1931, initiated 1957). He organizes the small groups of **mendicants** who travel together, and he decides on their place of residence for the four-month rainy season period (**cāturmāsa**). This is done each year in the month of Vaiśāka (April/May) following the **Akṣaya-tṛtīyā festival**. As of 1999, it was estimated that there was a total of 250 mendicants (29 monks and 220 **nuns**), who are concentrated in Mumbai and in Kacch, where there is a large lay community. There currently is one other **ācārya** named Kalāprabhasāgarasūri (born 1953, initiated 1969). Because of the small number of monks, there may only be nuns in residence during cāturmāsa. In this gaccha, nuns are allowed to preach. Their mendicants may be identified by black alms bowls, a practice reportedly fixed by Ācārya Gautamasāgarasūri (1863–1952) in 1948.

ANEKĀNTAVĀDA. Doctrine of non-one-sidedness or a multifaceted view of reality. It is based on the teachings of the **Tīrthaṅkaras** who, because of their omniscience (**kevala-jñāna**), experience direct knowledge of reality and are able to simultaneously apprehend all possible aspects of an object. Expression of this reality is difficult due to the inherent limitations of human language. In order to make statements about apparently mutually contradictory qualities, Jains have developed a system of formal argumentation that uses the doctrine of qualified assertion (**syādvāda**) for different philosophical standpoints (naya or **nayavāda**) in a system of sevenfold predication (**sapta-bhaṅgi-naya**). Thus, one is able to argue that a **soul** (**jīva**) is both permanent and impermanent, depending on the standpoint that one takes. According to Jains, the teachings of other religious traditions, such as Hinduism, which is based on permanence, and Buddhism, which is based on impermanence, both contain partial versions of the truth. This qualified acceptance of the views of others is seen as an extension of the principle of non-harming (**ahiṃsā**), especially in modern times. Many Jains today, both in the diaspora and India, are reinterpreting anekāntavāda as a generalized attitude of tolerance in situations of religious pluralism. However, it is important to recognize that in earlier times, even the most broad-minded of Jain authors, such as **Haribhadra**, pointed out the inadequacies of their opponents' views, which are one-sided (ekānta) because they did not recognize the multifaceted nature of reality.

AṄGA. Literally, "limb." A collection of 12 texts that comprise the main body of the Jain scriptural canon (**Āgama**). They are composed by the chief disciples (**gaṇadharas**) of a **Tīrthaṅkara** and are based on his teachings, which express the beginningless and uncreated truths of reality. **Śvetāmbaras** believe that 11 of these texts are extant. **Digambaras** believe that all of these texts have been lost. (For a listing of the individual texts, see "The Jain Scriptures," pp. xix–xxvi.)

AṄGABĀHYA. Literally, "outside the limbs." A collection of texts composed by mendicant elders (**sthaviras**) that comprise the subsidiary portion of the Jain scriptural canon (**Āgama**). The number and ordering of Aṅgabāhya texts vary according to **Śvetāmbara** sectarian tradition. **Digambaras** believe that all of these texts have been lost. (For a listing of the individual texts, see "The Jain Scriptures," pp. xix–xxvi.)

ĀṄGĪ. In **Śvetāmbara** temple worship (**pūjā**), the dressing of a consecrated **image** of a **Tīrthaṅkara** or of his guardian deities (**śāsana-devatās**) in ornaments and silver armor or in special clothing. Āṅgī is not performed in **Digambara** temple worship, where images are always unadorned.

ANUPREKṢĀ. A term used by **Digambaras** for reflection or **meditation** (**dhyāna**) on themes that emphasize the unsatisfactory nature of life in the cycle of rebirth (**saṃsāra**). The 12 reflections are impermanence, helplessness, the cycle of rebirth, solitariness, the isolated nature of the **soul** (**jīva**), the impurity of the body, the influx of **karma** (āsrava), the checking of the influx of karma (saṃvara), the elimination of karma (nirjarā), the nature of the universe, the rarity of attaining omniscience (**kevala-jñāna**), and the teachings of the sacred law. Reflection on these topics is believed to inhibit the influx of karma to the soul. *See also* BHĀVANĀ.

AṆUVRAT MOVEMENT. A movement founded in 1949 by the **Śvetāmbara Terāpanthī Ācārya Tulsī** to promote nonviolence (**ahiṃsā**), morality, and tolerance in society. This movement, which is designed to bring about the moral transformation of society, is nonsectarian. It is open to all who agree to abide by a code of ethical conduct in their everyday lives. This code, which is based on the Jain **lay vows** (**aṇuvratas**), emphasizes self-restraint and the propagation of friendship, unity, peace, and tolerance of the viewpoints of others. An international non-governmental organization (NGO) called Aṇuvrat Vishva Bharati has been established as an extension of this movement. *See also* VRATA.

AṆUVRATAS. Five lesser vows or limited vows of restraint (**vratas**) that may be taken by a **layperson**. They are the vows of non-harming (**ahiṃsā**), truthfulness (**satya**), taking only what is given (**asteya**), sexual restraint (**brahmacarya**), and non-possession (**aparigraha**). They are patterned after the five great vows (**mahāvratas**) of a **mendicant**

but are less restrictive in nature. Their purpose is to limit actions that harm other living beings and harm oneself by impeding spiritual progress. A person vows (1) not to perform prohibited actions oneself with body, mind, or speech (kṛta); (2) not to cause others to undertake such actions (kārita); and (3) not to approve of their performance (anumodana). Today, few Jains formally take one or more of these vows. Nevertheless, they represent the ideal conduct for a layperson.

APARIGRAHA. Non-possession. Aparigraha-**vrata** is the fifth of five mendicant vows (**mahāvratas**) and **lay vows** (**aṇuvratas**). For a **layperson**, it is interpreted as cultivating a feeling of non-attachment to possessions. In taking this vow, laypeople agree to abide by the limits that they have established on accumulated items, such as land, houses, money, clothing, furniture, and so forth. **Mendicants** vow to renounce all possessions. Henceforth, they may keep only those items deemed necessary for maintaining their mendicant life. **Śvetāmbaras** understand this to include mendicant garments, alms bowls, whisk brooms (**rajoharaṇa**), and other mendicant implements. For **Digambaras**, this includes only two items: a peacock-feather whisk broom (**piñchī**) and a water pot (**kamaṇḍalu**). Thus, in taking this vow, a Digambara **monk** (**muni**) gives up wearing clothing for the rest of his life and eats from the joined palms of his hands. Because **women** are prohibited from practicing **nudity**, in the Digambara tradition **nuns** (**āryikās**) do not observe this mendicant vow in its totality. Thus, the two traditions disagree about the stage of spiritual purity (**guṇasthāna**) attained by a nun. Śvetāmbaras believe both monks and nuns attain the stage of total restraint (sarva-virata, the sixth guṇasthāna). Digambaras maintain that a woman cannot progress past the fifth stage of partial restraint of a layperson (deśa-virata, the fifth guṇasthāna).

ĀRATĪ. Rite of offering lamps to the **image** of a **Tīrthaṅkara**. It includes the offering of a five-wicked lamp containing clarified butter or ghee (āratī) and a single-wicked ghee lamp containing camphor (maṅgaḷ dīvo). It is usually performed at the conclusion of external or material worship (dravya **pūjā**) or in a special temple ceremony performed in the early evening. It is thought to remove any negative **karma** that might have accrued during worship. This rite is performed in **Śvetāmbara Mūrtipūjaka** temples except those of the **A(ñ)cala Gaccha**. It is performed in **Digambara temples** in south India and in some Digambara Bīsapanthī temples in north India. *See also* AṢṬAKA PŪJĀ; AṢṬAPRAKĀRĪ PŪJĀ; PŪJĀ.

ARDHAPHĀLAKA. An early **mendicant lineage** that flourished in the region of **Mathurā** during the pre-Kuṣāṇa and Kuṣāṇa periods (mid-2nd century B.C.E. through 3rd century C.E.). **Monks** from this lineage are depicted here on āyāgapaṭas (votive tablets) and on the bases of **Tīrthaṅkara** images. They are named after their mendicant emblem, a half piece (ardha) of cloth (phālaka), that monks draped over their left forearms to cover their **nudity**. There are narratives of the origins of this group in several medieval texts. The *Bhadrabāhukathānakam*, "The Story of Bhadrabāhu," in the **Digambara Hariṣeṇa**'s *Bṛhatkathākośa* (10th century C.E.) is the earliest account of their origins. According to this story, because of a 12-year drought, monks in the area of Ujjayinī had to disperse, and some migrated to Sindh. Those who remained were forced to collect alms at night, and they gathered food in alms bowls, taking it back to their place of residence to eat after sunrise. In order to avoid frightening the householders, they would drape a small piece of cloth (ardhaphālaka) over their arms to cover their nudity. After the drought was over, some monks reaffirmed their vow of total nudity while others continued the practice of using a cloth. Subsequently, a group of these Ardhaphālaka monks migrated to south India and became known as the Yāpana Saṅgha.

The origins of the **Śvetāmbara** tradition, according to Digambaras, is associated with a group of these Ardhaphālaka monks living in Valabhī. The king told them that their attire was unsuitable and they should assume nudity according to the tradition. When they refused, the king said they should begin to wear proper clothing. This group of monks came to be known as the Kambaḷa-tīrtha ("The Sect That Uses a Blanket"), which also was called Śveta-paṭa (= Śvetāmbara). This story reflects the Digambara belief that monks originally practiced total nudity and began wearing clothing at a later time, a view that is not accepted by Śvetāmbaras.

It is not known what happened to this mendicant lineage. Ardhaphālaka monks are not depicted after the Kuṣāṇa period at Mathurā nor are they depicted elsewhere. Some scholars believe they were absorbed into the Śvetāmbara community at Mathurā and others believe that they were the precursors of the **Yāpanīyas**.

ARHAT. Literally, "one who is worthy of worship." A synonym for a **Jina** or **Tīrthaṅkara**, who teachers others the path to liberation (mokṣa-mārga). It is occasionally used as a synonym for a **kevalin**.

ARIṢṬANEMI. *See* NEMINĀTHA.

ĀRYIKĀ. Literally, "a **woman** worthy of respect." A general designation for a Jain **nun** in the **Digambara** tradition. An āryikā is initiated by a **monk** (a **muni** or an **ācārya**) and traditionally becomes a member of a male **mendicant's lineage**. Today, however, some act as independent group leaders. They may be given permission to initiate their own lay disciples, usually female, but occasionally males as well. *See also* MENDICANT HIERARCHY.

ĀŚĀDHARA (13th century C.E.). Digambara lay poet and scholar. He belonged to a merchant family that was associated with the **Mūla Saṅgha mendicant lineage** and with the rulers of Dhārā. His most famous work is entitled *Dharmāmṛta*. One section, *Sāgāra-dharmāmṛta*, discusses lay conduct (**śrāvakācāra**), and the other, *Anagāra-dharmāmṛta,* discusses mendicant laws and conduct. He is the only **layperson** to have written on these topics. Some believe that his writings were influenced by the **Yāpanīya** tradition. He apparently was the only authority who approved of administering vows of **nudity** to a **woman** on her deathbed in the context of a religious death through fasting (**sallekhanā**).

ĀŚĀTANĀ. A moral fault or sacrilegious act. As used in canonical texts, this term refers to any act of a younger **monk** that shows a lack of respect for an older monk. In texts describing the six obligatory duties (**āvaśyakas**), 33 transgressions of the ritual veneration of **mendicants** (guru-**vandana**) are listed. In time, this concept was applied to the ritual of **caitya-vandana**, or the veneration of the image of a **Tīrthaṅkara**. Later, this term came to signify a sacrilegious act performed in a **temple**. In **Śvetāmbara** medieval texts on lay conduct (**śrāvakācāra**), as many as 84 āśātanās are listed. They include acts, such as sleeping, laughing, sporting, quarreling, spitting, evil gossip, eating in a temple, and destruction of temple property. Later texts identify four categories of āśātanās: (1) faults with respect to knowledge, which include acts of disrespect associated with **manuscripts**; (2) faults with respect to **devas**, which include the 84 acts found in earlier texts; (3) faults with respect to the guru, which incorporate the 33 acts from the āvaśyaka texts; and (4) faults with respect to the **sthāpanācārya**, such as touching it with the feet, letting it drop on the ground, and so forth. This designation is not found in the **Digambara** śrāvakācāra texts, but they contain lists of acts that should be avoided in the presence of a mendicant. One can atone for these faults by performing appropriate expiations. Details of the various listings of the āśātanās in the śrāvakācāra texts may be found in *Jaina Yoga* by R. Williams (pp. 225–229).

ASSOCIATIONS OF JAINS IN INDIA. Beginning in the late 19th and early 20th centuries, a number of associations were established by the Jain lay community to address various religious and social concerns. The membership of many of these associations was exclusively of one **caste**, or was dominated by one caste, or was from one local area. However, there were several associations that were organized in an effort to represent Jains of one sectarian tradition throughout India. These all-India associations, which usually communicated with their members through the publication of magazines, attempted to create a sense of community that transcended state or region. However, their membership, and thus the focus of their activities, often was concentrated in the region where their headquarters was located. All of the organizations mentioned below are still in existence today.

There are several all-India **Digambara** associations with headquarters in north India. The Bhāratavarṣīya Digambara Jain (Dharmarakṣini) Mahāsabhā was founded in Caurasi (Mathurā) around 1895 by Rājā Lakṣmaṇadās and others. They publish the *Jain Gazette* (Hindi). The Akhil Bhāratavarṣīya Digambara Jaina Pariṣad was founded in 1923 in Delhi by **Brahmacārī Sītal Prasād**, **Champat Rai Jain**, and other reformers who disagreed with the Mahāsabhā's conservative stance on the independence of the **munis** from the **bhaṭṭārakas** and their opposition to the publication of Jain **scriptures**. They began publication of *Vīr*. More recently, in 1974 the Digambara Jain Mahāsamiti was established in Delhi. At the end of the 19th century, several regionally focused Digambara associations were established in south India that were instrumental in forging a larger sense of community. In 1895, the Bombay Regional Digambara Jain Sabhā was established, which published the newspaper *Jain Mitra*. In 1899, the Dakṣiṇ (southern) Mahārāṣṭra Jain Sabhā was founded to represent Digambara Jains of the southern Maratha Country of the Bombay Presidency, including Kolhapur State, Belgaum, and Sangli. They began publication of the magazine *Pragati āṇi Jinavijaya*.

Among **Śvetāmbaras**, the principal all-India association for the **Mūrtipūjaka** lay community is the Jain Śvetāmbara Conference, which was founded in 1902 in Bombay (now Mumbai) by Jains who had recently immigrated there. In 1905, they began publication of an English-language magazine, the *Jain Swetamber Conference Herald*. A nationwide organization of **Sthānakavāsī laypeople**, the Akhil Bhāratavarṣīya Śvetāmbara Sthānakavāsī Jain Conference, was founded in 1906 in Morvi, Gujarat. Because of differences in culture and language between Gujarati-speaking and Hindi-speaking Sthānakavāsīs, it split into two independent organizations in 1984. The Hindi-speaking organization currently is based in New Delhi and the Gujarati-speaking organization in Mumbai. The first formal organization of the **Terāpanthī** lay community, the Terāpanth Sabhā, was established in Calcutta in 1913 in response to a bill that sought to classify young Jain **mendicants** as professional beggars and imprison them if caught on the streets. This group continued to represent the interests of only the Calcutta community until, at the urging **Ācārya Tulsī**, it was transformed into a nationwide institution called the Akhil Bhāratīya Terāpanth Mahāsabhā. They hold a biannual meeting during the **maryādā mahotsava**, where a president is elected who acts as the leader of the lay community (sabhāpati).

The Bhārata Jain Mahāmaṇḍal was established in Delhi in 1899 as an ecumenical national organization of Śvetāmbaras, Digambaras, and Sthānakavāsīs. Originally known as the Jain Young Men's Association, in 1929 the Mahāmaṇḍal officially adopted the name All-India Jain Association. Its main office is currently in Mumbai but for a number of years it was headquartered in Lucknow. From 1904 to 1927, Jagmanderlāl Jaini edited its English-language publication, *Jain Gazette*. It also has a Hindi publication, *Jain Jagat* (= *Gazait*, or *Gazette*). Its president is appointed alternatively from lay members of the Śvetāmbara Mūrtipūjaka, Sthānakavāsī, Terāpanthī, and Digambara communities.

In the early years, most of these associations held conferences every year or two that were attended by thousands of lay Jains with the leading śeṭhs, or merchant-princes, of the host city providing the leadership and financial support. Some of the matters addressed at these conferences were related to practices that violated the principle of non-harming (**ahiṃsā**) or did not show appropriate restraint. For example, various marriage customs were addressed, including child marriage, the payment of bride-price, having more than one wife, widow remarriage, intercaste marriage, and non-Jain wedding rites. The worship of non-Jain deities, the observance of non-Jain festivals, such as Holī, the performance of Lakṣmī Pūjā on **Dīvālī**, and the observance of non-Jain practices at the time of death were also debated. Resolutions were adopted supporting **educational institutions**, the education of **women**, the preservation of **manuscripts**, and the publication of printed editions of sacred texts. Among image-worshipping Jains, the restoration of **temples** and the right of low-caste Jains to worship in higher-caste temples were subjects of concern. Occasionally, matters relating to the mendicant community were discussed, such as proper education of mendicants and giving mendicant initiation (**dīkṣā**) to young children.

ASSOCIATIONS OF JAINS IN THE DIASPORA. In the United Kingdom, the Jain Samaj was founded in 1973 in Leicester by families that had recently migrated to the United Kingdom from East Africa. Although it was founded jointly by **Śvetāmbara Mūrtipūjaka** Jains of the Osvāl and Śrīmālī **castes**, four years later many of the Osvāl families withdrew from the organization. In 1980, there was a partial reconciliation when the association was reconstituted as Jain Samaj Europe with membership open to any Jain living in Europe (website: www.jainsamaj.org). Its objective is to promote Jainism within the Jain community and in the society at large by organizing worship, educational, and social activities. An old church was purchased in downtown Leicester for the association's Jain Centre. A **temple** was constructed at this site and, in 1988, the consecrated **images** of three **Tīrthaṅkaras**, **Śāntinātha**, **Pārśvanātha**, and **Mahāvīra**, were installed here. *The Jain* is a periodical published by this organization. The Institute of Jainology (IoJ) was established in London in 1983 to coordinate Jain affairs internationally (website: www.jainology.org). Its goals are to provide a platform for interaction between different community organizations, to promote interfaith dialogue, to create an awareness of the Jain faith in the community at large, and to provide opportunities for scholarly research on Jainism.

In North America, the Federation of Jain Associations in North America (JAINA) was founded in 1981 (website: www.jaina.org). It is the umbrella organization of 62 local Jain associations (as of 2003) in the United States and Canada. Its objectives are to assist local Jain associations, to promote the establishment of new Jain associations in North America, to assist in the establishment of Jain temples, to promote religious and educational activities including **vegetarianism** and nonviolence (**ahiṃsā**), to promote charitable and humanitarian activities, and to establish liaisons with governmental agencies. It holds a biennial convention and publishes *Jain Digest*. There also are local Jain associations in a number of countries where Jains have migrated in smaller numbers, including Australia (Melbourne, Perth, and Sydney), Hong Kong, Kenya (Nairobi and Mombasa), and Japan (Kobe).

There are several associations for Jain youth living in the diaspora. Young Jains of the UK was originally formed in 1987 as the Young Oshwal Cultural Society and became an independent organization a few months later (website: www.youngjains.org.uk). It encourages the exploration of Jain philosophy and spirituality and its practical importance in everyday life. Young Jains of America (YJA) is an umbrella organization affiliated with JAINA (website: www.jya.org). Its objectives are to raise awareness of Jain values and to instill pride in Jain heritage. Its first biennial convention was held in 1994. Young Jain Professionals (YJP) also is affiliated with JAINA (website: www.YJPOnline.org). It is a forum for young Jain professionals to meet and to work with successful role models in the Jain community. It promotes the values of Jainism in professional and social life through sponsoring seminars on Jain ethics in science, medicine, business, and the arts, and encouraging socially responsible investing. Its first annual convention was held in 1998.

AṢṬAKA (AṢṬA-DRAVYA) PŪJĀ. Worship with Eight Substances. A rite of daily material worship (dravya **pūjā**) performed by **laypeople** in **Digambara temples** in south India, and in a modified form in Digambara **Bīsapanthī** temples in north India, in which eight substances are offered to the consecrated **image** of a **Tīrthaṅkara**. These substances are (1) lustration (**abhiṣekha**) with purified water or the five nectars (pañca-amṛta), (2) sandalwood paste, (3) flowers, (4) incense, (5) a lamp with camphor, (6) uncooked rice, (7) sweets, and (8) fruit or nuts. In the Digambara *Paümacariya* of Vimalasūri (1st–5th centuries C.E.), the oldest extant Jain purāṇa, elements of the eightfold pūjā are described, such as bathing the image and offering flowers, incense, and lamps.

There are regional differences in the performance of this ritual. In north India, laypeople may enter the inner sanctum and make the offerings themselves, although they usually do not touch the image itself. If the worshipper is standing, offerings are placed on a metal tray on the altar or on a high narrow table in front of the altar. If the worshipper is seated on the floor, the offerings are placed on a metal tray on a low table. Sanskrit **mantras** accompany each offering. One of the most popular liturgies in north India is the *Deva Śāstra Guru Pūjā* by the Braj poet **Dyānatrāy**. In Digambara temples in south India, laypeople do not enter the inner sanctum. Instead, a Jain priest (**Jaina Brahmin, Upādhye**) performs the daily rites of worship on behalf of the laypeople, although laity may perform these rites themselves in home shrines. The eight substances are still offered, although there is some regional variation in the manner in which the rituals associated with the offerings are performed. Due to the influence of Digambara **Terāpanthīs**, this ritual has been modified in many Bīsapanthī temples in north India. When lustration of the image is performed, the five nectars (pañca-amṛta) are generally not offered, but only a minimum amount of water is poured over the image. In some Bīsapanthī temples, the lustration is omitted entirely. In some the lamp ceremony is not performed, and there is no worship after dark.

AṢṬAMAṄGALA. Eight auspicious symbols. For **Śvetāmbaras**, they are the **svastika**, an extended, elaborately formed svastika (nandyāvarta), a mark in the center of a **Tīrthaṅkara**'s chest (śrīvatsa), a powder flask (vardhamānaka), a throne or seat (bhadrāsana), a pair of fish (matsya-yugma), a full pitcher (kalaśa), and a mirror (darpaṇa). For **Digambaras**, they are a gilded vase (bhṛṅgāra), a fly whisk (cāmara), a banner (dhvaja), a fan (vyajana), an umbrella (chatra), a seat of honor (supratiṣṭha), a full pitcher (kalaśa), and a mirror (darpaṇa). Although eight auspicious symbols are depicted on votive tablets (āyāgapaṭas) from the Kuṣāṇa period at **Mathurā** (2nd–3rd centuries C.E.), some of the symbols differ from the above-mentioned objects.

AṢṬĀPADA. *See* MOUNT AṢṬĀPADA.

AṢṬAPRAKĀRĪ PŪJĀ. Worship with Eight Objects. A rite of daily material worship (dravya **pūjā**) performed in a **temple** by **Śvetāmbara Mūrtipūjaka laypeople**. It is performed in a modified form by those affiliated with the **A(ñ)cala Gaccha**. Eight substances are offered to the consecrated **image** of a **Tīrthaṅkara**. These substances are (1) purified water or the five nectars (pañca-amṛta), (2) sandalwood paste, (3) flowers, (4) incense, (5) a lamp with camphor, (6) uncooked rice, (7) sweets, and (8) fruit or nuts. Laypeople may enter the inner sanctum and touch the image of a Tīrthaṅkara if they are in a state of ritual purity, have bathed, and are wearing appropriate garments reserved for worship. They must cover their mouths with a cloth to prevent impurities from being breathed onto the image.

The ritual actions and recitations associated with this worship are highly variable. However, worship normally takes place in the morning. The person utters the word **nisīhi** ("it is abandoned") when entering the temple and **circumambulates** the image in a clockwise direction (pradakṣinā) three times. The first three offerings are placed directly on the Tīrthaṅkara's image (aṅga pūjā). After cleaning the image to remove any substances left from previous worship, it is anointed with pure water, milk, or the five nectars (pañca-amṛta). A paste of sandalwood and camphor (having cooling properties) is dabbed on the image in nine places (navāṅgi pūjā): the great toes, knees, wrists, shoulders, head, forehead, throat, heart, and navel. Flowers are placed on the Tīrthaṅkara's lap, knees, shoulders, and head, and the image may be garlanded. The remaining five offerings are made in front of the image (agra pūjā). The worshipper waves incense and a lamp in front of the image. Three food offerings of rice, sweets, and fruit or nuts are offered on a low table or offering box in the main pavilion of the temple. The worshipper forms auspicious symbols with the rice. Often, this is a **svastika**, above which is placed in a horizontal row three dots symbolizing the Three Jewels (**Ratnatraya**) of right faith, right knowledge, and right conduct, which is surmounted with a crescent with a dot inside symbolizing liberated **souls (siddhas)** at the top of the universe. The other food offerings and coins are placed on the auspicious diagram. All food offered to a Tīrthaṅkara is permanently given up. It is never returned to the worshipper or consumed as a blessed substance (prasāda). Liquids that bathe the image are collected and may be used to anoint the forehead and eyes of the worshipper, but they are not consumed. At the completion of external or material worship (dravya pūjā), the worshipper utters the word nisīhi and commences with mental worship (bhāva pūjā). After worship of the Tīrthaṅkara has been completed, a layperson may worship images of ancillary deities, such as **yakṣas/yakṣīs**, various protector deities (**kṣetrapālas**), and images of deceased mendicant leaders.

In the **Kharatara Gaccha**, laywomen of childbearing years are prohibited from anointing a Tīrthaṅkara image with sandalwood paste. In the A(ñ)cala Gaccha, lamps and solid foods, such as fruits and nuts, are not offered to images of Tīrthaṅkaras, and evening worship is not performed in their temples. *See also* AṢṬAKA PŪJĀ; PŪJĀ.

ASTEYA. Not taking anything that is not given. The asteya-**vrata** is the third of five mendicant vows (**mahāvratas**) and **lay vows (aṇuvratas)**. A **layperson** agrees to accept only those items that are acquired through legitimate means or through inheritance. Refraining from all illegal or dishonest business practices is included in this lay vow. A **mendicant** agrees to accept only those items that are given by the laity.

ATICĀRA. Infraction of a vow (**vrata**). In the texts on mendicant conduct (Chedasūtras) and lay conduct (**śrāvakācāra**), five infractions are listed for each of the five mendicant vows (**mahāvratas**) and for each of the 12 **lay vows**, namely, the five **aṇuvratas**, the three **guṇa-vratas**, and the four **śikṣā-vratas**. For example, using false weights and measures is an infraction of the lay vow of truthfulness (satya-vrata). Expiations (prāyaścitta) vary in accordance with the nature and severity of the infraction, whether it was committed intentionally or accidentally, and with strong or weak volition. *See also* PRATIKRAMAṆA.

ĀTMAN. Self, **soul**, or that which is sentient. In some texts, it is used interchangeably with the term **jīva**. In other texts, especially those of the **Digambara** mystical tradition, it means an innate pure soul, which is visualized to be like that of a **siddha**, unaffected by **karmic** matter.

ĀTMĀRĀMJĪ, MUNI. *See* VIJAYĀNANDASŪRI.

AUSPICIOUS DREAMS. Dreams seen by the mother of a **Tīrthaṅkara** at the time of conception. In the **Śvetāmbara** tradition, there are 14 dreams: (1) a white elephant, (2) a white bull, (3) a lion, (4) the **goddess** Śrī, (5) a flower garland, (6) the full moon, (7) the rising sun, (8) a banner, (9) a vase full of water, (10) a lake adorned with lotuses, (11) the ocean of milk (often depicted by a ship), (12) a heavenly vehicle in which deities travel, (13) a heap of jewels, and (14) a fire. There are two additional dreams in the **Digambara** tradition: (15) a throne and (16) a pair of fish playing in a lake. Models of these objects are displayed in **temples** during the rituals celebrating a Tīrthaṅkara's conception and birth, and the dreams are frequently illustrated on Jain temples. *See also* KALYĀṆAKA.

AVASARPIṆĪ. Regressive half of the **cycle of time.**

ĀVAŚYAKAS. Six obligatory duties of a **mendicant** that are performed on a daily basis. They are recommended for a **layperson**, who may choose to perform them daily or occasionally during the year, especially during the four-month rainy season period (**cāturmāsa**). They are (1) attainment of equanimity (**sāmāyika**), (2) praising the 24 **Tīrthaṅkaras** (caturviṃśati-stava), (3) veneration of mendicants (guru-**vandana**), (4) confession (**pratikramaṇa**), (5) abandoning the body (**kāyotsarga**), and (6) renouncing certain foods or activities for a specific period of time (**pratyākhyāna**). Mendicants have written ritual manuals, which are based on ancient texts and their **commentaries**, that are used today for these rites. The ritualized formulae and gestures that accompany these rites vary among **Śvetāmbaras** and **Digambaras** and among image-worshipping and non-image-worshipping traditions. Although described as separate rituals in early texts such as the *Āvaśyaka Sūtra*, today several rites are performed as an integrated whole. For instance, the rituals of guru-vandana, caturviṃśati-stava, and pratyākhyāna may be performed as part of pratikramaṇa. Some Digambara authors, such as **Jinasena** (9th century), recommend six daily activities (karmans) for laypeople in place of the āvaśyakas: (1) worship of the Tīrthaṅkaras (deva-pūjā), which incorporates caturviṃśati-stava and aspects of sāmāyika, (2) veneration of mendicant teachers (guru-upāsti), (3) study of the scriptures (svādhyāya), (4) observing vows and restraints of a layperson (saṃyama), (5) austerities (**tapas**), and (6) giving to worthy recipients (**dāna**).

ĀYAMBIL (Skt., **ĀCĀMĀMLA**). A practice undertaken by **Śvetāmbaras** of eating one meal a day of bland foods that are considered to be "sour," such as boiled rice, gruel, and barley meal. These foods are prepared without using any oil, ghee, sugar, salt, or curds, and they do not contain any dry or green fruits. In areas with large Jain populations, there are special eating halls where suitable food is prepared on a daily basis. Some **mendicants** observe this **fast** throughout their life. For **laypeople**, the most popular time for observing this fast is during the nine-day **festival** of **Olī**, which takes place twice a year.

AYOGA KEVALIN. Kevalin without activity. *See* SAYOGA KEVALIN.

– B –

BĀHUBALI. The second son of **Ṛṣabha**, the first **Tīrthaṅkara** of this era, and his wife Sudanā. When Ṛṣabha renounced the household life and appointed his eldest son, **Bharata**, as king, he gave portions of his territory to his other sons. After receiving the special weapon of a universal emperor (**Cakravartin**), Bharata undertook a campaign to conquer the entire world. His other brothers ceded their territories to him when they renounced the household life under Ṛṣabha. However, Bāhubali refused to give up his land, and they engaged in a duel. As Bāhubali raised his fist to strike the killing blow, he realized that wealth and kingship had no meaning if it entailed the death of his brother. Bāhubali immediately renounced the household life. He stood motionless in the forest for so long with his arms at his side in the meditative posture called **kāyotsarga** that creepers entwined his arms and legs and anthills covered his feet. After a year in **meditation** (**dhyāna**), he overcame his passions (**kaṣāyas**) and attained omniscience (**kevala-jñāna**). According to some **Digambara** sources, he was the first person to attain liberation (**mokṣa**) in our era. However, other texts state that it was Anantavīrya, a son of Bharata. Today, Bāhubali is worshipped primarily by Digambaras at numerous sites throughout India where colossal **images** of him have been erected. The most famous of these is at

Śravaṇa Beḷgoḷa where approximately every 12 years tens of thousands gather for a head-anointing ceremony (**mastakābhiṣeka**).

BALADEVA (BALABHADRA). One of the five categories of the 63 illustrious men (**śalākā-puruṣas**) in **Universal History** texts and other Jain narratives. They are the older half brothers of the **Vāsudevas**, having the same father and different mothers. Like Vāsudevas, they are Half-Cakravartins, with half the status and power of full universal emperors (**Cakravartins**). In **Bharata-kṣetra** (the part of the universe where we are said to live), nine Baladevas are born in each progressive and regressive half-**cycle of time**. In this era, they are (1) Acala (Dig., 2nd Baladeva), (2) Vijaya (Dig., 1st Baladeva), (3) Sudharma (or Bhadra), (4) Suprabha, (5) Sudarśana, (6) Ānanda (Dig., Nandīṣeṇa), (7) Nandana (Dig., Nandimitra), (8) Rāma (= Padma), the hero of Jain *Rāmāyaṇa* (in Jain narratives, it is Lakṣmaṇa, not Rāma, who kills Rāvaṇa), and (9) Baladeva (= Rāma, Balarāma, Balabhadra), the elder brother of Vāsudeva Kṛṣṇa. They are righteous Jains who firmly observe the central Jain ethical principle of non-harming (**ahiṃsā**). Because of this, after renouncing the world and becoming Jain **mendicants**, they usually attain liberation (**mokṣa**), but they also may be reborn as a heavenly being (**deva**) in one of the heavenly abodes. All of the Baladevas mentioned above attained liberation at the end of life, except for Baladeva, who was reborn in the Brahmaloka.

BANARAS (BENARES, KĀŚĪ, VĀRĀṆASĪ). In Jainism, the birthplace of **Pārśvanātha**, the 23rd **Tīrthaṅkara** of this era. Located on the northern bank of the Ganges River, it is one of most ancient cities in the world that is still inhabited. Jains do not consider dying in Banaras to be auspicious or to assure liberation from rebirth (mokṣa), nor do they come here on **pilgrimage** to bathe in the Ganges. Banaras has long been a center of traditional scholarship. In the early 20th century, several Jain **educational institutions** were established here, including Syādvāda Jain Mahāvidyālaya, Pārśvanātha Mahāvidyāśrama, and Yaśovijaya Jain Pāṭhśālā. At this time, there was an active intellectual community of **Digambara paṇḍits** living here. It is also the site of Banaras Hindu University, where many Jain scholars have studied.

BANĀR(A)SĪDĀS(A) (1586–1643). Lay reformer and mystical poet of the **Adhyātma movement**. He was born in Jaunpur, Uttar Pradesh, into a family of Jain merchants of the Śrīmālī **caste** who were associated with the **mendicant lineage** of the **Śvetāmbara Mūrtipūjaka**

Kharatara Gaccha. He studied grammar and composition under several lay scholars (**paṇḍits**) and religious subjects with a Kharatara Gaccha **monk**. He was first exposed to ideas associated with the Adhyātma movement in 1598 when he was 12 years old, but he continued to participate in Śvetāmbara rituals for a number of years. He became a trader in north India and settled in Āgra.

Around 1633 Banārsīdās read **Kundakunda**'s *Samayasāra* and experienced a crisis of faith about the rituals that he had engaged in. He became involved with a discussion circle of **laymen** in Agra who gathered in the **Digambara temple** in the Shahganj neighborhood to study texts of the Digambara mystical tradition authored by Kundakunda, **Yogīndu**, and Rāmasiṃha Muni, and to compose their own religious poetry. He became one of the leaders of this circle and of the Adhyātma movement that grew out of it and other study circles in north India.

In 1635, at the Agra study circle there was a series of lectures on the *Gommaṭasāra* that included details of the 14 **guṇasthānas**, or levels of spiritual purity. Banārsīdās learned that different ritual practices are appropriate for different levels, and that at the higher levels inner spiritual transformation and contemplation on the purity of the **soul** should be emphasized. In 1636, he composed *Samaysāra Nāṭaka*, a Hindi rendering of Kundakunda's *Samayasāra*. He also wrote *Ardhakathānaka* ("Half-a-Story"), which is the first Hindi autobiography. He wrote it when he had lived approximately half of the 110-year life span traditionally allotted to humans in Jainism. In addition to detailing his spiritual progress, this work is an important source of information about business and politics in north India in the 17th century. In 1644, Jagjīvanrām compiled his Hindi poetry into a single collection entitled *Banārasī Vilās*. *See also* TERĀPANTHĪ (Dig.); ṬOḌARMAL.

BHADRABĀHU. There is much confusion about the name Bhadrabāhu, which appears in **Śvetāmbara** and **Digambara mendicant lineage** lists, in Śvetāmbara and Digambara narratives, in Śvetāmbara **commentaries**, and in an inscription at **Śravaṇa Beḷgoḷa** from around 600 C.E. Most scholars believe that there were at least two Bhadrabāhus and some believe that there were three. Digambaras and Śvetāmbaras agree that the first Bhadrabāhu was the last person to know all 14 ancient texts called the **Pūrvas** and that after him only 10 Pūrvas were known. In some of the lists, he is the fifth elder (**sthavira**) in the mendicant lineage established by **Mahāvīra** and is said to have died either 162 years or 175 years after the death of Mahāvīra.

There are several versions of his life story in Digambara sources, all of which were composed many centuries after his death. Some Digambara accounts mention his migration from Pāṭaliputra (now Patna) in Magadha to the south along with Candragupta Maurya (320 B.C.E.–293 B.C.E.), the founder of the Mauryan dynasty. It is thought that a large portion of the mendicant community left the north at this time because of a severe famine in Magadha and that Candragupta Maurya had renounced the throne to become a Jain **monk**. It is believed that Bhadrabāhu and Candragupta undertook a religious death through fasting (**sallekhanā**) at Śravaṇa Beḷgoḷa. In a Kannada version, Candragupta is called Samprati Candragupta (fl. 200 C.E.), who would have been the grandson of Aśoka. The migration takes place from Ujjain, the capital of Avantī. Because of his advanced age, Bhadrabāhu remained behind and died in Avantī.

There is an inscription from the 6th or 7th century at Śravaṇa Beḷgoḷa in which two Bhadrabāhus are mentioned. It states that Bhadrabāhusvāmī foretold a calamity lasting for 12 years in Ujjain and the entire community left the north and came to the south. He was in a lineage of great men. Beginning with Jambū, the fifth **mendicant** listed is Bhadrabāhu, who is followed in the list by eight names, concluding with "and other teachers." The inscription also mentions an **ācārya** named Prabhācandra who undertook a fast ending in death.

The scholar M. D. Vasantha Raj has concluded that there were three Bhadrabāhus and two migrations to the south. According to him, the first Bhadrabāhu, the knower of the 14 Pūrvas, was a contemporary of Candragupta Maurya as mentioned above. The second Bhadrabāhu, who had complete knowledge of eight **Aṅga** texts and partial knowledge of the others, was a contemporary of King Vikramāditya who ruled Ujjain in the 1st century B.C.E. It is said that he was the brother of the astrologer Varāhamihira. The third Bhadrabāhu, who had complete knowledge of the first Aṅga and partial knowledge of the others, migrated to Śravaṇa Beḷgoḷa, having predicted the calamity in Ujjain. He undertook sallekhanā there, dying in 106 C.E. He was assisted by Prabhācandra, who later undertook sallekhanā himself.

According to Śvetāmbara accounts, Bhadrabāhu did not go to the south at the time of a famine. Instead, he was practicing **meditation** in Nepal. After the famine ended, a council was convened by **Sthūlabhadra** at Pāṭaliputra to recite the sacred texts. When it was discovered that no one present had knowledge of the Pūrvas, Sthūlabhadra was sent to Nepal to learn them from Bhadrabāhu. Eventually, the two of them left Nepal and came to Pāṭaliputra, where Bhadrabāhu later died. The name Bhadrabāhu is mentioned in other contexts. It is said that Bhadrabāhu was the author of three Chedasūtras, the *Bṛhatkalpa, Vyavahāra*, and *Niśītha Sūtras*, texts on mendicant law in the Śvetāmbara canon. It is also said that Bhadrabāhu was the author of the ***Kalpa Sūtra*** and of 10 important verse commentaries (niryuktis) on Śvetāmbara canonical texts. Some have identified the author of the Chedasūtras as Bhadrabāhu I and the author of the *Kalpa Sūtra* and niryuktis as Bhadrabāhu II. Some believe that Bhadrabāhu II flourished in the 1st century C.E. However, Suzuko Ohira has concluded that Bhadrabāhu II, the author of the niryuktis, foretold a famine at Ujjain, after which the final council of Valabhī was convened (453 or 466 C.E.).

BHADRAṄKARAVIJAYAGAṆI, PAṄNYĀSA (1903–1980). Śvetāmbara Mūrtipūjaka scholar-**monk** of the **Tapā Gaccha**. He was born in Patan, Gujarat, and was named Bhagavan Dās. He was brought up in Bombay (now Mumbai) where his father was working. In 1928, Ācārya Vijayadhānasūri came to Bombay. Among the monks traveling with him was his disciple Muni Rāmavijaya. Impressed by the discourses of Muni Rāmavijaya, Bhagavan Dās began studying the works of **Mahopādhyāya Yaśovijaya**. Two years later he was initiated by Rāmavijaya as Bhadraṅkaravijaya. Not wanting to be appointed **ācārya**, he accepted the rank of **paṅnyāsa** in 1940. He was one of the leading intellectuals in the Tapā Gaccha in the 20th century. He was well versed in rituals and was known for his austerities and long periods of **fasting**, including several six-month **āyambil** fasts. He wrote several important works on various aspects of ritual, including *Pratimā Pūjan*, *Tattvadohan*, and *Paramātmā Darśan*. He coauthored a **commentary** on the *Pratikramaṇa Sūtra* that was included in a recommended curriculum for Tapā Gaccha monks. He traveled extensively in the Marwar area of Rajasthan and spent the last years of his life in Patan.

BHAGAVATĪ SŪTRA. "The Venerable." Also called *Vyākhyāprajñapti Sūtra*, "Proclamation of Explanations." It is the fifth **Aṅga** in the **Śvetāmbara** scriptural canon (**Āgama**). It is the longest canonical text, which scholars believe is a composite of portions that are older and portions that originated closer to the final Council of Valabhī. It is composed in the form of answers by **Mahāvīra** to numerous questions posed by one of his **gaṇadharas, Indrabhūti Gautama**, on a wide variety of topics relating to Jain doctrine and ascetic practices. The answers are qualified from a specific viewpoint. The concept that all statements are subject to qualifications (**syādvāda**) is later developed into a system of argumentation that is a cornerstone of Jain philosophy. It also contains fragmented narratives of Mahāvīra's life, including his association with the **Ājīvika** leader **Makkhali Gosāla**.

BHAIRAV(A). A non-liberated male guardian deity who protects **temple** precincts. Originally, he was a fierce manifestation of the Hindu god Śiva, who was converted to Jainism. He is depicted as a mustached warrior with a bow and arrow. *See also* ADHIṢṬHĀYAKA DEVAS; NĀKOṚ(Ḍ)A BHAIRAVA.

***BHAKTĀMARA STOTRA*.** Hymn of praise composed by Mānatuṅga that is dedicated to **Ṛṣabha** or **Ādinātha**, the first **Tīrthaṅkara** of this era. The title "Devoted Gods" comes from the first verse of the hymn, which describes the gods bowing in devotion to Ādinātha. Composed in Sanskrit, it is one of the few texts that is accepted by both **Śvetāmbaras** and **Digambaras**. The Śvetāmbara version contains 44 verses and the Digambara version 48 verses, with the four additional verses describing additional miracles (atiśayas) that appear when a Tīrthaṅkara attains omniscience (**kevala-jñāna**).

According to hagiographical accounts, Mānatuṅga was a court poet associated with either King Bhoja in Ujjain or King Harṣa in **Banaras**. Some scholars, including M. A. Dhaky and Jitendra Shah, have concluded that he was not a court poet but a Śvetāmbara devotional poet who lived in the second half of the 6th century C.E. According to traditional accounts, in order to demonstrate the power of this hymn to the king, Mānatuṅga was bound in chains. As he recited each verse, one of the chains broke, and ultimately he was freed from his bondage.

Beginning in the 14th century, many **commentaries** have been written on this text that relate the worldly benefits attained from reciting or **meditating** on this hymn. Its popularity gave rise to a number of devotional hymns to other Tīrthaṅkaras that incorporated portions of its verses or imitated its style. The most famous of these is the *Kalyāṇamandira Stotra*, which is devoted to **Pārśvanātha** and is also accepted by both Śvetāmbaras and Digambaras. The *Bhaktāmara Stotra* was incorporated into the Jain tantric tradition. Both Śvetāmbara and Digambara **manuscripts** contain diagrams of **yantras** along with the ritual formulas (ṛddhis and **mantras**) that accompany the recitation of each verse.

Beginning in the 17th century, numerous vernacular translations have been published and recently there have been several English translations. In the Śvetāmbara **Mūrtipūjaka** community, this hymn has been expanded into an elaborate collective temple ritual called the

Bhakāmara Stotra Mahāpūjā, which was devised by Ācārya Vijayavikramasūri in the 1970s. It is performed by a lay ritual specialist on special occasions, such as the anniversary of a death, the completion of a lengthy **fast**, or a **laywoman** renouncing the world to become a **nun**.

BHARATA. The eldest son of **Ṛṣabha**, the first **Tīrthaṅkara** of this era, and his wife Sumaṅgalā. When Ṛṣabha renounced the household life, he appointed Bharata to succeed him as king. At the time that his father attained omniscience (**kevala-jñāna**), a special weapon (cakra) appeared in his armory, a sign that he had become the first universal emperor (**Cakravartin**) of this era. He is depicted as an ideal Jain king who adhered to the lay vows of non-harming (**ahiṃsā**) and non-possession (**aparigraha**) by ruling justly and remaining unattached to his wealth. He is credited with establishing the occupational **caste** of priests (**Brahmin** varṇa). **Śvetāmbaras** believe that he attained omniscience after the death of Ṛṣabha without having first renounced the household life, but **Digambaras** believe that he renounced prior to attaining omniscience. According to the Digambara ***Mahāpurāṇa***, he and Ṛṣabha are the last patriarchs (**kulakaras**) of this era.

BHARATA-KṢETRA. In Jain cosmography, one of seven continents located on the island-continents inhabited by humans. There are a total of five Bharata-kṣetras: one on the island-continent of **Jambūdvīpa** and two each on the island-continents of Dhātakīkhaṇḍa and Puṣkaravara. The Bharata-kṣetra located on the island-continent of Jambūdvīpa is the part of the universe where we are said to live. Bharata-kṣetra is one of the **karma-bhūmi** lands. *See also* MADHYA-LOKA.

BHĀRATAVARṢĪYA DIGAMBARA JAIN (DHARMARAKṢINI) MAHĀSABHĀ. *See* ASSOCIATIONS OF JAINS IN INDIA.

BHĀṢYA. *See* COMMENTARY.

BHAṬṬĀRAKA. Venerable One or Learned One. (1) A term of respect that was used in earlier times for a learned **monk** in both the **Śvetāmbara** and **Digambara** traditions. (2) As it is used today, the title of a man who was chosen as the head of a group of Digambara **munis** who lived permanently in a **monastery** (maṭha) and who in the course of time gave up the practice of total **nudity**. Although there is evidence that Digambara **mendicants** in the **Drāviḍa Saṅgha** lived a sedentary life in the 5th century C.E., it is not known when this practice became widespread or when the institution of the bhaṭṭāraka first arose. However, it appears that many monks abandoned the practice of total nudity in the 13th or 14th century. An inscription dated 1363 C.E. states that the Delhi bhaṭṭāraka donned a cloth in 1333. A 16th-century text mentions that Muslims harassed Digambara monks for appearing naked in public, so Bhaṭṭāraka Vasantakīrti instructed his disciples to wear clothes when in public and return to nudity when inside the monastery. **Nāthūrām Premī** has speculated that Vasantakīrti may have lived in Chittor in 1207 and that some bhaṭṭārakas might have been **Yāpanīyas**, whose monks covered their nudity with a small piece of cloth when in populated areas. Over time, bhaṭṭārakas became celibate clerics who took lesser vows and who wore orange-colored robes both inside and outside the monastery, removing them only when eating and when initiating another bhaṭṭāraka.

During medieval times, there were 36 separate seats of authority or thrones for bhaṭṭārakas throughout India. They could own property and were responsible for the administration of temple complexes, including **manuscript libraries** and residences (maṭhas). They also were responsible for the installation of **images**, for conducting various rituals, for supervising **lay vows**, and for education of the community. Each bhaṭṭāraka was associated with a specific local **caste**, and he served as a judge in caste disputes and represented his community at the Rajput and Muslim courts. Like a **śrīpūjya** in the Śvetāmbara tradition, he had a throne in his principal place of residence, rode in a palanquin, was accompanied by parasols and fly whisks, and was given other royal insignia at the time of installation. Some served as advisors to kings.

In the 17th century, lay Jains who were part of the **Adhyātma movement** in north India and those associated with the Digambara **Terāpanthī** tradition in Jaipur rejected the authority of bhaṭṭārakas, and their numbers began to decline. In the 20th century, all bhaṭṭāraka seats in north India had become extinct. However, bhaṭṭārakas are still an important part of the Digambara community in south India. Because bhaṭṭārakas are not prohibited from using mechanized transport, they travel throughout India, representing the community at official functions and engaging in educational and publishing activities. They also travel abroad and serve the diaspora community. They no longer have disciples among the munis and **āryikās**, who are independently organized and of higher religious status. Traditionally, a bhaṭṭāraka nominates a successor from among his disciples. If he fails to do this, a committee of laypeople is formed to select a new bhaṭṭāraka. Today, 10 seats (maṭhas) in south India are occupied. The hereditary name for the bhaṭṭāraka is in parentheses following the location of the seat. In

Karnataka, there are seats at **Hombuja** (Devendrakīrti), Karkala (Lalitakīrti), **Mūḍbidrī** (Cārukīrti), Simhanagadde or Narasimharajapura (Lakṣmīsena), Sode (Akalaṅka), and **Śravaṇa Beḷgoḷa** (Cārukīrti). In Maharashtra, there are seats at Kolhapur and Bahubalī (Lakṣmīsena and Jinasena). In Tamil Nadu there is a seat at Melchittamur. Recently, a maṭha south of Mysore has been revived with the support of the Śravaṇa Beḷgoḷa bhaṭṭāraka.

BHĀVA. The feeling, sentiment, mental attitude, or intention that underlies a ritual action. This term can be used in the context of ritual act, such as worship (**pūjā**), gifting (**dāna**), or austerities, such as **fasting**. It is thought that one's intention has a direct relationship with the efficacy of an act, and the same action can have different consequences depending on one's mental attitude. For example, if worship of a **Tīrthaṅkara** is undertaken with the thought of some worldly gain, spiritual progress will not be made, nor will it bring prosperity or merit (**puṇya**), since these are granted only by non-liberated deities, such as **yakṣa/yakṣīs** and guardian deities (**kṣetrapālas**). The appropriate mental attitude or bhāva underlying a fast is the removal of **karma** from the **soul** (**jīva**), not the desire for a specific worldly outcome, such as the welfare of one's family, even though this may be obtained. Ritual acts, including reciting prayers and **mantras**, should not be performed mechanically but with an underlying conviction or bhāva. The proper bhāva for a **mendicant** performing an action is the absence of all attachments and desires. This term is also used in the sense of bhāva pūjā, internal or mental worship.

BHĀVANĀS. Contemplation or **meditation**. This term is used in several ways in Jainism. (1) It is a designation used by **Śvetāmbaras** for the 12 themes of meditation that are called **anuprekṣās** by **Digambaras**. (2) It is a designation used by Śvetāmbaras and Digambaras for a list of 25 observances or supporting practices that strengthen the mendicant vows (**mahāvratas**). There are five observances for each of the five mendicant vows. They are listed in the ***Tattvārtha Sūtra*** (Dig., sūtras 7.3–7.8; Śvet. **Umāsvāti's commentary** to 7.3). (3) A designation used by Digambara authors of medieval texts on lay conduct (**śrāvakācāra**) for 16 mental attitudes, or observances, to be followed in order to achieve progress in spiritual life. They are identical with the list of 16 virtues in the *Tattvārtha Sūtra* (Śvet. 6.23; Dig. 6.24) that lead to the binding of the variety of **karma** that causes rebirth as a **Tīrthaṅkara**.

BHAVANAVĀSĪ DEVAS. A class of demigods who reside in a mansion (bhavana). These deities are also called Kumāras because their lives are like those of princes. Most are named after the animal or natural phenomenon with which they are associated. There are 10 classes of these deities: asurakumāra (demon), nāgakumāra (cobra), vidyutkumāra (lightning), suparṇakumāra (vulture), agnikumāra (fire), vātakumāra (storms), stanitakumāra (thunder), udadhikumāra (oceans), dvīpakumāra (islands), and dikkumāra (cardinal directions). The mansions of the asurakumāras are located in the upper level of the first hell. The mansions of the other classes of deities are located either between earth and hell regions or between earth and heavenly regions. *See also* DEVA; NĀRAKI.

BHAVYA. A **soul** (**jīva**) that has the inherent capacity of attaining liberation (**mokṣa**) from the cycle of rebirth (**saṃsāra**) because it has the quality of **bhavytva**. *See also* ABHAVYA.

BHAVYATVA. A quality that exists in some **souls** (**jīvas**), rendering them capable of attaining liberation (**mokṣa**). In order for this quality to be activated, one must encounter appropriate external conditions, such as seeing a **Tīrthaṅkara** or viewing his **image**, hearing the teachings of a Tīrthaṅkara, or remembering one's past lives. When this quality is awakened, the soul's energy (vīrya) is directed away from delusion (mithyātva) toward proper insight (**samyak-darśana**) and liberation (mokṣa). There is no guarantee that a soul with bhavyatva will encounter the appropriate conditions for its activation. Thus, some souls with this quality may never attain liberation. Those souls that lack this quality, called **abhavyas**, are not capable of attaining either proper insight or liberation.

BHIKṢU, ĀCĀRYA (MUNI BHĪKHANJĪ) (1726–1803). Founder and first mendicant leader of the **Śvetāmbara Terāpanthī** tradition known also by his given name of Bhīkhan. He was born in the village of Kantaliya near Sojat, Rajasthan, into a **Mūrtipūjaka** Bīsa Osvāl family. In 1751, after the death of his wife, he was initiated into the **Sthānakavāsī mendicant lineage** headed by Ācārya Raghunātha (1706 or 1708–1790). In 1760, he and four other **monks** split from this group over disagreements about lax mendicant conduct and about the spiritual efficacy of meritorious actions undertaken by the Sthānakavāsī lay community. He believed that charitable giving and assistance to non-mendicants commonly undertaken by Jain **laypeople** to gain merit (**puṇya**) might be positive from a worldly point of view (**vyavahāra**

naya), but they were negative from the absolute point of view (**niścaya naya**) because they did not lead to liberation (**mokṣa**). During his lifetime, he initiated 49 monks and 56 **nuns** and developed a detailed set of rules for mendicant conduct (*Maryādā Patra*), including the rule that there will be only one **ācārya** and that all **mendicants** must abide by his decisions. Five historic sites related to his life have become **pilgrimage** sites for Terāpanthīs. They are his birth at Kantaliya, his enlightenment experience at Rajnagar, his separation from the Sthānakavāsīs at Bagri, his self-initiation and the founding of the Terāpanth at Kelva, and his death at Siriyari.

BHOGA-BHŪMI. In Jain cosmography, a realm (bhūmi) of enjoyment (bhoga) where one's needs are satisfied without effort. Because all necessities are provided by 10 kinds of wish-fulfilling trees, people do not engage in agriculture or occupational crafts. There is a minimum of suffering and people are not motivated to attain liberation (**mokṣa**). Therefore, **Tīrthaṅkaras** are never born in these lands and humans cannot attain liberation there. The continents of Haimavata, Hari, the Devakuru and Uttarakuru regions of **Mahāvideha**, Ramyaka, and Hairaṇyavata are bhoga-bhūmi lands. There is one set of these continents located on the island-continent of **Jambūdvīpa**, and two sets each on island-continents of Dhātakīkhaṇḍa and Puṣkaravara. There also **are** islands in the oceans that are bhoga-bhūmi realms. None of the bhoga-bhūmi lands are subject to the **cycle of time**. *See also* KARMA-BHŪMI; MADHYA-LOKA.

BHOGOPABHOGA-PARIMĀṆA-VRATA. One of three specialized vows of restraint of a **layperson (guṇa-vratas)**. It entails refraining from practicing certain professions, eating certain foods normally allowed for a layperson, and drinking unfiltered water. It also prohibits eating or cooking at night. *See also* VRATA.

BHŪTABALI. *See ṢAṬKHAṆḌĀGAMA.*

BĪSAPANTHĪ (VĪSĀPANTHĪ or VIŚVAPANTHĪ). Followers of the "Twenty-fold Path" or "Universal (Viśva) Path." One of the two main **Digambara** sectarian traditions in north India today, including Madhya Pradesh, Rajasthan, and Uttar Pradesh. The division of the Digambara lay community in north India took place in the mid-17th century with the **Adhyātma movement** in Agra and other north Indian cities and the subsequent establishment of a separate sectarian tradition known as **Terāpanth**. When the name Terāpanth came into use, the **bhaṭṭārakas** in north India called their system Bīsapanth. They accept the authority of bhaṭṭārakas as religious teachers and leaders while Terāpanthīs do not. Bīsapanthīs worship **images** of **Tīrthaṅkaras** as well as non-liberated deities, such as **kṣetrapālas** and **yakṣa/yakṣīs**. As part of worship, they offer eight objects (**aṣṭaka pūjā**), either while seated or standing, perform the lamp ceremonies (**āratī**), and worship in **temples** after dark. The Bīsapanthī-Terāpanthī division does not exist in Karnataka, southern Maharashtra, and Tamil Nadu. Here, the Digambara community has continued to accept the authority of bhaṭṭārakas. The decline of bhaṭṭārakas in the 20th century and the revival of the institution of naked **munis**, who do not identify themselves as Bīsapanthī or Terāpanthī, have lessened the differences between these two sectarian traditions.

BRAHMACĀRĪ/BRAHMACĀRIṆĪ. A man/**woman** who practices total **celibacy**. In taking the fourth mendicant vow (**brahmacarya-vrata**), a **mendicant** agrees to remain celibate. A **layperson** may observe this restraint either informally or formally by taking a vow of lifelong celibacy. In taking this vow, a layperson attains a stage of renunciation called brahmacarya **pratimā** (Śvet., 6th or 8th pratimā; Dig., 7th pratimā). Often celibate laypeople wear only simple white clothing. The social institution of brahmacārī/brahmacāriṇī, or semi-renouncers who are technically lay but act much like mendicants do, is largely a **Digambara** phenomenon.

BRAHMACARYA. **Celibacy** or restraint in sexual activity. The brahmacarya-**vrata** is the fourth of five mendicant vows (**mahāvratas**) and **lay vows** (**aṇuvratas**). In taking this vow, a **layperson** agrees to refrain from all sexual activity outside of marriage and to practice moderation within marriage. A **mendicant** vows to remain celibate, to avoid touching those of the opposite **gender**, and to limit social contact with them. A layperson may also take a vow of lifelong celibacy, thereby attaining a stage of renunciation known as the brahmacarya **pratimā** (Śvet., 6th or 8th pratimā; Dig., 7th pratimā).

BRAHMADEVA. The **yakṣa** of Śītala, the 10th **Tīrthaṅkara** of this era, whose **image** is surmounted on a pillar called a **Brahmadevastambha**. This yakṣa is the protector deity of Nitani in Karnataka.

BRAHMADEVASTAMBHA. A monolithic pillar erected at **Digambara** sacred sites, primarily in south India. Similar in appearance to a **mānastambha**, it is surmounted by the seated **image** of **Brahmadeva**, the **yakṣa** of Śītala, the 10th **Tīrthaṅkara** of this era. On the base of the pillar, Brahmadeva is depicted riding a horse, with a sword in his right hand. These pillars may be erected in front of the main entrance to a **temple**. However, unlike mānastambhas, they also may be erected in front of colossal images of **Bāhubali**. The earliest of these pillars dates from the 14th century.

BRAHMIN. A member of the occupational class of priests and scholars in the ancient system of social organization (varṇa). In the Hindu tradition, male members of this class could study the vedas, become priests, and perform vedic rituals for themselves and for others. According to the *Ādipurāṇa* of **Jinasena** (9th century), the Brahmin varṇa was established by the Universal Emperor (**Cakravartin**) **Bharata** by selecting those **laymen** from the existing three varṇas whose actions minimized harm (**hiṃsā**) to other living beings. In south India, temple priests who perform rituals in **Digambara temples** are known as **Jaina-Brahmins**. The English spelling of "Brahmin" is a corruption of the Sanskrit word Brāhmaṇa. *See also* CASTE.

BṚHAT SAUDHARMA TAPĀ GACCHA. *See* TRISTUTI GACCHA.

BUDDHA. The Awakened One, the title of Siddhārtha Gautama, who founded the religious tradition known as Buddhism. The dates of his life have been the subject of considerable scholarly debate. Some believe he lived around 563–483 B.C.E., while others have dated him up to a century later. He was born into a **Kṣatriya** family and was raised in Kapilavastu, the capital of a small republic of the Śākyas, which is in present-day Nepal. He renounced the household life and went to live in the Ganges Valley where he studied with a number of teachers, experimenting with various **meditational** techniques and practicing severe austerities (**tapas**). He decided that emaciating his body by **fasting** was not conducive to enlightenment and so he adopted a middle path between extreme asceticism and excessive indulgences of the household life. After six years, at the age of 35, he attained enlightenment. He spent the next 45 years organizing his community of renouncers and teaching about the cause of suffering and the way to end all suffering.

Gautama the Buddha was a contemporary of **Mahāvīra**. Although both preached in the Ganges Valley, there is no evidence that they ever met. However, a Buddhist text called *Sāmaññaphala-sutta* ("Fruits of the Life of a Śramaṇa") contains an account of six "heretical" **śramaṇa** (non-brahmanical) teachers who were contemporaries of the Buddha. One of these is Nigaṇṭha Nātaputta. Nigaṇṭha (Skt., **Nirgrantha**, "one who is free from bonds") is the name for Jain **mendicants** in early times, and Nātaputta (Skt., Jñātṛputra) is the name of Mahāvīra. According to this account, he taught a fourfold system of restraint (**cātuyāma-saṃvara**), although in Jain texts this teaching is associated with Mahāvīra's predecessor, **Pārśvanātha**. Like Mahāvīra and the other śramaṇa teachers, the Buddha rejected the authority of the Vedas, the efficacy of the vedic sacrifice, and the spiritual superiority of **Brahmins**.

BUDDHISĀGARASŪRI, ĀCĀRYA (1874–1925). Śvetāmbara Mūrtipūjaka Tapā Gaccha mendicant leader. He was born in Vijapur, a town near Mahudi, Gujarat, and was named Bechardās Śivdās Paṭel. Although born into a Hindu family, he went to Yaśovijayajī Jain Sanskrit Pāṭhśālā in Mehsana. He came under the influence of Muni Ravisāgar, the leader of a small group of fully initiated monks (**saṃvegī sādhus**) in the Sāgara branch of the Tapā Gaccha. In 1900, he was initiated as Buddhisāgara by Ravisāgara's disciple, Muni Sukhasāgara. In 1913, the Mūrtipūjaka community of Pethapur installed him as **ācārya**. He is said to have authored 108 works in Sanskrit and Gujarati, and he is famous for his preaching. He is equally renowned for his yogic powers and for attaining a direct vision of a deity named **Ghaṇṭākarṇa Mahāvīra**. This occurred in 1898 in the town of Mahudi after Ravisāgara gave him the secret Ghaṇṭākarṇa Mantra. The following day, he established an anthropomorphic **image** of Ghaṇṭākarṇa there, which has become a popular **pilgrimage** site among Gujarati Jains. In the early 1920s, he composed two ritual manuals for the worship of this deity. The sublineage (**samudāya**) established by his successors is one of the more influential in the Tapā Gaccha today.

BÜHLER, GEORG (1837–1898). Philologist. Born in Borstel in the province of Hanover, Germany, he studied classical languages and archeology at Göttingen University. After receiving a Ph.D. in 1858, he continued his Sanskrit studies in Paris, London, and Oxford. In 1863, he was appointed professor of Oriental languages at Elphinstone College, Bombay (now Mumbai) and, in 1868, he assumed the post of Educational Inspector of Gujarat and Officer in Charge of the Search for Sanskrit manuscripts in the Bombay Presidency. In this capacity, he was responsible for cataloging **manuscript libraries** and procuring manuscripts. Accompanied by **Hermann Jacobi**, he traveled through Rajasthan to **Jaisalmer** in 1873–1874. With the assistance of the **Kharatara Gaccha Śrīpūjya** Jinamuktisūri, Bühler and Jacobi became the first foreigners to gain limited access to the Jain manuscript libraries there. In his travels, he obtained numerous Jain manuscripts, including copies of most of the 45 **Śvetāmbara Āgamas**. Bühler sent some 500 Jain manuscripts to the Royal Prussian State Library in Berlin, where they were cataloged by **Albrecht Weber**. Bühler left India in 1880, assuming the position of Professor of Sanskrit and Indology at the University of Vienna, which he held until his death. In a lecture given to the Vienna Academy in 1887 entitled *Über die indische Sekte der Jaina* (translated as *On the Indian Sect of the Jainas*, London, 1903), Bühler supported Jacobi's view that Jainism had always been an independent ascetic tradition. He based his arguments on inscriptions from Kaṅkālī Ṭīlā at **Mathurā**. Bühler encouraged Dr. J. Burgess to reopen this site, and he published reports on the findings, including translations and interpretations of Jain inscriptions. He also is known for his pioneering work on Prākrit **languages**. A bibliography of his writings has been published in the *Encyclopedia of Indo-Aryan Research* (1899).

– C –

CAILLAT, COLETTE (1921–). Indologist. Born near Paris in Saint-Leu-la-Foret (Val d'Oise, France), she completed her university studies in classical humanities in Paris and taught in various high schools from 1945 to 1952. From 1952 to 1960, as a member of the Centre National de la Recherche Scientifique, she studied comparative grammar of Indo-European languages and Indology with a number of professors, including Louis Renou and **Walther Schubring**, and conducted research on Middle-Indic linguistics and Jainism. She taught Sanskrit and comparative grammar at the University of Lyon and received a Doctorat d'Etat ès Lettres et Sciences Humaines degree for her theses "Les expiations dans le rituel ancien des religieux jaina" (translated as *Atonements in the Ancient Ritual of the Jaina Monks*, L. D. Series no. 49) and "Vavahāra Sūtra 1–3, Texte, Traduction, Commentaire." Since 1967, she has held the chair of Civilisation d'Inde et du Sud-est asiatique at the University of Paris (Sorbonne, later Paris-3). In addition to her extensive research on mendicant rituals, including Jain canonical and commentarial literature, she has translated Jain Prākrit and Apabhraṃśa texts into French and has written a number of articles on Pāli, Prākrit, and Middle-Indic **languages**. A bibliography of her works prior to 1987 has been published in *Indologica Taurinensia*, vol. 14 (Professor Colette Caillat Felicitation Volume, 1987–1988).

CAITYA-VANDANA. Rite of veneration of the **image** of a **Tīrthaṅkara**. It is an expansion of the obligatory action (**āvaśyaka**) of the "Hymn of Praise to the Twenty-Four [Tīrthaṅkaras]" (caturviṃśati-stava). It incorporates other obligatory actions of ritualized confession (**pratikramaṇa**) and abandoning the body (**kāyotsarga**). It consists of recitations in Prākrit and ritualized actions performed in a fixed order while facing an image of a Tīrthaṅkara. The observance of this rite is identical for **mendicants** and **laypeople**. Laypeople may perform this rite as part of internal worship (bhāva **pūjā**) after finishing material worship (dravya pūjā). *See also* AṢṬAKA PŪJĀ; AṢṬAPRAKĀRĪ PŪJĀ; PŪJĀ.

CAITYAVĀSĪ. Temple-dweller. A term used for **mendicants** who lived a permanent and sedentary life in a **temple** (caitya) or in a subsidiary building at the temple complex, such as a lodging house (**upāśraya**) or a **monastery** (maṭha). In so doing, they did not adhere to the itinerant lifestyle proscribed in the **scriptures**. They safeguarded temples, and some of them owned property and used money. It is not known when this practice began, but by the 11th century, there is mention of debates between temple-dwelling mendicants and mendicants called forest-dwellers (**vanavāsīs**), who lived an itinerant lifestyle. There have been repeated efforts to reform such mendicant practices. In the **Śvetāmbara** community, these sedentary monks came to be known as **yatis** and their mendicant leaders had the title **śrīpūjya**.

CAKRAVARTIN. One of the five categories of the 63 illustrious men (**śalākā-puruṣas**) in Jain **Universal History** texts and other Jain narratives. They are universal emperors who are said to be the Lords of Six Continents. In **Bharata-kṣetra** (the part of the universe where we are said to live), 12 universal monarchs are born in each progressive and regressive half-**cycle of time**. In this era, they were (1) Bharata, (2) Sagara, (3) Maghavan, (4) Sanatkumāra, (5) Śānti, (6) Kunthu, (7) Ara, (8) Subhūma, (9) Padma, (10) Hariṣeṇa, (11) Jayasena, and (12) Brahmadatta. Three of them, Śāntinātha, Kunthunātha, and Aranātha, renounced the world and became **Tīrthaṅkaras**. Of the remaining nine, seven were just rulers who were devout followers of Jainism. At the end of their lives, they renounced their thrones and became Jain **monks**. Some attained liberation (**mokṣa**) and others were reborn as heavenly beings (**deva**) in one of the heavenly abodes. However, Subhūma ruled unjustly and committed acts of excessive violence (**hiṃsā**) and Brahmadatta remained attached to sense-pleasures. Both were reborn as hell-beings (**nāraki**) in the seventh hell.

CAKREŚVARĪ. *See* YAKṢA/YAKṢĪ.

CAMPĀBAHEN MĀTĀJĪ (1918–1993). Spiritual leader of the **neo-Digambara Kānjī Svāmī Panth** and the only **woman** to head a Jain sect. She was born in rural Gujarat and showed an early interest in spiritual matters. After studying Jain doctrine and practicing **meditation**, she became a follower of **Kānjī Svāmī** while he was still a **Sthānakavāsī monk**. In 1932, she stated that she had fully experienced her inner **soul** and later that she remembered her previous births. She reportedly told Kānjī Svāmī that in a past life the two of them had lived in **Mahāvideha** and were present when **Kundakunda** came there to hear **Sīmandhara Svāmī** preaching. An assembly hall (**samavasaraṇa**) of Sīmandhara has been constructed at Songadh, Gujarat, which is based on her description of his assembly hall in Mahāvideha. After Kānjī Svāmī's death, she revealed to his followers that he will be reborn as the **Tīrthaṅkara** Suryakīrti on the island-continent of Dhātakīkhaṇḍa.

CAMPĀPŪRI. **Pilgrimage** site near the town of Bhagalpur, Bihar. Tradition holds that it is the birthplace of Vāsupūjya, the 12th **Tīrthaṅkara** of this era, who also attained omniscience (**kevala-jñāna**) and liberation (**mokṣa**) here.

CANDANĀ. Head **nun** (**pravartinī**) in the **mendicant lineage** established by **Mahāvīra**. In her youth, she was adopted by a merchant and imprisoned by his jealous wife. During this time, she broke a five-month **fast** of Mahāvīra by meeting his predetermined conditions for accepting food while on his alms-gathering rounds. She later requested initiation from Mahāvīra. Traditional accounts state that there were 36,000 nuns (**sādhvīs**) under her supervision. According to **Śvetāmbaras**, she attained liberation (**mokṣa**). According to **Digambaras**, she was reborn as a god (**deva**) in the Acyuta heaven.

CANDANĀ, ĀCĀRYA (1937–). Śvetāmbara Sthānakavāsī mendicant leader. Initiated in 1951 at the age of 14, she studied Jain **scriptures** and Sanskrit literature, earning the degree of Darśanācārya. With her appointment as **ācārya** by **Amar Muni**, she became the first and only **nun** in the history of Jainism to have attained this rank. Her appointment has been controversial and is not accepted by some in the community. In 1973, she founded the Veeryatan institution at Rajgir, Bihar. Based on the philosophy of compassion in action, the goals of this non-governmental organization (NGO) are to provide humanitarian service and education and to promote spiritual development. An eye clinic with a hospital and training in ophthalmology, a polio clinic, and a general outpatient clinic have been established here. A **meditation** and spiritual development center has been established near Pune. Veeryatan International was formed in 1995 to promote education in traditional cultural values of the community and to organize volunteer service in India.

CASTE. English term, derived from the Portuguese word "casta" (color, race) that for several centuries has been used to describe the various social groups or classes in India. This term is often used for the fourfold varṇa system of a divinely sanctioned hierarchical social organization of **Brahmins** (priests and scholars), **Kṣatriyas** (warriors and rulers), **Vaiśyas** (merchants and agriculturists), and **Śūdras** (laborers and craftspeople). Jains have rejected the Hindu varṇa system in which rank is dependent on birth and Brahmins are religiously superior to other classes. However, it is likely that Jains always have accepted a system of caste hierarchy for social purposes. Jainism has taught that the fourfold division of classes (varṇas) was created out of need for social organization and was not religiously sanctioned. According to the *Ādipurāṇa* of **Jinasena** (9th century), it was **Ṛṣabha**, as the first king of this era, who established the Kṣatriya varṇa in response to deteriorating living conditions during his time. He then taught the other people agriculture and crafts and organized them into the Vaiśya and Śūdra varṇas. After Ṛṣabha had renounced the household life, it was his son King **Bharata** who later established the Brahmin varṇa by selecting those **laymen** from the existing three varṇas whose actions minimized harm (**hiṃsā**) to other living beings. The term caste is also used for sub-caste groups called **Jāti** or Jñātī.

CATUḤ-ŚARAṆA. The Four Refuges. Verses of prayer in which one takes refuge in the enlightened teachers (**Arhats**), in liberated **souls** (**siddhas**), in **mendicants** (**sādhus**), and in the Holy Law (**dharma**).

CĀTURMĀSA. The four-month rainy season period when **mendicants** cease their travels and live in a fixed place of residence. This period officially begins on the 14th day of the bright half of Āṣāḍha (June/July) and ends on the full moon day of Kārtika (October/November). Some months in advance, the lay community formally invites a small group of mendicants to stay in their town for the rainy season. Because **laypeople** have the opportunity to meet with mendicants and listen to sermons (**pravacana**) on a daily basis, they may be inclined to take various vows of restraint, including **fasting** or specific **dietary restrictions**, not eating after dark, sitting in **meditation** each day, or studying sacred **scriptures.**

CĀTUYĀMA-SAṂVARA (CĀTURYĀMA-DHARMA). Law of fourfold restraint. According to **Śvetāmbara** canonical texts, four vows were taken by the **mendicant** followers of **Pārśvanātha**: refraining from all violence (**ahiṃsā**), untruthfulness (**satya**), taking things not given (**asteya**), and accumulating possessions. The meaning of the fourth restraint, called "bahiddhādāṇa," is obscure. Although some scholars believe that the mendicant followers of Pārśva did not practice **celibacy**, commentators state that the fourth vow includes restraint regarding possessions and contact with **women** (whom they classify as possessions). This term is not found in **Digambara** texts, which state that during the time of Pārśva there was a single vow of refraining from all karmically harmful acts (sāmāyika-saṃyama). **Mahāvīra** made this vow more explicit by preaching the five great vows (**mahāvratas**) for his mendicant followers. Śvetāmbaras and Digambaras agree that at certain times mendicants need to be given a more explicit set of vows. Thus, in our location of the universe, in each ascending and descending half-**cycle of time** (utsarpiṇī, avasarpiṇī), the first and last **Tīrthaṅkaras** always teach the five great vows while the remaining 22 Tīrthaṅkaras always teach the limited vows of restraint.

CELIBACY. Abstention from sexual activity. A vow of celibacy (**brahmacarya-vrata**) is one of the five great vows (**mahāvratas**) taken during initiation into mendicancy (**dīkṣā**). According to **Śvetāmbara** canonical texts, four vows were taken by the **mendicant** followers of the 23rd **Tīrthaṅkara, Pārśvanātha**, which did not include a separate vow of celibacy. Therefore, some scholars believe that prior to the time of **Mahāvīra**, Jain mendicants were not required to practice celibacy. However, commentators interpret the fourth vow, which is associated with the accumulation of possessions, to include all contact with **women** because they were part of a man's household and thus technically were "possessions." **Laypeople** who are not married are expected to remain celibate. Occasionally, a person who has not yet married may take a vow of lifelong celibacy at a young age. A married person may be celibate for limited periods of time, for example, while performing a **fast**. As they grow older, some couples decide to remain celibate for the rest of their lives. They may do so informally or they may take the vows of a **brahmacārī**.

CHITRABHANU (1922–). **Śvetāmbara Mūrtipūjaka** spiritual leader. Born in a small town in Rajasthan, he was initiated as Muni Candraprabhasāgara in 1940. He spent the first five years of mendicancy in silence and **meditation**. In 1970, he broke with the prohibition against travel by mechanical conveyance when he attended the Second Spiritual Summit Conference in Geneva. He came to New York the following year and subsequently returned to the household life and married his longtime student Pramodā. He founded the Jain Meditation International Center in New York City, which currently has 57 branches in the United States, Canada, India, Japan (Kobe), Singapore, the United Kingdom, and in Africa. He is the author of numerous books on nonviolence (**ahiṃsā**), world peace, meditation, and the practice and philosophy of Jainism.

CIRCUMAMBULATION. The tradition of walking around (pradakṣiṇa) a sacred structure, such as a **temple**, a sacred **image**, or a **mendicant**. One walks in a clockwise direction, keeping the object of veneration on one's right as a way of expressing respect.

COMMENTARY. There are four types of classical commentaries on the **Śvetāmbara** scriptural canon (**Āgamas**). The oldest are the niryuktis (Pkt., nijjutti), concise verse explanations written in Prākrit. Tradition attributes the authorship of all 10 niryuktis to **Bhadrabāhu** (ca. 1st century C.E.), but there is evidence that they were subject to interpolation. Niryuktis were expanded into more detailed commentaries called bhāṣyas (Pkt., bhāsa), written in Prākrit verse, and cūrnīs (Pkt., cuṇṇi), written in Prākrit prose with some Sanskritization. These three strata of exegesis sometimes are intermingled in extant texts. Sanskrit prose commentaries, called vṛtti or ṭīkā, provide a traditional running explanation of the verses in the root text. **Haribhadra** (8th century) wrote the earliest Sanskrit commentaries. Śilāṅka (9th century) wrote Sanskrit commentaries on the ***Ācārāṅga Sūtra*** and ***Sūtrakṛtāṅga Sūtra***, and

Abhayadevasūri (11th century) on the remaining nine **Aṅgas**. Exegetical literature on the Śvetāmbara Āgamas written in Gujarati (ṭabo, bālāvabodha) date from the 13th century. Commentaries may contain extensive narrative literature and occasionally have attained the status of a root text. For example, two niryuktis have been incorporated into the Śvetāmbara subsidiary canon (**Aṅgabāhya**). The earliest extant commentaries on the **Digambara Siddhānta** are prose ṭīkās written in Jain Śaurasenī and Sanskrit by **Vīrasena** (9th century C.E.). *See also* LANGUAGES.

CONSCIOUSNESS. Translation of the Sanskrit term caitanya. Consciousness, or awareness, is a defining quality (**guṇa**) of the **soul** (**jīva**). It is the quality that distinguishes the substance (**dravya**) that is sentient (jīva) from the substances that are non-sentient (**ajīva**), such as matter (**pudgala**). It is because of this quality that a soul can be the knower of other objects and of itself. Application of consciousness is twofold: (1) perception (**darśana**), or indistinct awareness of an object; and (2) knowledge (**jñāna**), or comprehending the details of an object. Prior to attaining omniscience (**kevala-jñāna**), perception and knowledge operate in sequence. Therefore, they are classified as two distinct qualities of the soul.

COSMOGRAPHY. *See* LOKA-ĀKĀŚA.

CREMATION. *See* FUNERAL.

CŪRNĪ. *See* COMMENTARY.

CYCLE OF TIME. Jains believe that in certain areas of the occupied universe (**loka-ākāśa**), time is cyclical, and living conditions improve and decline. For human beings, there is a gradual increase in knowledge, length of life span, stature, pleasure, morality, and spirituality during the progressive half of the cycle (utsarpiṇī) and a decrease in these during the regressive half of the cycle (avasarpiṇī). Together these two half-cycles constitute a complete cycle of time (kalpa). These two half-cycles last for a vast, but finite, number of years and follow each other in unbroken succession. There is no period of demanifestation (pralāya) and re-creation of the universe at the end of these cycles. However, after an uncountable (asaṁkhyāta) number of progressive and regressive cycles, there is an abnormal regressive cycle called a huṇḍāvasarpiṇī, when extraordinary events take place.

The regressive half of the cycle is divided into six stages: (1) extremely happy (suṣamā-suṣamā), (2) happy (suṣamā), (3) more happy than unhappy (suṣamā-duṣamā), (4) more unhappy than happy (duṣamā-suṣamā), (5) unhappy (duṣamā), and (6) extremely unhappy (duṣamā-duṣamā). These six stages are reversed for the progressive half of the cycle. Liberation (**mokṣa**) is possible only during the third and fourth stages of these half-cycles, when there is not an abundance of either happiness or unhappiness.

The continents of **Bharata-kṣetra** (where we are said to live) and Airāvata-kṣetra experience cyclical time. We are currently in the fifth or unhappy (duṣamā) stage of a regressive cycle that is a huṇḍāvasarpiṇī. It began less than three years after the death of **Mahāvīra**, the 24th and final **Tīrthaṅkara** of this era. Thus, liberation is not possible for humans who are born here at this time. However, there is a continent called **Mahāvideha** where liberation is always possible because time is not cyclical and conditions are always suitable for the birth of Tīrthaṅkaras.

– D –

DĀDĀ BHAGAVĀN. *See* PAṬEL, AMBĀLĀL.

DĀDĀGURUS. Four distinguished mendicant leaders (**ācāryas**) of the **Śvetāmbara Mūrtipūjaka Kharatara Gaccha** (11th–17th centuries) who are worshipped by Śvetāmbaras associated with the Kharatara Gaccha. They are **Jinacandrasūri**, **Jinacandrasūri II**, **Jinadattasūri**, and **Jinakuśalasūri**. As the name Dādā ("Grandfather") suggests, they are viewed as the patriarchs of this **mendicant lineage**.

As ascetics who have not yet attained liberation (**mokṣa**), they remain active in this world and are available to assist worshippers in times of crisis and to grant worldly benefits, such as wealth, health, and offspring. Since the time of their deaths, they have been worshipped in the traditional form of footprint images (pādukās). More recently, anthropomorphic **images** of them have been installed in Kharatara Gaccha **temples** and also in shrines in Dādābāṛīs, gardens or complexes outside a town. Some mark the place of a Dādāguru's cremation or where he has miraculously appeared after death and others commemorate the four Dādāgurus collectively. Hagiographical accounts describe their magical powers acquired through **yoga**, and the miraculous events associated with their lives are illustrated on the walls of their shrines.

Images of the Dādāgurus are distinguished from those of the **Tīrthaṅkaras** by their mendicant implements and their posture. When worshipping the Dādāgurus, the images of Tīrthaṅkaras are always worshipped first, since the Tīrthaṅkaras are superior, having attained liberation.

There are several important differences in rituals of worship for the Dādāgurus and for the Tīrthaṅkaras. When worshipping the Dādāgurus, in forming the auspicious symbols with rice, a flag is substituted for the crescent and dot, which signify liberated beings. Rituals may include verses to invoke the Dādāgurus to be present, which are absent in the worship of the liberated Tīrthaṅkaras. A portion of the food offered to the Dādāgurus is returned to worshippers as prasāda and may be consumed outside the temple complex, which is not done with offerings to the Tīrthaṅkaras. Mondays and full-moon days are considered the most appropriate times for their worship.

DAKṢIṆ MAHĀRĀṢṬRA JAIN SABHĀ. *See* ASSOCIATIONS OF JAINS IN INDIA.

DĀNA. Ritual or religious gifting. The survival of the Jain community is dependent upon religious gifting because Jain **mendicants** must obtain all requisites of life, including food, from **laypeople**. If done properly, there is an increase in merit (**puṇya**) and the destruction of harmful (pāpa) **karma** for the donor. Authors of the medieval texts on lay conduct (**śrāvakācāra**) agree that spiritual benefits for the donor are dependent on four factors. (1) Having an appropriate disposition or sentiment (**bhāva**) when giving. It is generally agreed that gifting should be done without any desire for worldly gain, with a peaceful mind, without anger, deceit, envy, or pride. (2) The manner of giving includes factors, such as showing appropriate respect for the recipient, giving at the appropriate time (e.g., food during the day but not at night), and so forth. (3) The nature of the gift should be appropriate for the recipient. (4) The nature of the recipient. The most merit is earned from giving to the most worthy recipient. According to **Hemacandra**, religious gifting includes all money or goods donated by Jains upon seven fields of merit: Jain **images**, Jain **temples**, Jain texts, Jain mendicants (male and female), and Jain laypeople (male and female). These are accepted by **Śvetāmbara Mūrtipūjakas** and **Digambaras** as worthy recipients. Neither **Sthānakavāsīs** nor Śvetāmbara **Terāpanthīs** accept Jain images or Jain temples as appropriate fields of gifting. Terāpanthīs believe that giving to laypeople and giving to charitable projects such as animal shelters (**pāñjrāpoḷs**), which are done out of compassion, may be beneficial from a societal perspective, but they are not beneficial from a religious perspective and do not result in the accumulation of merit for the donor.

Some Jains do not use the verb "to give" in describing dāna because giving is often associated with a donor of higher status and a recipient of lower status. In the religious hierarchy, Jain mendicants have a higher status than laypeople. The act of giving also implies some sort of exchange, which is not the intent here. By receiving a gift, a mendicant is not indebted to reciprocate in any manner. A donor may acquire merit as a result of giving to a mendicant, but this is inherent in the law of karma. It is not something that is given by the mendicant. A layperson may receive the "gift" of knowledge (jñāna dāna) or the "gift" of fearlessness (abhaya dāna) from a mendicant. However, teaching is the duty (**dharma**) of a mendicant, and religious study and teaching are forms of internal asceticism (**tapas**).

DĀNA-VRATA. One of four vows of spiritual discipline of a **layperson** (**śikṣā-vratas**). One agrees to give alms regularly to **mendicants**. This vow also governs proper conduct of laypeople toward mendicants. One must know the qualities of a proper donor and endeavor to embody them, and know what should be given, to whom it should be given, and the manner in which it should be given. *See also* VRATA.

DAṆḌA. A long wooden staff that is carried by **Śvetāmbara Mūrtipūjaka mendicants**. The top portion is carved with a simple design. The tip is curved to resemble **Mount Meru**. Below this are carvings representing the three worlds (triloka) or the Three Jewels (**Ratnatraya**), the auspicious symbol of a full water pot (kalaśa), and five horizontal lines symbolizing either the five who are worthy of worship (**parameṣṭhin**) or the five great vows (**mahāvratas**).

DARŚANA. This term has two meanings. (1) The reverential viewing or sight of **images** of **Tīrthaṅkaras** and non-liberated deities (**devas**), and the reverential viewing of Jain **mendicants** (**sādhus/sādhvīs**). (2) Perception, which is the quality (**guṇa**) of the **soul** (**jīva**) that ascertains an indistinct awareness of an object. In cognition (upayoga), or the application of **consciousness** (caitanya), it operates in association with the knowledge (**jñāna**) quality of the soul, which ascertains the details of an object. Like other qualities of the soul, perception constantly undergoes change or modification (pariṇāma), acquiring new modes (paryāya) and losing old modes. These modes are expressed as four types of perception. Each is affected by a specific variety of obscuring (āvaraṇīya) **karma**, which is named in accordance with the type of awareness that it obstructs. (1) Mati-darśana is awareness acquired through the senses, including the mind. All living beings, even the most elementary one-sensed beings (**ekendriya**), have some degree of sensory perception, experienced through the sense of touch. (2) Śruta-darśana is perception associated with language and reasoning by interpreting words, writing, and gestures. All five-sensed beings with a mind (i.e., with the capacity to reason) have some degree of this type of perception. (3) Avadhi-darśana, awareness of objects beyond the normal range of the senses, is not actually a type of perception, since it is not associated with any of the sense organs. It may be understood as a type of indistinct awareness that precedes detailed extrasensory knowledge. (4) Kevala-darśana likewise is not associated with any sense organs but is present in a soul that has attained omniscience (**kevala-jñāna**). It forms a unitary cognitive function with kevala-jñāna, so that the omniscient soul is simultaneously aware of itself and others.

DAŚA-LAKṢAṆA-PARVAN. Festival of Ten Virtues. Honoring the cultivation of religious restraints, this is the most important event in the **Digambara** ritual calendar. This 10-day festival begins on the fifth day of the bright half of Bhādrapada (August/September). During this time, many Digambaras observe some form of voluntary **dietary restrictions**. They may vow to eat only once a day, or **fast** completely on the first and last days. Some eat nothing and drink only boiled water for these 10 days. In this way, for a short time, a **layperson**'s discipline becomes closer to that of a **mendicant**'s. There is a recitation of the 10 chapters of the ***Tattvārtha Sūtra*** and a daily sermon dedicated to one of the 10 virtues: forgiveness, humility, honesty, purity, truthfulness, self-restraint, asceticism, study, detachment, and **celibacy**. The final day, called Ananta-caturdaśī (Endless Fourteenth), which is associated with the 14th **Tīrthaṅkara**, Ananta, is the most sacred day of the year for Digambaras. Most fast on this day and perform the annual ceremony of communal confession called kṣamāpanā ("Asking for Pardon"). It is similar to the **Śvetāmbara** ceremony of **saṃvatsarī-pratikramaṇa**. *See also* PARYUṢAṆA.

DEATH. In Jainism, death is viewed as a time of transition of the **soul** (**jīva**) from one state of existence to another. Death of the physical body takes place when the **karma** that determines life span (āyu karma) comes to an end. For a person who has attained omniscience (**kevala-jñāna**), this transition is one of liberation (**mokṣa**) from the cycle of rebirth (**saṃsāra**). For most, however, death is a transition from one embodiment to another.

The manner in which one dies is important because one's mental state at the time of death could affect, positively or negatively, one's destiny in the next life. Violent deaths, including self-inflicted death or suicide through poison, hanging, fire, weapons, and so forth, are to be avoided because they entail violence (**hiṃsā**) and lead to the binding of those karmas that cause bad rebirths. It is best to die in a calm mental state with a minimum of agitation and fear. Confession of past transgressions, chanting sacred **mantras**, especially the **Namaskāra Mantra**, and focusing one's thoughts on the **Tīrthaṅkaras** are helpful in this regard. Some **mendicants** who are in the final stages of a terminal illness or who have a serious infirmity that hinders the observance of their mendicant vows (**mahāvratas**) choose to end their life by a religious death through fasting (**sallekhanā**). **Laypeople** may also choose to end their lives in this manner in the case of terminal illness. *See also* FUNERAL.

DELEU, JOZEF (1925–1994). Philologist and Indologist. Born in Alveringem in West-Flanders, Belgium, he received a B.A. in Germanic philology from Rijksuniversiteit, Ghent, in 1948. While teaching Dutch and English, he continued studying Sanskrit and reading Jain texts. In 1957, he was awarded a Ph.D. for his thesis on Rājaśekhara's *Prabandhakośa.* He was a research fellow of the National Foundation for Scientific Research at the University of Ghent and, in 1959, he studied Jain Prākrit with **Ludwig Alsdorf** and **Walther Schubring** at the University of Hamburg. In 1981, he was appointed professor in Old-Middle- and New-Indo-Aryan **languages** at the State University of Ghent. He was a pioneer in a literary genre called Prabandha, including its language and its importance as semi-historiographical works. Deleu worked with Walther Schubring to prepare a critical edition, English translation, critical notes, and glossary for chapters 1–3 of the *Mahāniśītha Sūtra.* His most influential work is *Viyāhapannatti (Bhagavaī): The Fifth Anga of the Jaina Canon* (1970), which contains an extensive introduction, an account of its contents, and an index to proper names and technical terms. This work has prompted further studies on this important canonical text. A bibliography of his main works has been published in *Jain Studies in Honour of Jozef Deleu* (1993).

DELVARA. *See* MOUNT ĀBŪ.

DERĀVĀSĪ. A term used in certain parts of India for **Śvetāmbaras** who venerate or worship **images** of **Tīrthaṅkaras** in **temples**, although literally it means one who dwells (vāsī) in a Jain temple (derāsar). **Mandir Mārgī** and **Mūrtipūjaka** are other designations for this group of Śvetāmbaras.

DEŚĀVAKĀŚIKA-VRATA. One of four vows of spiritual discipline of a **layperson** (**śikṣā-vratas**). One agrees to observe more stringent restrictions on travel for a limited time (e.g., 12 hours, a day or two) than are agreed to in the **dig-vrata**. For example, a person might agree to remain at home, or in one room, and not to contact anyone outside. One might agree to go no farther than the **temple** during the four-month rainy season period (**cāturmāsa**). *See also* VRATA.

DESIRE. *See* KAṢĀYA.

DEVA. **God** or heavenly being. This term is used as a referent for two classes of beings. (1) Those who are worthy of honor. The foremost of these are the **Arhats** or **Tīrthaṅkaras** and the disembodied perfected **souls** (**siddhas**) that have attained liberation (**mokṣa**) from the cycle of rebirth (**saṃsāra**) through their own efforts. In this sense, deva is translated as God. Others are worthy of honor because of their exemplary conduct. These include **monks**, who may be called Gurudev, and kings or rulers (Mahārāj), which is an honorific title for a monk.

(2) One of the four states of existence in the cycle of rebirth. In this sense, deva may be translated as heavenly being, god/**goddess**, or deity. One attains rebirth as a heavenly being because of austerities or meritorious actions performed in the previous life that are characterized by a minimum of violence (**hiṃsā**) and passions (**kaṣāyas**). When the soul arrives at its destination in a heavenly abode, the body of a heavenly being is formed instantaneously without the need for parents. It is composed of a special type of matter that can assume different shapes at will and that can travel unimpeded through space. All heavenly beings have an innate capacity of extrasensory perception. Although their lives are predominately pleasurable, heavenly beings cannot attain liberation. When their predetermined life span comes to an end, they are reborn again on earth either as a human being or as an animal (**tiryañc**). There are four main classes of heavenly beings: **bhavanavāsī devas, jyotiṣka devas, vaimānika devas**, and **vyantaravāsī devas**. In addition, there are various local deities such as **kṣetrapālas**, who are guardians of **temple** precincts, and **yakṣa/yakṣī**, who are tutelary deities of Tīrthaṅkaras. *See also* ADHIṢṬĀYAKA DEVAS; PARAMĀTMAN.

DEVAGUPTASŪRI, ĀCĀRYA. *See* JÑĀN(A)SUNDAR(A), MUNI.

DEVENDRASŪRI, ĀCĀRYA (d. 1270). Śvetāmbara Mūrtipūjaka Tapā Gaccha mendicant leader. He was the pupil of Jagaccandra, the founder of the Tapā Gaccha. He is the author of five of the *Karmagrantha*s (the sixth was written by Candramahattara), which today are the most widely read of the Śvetāmbara works on Jain **karma** theory. In the generation after Jagaccandra, there was a split in the Tapā Gaccha over lax mendicant practices, and Devendrasūri became the leader of the more strict Lodhī Pośāl (= Skt. Laghu Posala, "Small Monastery") branch of **saṃvegī sādhus**. Although mendicants today do not trace direct pupillary descent from him, Devendrasūri is considered to be an ancestor of the current Tapā Gaccha.

DHARAṆA (DHARAṆENDRA). The **yakṣa** of **Pārśvanātha**. In his previous life, Dharaṇa had been a cobra who lived in **Banaras**. Pārśva saw an ascetic performing the penance of five fires. By means of his clairvoyant knowledge, Pārśva knew that there was a snake in the burning log, so he had the wood removed from the fire and cut it open. The cobra died while absorbed in **meditation** listening to the holy Jain litany (**Namaskāra Mantra**). He was reborn as the king (**Indra**) of the nāgakumāra gods, a class of **bhavanavāsī devas** that assume the form of cobra deities (nāgas). Dharaṇa sheltered Pārśvanātha from a torrential rain caused by the Asura Meghamālin (Śvet.) or Samvara (Dig.) by forming a canopy over him with his expanded hood. According to **Digambara** versions, there also was a female cobra in the log. She died at the same time and was reborn as **Padmāvatī**, who became the **yakṣī** of Pārśvanātha.

DHARASENA. *See ṢAṬKHAṆḌĀGAMA.*

DHARMA. (1) The term dharma has become, in modern usage, the Indic equivalent of the Western term religion, or Jain dharma. It is commonly used in the expression "ahiṃsā paramo dharmaḥ (nonviolence is the highest religion)." It also is used in the sense of duty. For example, it is the dharma of mendicants to teach. (2) The principle of motion, sometimes written as dharma-dravya. It is one of the substances (**dravya**) that is non-material and non-sentient (**arūpi-ajīva**). *See also* ADHARMA-DRAVYA.

DHARMADĀSA, MUNI (ca. 1645–1703, or 1717). One of the five principal reformers (pañca-munis) in the non-image-worshipping **Śvetām-**

bara sectarian tradition that today is known as **Sthānakavāsī**. In 1661, under the influence of **Muni Lavajī** and **Muni Dharmasiṃha**, he split with a lay movement of unknown origin called the Ekāl Pātriyā Panth. Through self-initiation, he founded his own tradition called Bāīstolā, or "Twenty-two Schools."

DHARMASIṂHA, MUNI (1599–1671). One of the five principal reformers (pañca-munis) in the non-image-worshipping **Śvetāmbara** sectarian tradition that today is known as **Sthānakavāsī**. He was a merchant who broke with the **Loṅkā Gaccha** over a disagreement about their lax mendicant practices and support of temple worship. He founded the Āṭha Koṭī ("Eight Class") tradition and wrote vernacular **commentaries** (ṭabo) on the Śvetāmbara **Āgamas**. He introduced a special rite of confession (**pratikramaṇa**) for his lay followers.

DHARMASŪRI, ĀCĀRYA VIJAYA. *See* VIJAYADHARMASŪRI, ĀCĀRYA.

DHYĀNA. Concentration of the mind or **meditation** upon a single object for a period of time, up to 48 minutes. Dhyāna is one of six internal austerities (**tapas**) that remove **karma** from the **soul** (**jīva**). According to the *Tattvārtha Sūtra* (9.27–46), there are four types of concentration. The first two are concentrations that are characteristic of those with attachment, hatred, anger, and greed. Because they are not conducive to liberation (**mokṣa**) and are to be avoided, some authors of classical works on meditation do not include the first two types in discussions of meditational practices.

1. Sorrowful concentration (ārta-dhyāna) focuses on thoughts about avoiding contact with objects that give rise to pain and having contact with objects that give rise to pleasure.
2. Cruel concentration (raudra-dhyāna) focuses on activities that are to be avoided, such as harming, lying, stealing, sexuality, and safeguarding of possessions.
3. Virtuous concentration (dharma-dhyāna) focuses the mind on the general features of worldly existence, including the essence of the **scriptures**, the nature of suffering, the effects of the fruition of karma, and the nature of the universe. There is a difference of opinion among the commentators regarding who may engage in this meditation, but all agree that a person must have attained a proper view of reality (**samyak-darśana**), or the fourth stage of spiritual purity (**guṇasthāna**).
4. There are four types of pure concentration (śukla-dhyāna). The

first two are undertaken by those in the 7th through the 12th guṇasthānas. The mind gradually shortens its field of concentration. In the first type of pure concentration (pṛthaktva-vitarka-savicāra), the mind focuses on the various aspects or modes of an entity, such as the origination, continuity, and disappearance of a particular entity from a number of philosophical standpoints (**nayas**). Objects of this meditation include suffering and its conditions, the unsatisfactory nature of worldly existence, the endless continuity of the world, and impermanence. In the second type (ekatva-vitarkāvicāra), the mind focuses on a single mode (ekatva) of an entity, and there is no movement of the mind to other standpoints. The last two types of pure concentration are undertaken only by an omniscient being in the 13th guṇasthāna (**sayoga kevalin**) at the very end of life, just prior to attaining final liberation. However, this is not meditation in the conventional sense, because there is no need for an omniscient being to concentrate his mind on an object or to think. The purpose of these two meditational states is to bring to an end all activities of the body. In the third type of śukla-dhyāna, the gross and subtle activities of the mind and the sense organ of speech are stopped, and the gross activities of the body are stopped. In the fourth type of śukla-dhyāna, all subtle activities of the body are stopped, and the soul attains the 14th guṇasthāna, omniscience without activity (**ayoga kevalin**). The soul remains in this stage for a few moments before leaving the body and attaining its final abode as an disembodied perfected soul (**siddha**) in the siddha-loka or īśat-prāgbhārā-bhūmi, which is located above the heavenly realms, at the very edge of the occupied universe (**loka-ākāśa**).

There are other types of meditational practices that have been developed in recent times, including **prekṣā-dhyāna**, which was introduced by the **Śvetāmbara Terāpanthī Ācārya Mahāprajña** and the Arhum Yoga system of meditation, which was introduced by the **Sthānakavāsī Ācārya Sushil Kumar**.

DIETARY RESTRICTIONS. In keeping with the principle of non-harming (**ahiṃsā**), Jains are advocates of a strict vegetarian diet. In general, the diet of a **mendicant** is more restrictive than that of a **layperson**. There is not a single list of restrictions that is followed by all Jain mendicants. Dietary rules vary according to sectarian tradition and mendicant lineage (**gaccha**). For laypeople, foods that are not fit to be eaten (abhakṣyas) are outlined in medieval texts on lay conduct (**śrāvakācāra**). Meat of any type must not be eaten, including poultry and fish. This prohibition includes eggs and the flesh of animals that have died a natural death. Alcohol, honey, and the five kinds of figs (udumbàra) also are prohibited. Foods that are moist, decaying, or fermented are said to be the breeding ground for numerous **souls (jīvas)** embodied as the most elementary form of life, called **nigoda**. Lists of other foods that should not be consumed vary from text to text. However, they include those plants that are inhabited by an infinite number of souls (called ananta-kāyas or sādhāraṇa), rather than just a single soul. These are root vegetables and bulbs, such as carrots, radishes, onions, and garlic. Potatoes are also included in this category, although they were not grown in India when these texts were written. Foods with a large number of seeds, such as pomegranates and eggplant, are not to be eaten because there is a risk of destroying a soul in each of the seeds. Eating after dark (rātri-bhojana) is to be avoided for a number of reasons. In addition to being bad for one's health, insects are attracted to the cooking fire, and numerous life-forms that come out at night might fall into the food.

Some laypeople still observe most of the traditional dietary restrictions, including not eating after dark. Some observe them on certain days. Others eat some or all of the fruits and vegetables on these lists of suggested restrictions. Meat eating, however, is strongly condemned by virtually all Jains, and many also consider alcohol to be unacceptable. The consumption of dairy products, such as milk, curds, and clarified butter (ghee), are not prohibited in the medieval texts. In recent times, out of concern for the treatment of cows in commercial dairy farming, some Jains in the diaspora and in India now observe a vegan diet and discourage the use of dairy products in temple rituals.

Some Jains choose to refrain from eating foods that are normally allowed for a layperson. For example, some do not eat green or leafy vegetables on the eighth and 14th day of each lunar fortnight, which are especially auspicious times for religious activities. Some do not eat them during the four-month rainy season period (**cāturmāsa**) or during **Paryuṣaṇa** (Śvet.) or **Daśa-Lakṣaṇa-Parvan** (Dig.). **Women** and older people tend to be more strict about dietary practices than men and younger people.

DIGAMBARA. Sky-clad. One of the two main Jain sectarian traditions that exist today. The name is derived from their male **mendicants (munis)** renouncing all possessions, including clothing, and practicing total **nudity**, clothed (ambara) in the directions or the sky (dik = dig). In north India today, the Digambara community is broadly divided into two sectarian traditions, the **Bīsapanthīs**, who accept the authority of **bhaṭṭārakas**, and the **Terāpanthīs**, who do not. In addition, there are several smaller Digambara groups that were established in north India, including the **Tāraṇ Svāmī Panth**, which originated in the Bundelkhand region of central India, and the Gumān Panth of Jaipur, Rajasthan (which often is considered to be a branch of the Digambara Terāpanthīs). Two Digambara sectarian traditions arose in the 20th century in Gujarat: those who follow the teachings of **Śrīmad Rājacandra**, who sometimes are called the **Kavi Panth**, and those who follow the teachings of **Kānjī Svāmī**, or the **Kānjī Svāmī Panth**. In south India, the Bīsapanthī-Terāpanthī division is not found, and the Digambara community continued to accept the authority of bhaṭṭārakas. Historically, Digambaras have lived in southern Maharashtra and Karnataka and in urban areas of northern and central India. *See also* ADHYĀTMA MOVEMENT; NEO-DIGAMBARA; ŚVETĀMBARA.

DIGAMBARA JAIN MAHĀSAMITI. *See* ASSOCIATIONS OF JAINS IN INDIA.

DIG-VRATA. One of three specialized vows of restraint of a layperson (**guṇa-vratas**). One voluntarily sets limits on the distance of travel. This can be expressed in terms of geographical boundaries or by a specific radius from one's home. Today, this vow may include restrictions on long-distance forms of communication, such as telephone calls, letters, and e-mail. One can take this vow for a specified time (e.g., the four months of the rainy season) or for the remainder of one's life. *See also* VRATA.

DĪKṢĀ. Initiation into mendicancy. Requirements for initiation vary according to sectarian tradition and also among the various **mendicant lineages**. For example, Jain texts state that eight is the minimum age for initiation. However, some mendicant leaders (**ācāryas**) today do not initiate anyone under the age of 18. Some ācāryas will initiate minors if permission is given by the parents. Some restrict initiation to members of the merchant **castes** and among **Digambaras** in south India to merchant and agricultural castes. For **Śvetāmbaras** one properly initiated **monk (sādhu)** of any rank is required for an initiation ceremony, and he initiates both men and **women**. Often, it is the ācārya who gives permission for initiation and performs the ceremony. Among Digambaras, there are cases where, in the absence of qualified monks (**munis**), individuals who have practiced the vows leading to monkhood have initiated themselves by giving up all clothing, which is a sign of a **layperson**. The rituals of initiation vary according to sectarian tradition.

In the Śvetāmbara **Mūrtipūjaka** community, some rituals are performed in private and some in public. The private portion is fixed by tradition and is uniform for all Mūrtipūjaka **mendicants**. It consists of a series of questions and answers and the recitation of a set of binding vows (**vratas**) in Prākrit. The public portion varies according to local customs. Usually, several days before initiation, the prospective mendicant is feasted, which generates merit (**puṇya**) for the lay donors. The day before initiation, he or she symbolically gives away all accumulated wealth in a public procession, which replicates the yearlong renunciation of wealth (varṣī dāna) by the **Tīrthaṅkaras**. On the day of initiation, the initiate comes into a gathering of the lay and mendicant community dressed in the clothes of a groom (e.g., like a prince wearing a turban) or a bride, and is presented with mendicant garments and implements. After the private portion of the ceremony, the initiate returns wearing mendicant garments. While shielded from public view, the tuft of hair on the crown of the head is removed by hand and the initiate is given a new name. The person who breaks the **fast** of the newly initiated mendicant acquires great merit (puṇya).

After this initial initiation, called the prāvrajyā bhagavatī dīkṣā ("blessed initiation"), there is a period of austerities, fasting, and study of the *Daśavaikālika Sūtra* (describing rules of mendicant conduct) and the *Āvaśyaka Sūtra* (describing the six daily obligatory rites), which may last for up to six months. During this time, the initiate does not go on food-gathering rounds (**gocarī**) but receives food collected by other members of the group. If the initiate remains firmly resolved to lead a mendicant life, he or she takes the final initiation, called the vaḍī dīkṣā ("great initiation"). In this rite, the mendicant formally takes the five great vows (**mahāvratas**) and agrees to remain in a state of **sāmāyika** for the rest of his or her life.

In the Digambara community, there is a gradation of mendicancy beginning with the 11th stage of renunciation (**pratimā**) of a layperson, which for men consists of two stages. In the first stage, a man or woman is initiated as a **kṣullaka** or kṣullikā, respectively. The aspirant formally takes the five lesser vows (**aṇuvratas**), which are interpreted more severely than for less advanced laypeople, and agrees to abide by the **guṇa-vratas**, **śikṣā-vratas**, and the pratimās. At initiation, they are given mendicant implements (**piñchī** and **kamaṇḍalu**) and garments in accordance with their **gender**. Men are permitted to wear an undergarment and two outer garments, and women wear a white sari. In the second stage, a man is initiated as an **ailaka** and wears only a loincloth. Although technically they are advanced laypeople, these renunciants are viewed as novice mendicants since they have undertaken formal initiation and live with other mendicants of the same gender. The final stage of mendicancy for a man or woman is initiation as a muni or **āryikā**, respectively, in a public ceremony witnessed by the lay and mendicant communities, including the plucking by hand of one's head and facial hair (**keśa-loñca**). In becoming a muni, a man takes the five great vows (mahāvratas) and in keeping with the fifth vow of non-possession (**aparigraha**) discards all clothing. In becoming an āryikā, a woman takes the fifth vow of non-possession in a modified form, and she wears a white sari for the rest of her life. Because her vows of non-possession are less stringent than those of a muni, an āryikā is technically not a full-fledged mendicant and does not have the same spiritual status as a naked muni.

DILWARA. *See* MOUNT ĀBŪ.

DĪVĀLĪ (DĪPĀVALĪ). Festival of Lights. For the Jain community, it commemorates the day on which **Mahāvīra** attained final liberation (**mokṣa**). It takes place on the 15th day of the dark half of Āśvina (September/October). According to tradition, on this night the kings in the Ganges Valley lit lamps in recognition of the light of knowledge that had been extinguished by Mahāvīra's death. Although great merit (puṇya) may be acquired by **fasting**, most **laypeople** today gather with family and friends for a festive meal. On this evening, some worship the **goddess** Lakṣmī, who is associated with wealth and auspiciousness. The following day, the first day of the bright half of Kārtika (October/November), marks the New Year. **Indrabhūti Gautama**, a chief disciple (**gaṇadhara**) of Mahāvīra, attained omniscience (**kevala-jñāna**) on this day. Some laypeople go to the **temple** to light lamps in front of Mahāvīra's **image** and to recite a hymn honoring all liberated beings (**siddhas**). Some go on **pilgrimage** to **Pāvāpurī** and spend the night at the site of Mahāvīra's liberation.

DIVYADHVANI. Divine Sound. The sound (dhvani) that emanates from the mouth of a **Tīrthaṅkara** after attaining omniscience (**kevala-jñāna**). **Digambaras** believe this sound is unarticulated, that it is a blend of all sounds, similar to **Oṃ**, and that only **gaṇadharas**, the chief disciples of a Tīrthaṅkara, are able to understand it. According to **Śvetāmbaras**, this sound takes the form of the Ardhamāgadhī **language**. It is divine (divya) because it can be understood not only by humans, regardless of their spoken language, but also by various five-sensed animals with the capacity to reason.

DOSHI, BECARDĀS (1889–1982). Śvetāmbara paṇḍit. Born in Vallabhipur, Gujarat, he attended Yaśovijaya Jain Pāṭhśālā in **Banaras**, where he assisted Paṇḍit Hargovindās Sheth in editing the Yaśovijayajī Jaina Granthamālā series. After passing the Nyāyatīrtha and Vyākaraṇatīrtha examinations in 1914, he went to Sri Lanka (Ceylon) to study Pāli and Buddhism. He returned to Gujarat in 1915. He wanted to translate the Śvetāmbara **Āgamas** into Gujarati, but this project met with much resistance from orthodox Jain **mendicants** and their lay followers. After the publication of the ***Bhagavatī Sūtra***, he lost his position at the Mahāvīra Jain Vidyālaya, Bombay (now Mumbai). In 1921, he began working with **Paṇḍit Sukhlāl Saṅghavī**, assisting him in editing and translating the *Sanmati-tarka-prakaraṇa* of **Siddhasena Divākara**. After being jailed for his editorship of Mahātmā Gāndhī's periodical *Navajīvana*, Doshi was prohibited from entering British-ruled territories. After this ban was lifted in 1936, he returned to Ahmedabad and became a lecturer at the L. D. Arts College and began editing the periodical *Jainaśāsana*. After his retirement he was associated with the L. D. Institute of Indology. *Aspects of Jainology: vol. 2., Pt. Bechardās Doshi Commemoration Volume* contains a bibliography of his works (pp. 13–22, in Gujarati).

DRĀVIḌA (DRAMILA) SAṄGHA. An extinct **Digambara mendicant lineage.** According to the *Darśanasāra*, written by Devasena of the **Mūla Saṅgha** at the beginning of the 10th century, the Drāviḍa Saṅgha was founded at Madurai, Tamil Nadu, by Vajranandin (d. 469 C.E.), a disciple of Pūjyapāda. Inscriptions dating from the 10th century indicate that this group was influential in Karnataka and Mysore. Little is known about their mendicant practices aside from Devasena's criticism of their sedentary life, eating certain plants, and bathing. This group apparently died out in the late medieval period.

DRAVYA. Substance. There are three main categories of substances: (1) the non-material, sentient Self or **soul** (**jīva**); (2) non-sentient matter (**pudgala**); and (3) and the non-sentient, non-material substances of space (ākāśa), the principle of motion (**dharma**-dravya), the principle of rest (**adharma**-dravya), and (according to some) time (kāla). The substance serves as a substratum for different defining qualities or characteristics (**guṇas**), which have various aspects or modes (paryāyas). For example, the substance matter (pudgala) is the substratum for the four defining qualities (guṇas) of color, taste, smell, and palpability. Although these four qualities are always present in matter, they are constantly changing because they undergo modifications (pariṇāma), acquiring new modes (paryāya) and losing old modes. For example, the color of matter may change from red (one mode) to blue (another mode), or its taste may change from bitter to sour. Therefore, a substance is eternal when viewed from the perspective of the substance itself and from the perspective of its qualities because neither of these aspects will ever cease to exist. A substance and its qualities are non-eternal when viewed from the perspective of modes because the modes are constantly changing.

DYĀNATRĀY(A) (1676–1726). **Digambara** mystical poet. He was born in Agra into an Agarvāl family from the village of Lalpur. At the age of 13 he began studying Sanskrit, Prākrit, and Jain **scriptures** with Paṇḍit Bihārīdās and Paṇḍit Mānsiṃha. He married when he was 16 and had seven sons and three daughters. He lived in Agra and Delhi, and met circles of laymen who were associated with the **Adhyātma movement**. He composed liturgies in Brajbhasha for many **pūjās**. His most popular liturgy is addressed to the worship of the triad of **god**, scripture, and teacher. It is recited by many north Indian Digambaras in their daily eightfold temple worship (**aṣṭaka pūjā**). Other liturgies are addressed to the 20 **Tīrthaṅkaras** living elsewhere in the universe, to the disembodied liberated **souls** (**siddhas**), to the island-continent of **Nandīśvara**, to those places where the Tīrthaṅkaras attained liberation (**mokṣa**), and to the **goddess Sarasvatī**. These liturgies are still popular among Digambaras in Hindi-speaking areas of north India today. Dyānatrāy also authored some 90 separate devotional poems (pads). He was influenced by earlier mystical authors, such as **Kundakunda** and **Yogīndu**, and their emphasis on the necessity of distinguishing between the soul and everything else, and the realization that there is no fundamental difference between one's own soul and the souls of the omniscient Tīrthaṅkaras and siddhas. He was also inspired by Jain devotional poetry, such as the ***Bhaktāmara Stotra*** and by Hindi poetry of the poet-saints, such as Kabīr, Nānak, and Ravidās.

– E –

EDUCATIONAL INSTITUTIONS OF JAINS. Early in the 20th century, Jains began to establish a number of educational institutions for religious and secular education of their community. Since **Digambaras** and

Śvetāmbaras have separate literatures, each has established its own religious schools, or pāṭhśālās, and associated examination boards for Nyāyācārya, Nyāyatīrtha, Sāhityācārya, and Śāstrī degrees.

Within the Śvetāmbara community, the Yaśovijaya Jain pāṭhśālās was established in Mandal, Gujarat, in 1902 by **Ācārya Vijayadharmasūri**, and the following year it was moved to **Banaras**. This was the first Jain educational institution in this city renowned for its traditional brahmanical scholarship. Ācārya Vijayadharmasūri also established the Vīra-Tattva-Prakāśaka Maṇḍal in Bombay (now Mumbai) in 1920, which was moved to Shivpuri in 1924. This college prepared students for examinations in Jain history, literature, philosophy, and logic. The Pārśvanātha Vidyāpīṭh (also called the Pārśvanātha Vidyāśram Śodha Saṃsthāna Jain Institute) was established in Banaras in 1937 under the auspices of the (**Sthānakavāsī**) Sohanlāl Jain Dharma Pracārak Samiti of Amritsar. This postgraduate research institute for students working on Jain studies has published a number of works, including the six-volume *Jain Sāhitya kā Bṛhad Itihāsa*. It also publishes the periodical *Śramaṇa*. Jain Vishva Bharati was founded at Ladnun, Rajasthan, under the inspiration of **Ācārya Tulsī** of the Śvetāmbara **Terāpanth**. Established in 1970, it became a university in 1991.

Within the Digambara community, the Syādvāda Jain Mahāvidyālaya was established in Banaras in 1905. Over the years, many influential Digambara **paṇḍits** have been educated here, and it became a vibrant intellectual center for the community. In association with this university, the Bhāratavarṣīya Digambara Jain Vidvat Pariṣad (India Digambara Jain Scholars Assembly) was established in 1944. It is a forum for scholars in the Digambara community to meet once a year to review the works of other members.

Gurukulas are residential schools that prepare students for university courses and also impart sectarian religious instruction. The Mahāvīra Jain Vidyālaya was established in Bombay (now Mumbai) in 1915 by the Śvetāmbara **Mūrtipūjaka Ācārya Vijayavallabhasūri**. This school now has branches in eight cities, including Ahmedabad and Pune. Another well-known Śvetāmbara institution is the Yaśovijaya Jain Gurukula at Palitana, Gujarat. The Digambara **Ācārya Samantabhadra** established several elementary and secondary boarding schools. The Mahāvīra Brahmacaryāśram was established in 1918 at Karanja (Akola), Maharashtra, and the Bāhubali Brahmacaryāśram at Kumbhoj (Kolhapur), Maharashtra, in 1934. Although the boarding-houses and scholarship funds for these schools are reserved for Digambara Jains, free education is offered to local children irrespective of religious affiliation.

EKENDRIYA. One-sensed beings. The most elementary life-forms, which experience the world through the sense of touch. This category includes all types of vegetable life (vanaspati-kāya), including the **nigoda**. It also includes single-sensed organisms with the elements themselves as their bodies. They are called earth-bodied beings (pṛthvī-kāyika), water-bodied beings (āpo-kāyika), fire-bodied beings (tejo-kāyika), and air-bodied beings (vāyu-kāyika). Like nigodas, their bodies are of two types. They may be composed of matter that is gross (bādara), or matter that is so subtle and fine (sūkṣma) that they can exist anywhere in the occupied universe **(loka-ākāśa)**. **Mendicants** must avoid harming all living beings, including those with one sense. Therefore, there are detailed discussions in early Jain texts about all forms of life, including the various one-sensed beings. *See also* TIRYAÑC.

ENLIGHTENMENT. *See* KEVALA-JÑĀNA.

– F –

FAST. A voluntary act of restraint in which one abstains from, or places restrictions on, the consumption of food and water. **Vrata** is a general term for a Hindu fast. Some Jain **laypeople** undertake certain Hindu fasts because they are considered efficacious for the attainment of worldly desires. **Tapas** (literally, austerity) or tapasyā are general terms for a Jain fast. Both **mendicants** and laypeople may engage in various types of Jain fasts. Austerities, such as fasting, are observed in order to remove **karma** from the **soul (jīva)**. One also gains merit **(puṇya)** by fasting. Although **sallekhanā** is often called a religious death through fasting, this is a supplementary vow, not a fast.

Prior to undertaking a Jain fast, a person must make a vow, or a formal statement of intent (Skt., **pratyākhyāna**, Pkt. pacakkhāṇa). If possible, this vow is made in the presence of a mendicant, but it also may be made before the image of a **Tīrthaṅkara**, a photograph of a mendicant, or a **sthāpanācārya**. In the Jain tradition, a one-day fast lasts approximately 36 hours. It begins at sundown on the preceding day, continues throughout the fasting day, and ends 48 minutes after sunrise on the following day.

An upavāsa is a fast in which one takes no food or water or in which one takes only boiled water. It may be observed for one day or for a more extended period. Some undertake a water-only upavāsa for eight consecutive days during **Paryuṣaṇa** (Śvet.) or 10 consecutive days during **Daśa-Lakṣaṇa-Parvan** (Dig.). Many Jains observe a one-day fast on the final day of these **festivals**. Some may fast for longer periods, such as the monthlong upavāsa in which one consumes only water.

Regulated forms of eating include limits on the quantity and/or types of food that are consumed. People may vow to eat only once a day or twice a day, not to eat from sunset to 48 minutes after sunrise, to refrain from eating green or leafy vegetables on certain days each month, or to eat only bland food (**āyambil**). Some fasts are combinations of these. For example, in undertaking the Varṣī Tapas, which lasts for one year and ends on **Akṣaya-Tṛtīyā**, a person observes an upavāsa on one day and on the next day eats once a day.

Among laypeople, it is more common for **women** to fast than it is for men. Fasting is a way for a laywoman to demonstrate her piety and religious purity, to gain merit, to gain prestige for herself and her family, and to ensure the health and well-being of her husband and her family. For unmarried women of marriageable age, it is a way to publicly demonstrate her piety and to obtain a good husband. However, one should not undertake a Jain fast with a specific intent in mind or to fulfill a contractual vow to a deity. A layperson may fast in the home. However, longer fasts are usually undertaken collectively with other men or women (depending on one's gender) in a mendicant dwelling-hall (**upāśraya**, sthānaka). In some fasts, such as the **upadhāna tapas**, a layperson temporarily observes many of the mendicant restraints.

The breaking of an extended organized fast is a time of public celebration with families sponsoring special fast-breaking ceremonies. Photographs of the fasters may be published in the local newspaper and they may be taken on parade in the vicinity of the temple. Giving food to a person who has engaged in an extended fast is a way of acquiring merit. People may come for auspicious viewing (**darśana**) and there is often singing, dancing, and feasting. It is also a time of religious gifting (**dāna**) to the **temple** or mendicant community and gifts are usually given to others who performed the fast.

FESTIVAL. A day that is marked by special religious observances. The ceremonies vary in accordance with the specific festival. For a listing of the individual festivals that are discussed in the dictionary, see the Jain Festival Calendar in the appendix (p. 246).

FUNERAL. After **death**, a body is usually cremated. Traditionally, shortly after death, the body is carried to the cremation ground by male relatives and is placed on a pyre of wood. A funeral ceremony is conducted in association with cremation. Typically, **women** do not take part in cremation rites. After returning home, participants bathe and ritually purify themselves by reciting sacred **mantras**. For several days after the funeral, relatives and close friends gather in the home of the deceased and comfort the family by singing devotional hymns (**stavan**). A formal period of mourning is observed, often for three days, but it may continue for two weeks. Among image-worshipping Jains, this period ends with a visit to the **temple** and religious gifting (**dāna**). Because Jains believe that rebirth is virtually instantaneous and there is no intermediate state of existence, there is no need to perform elaborate post-cremation rituals for the benefit of the deceased, like the ancestral rites of śrāddha in Hinduism. However, ceremonies may be held in remembrance of the deceased, especially on the anniversary of their death.

The funeral of a **mendicant** is an opportunity for a **layperson** to gain merit (**puṇya**). In some Jain communities, the various rites, such as carrying the palanquin and lighting the fire, may be auctioned off, and the donors accrue merit from performing these rites. Memorial or commemorative shrines called samādhi mandir (Śvet.) or niṣidhi (Dig.) are sometimes built at the cremation site of an important or charismatic mendicant. Historically, memorials have been erected for those undertaking a religious death through fasting (**sallekhanā**). A number of these memorials are found in south India, especially in the area of **Śravaṇa Beḷgoḷa**.

– G –

GACCHA. "Tree," but traditionally given the derivation of "going" or "traveling together." (1) A term used by **Śvetāmbara Mūrtipūjakas** for the largest groups, or basic divisions, of their **mendicant lineages**. This term has been translated as group, order, or monastic tradition, but usually not as school or sect because gacchas differ more on mendicant praxis than on doctrinal issues. Gaccha gradually replaced the terms **gaṇa** and kula for these basic divisions. A new gaccha was formed when a group of mendicants split with their mendicant leader (**ācārya**) over lax mendicant praxis or, less frequently, over doctrinal issues. In medieval times, there were a large number of gacchas, 84 according to traditional accounts. Each had a community of lay followers. There are only a few Mūrtipūjaka gacchas in existence today. Listed in order of approximate size as of 1999, they are the **Tapā Gaccha** (6,027), the

A(ñ)cala Gaccha (250), the **Kharatara Gaccha** (229), the **Tristuti Gaccha**, or Saudharma Bṛhat Tapā Gaccha (190), the Pārśvacandra Gaccha (74), and the Vimala Gaccha (41). The Pārśvacandra and Vimala Gacchas were originally a branch and subbranch, respectively, of the Tapā Gaccha, and some consider them to still be within the Tapā Gaccha. In earlier times, each gaccha was subdivided into smaller groups that were all under the central authority of one head ācārya. Today, only the A(ñ)cala Gaccha is centrally organized. The other gacchas are subdivided into smaller independent groups, called **samudāyas** and **parivāras**, that have their own ācāryas. (2) A term used in earlier times by **Digambaras** to denote a subdivision within a mendicant lineage. *See also* ĀGAMIKA GACCHA; KAḌUĀ GACCHA; LOṄKĀ GACCHA; PŪRṆIMĀ GACCHA; UPAKEŚA GACCHA.

GAṆA. (1) In early **Śvetāmbara** sources, gaṇa ("troop") was the largest unit, or basic division, of **mendicant lineages**. This term was gradually replaced by **gaccha**, although on occasion it has been used interchangeably and simultaneously with gaccha. (2) In **Digambara** sources, gaṇa was a smaller grouping of mendicants within a **saṅgha**. (3) Among Śvetāmbara **Terāpanthīs**, the term for their undivided mendicant community, which is headed by a single mendicant leader (**ācārya**).

GAṆADHARA. Literally, "supporter of the mendicant order (**gaṇa**)." Gaṇadharas are the chief disciples of a **Tīrthaṅkara** and are the first mendicants to join his order. They have the ability to properly understand the teachings of a Tīrthaṅkara. Based on his sermons, the gaṇadharas compose the 12 **Aṅgas** and the 14 **Pūrvas** of Jain canon (**Āgama**). A gaṇadhara serves as a leader of a "troop" (gaṇa) of mendicants until he attains omniscience (**kevala-jñāna**). After this, he ceases his activities as a mendicant leader.

Mahāvīra had 11 gaṇadharas, all of whom were from **Brahmin** families. They were the leaders of nine gaṇas (two gaṇas had coleaders). **Indrabhūti Gautama** was the first of Mahāvīra's gaṇadharas. **Digambara mendicant lineages** trace their descent from him. With the exception of the **Upakeśa Gaccha**, all **Śvetāmbara** mendicant lineages in existence today trace their descent from the gaṇa led by **Sudharman**, the last of Mahāvīra's gaṇadharas to attain omniscience. The Upakeśa Gaccha, which as of 1998 had only one celibate **yati**, traces its lineage to the mendicant order established by **Pārśvanātha**, the 23rd Tīrthaṅkara of this era.

GĀNDHĪ, VĪRCAND RĀGHAVJĪ (1864–1901). Śvetāmbara scholar of Jainism. Born in Mahuva, Kathiawar, Gujarat, he received a B.A. from Elphinstone College, Bombay (now Mumbai). In 1885, he became the first honorary secretary of the Jain Association of India and worked for the abolition of a poll tax levied on pilgrims at Palitana. He was appointed by **Ācārya Vijayānandasūri** to represent the Jain community at the World's Parliament of Religions in Chicago in 1893. In introducing Jainism to Western audiences, he maintained that it was an independent tradition that predated Buddhism. His lecture to the Parliament entitled "The Philosophy and Ethics of the Jains" outlined the major tenets of the faith. After the Parliament ended, he traveled to other cities lecturing on Jainism and Indian philosophy. He returned to the United States in 1896 and 1899 and established the Gandhi Philosophical Society, the School of Oriental Philosophy, and the International Society for the Education of Women in India. He lived for a time in England and became a barrister. He founded the Jain Literature Society in London. Herbert Warren, its honorary secretary, wrote *The Jaina Philosophy* (1910), *Jainism in Western Garb* (1912), and *The Karma Philosophy* (1913) based on Gāndhī's lectures. *See also* ASSOCIATIONS OF JAINS IN INDIA.

GAṆIN. The title of a **monk** who is the leader of a small group of monks who live and travel together. Today, this position may be combined with that of the **paṁnyāsa**. This title, which also is written as "gaṇi," may be appended to the name of a mendicant who holds this position. *See also* MENDICANT HIERARCHY.

GAUTAMA, INDRABHŪTI (GAUTAMA SVĀMĪ). A **Brahmin** who became the first of the 11 chief disciples (**gaṇadharas**) of **Mahāvīra**. Like Ānanda, the chief disciple of Gautama the **Buddha**, he was unable to attain enlightenment or omniscience (**kevala-jñāna**) because of his close attachment to his master. Therefore, along with Gaṇadhara **Sudharman**, he continued to lead the mendicant community after the other gaṇadharas had attained omniscience. He attained omniscience on the day that Mahāvīra attained final liberation (**mokṣa**). He lived another 12 years and attained final liberation at the age of 82 at Rājagṛha.

Since medieval times he has been a popular figure of worship among **Śvetāmbaras**. By the 9th century, his biographies included characteristics associated with the Hindu god Ganeśa, including the power to remove obstacles and to make things increase, a fondness for food, and an association with auspicious and desirable goals of this life, such as an increase in prosperity. The earliest known **image** of him, dating from

1277 C.E., is in the Pārśvanātha temple in Bhildiya in northern Gujarat. Images of Gautama are worshipped in hundreds of Śvetāmbara temples today. He is frequently depicted in **manuscripts** of the ***Kalpa Sūtra*** seated in **meditation** surrounded by symbols of prosperity and good fortune. On the first day of the Jain New Year, which coincides with **Dīvālī**, many Śvetāmbara businessmen write Gautama's name on the opening page of their new account books to ensure prosperity in the coming year.

GENDER. Jain texts refer to three biological genders (liṅgas): male (puṃ-liṅga), female (strī-liṅga), and neither male nor female (napuṃsaka-liṅga), which corresponds to a hermaphrodite. The biological genders are the result of a variety of **karma** that is responsible for the formation of the body (nāma karma). The texts also describe three psychological sexual cravings called **vedas**: desire for **women** (puṃ-veda), desire for men (strī-veda), and desire for both men and women (napuṃsaka-veda). These are caused by varieties of conduct-deluding (cāritra mohanīya) karmas and are classified a type of feeling or emotion (**no-kaṣāya**). Although there usually is a correspondence between the biological gender and sexual inclinations (e.g., a man has puṃ-veda, or desire for a woman), this need not be the case, and sexual inclinations can change in the course of a lifetime. The subject of biological gender has occupied an important place in debates among **Śvetāmbaras** and **Digambaras** over the question of spiritual liberation of women (**strī-mokṣa** or strī-nirvāṇa).

GHAṆṬĀKARṆA MAHĀVĪR(A). Bell-Ears the Great Hero. One of 52 heroes, called Vīrs or Vīras, powerful non-liberated male deities that protect Jains and defeat the enemies of the Jain community. He shares many features with the Hindu god Hanumān. One of the earliest **Śvetāmbara** texts describing his worship, the Sanskrit *Ghaṇṭākarṇa Mantra Stotra*, was composed in the 16th century by Vimalacandra. Initially, Ghaṇṭākarṇa was propitiated in private **tantric** rituals aimed at gaining the powers of this deity, which include protection, curing diseases, and increasing one's material wealth. After **Buddhisāgarasūri** (1874–1925) attained a vision of Bell-Ears, he established an anthropomorphic **image** in a shrine at Mahudi, in northern Gujarat. This has become the center of his devotional cult among Śvetāmbaras. On the day before **Dīvālī**, the 14th day of the dark half of Āśvina (September/October), a special fire ceremony is performed in front of his image.

GIRNĀR. *See* MOUNT GIRNĀR.

GOCARĪ. Literally, "wandering like a cow." A term for a **Śvetāmbara mendicant**'s food-gathering rounds. When collecting food, mendicants behave in the manner of a cow by wandering randomly without any preconceived thought or planning and gathering only a small amount of food in their alms bowls at each stop. Approaching whichever house they happen to encounter first is in keeping with their mendicant vow of non-harming (**ahiṃsā**) because they avoid the harm that would have been committed had they consumed food that was prepared specifically for them. They also avoid placing any undue hardship on one household by taking large amounts of food. Except when **fasting**, Śvetāmbara mendicants usually gather food twice a day, around 11 a.m. and sometime in the late afternoon. They may collect food for other mendicants in their group. They eat together at their place of residence after performing expiations for any faults they might have committed while gathering alms. All food must be consumed prior to sundown. *See also* ĀHĀRA-DĀNA.

GOD. English translation of the Sanskrit terms **paramātman** (Supreme Soul) and **deva** when used as a designation for **Arhats** or **Tīrthaṅkaras**, or for disembodied perfected **souls** (**siddhas**) that have attained liberation (**mokṣa**) from the cycle of rebirth (**saṃsāra**). Jainism sometimes has been described as an atheistic religion because there is no belief in a Supreme God, as in the monotheistic traditions of Christianity, Islam, and Judaism, that is the creator of the universe and the judge of one's destiny in the next life. There is no Absolute, Universal Soul (brahman), or a supreme creator god, such as Viṣṇu and Śiva in the Hindu traditions, that has never been bound in the cycle of rebirth. The elevated status of Tīrthaṅkaras and siddhas as God is associated with their attainment of liberation through their own efforts. Although they are worthy of honor and worship, Supreme Souls do not intervene to assist worshippers in worldly matters. They do not forgive transgressions, mitigate the effects of **karma** on the soul (**jīva**), or grant liberation through bestowing grace on those who worship them.

GODDESS. English translation of the Sanskrit term devī. Because goddesses have not attained liberation (**mokṣa**) from the cycle of rebirth (**saṃsāra**), they are able to respond to the worldly requests of their worshippers. Although goddess worship became popular in medieval times, **Sarasvatī** is mentioned in the **Śvetāmbara** ***Bhagavatī Sūtra***, and a Sarasvatī **image** dated 132 C.E. has been found at **Mathurā**. See also

AMBIKĀ; JVĀLĀMĀLINĪ; KŪṢMĀNDINĪ; MAHĀVIDYĀS; PADMĀVATĪ; YAKṢA/YAKṢĪ.

GUṆA. Quality. *See* DRAVYA.

GUṆASTHĀNA. Fourteen stages of spiritual development or stages of purification of the **soul** (**jīva**). *See* appendix.

GUṆATRAYA. The Three Qualities. *See* RATNATRAYA.

GUṆA-VRATAS. Three specialized vows of restraint that a **layperson** may take that supplement or reinforce the five lesser vows (**aṇuvratas**). By limiting the scope of one's activities even further, the potential to cause harm is reduced. *See also* ANARTHA-DAṆḌA-VRATA; BHOGOPABHOGA-PARIMĀNA-VRATA; DIG-VRATA; VRATA.

GUPTI. Progressive curbing of activities of body, speech, and mind practiced by a **mendicant** in order to prevent the influx (saṃvara) of new **karma** and to prepare for advanced **meditational** states. This entails remaining motionless for hours, observing long periods of silence, and practicing one-pointed mental concentration. *See also* SAMITI.

GURUṆĪ. The title of a **nun** who is the leader of a small group of nuns who live and travel together. She often is appointed for life with the approval of the male mendicant leader (**ācārya**) supervising her group. She usually is succeeded by the most senior nun in her lineage. The title of mahattarā is occasionally used today for this position. In earlier times, it may have been a title for an aged and venerable nun who had spiritual and administrative responsibilities. This rank has never existed among **Śvetāmbara Terāpanthīs**. *See also* MENDICANT HIERARCHY.

– H –

HARA, MUNI (17th century). One of the five principal reformers (pañcamunis) in the non-image-worshipping **Śvetāmbara** subsect that today is known as **Sthānakavāsī**. He broke with the **Loṅkā Gaccha** over a disagreement about their lax mendicant practices and their support of temple worship. He founded the Sādhumārgī tradition, a branch of the extinct Koṭā Sampradāya.

HARIBHADRA (ca. 7th–8th centuries C.E.). Śvetāmbara mendicant leader and author of many important philosophical texts. Two traditional dates of his death are 478 and 529 C.E.; however, his familiarity with the Buddhist Dharmakīrti would indicate a date after 650 C.E.

Haribhadra identifies himself as a pupil of Jinabhadra (Jinabhaṭa) and Jinadatta of the Vidyādhara Kula. There are several stories of his life. According to the earliest (ca. 12th century), Haribhadra was a learned **Brahmin** who boasted that he would become the pupil of anyone who uttered a sentence that he could not explain. Upon hearing a verse recited by a Jain **nun** named Yākinī Mahattarā that he could not understand, he was sent to her preceptor (Jinabhaṭa), who promised to instruct him if he would take initiation. He did so, taking the title Yākinīputra ("Spiritual Son of Yākinī"). The second account, which is similar in certain respects to the biography of **Akalaṅka**, reflects the animosity between Buddhist and Jain **mendicants** at this time. Haribhadra had two nephews who were his pupils. They went to study logic secretly in a Buddhist monastery and fled when they were discovered. One nephew was killed by the Buddhists and the other died of grief. Haribhadra engaged these Buddhist monks in a philosophical debate, and upon winning, he forced them to jump into a vat of hot oil. His preceptor ordered him to undertake severe penances for his display of anger and attachment. He took as his title Virahāṅka ("Having Separation, Viraha [from his nephews], as a Distinguishing Characteristic").

Although tradition ascribes around 1,400 works to him, he probably authored around a hundred, some of which are among the most highly regarded works in Jainism. On the basis of language and subject matter, some scholars believe there were two Haribhadras. One used the epithet Virahāṅka (ca. 6th century) and the other, who was a temple-dwelling monk (**caityavāsī**), called himself Yākinīputra (ca. 8th century). However, scholars within the Śvetāmbara community have supported a sole author for these works.

Haribhadra's most important works include *Dharmabindu*, which outlines duties of a **layperson**, rules for mendicants, and the bliss of liberation (**mokṣa**); *Dhūrtākhyāna*, a satire on Hinduism; *Pañcāśaka*, a Prākrit work discussing ritual and spiritual matters; and *Samarāiccakahā*, a narrative about the effects of **karma** in the context of an enduring enmity among its characters that unfolds through a series of rebirths. However, Haribhadra is best known for his writings on philosophy and **yoga**. These include *Anekāntajayapatākā*, in which he advances arguments for the doctrine of manifold aspects (**anekāntavāda**); and *Ṣaḍdarśanasamuccaya* ("Compendium of Six Philosophies"), in which he compares Jain philosophy with other schools of Indian philosophy. He wrote three works on yoga, *Yogabindu*, *Yogadṛṣṭisamuccaya*, and *Yogaśataka*, in which he compares Jain yoga with other yogic systems prevalent in India at this time. He also wrote the first Sanskrit **commentaries** on Śvetāmbara canonical texts (**Āgamas**).

In works such as these, Haribhadra established Sanskrit, rather than Prākrit, as the intellectual **language** of Jainism. He was able to use his familiarity with the techniques of brahmanical learning to benefit Jainism by writing in the style of classical brahmanical scholarship. He is noted for his respect of other religious traditions. However, ultimately he supported Jainism and its doctrine of manifold aspects, arguing that other religions were ultimately flawed because they represented only a one-sided view of reality. He is one of the few Jain scholars to have written a commentary on a non-Jain text, the *Nyāyapraveśa* of the 5th-century Buddhist logician Dignāga.

HARINEGAMESĪ. In the **Śvetāmbara** tradition, a demigod who is the commander of Śakra's (**Indra**'s) celestial army. He transferred the embryo of **Mahāvīra** from the womb of a **Brahmin woman**, Devānandā, to the womb of a **Kṣatriya** woman, Triśalā. He is depicted as a male with a human body and the head of a goat or an antelope, and he carries the embryo, which looks like a mango fruit or a stylized cloud, in the cupped palms of his hands. This scene is depicted on Kuṣāṇa-period sculptures at **Mathurā** (2nd–3rd centuries C.E.).

HARIṢEṆA (10th century C.E.). Digambara author of the *Bṛhatkathākośa*. This collection of narratives contains the *Bhadrabāhukathānakam* ("The Story of Bhadrabāhu,"), which is the earliest legendary Digambara account of a major schism in the Jain mendicant community during the time of **Bhadrabāhu**. It describes the formation of the **Ardhaphālaka** and **Yāpanīya Saṅghas** and the establishment of a twofold mode of mendicancy, the **jina-kalpa** and the **sthavira-kalpa**.

HASTĪMAL, ĀCĀRYA (1910–1991). Śvetāmbara Sthānakavāsī mendicant leader. He was born in Jodhpur, Rajasthan. In 1920, in Ajmer, Ācārya Śobhācandra initiated him as Sant Hastīmal in the lineage of **Ratnacandra** and, in 1930, he was appointed **ācārya**. He translated a number of **Āgamas** into Hindi and wrote **commentaries** on them. He also wrote a four-volume history of the Jain religion entitled *Jain Dharma ka Maulika Itihāsa*. *Concept of Prayer* is an English translation of his discourses on prayer. He initiated 31 **monks** and 54 **nuns**. A bibliography (in Hindi) of his works and a list of institutions and organizations established by him have been published in *Ācārya Hastī* (Jaipur, 1992).

HEMACANDRA (1089–1172 C.E.). Śvetāmbara mendicant leader and consolidator of Jain literature and philosophy, whose epithet was "Omniscient One of the Kali Yuga." He was born into a Jain merchant family in Dhandhuka, a village near Ahmedabad, Gujarat, and was named Caṅgadeva. He was given to a Śvetāmbara **ācārya** named Devacandra and was initiated as Muni Somacandra while still a young boy. After mastering the various traditional branches of Indian learning, he was appointed ācārya in 1108 and was given the name Hemacandra.

Jayasiṃha Siddharāja, a king in the Caulukya dynasty who ruled Gujarat from his capital in Patan from 1092–1141, appointed him as a court scholar and historian. He commissioned Hemacandra to write a history of the dynasty and a Sanskrit grammar called *Siddhahaima*, which is still used by Śvetāmbara **mendicants** today. When dissention arose in the royal family, it is reported that Hemacandra hid the king's nephew Kumārapāla under a pile of manuscripts as he was fleeing for his life. After Siddharāja's death, Kumārapāla returned to Patan and Hemacandra validated his claim to the throne. Hemacandra persuaded the king to abstain from meat and alcohol and to issue edicts banning the killing of animals in his kingdom.

Hemacandra's most important works are *Triṣaṣṭiśalākāpuruṣacaritra* ("The Lives of Sixty-Three Illustrious Persons"), the largest surviving example of the Jain literary genre called **Universal History**, and *Yogaśāstra*, in which various aspects of **yoga** are discussed, providing a summary of his views on Jainism.

HIṂSĀ. Violence or harming. In the ***Tattvārtha Sūtra***, violence (hiṃsā) is defined as taking away life by actions of the body, speech, or mind that are done out of carelessness and are influenced by passions (**kaṣāyas**). Killing other living beings and engaging in actions that are hurtful to others, such as stealing, lying, and so forth, are karmically harmful to oneself as well because they cause the binding of inauspicious varieties (pāpa-prakṛti) of **karma** with the **soul (jīva)**. They lead to rebirth as a hell-being (**nāraki**) or an animal (**tiryañc**), which are characterized by a preponderance of suffering and are not conducive to spiritual progress.

The life of a **layperson** is always associated with some degree of violence because one must cook and engage in an **occupation**, and these activities harm one-sensed beings (**ekendriya**). The authors of the medieval texts on lay conduct (**śrāvakācāra**) view the household life as a compromise in which moderation is encouraged and unnecessary harmful actions are to be avoided. In these texts, four categories of hiṃsā are identified. Intentional or premeditated violence (saṃkalpajā-hiṃsā), such as murder or the intention with which a hunter might stalk his prey, is not permitted under any circumstances. Violence associated with household activities, such as cooking and cleaning (ārambhajā-hiṃsā), and violence associated with carrying out one's profession (udyogī-hiṃsā) cannot be avoided, but they should be minimized whenever possible. Violence associated with self-defense (virodhī-hiṃsā) is permissible for a layperson. For example, a king may take up arms against his enemies to protect himself and to protect his kingdom. Some authors maintain that harm done for the sake of religion, such as building a **temple**, for bodily organs, such as eating for nourishment, and for producing food, such as farming, are permissible for a layperson. *See also* AHIṂSĀ.

HĪRAVIJAYASŪRI, ĀCĀRYA (1527–1596). Śvetāmbara Mūrtipūjaka Tapā Gaccha mendicant leader. Famous for his charismatic preaching, he was summoned to the Mughal emperor Akbar's court in Agra. He told Akbar that the true religion taught compassion for all living beings. Although he did not convert Akbar to Jainism, Akbar issued a decree freeing all prisoners and caged birds, and he banned the slaughter of animals on the Jain **festival** of **Paryuṣaṇa**. There are no important writings attributed to him. A memorial shrine (samādhi mandir) was erected at the site of his cremation near Diu, Gujarat, and **images** of him are worshipped in some Tapā Gaccha **temples** today.

HOMBUJA (HUMCHA). Small town in the Shimoga district of Karnataka that is a **pilgrimage** site for **Digambaras**. It is famous for a Digambara **temple** dedicated to **Pārśvanātha** that houses an **image** of the **Yakṣī Padmāvatī**, which is believed to have special powers. Although the earliest inscriptions here date from the 9th century, it is said that this site was established by Jinadatta (ca. 7th–8th centuries C.E.), a prince of **Mathurā**, who was forced to flee to the south. He is said to be the founder of the Jain Sāntara dynasty. At the urging of his teacher, he took this image of Padmāvatī with him. After being told in a dream that he should establish his capital here, he built two temples dedicated to Pārśvanātha with Padmāvatī as the presiding tutelary deity. The temple currently housing this ancient image of Padmāvatī was erected by Vīra Sāntara in 1061, probably as a replacement for the original temple built by Jinadatta. An image of Pārśvanātha and the **Yakṣa Dharaṇendra** (which originally was an image of Yakṣa Sarvānubhūti) also are enshrined in the main sanctum. Other early temples include a stone temple named Guddaḍa-basti, which was dedicated to **Bāhubali**. Erected on top of a hill in 897 C.E. by Vikrama Sāntara I, it was demolished in recent times and replaced by a concrete temple. He also erected the Sūḷe-basti, which houses an image of **Mahāvīra** that is no longer worshipped because it has been broken. A temple dedicated to Pārśvanātha was erected in 950 C.E. Hombuja is the seat of a **bhaṭṭāraka** known by the hereditary name of Devendrakīrti.

– I –

IMAGE. Jains in the **Śvetāmbara** image-worshipping (**Mūrtipūjaka**) community and most **Digambaras** venerate the images of **Tīrthaṅkaras** in **temples** and in home shrines. Some of these images are cast using metal alloys, such as copper or bronze, and others are carved from stone, such as marble or crystal. By the beginning of the common era, there is physical evidence for the worship of Tīrthaṅkara images, although according to tradition this practice is beginningless in time. An inscription found in the Hāthīgumphā cave on Udayagiri Hill outside of Bhubaneswar, Orissa, which has been dated to the late 1st century B.C.E. or the early 1st century C.E., states that in the 12th year of his reign, Mahāmeghavāhana King Khāravela of the Chedi dynasty "brought Kāliṅga Jina that had been taken away by King Nanda" back to his capital. This image would have dated from the 4th century B.C.E. because the Nanda dynasty was ruling Magadha from their capital at Pāṭaliputra (Patna, Bihar) when Alexander the Great entered northwestern India in 327 B.C.E. Two stone headless torsos of images found at Lohanipur, near Patna, which many believe are Tīrthaṅkaras, have been dated to the early centuries C.E. In Chauṣa, Bihar, six seated and 10 standing bronze Tīrthaṅkara images have been found, most of which date from the early Gupta period (4th century C.E.). A number of images of Tīrthaṅkaras and other Jain deities have been found at **Mathurā** from the pre-Kuṣāṇa and Kuṣāṇa periods (mid-2nd century B.C.E. through 3rd century C.E.). The earliest representations here are carved on two-dimensional plaques known as āyāgapaṭas, and later representations are three-dimensional figures. Prior to the 5th century, when cognizances identifying the individual Tīrthaṅkaras begin to be carved on the base of the image, it usually is not possible to identify which Tīrthaṅkara is represented because their features are identical. However, **Ṛṣabha** can be recognized by long hair hanging on his shoulders and **Pārśvanātha** by a canopy of snake-hoods over his head.

Tīrthaṅkaras are depicted in only two postures: seated in the classic lotus position (padmāsana), which represents the Tīrthaṅkara preaching in the assembly hall (**samavasaraṇa**), and standing in the **kāyotsarga** posture, which represents abandoning the body. Some seated images show the Tīrthaṅkara simultaneously facing in the four cardinal directions. Some images have an auspicious symbol called a śrīvatsa on the chest, which represents a curl of hair. Several Tīrthaṅkaras may be represented together, and sometimes all 24 Tīrthaṅkaras of our era are collectively represented. Tīrthaṅkaras are sometimes shown with an attendant **yakṣa/yakṣī** pair.

Prior to the 5th century, all extant images of Tīrthaṅkaras are nude. The earliest image of a Tīrthaṅkara with lower garment, which has been dated to the 5th century, was found at Akota (near Baroda). On seated Śvetāmbara images, clothing is depicted by folds of the lower garment, which are visible under the ankles. Clothed images became the standard representation for Śvetāmbara images in the following centuries. Also in the 5th century, Śvetāmbaras began to depict Tīrthaṅkaras with eyes gazing outward. Most Śvetāmbara images are adorned with large enamel eyes on top of the carved ones, so that even from a distance a worshipper can interact with the image. They are often elaborately ornamented, like a king. Digambara images are unornamented and their eyes gaze downward, symbolizing their non-interaction with the world.

After an image has been consecrated, it must be worshipped on a daily basis. The image of a Tīrthaṅkara represents the ultimate ideal, that of a human being who has overcome all passions (**kaṣāyas**) and has attained liberation (**mokṣa**). Through meditative contemplation during acts of worship (**pūjā**), a person tries to embody these qualities. Like all disembodied souls that have attained liberation (**siddhas**), the souls of the Tīrthaṅkaras permanently reside at the apex of the occupied universe (**loka-ākāśa**) in total isolation from all other souls. They do not interact with worshippers here on earth and they do not enter into the images.

Tīrthaṅkara images are not the only objects of worship. In addition to yakṣas and yakṣīs, there may be images of other non-liberated deities in temples, including **Sarasvatī** and the various protector deities (**kṣetrapālas**) who safeguard temples and shrines. In Śvetāmbara temples, images of the **gaṇadharas Indrabhūti Gautama** and **Sudharman** are frequently found. They are shown preaching, often seated cross-legged but sometimes standing. Unlike a Tīrthaṅkara, a gaṇadhara is depicted with mendicant implements, namely, a whisk broom (**rajoharaṇa**) and a mouth cloth (**muhpattī**) that is held in one hand. Some Śvetāmbara temples contain the images of deceased **monks** and, in recent times, of deceased **nuns**. Like the gaṇadharas, they are shown with mendicant implements and they may be holding a sacred text. In **Kharatara Gaccha** temples, images of the four **Dādāgurus** are worshipped. Images of **Marudevī**, the mother of Ṛṣabha, are found in Śvetāmbara temples at important pilgrimage sites, such as **Mount Śatruñjaya** and **Rāṇakpur**. Among Digambaras, colossal images of **Bāhubali** are worshipped. In both sectarian traditions, Tīrthaṅkaras and deceased mendicants may be worshipped in the form of carved footprint images (pādukās).

INDRA. King of the gods. In Jainism, there are three meanings for the word Indra. (1) As a group, Indras are the kings or rulers of the lower heavenly realms called the Kalpa Heavens, where a class of heavenly beings called **vaimānika devas** dwell. There are a total of 64 Indras living in these realms. (2) Indra is the name for the god who is also called Śakra (Śvet.) or Saudharma (Dig.), who is the ruler (Indra) of the first Kalpa Heaven called Saudharma. It is this Indra who leads the other gods in the celebrations of the five auspicious moments (**kalyāṇakas**) in the life of a **Tīrthaṅkara**. In temple rituals, a **layman** assumes the role of Indra and his wife that of Indrāṇī (Indra's wife) during the reenactment of the god's celebration of the conception and birth of a Tīrthaṅkara. (3) Indra is a title for a hereditary priest (**Jaina Brahmin**, **Upādhye**) who officiates in a **Digambara** temple in south India.

INDRABHŪTI GAUTAMA. *See* GAUTAMA, INDRABHŪTI.

INSTITUTE OF JAINOLOGY. *See* ASSOCIATIONS OF JAINS IN THE DIASPORA.

– J –

JACOBI, HERMANN (1850–1937). Indologist. Born in Cologne, Germany, he studied Sanskrit and comparative linguistics in Berlin under **Albrecht Weber**. He received a Ph.D. from Bonn University in 1872. In 1873–1874, he traveled to India, where he accompanied **Georg Bühler** on his trip through Rajasthan to collect manuscripts. He and

Bühler were the first foreigners to gain limited access to the Jain **manuscript libraries** in **Jaisalmer**. After returning to Germany in 1875, he became a professor at the University of Münster, moving to Kiel in 1885 and Cologne in 1899, where he remained until his retirement in 1922. Utilizing the manuscripts in the Royal Prussian State Library in Berlin, he translated important **Śvetāmbara** canonical texts into German and English. In an article entitled "Mahāvīra and His Predecessors" (*Indian Antiquary* 1880), he established the historicity of the 24th **Tīrthaṅkara**, **Mahāvīra**, by identifying him with **Nirgrantha** (= Pkt., Nigaṇṭha) Nātaputta, mentioned in the Buddhist *Sāmañña-phala-sutta*. He challenged the view held by many Western scholars, such as Auguste Barth, Christian Lassen, and Albrecht Weber, that Jainism was an offshoot of Buddhism. Based on the identification of the fourfold restraint (**cātuyāma-saṃvara**) mentioned in Buddhist texts with the teachings of the 23rd Tīrthaṅkara, **Pārśvanātha**, he argued that Jainism predated Buddhism. On a trip to India in 1913–1914, he was awarded the title Jaina Darśana Divākara ("Sun of Jain Doctrine") at the All India Jain Literary Conference in Jodhpur, held under the auspices of **Ācārya Vijayadharmasūri**. His observations on the Jain community from this trip are summarized in *Der Jainismus* (1915). There is a bibliography of his works in *Beiträge zur Literaturwissenschaft und Geistesgeschichte Indiens*, edited by Willibald Kirfel (Bonn, 1926).

JAIN(A). The term for those who accept the teachings of the omniscient **Jinas** or **Tīrthaṅkaras** and are followers of the religion called Jainism. **Nirgrantha** (Pkt., Nigaṇṭha) was the term used in earlier times for itinerant Jain **monks**. Sometime in the early centuries of the common era, the term Jain came into use for these monks and their lay followers. By the 9th century, the words "may the Jaina teaching prosper" appear in inscriptions. In modern north Indian languages, this word is pronounced like the name "Jane" and often is transliterated as "Jain." In modern south Indian languages, where the Sanskritic pronunciation has been retained, the diphthong "ai" is pronounced like the English word "eye," the final short "a" is pronounced, and the word often is transliterated as "Jaina." In recent scholarly writing, Jain is found more frequently.

JAIN, CAINSUKHDĀS. *See* NYĀYATĪRTHA, CAINSUKHDĀS JAIN.

JAIN, CHAMPAT RAI (1867–1942). Digambara scholar of Jainism. Born in Delhi, he graduated from Mission College (now St. Stephen's College) in 1885. He went to England to study law and returned to India after completing his studies in 1897, settling in Hardoi, Uttar Pradesh. Shortly after his return, he began studying Jain texts and also read about Christianity, Judaism, Hinduism, and Islam. After returning to England in 1913, he began writing a number of books in English on various aspects of Jainism, including logic and philosophy, law and culture, and lay conduct, as well as introductory works. In *The Key of Knowledge*, he compares Jain philosophy and religion with Christianity, Judaism, Hinduism, and Islam. He established the Jain Library in London to further the knowledge of Jainism in Europe. He returned to India in 1938, and shortly before his death established the Jain Academy of Wisdom and Culture in Delhi. He also was one of the founders of the Akil Bhāratavarṣīya Digambara Jain Pariṣad (est. 1923). *See also* ASSOCIATIONS OF JAINS IN INDIA.

JAIN, HĪRĀLĀL (1898–1973). Digambara scholar of Jainism and Prākrit **languages**. Born in Gangai, Madhya Pradesh, he received an M.A. from Allahabad University in 1925, where he studied Sanskrit and Prākrit languages. He was appointed assistant professor at King Edward College, Amaravati. He was awarded a D. Litt. from Nagpur University in 1944 and became a professor at Morris College, Nagpur. He served as the director of the Post-graduate and Research Institute of Prākrits and Jainology at Muzaffarpur from 1955 to 1960 and was head of the Department of Sanskrit, Pāli, and Prākrit at Jabalpur University from 1961 until his retirement in 1969. Along with **Ādināth Upādhye**, he edited a number of classical Digambara texts, including the ***Ṣaṭkhaṇḍāgama***. He is the author of *Bhāratīya Samskṛti me(m) Jain Dharma kā Yogadān* ("Contributions of Jainism to Indian Culture"). He also wrote numerous articles on Jain philosophy, history, and literature.

JAIN, JAGDISH CHANDRA (1909–1994). Scholar of Jainism and Prākrit **languages**. Born in Baseda, Uttar Pradesh, he attended Syādvāda Jain Mahāvidyālaya, **Banaras**, where he studied Sanskrit, Prākrit, literature, philosophy, and logic, passing his Śāstrī examination in 1925. He received an M.A. in philosophy from Banaras Hindu University in 1932 and was professor of Hindi at Ramnarain Ruia College, Bombay (now Mumbai). He was awarded a D.Litt. from the University of Bombay in 1945. After his retirement in 1968, he became a research professor in the Department of Indology, University of Kiel, Germany, where he worked with **Ludwig Alsdorf** and Klaus Bruhn. He also lectured at universities in the United States and Brazil. Among his numerous writings, he is noted for *Life in Ancient India as Depicted in* *the Jain Canon and Commentaries* (1947, rev. ed. 1984) and *The Vasudevahiṇḍi: An Authentic Jain Version of the Bṛhatkathā* (1977). His collected papers have been published in *Studies in Early Jainism* (1991). *Jainism and Prakrit in Ancient and Medieval India* contains a bibliography of his works.

JAIN, MAHENDRA KUMAR (1911–1959). Digambara scholar of Jainism. Born in Khurai, Madhya Pradesh, he attended Hukam Chand Mahāvidyālaya, Indore, passing the Śāstrī and Nyāyatīrtha examinations. In 1930, he joined Syādvāda Jain Mahāvidyālaya, **Banaras**, where he taught philosophy for 13 years. He received a D.Litt. from Banaras Hindu University and was appointed lecturer in Buddhist philosophy. He was associated with Bhāratīya Jñānapīṭha publishers from its inception in 1944 and edited its journal, *Jñānodaya*. He joined the faculty of Vārāṇasī Sanskrit University, where he taught Jain philosophy. He edited a number of classical Jain texts and is the author of *Jain Darśan*.

JAIN SAMAJ EUROPE. *See* ASSOCIATIONS OF JAINS IN THE DIASPORA.

JAIN, SĪTAL PRASĀD. *See* **SĪTAL PRASĀD, BRAHMACĀRĪ**

JAIN ŚVETĀMBARA CONFERENCE. *See* ASSOCIATIONS OF JAINS IN INDIA.

JAIN VISHVA BHARATI INSTITUTE. An institution of higher education located at Ladnun, Rajasthan. Established in 1970 under the inspiration of the **Ācārya Tulsī**, the ninth mendicant leader of the **Śvetāmbara Terāpanthīs**, it became a university in 1991. It promotes the values of Jainism by incorporating learning and research with training in nonviolence (**ahiṃsā**), non-possession (**aparigraha**), and the doctrine of manifold aspects (**anekāntavāda**). As of 2003, it has the following departments: Jainology and Comparative Religion and Philosophy, Department of Science and Living, **Prekṣā-Dhyāna** and **Yoga**, Nonviolence and Peace, Prākrit and Āgama Studies, and Social Work. The campus at Ladnun functions as the physical center of the Śvetāmbara Terāpanthī sectarian tradition.

JAINA. Acronym for Federation of Jain Associations in North America. *See* ASSOCIATIONS OF JAINS IN THE DIASPORA.

JAINA BRAHMIN. A Jain who is employed as a temple priest in **Digambara temples** in south India. Depending on the area, they may be called arcaka, **Indra**, Jaina Brahmin, paṇḍita, purohita, or **Upādhye**. They are Jain by birth and are hereditary ritual specialists who form a distinct Jain **caste**. These families may have descended from vedic **Brahmins** who converted to Jainism or from a group of Jain laymen who were appointed to this position because of their merit or advanced spiritual status. They perform the required daily rites of worship (**pūjā**) to the consecrated **images** of the **Tīrthaṅkaras** on behalf of **laypeople**. They also perform ceremonies associated with rites of passage (**saṃskāras**), such as weddings, and sometimes administer vows to laypeople. As part of their compensation, they receive the food that is offered to the Tīrthaṅkaras. Because Jains are forbidden from consuming this food, Jains from other castes traditionally do not intermarry with the families of temple priests. Families of hereditary temple priests are not found in north India, where Digambara laypeople perform temple worship themselves.

JAINI, PADMANABH S. Scholar of Jainism and Buddhism. He was born in Nellikar, a small town near **Mūḍbidrī**, Karnataka, into a **Digambara** family. After completing his elementary education, he attended Mahāvīra Brahmacaryāśram Jaina Gurukula at Karanja, Maharashtra, which was founded by Brahmacārī Devcand Kastūrcand Śāh (**Muni Samantabhadra**). Here he studied many basic Jain texts and met some of the renowned Digambara **paṇḍits** of this period. He then attended the Arts College at Nasik (affiliated with the University of Bombay), where he received a B.A. degree in Sanskrit and Prākrit.

After graduation in 1947, he was invited by Paṇḍit **Sukhlāl Saṅghavī** to study philosophy and logic with him in Ahmedabad. Thus, he became familiar with both the Digambara and **Śvetāmbara** textual traditions. Saṅghavi encouraged him to study the Buddhist Pāli canon for a comparative insight into the Jain **scriptures**. He studied as a layman at the Vidyodaya Pirivena, a Buddhist monastic training center in Sri Lanka (then, Ceylon). During his two years there, he concentrated his studies on the Abhidharma Piṭaka, which became his main area of scholarly expertise in Buddhist studies.

He was appointed to a lectureship in Pāli at Banaras Hindu University in 1952 and in 1956 at the School of Oriental and African Studies (SOAS), University of London, where he received a Ph.D. for his edition of the *Abhidharmadīpa*. Eventually, he moved to the University of Michigan, Ann Arbor, and in 1972 to the University of California at Berkeley. He was professor of Buddhist Studies in the Department of

South and Southeast Asian Studies there until his retirement in 1994, afterward becoming professor in the Graduate School.

Jaini's publications on Jainism began in the 1970s with a number of articles focusing on comparative aspects of Buddhism and Jainism. He is best known for *The Jaina Path of Purification* (1979), a survey text on Jainism, and *Gender and Salvation: Jaina Debates on the Spiritual Liberation of Women* (1991). His articles have been republished in *Collected Papers on Jaina Studies* (2000) and *Collected Papers on Buddhist Studies* (2001). A bibliography of his works as of 2002 may be found in *Jainism and Early Buddhism: Essays in Honor of Padmanabh S. Jaini* (2003).

JAISALMER. A city in the Thar desert of western Rajasthan that is famous for its valuable collection of manuscripts housed in seven **manuscript libraries**. The oldest **temple**, which is dedicated to **Pārśvanātha**, was constructed at the beginning of the 13th century and rebuilt early in the 15th century after being destroyed by Muslim invaders. Today, there is a large complex of temples carved in yellow sandstone, including those dedicated to **Ṛṣabha**, Sambhava (third **Tīrthaṅkara**), **Śāntinātha**, and **Mahāvīra**. In the manuscript libraries are stored palm-leaf manuscripts from the 10th century, as well as the oldest known Indian paper manuscript, dating from 1189. The largest manuscript library, which is located in the underground vaults of the temple of Sambhava, was founded by Muni Jinabhadra in 1551. Many valuable manuscripts from Patan and Cambray were taken here at the time of Muslim invasions. The manuscript collections in these temple libraries have been catalogued by a team headed by **Muni Puṇyavijaya**. In the 1990s, **Muni Jambūvijaya** organized a project to preserve many of the valuable manuscripts by scanning them, and he prepared a new manuscript catalogue of these collections.

JAMBŪ. In traditional lineage accounts, the first elder (**sthavira**) in the **mendicant lineage** established by **Mahāvīra**. He learned the sacred **scriptures** from **Gaṇadhara Sudharman**. After leading the community for eight years, he attained omniscience (**kevala-jñāna**) and liberation (**mokṣa**) 64 years after the death of Mahāvīra. He was the last person to attain liberation in the current descending **cycle of time** (avasarpiṇī).

JAMBŪDVĪPA. In Jain cosmography, the innermost island-continent in the middle realm (**madhya-loka**). It is named after the rose-apple tree (jambū) located atop **Mount Meru** at the center of the island. It is comprised of seven continents separated by six east-west oriented mountain ranges. From south to north, these continents are named **Bharata-kṣetra**, Haimavata, Hari, **Mahāvideha** (Videha), Ramyaka, Hairaṇyavata, and Airāvata-kṣetra. Bharata-kṣetra and Airāvata-kṣetra are subject to **cycles of time**, where living condition improve and decline. On the others, time is not cyclical and living conditions remain constant. Some of these are **bhoga-bhūmi** lands, where all one's needs are satisfied without effort, and others are **karma-bhūmi** lands, where one must labor in order to survive.

JAMBŪVIJAYA, MUNI (1923–). Śvetāmbara Mūrtipūjaka scholar-**monk** of the **Tapā Gaccha**. Born in Mandal, Gujarat, he was named Cinubhāī Bhogībhāī. His father, Bhogīlāl Mohanlāl Joītārām (1895–1959), took a vow of lifelong **celibacy** in 1925, and in Ahmedabad in 1932 he was initiated as Muni Bhuvanvijaya by Ācārya Vijayasiddhisūri (1855–1959). In Ratlam in 1937, at the age of 14, Jambūvijaya took initiation from Bhuvanvijaya, who became his teacher. Jambūvijaya's mother, Aṇibahen Popaṭlāl (1894–1995), took initiation as Sādhvī Manoharaśrījī in Ahmedabad in 1939 from Ācārya Vijayanītisūri. She became a disciple of Sādhvī Lābhaśrījī, who had been her elder sister. All four of her siblings took initiation, and in her extended family there have been a number of initiations. Jambūvijaya later studied under **Muni Puṇyavijaya** and assisted him in cataloging **manuscript** collections and in editing the Śvetāmbara **Āgamas** for publication. He is one of the most respected scholarly monks and has assisted a number of Western scholars in their research. He has edited a number of texts, including the *Dvādaśara-nayacakra* of Mallavādikṣāśramaṇa (5th century C.E.). After the death of Muni Puṇyavijaya, he became the chief editor of the ongoing Jaina Āgama Series.

JĀTI/JÑĀTI. Social class or **caste** fixed by birth. A term for an endogamous group within the caste or varṇa system. Some scholars believe that Jains developed a caste system in later times under the influence of the surrounding Hindu community. Others think that caste hierarchy always has been accepted for social purposes. Although the term jāti is found in some of the earliest Jain texts, most of the caste groups in existence today date from medieval times. Some are named after the towns or regions where they are said to have arisen. Castes with origins in north India include the **Śvetāmbara** Śrīmālīs, Osvāls, and Porvāls, and the **Digambara** Agravāls (Agarvāls) and Khaṇḍelvāls. Each is subdivided into the higher-ranked Vīśā or Bīsā (literally, 20), who historically have claimed social superiority because of their perceived greater wealth, and the lower-ranked Daśā (literally, 10). All of these castes include Hindu Vaiṣṇavas, but Jains are more numerous. Castes with origins in south India, which are exclusively Digambara, include Śetavālas (Saitavāla), Chaturtha, Pañchama, and Bogāra. Within the south Indian Digambara community, there is a separate caste of hereditary temple priests called **Upādhye** who do not intermarry with other castes.

In the 20th century, the bounded nature of these caste groupings began to break down. Intermarriage among castes has become more common, although in India Śvetāmbaras and Digambaras tend not to intermarry. In spite of the view of caste as being a measure of social but not religious status, there is evidence that in the past some castes were not given mendicant initiation (**dīkṣā**). Early in the 20th century, there was a debate within the Jain community over the practice of not allowing Daśā castes to enter Jain temples. This practice was ended, and Jains of all castes may worship in Jain temples throughout India.

JAYA, ĀCĀRYA (MUNI JĪTMAL) (1803–1881). Fourth mendicant leader of the **Śvetāmbara Terāpanthī** tradition. Born in the village of Royat, Rajasthan, he took initiation in 1812 along with his mother and two brothers. After being appointed as **ācārya** in 1852, he established a number of traditions within the Terāpanthī community. These include the annual celebration of the death of **Ācārya Bhikṣu**, the first Terāpanthī mendicant leader, and the celebration of his own succession as ācārya. He also instituted an annual meeting of all **mendicants** called **maryādā mahotsava**. He consolidated the rules of mendicant conduct into the version used by mendicants today, including the 13 essential rules of the order that are recited every morning. He also introduced the office of chief nun (**sādhvī pramukhā**). He established libraries by encouraging mendicants to copy **manuscripts**. His own writings include a collection of anecdotes related to Ācārya Bhikṣu. He also translated the ***Bhagavatī Sūtra*** into Rajasthani.

JINA. Spiritual Victor. An epithet used by Jains for a human being who attains omniscience (**kevala-jñāna**) through his own efforts and who teaches others the path to liberation (mokṣa-mārga). In early times, this term was used by other groups of **śramaṇas**, such as the **Ājīvikas** and Buddhists, for their mendicant teachers. It is a synonym for a **Tīrthaṅkara**.

JINACANDRASŪRI, ĀCĀRYA (1140–1166). Śvetāmbara Mūrtipūjaka Kharatara Gaccha mendicant leader and the second **Dādāguru**. He is also called Maṇidhārī because of a jewel (maṇi) on his forehead that emanated magical powers. He was born in Vikrampur and was named Sūrya Kumār. Initiated at the age of six by **Jinadattasūri**, he excelled in scholarship and was appointed **ācārya** when he was just eight. Through his teachings, he converted many non-Jains, and a number of lay followers joined his mendicant order. Like the other Dādāgurus, he is famous for his magical powers, which he used to subdue non-Jain deities and for the benefit of the Jain community. A shrine has been constructed at the site of his cremation near Delhi, which is known as Mehraulī Dādābāṛī.

JINACANDRASŪRI II, ĀCĀRYA (1537–1612). Śvetāmbara Mūrtipūjaka Kharatara Gaccha mendicant leader and the fourth **Dādāguru**. He is sometimes called Akbar Pratibodhaka ("Influencer of Akbar") to distinguish him from his predecessor. He was born in Khetasar, a village in the region of Jodhpur, Rajasthan, and was named Sultān Kumār. He asked to be initiated after hearing the preaching of the leader of the Kharatara Gaccha. He was appointed **ācārya** in 1555. He is noted for reestablishing strict rules of mendicant conduct and for defending the Kharatara Gaccha against critics, especially those in the **Tapā Gaccha**. He was invited to the Mughal emperor Akbar's court in 1591 and was influential in Akbar's decision to protect Jain **pilgrimage** sites and to prohibit the slaughter of animals during **Paryuṣaṇa**. His teachings on non-harming (**ahiṃsā**) may have saved the life of an infant granddaughter of Akbar whom court astrologers had suggested should be killed. Instead, Akbar had a special ceremony performed in a Jain temple to rectify the astrological problems. Most of Jinacandrasūri's miracles are associated with incidents that are reported to have occurred in Akbar's court. He died in the Marwari village of Bilada.

JINADATTASŪRI, ĀCĀRYA (1075–1154). Śvetāmbara Mūrtipūjaka Kharatara Gaccha mendicant leader and the first **Dādāguru**. He was born in Dholka, Gujarat, and was named Somacandra. He was initiated as a child at the request of a senior **monk** who came to know of auspicious marks on his body that were indicative of greatness. He succeeded **Jineśvarasūri** as **ācārya** in 1112, and under his guidance the mendicant community grew rapidly. He initiated large numbers of temple-dwelling monks (**caityavāsī**) and converted many non-Jains. Like the other Dādāgurus, he is famous for his magical powers, which he is said to have acquired through asceticism and from his discovery of a hidden text written centuries earlier. Most of his miracles are associated with subduing the various non-Jain deities with supernatural powers and with the protection of the Jain community. It is reported that at the time of his cremation, his clothing and mouth cloth (**muhpattī**) did not ignite and that they were preserved in **Jaisalmer**. A shrine was established at the site of his cremation in Ajmer, which is known as the Dādābāṛī. It is believed that he was reborn as a heavenly being (**deva**) and that in his next birth he will be reborn in **Mahāvideha** and will attain liberation (**mokṣa**).

JINA-KALPA. A mode of mendicant life like that of the **Jina**. During the time of **Mahāvīra**, there were two modes of life that **monks** could follow. They could live as part of an organized mendicant community (**sthavira-kalpa**) or they could choose to leave the community and live in isolation, either alone or with several other monks (jina-kalpa). This was how Mahāvīra lived after renouncing the household life until he attained omniscience (**kevala-jñāna**) and established his own community (**tīrtha**) of **mendicants** and **laypeople**. This mode of life was not permitted for **nuns**. A jina-kalpa monk was not subject to the supervision of a mendicant leader (**ācārya**) in matters like confession. **Śvetāmbaras** and **Digambaras** agree that this mode of mendicancy came to an end with the death of **Jambū**, which took place 64 years after the death of Mahāvīra. They also agree that this mode of mendicancy was more severe than living in a mendicant community. However, they disagree over what this entailed.

Although all Śvetāmbara monks are now required to wear clothing and to use alms bowls, this was not always the case. According to Śvetāmbara sources, sthavira-kalpa monks were required to wear at a minimum three pieces of clothing, but jina-kalpa monks could wear three pieces of clothing, or two pieces, or just a single cloth. If they were young and in good health, they could abandon clothing altogether and live naked, like **Ṛṣabha** and Mahāvīra, the first and last **Tīrthaṅkaras** of this era. They also had the option of giving up mendicant implements, such as alms bowls. In accordance with their interpretation of the mendicant vow (**mahāvrata**) of non-possession (**aparigraha**), all Digambara monks practiced total **nudity** and none used alms bowls, irrespective of whether they followed the sthavira-kalpa or jina-kalpa mode of mendicant life.

JINAKUŚALASŪRI, ĀCĀRYA (1280–1332). Śvetāmbara Mūrtipūjaka Kharatara Gaccha mendicant leader and the third **Dādāguru**. He was born in the Marwari village of Garh Sivana, Rajasthan, and was named Karmaṇ. He was acquainted with the ascetic life at an early age because his paternal uncle was the head of the Kharatara Gaccha. Around 1290, he took initiation and was given the name Kuśalakīrti. Noted for his scholarship, he was appointed **ācārya** in 1320. He participated in two large **pilgrimages** sponsored by prominent businessmen to **Mount Śatruñjaya** and **Mount Girnār** during which he consecrated many **images**, including those of previous Kharatara Gaccha ācāryas. He was invited by Jains to come to Sindh to rectify problems within the community, and he brought about a revival of Jainism there. He brought two Hindu deities, White Bhairava and Black Bhairava, under his control. He is often portrayed with these two deities, who are shown paying homage to him. He died at Devrajpur in Sindh. Since then, there have been numerous reports of his appearance to devotees. The most famous of these occurred in Sindh, where he is said to have prevented a boat from sinking.

JINASENA (ca. 770–850 C.E.). Digambara mendicant leader. He was born into a **Brahmin** family and while still young took initiation into the Pañcastūpānvaya mendicant lineage (later known as the Sena Gaṇa), which probably originated in **Banaras**. Mendicants in this lineage, who subsequently migrated to **Śravaṇa Beḷgoḷa**, were noted for their expertise in the doctrine of **karma**. Amoghavarṣa (815–877 C.E.), a Rāṣṭrakūṭa king who became a devout Jain and renounced the kingdom for a religious life, was one of his disciples. Around 820 C.E., Jinasena completed an important **commentary** begun by his teacher, **Vīrasena**, entitled *Jayadhavalā* on the ***Kaṣāyaprabhṛta***. He also is known for his work in the genre of Jain **Universal History**. He and his disciple Guṇabhadra wrote the ***Mahāpurāṇa***, which contains traditional accounts of the lives of the 63 exemplary men (**śalākā-puruṣas**) in this current descending **cycle of time** (avasarpiṇī), including the 24 **Tīrthaṅkaras**. In the context of the life story of the **Ṛṣabha**, Jinasena introduced into Jainism a number of Hindu ritual practices and secular life-cycle rites (**saṃskāras**). Some scholars have associated Jinasena with the Hinduization of Jainism. Others believe that his efforts were aimed at establishing a facade of social conformity by the Jain community within the dominant Hindu society. In introducing elements within these rites that were unique to Jainism, he facilitated the preservation of the Jain religious community with its own **temples**, rituals, and ritual specialists.

JINAVIJAYA, MUNI (1888–1976). Śvetāmbara Mūrtipūjaka scholar-**monk** of the **Tapā Gaccha**. He was born in Rupaheli, Rajasthan, and was named Kiśan Singh. After the death of his father in 1899, he stayed with the **Sthānakavāsī** mendicant community and began his education. In 1903, at the age of 15, he was initiated as a Sthānakavāsī monk. However, he discovered that he would have more opportunities for education if he could study with the **paṇḍits** who taught the monks in the Mūrtipūjaka community. Therefore, he left his mendicant community and, in 1910, he took a second initiation as Muni Jinavijaya from Muni Sundaravijaya in the Vallabha Samudāya, which was headed by **Ācārya Vijayavallabhasūri**. At Mehsana he came into contact with Ācārya Kāturvijaya and his disciples Muni Cāturvijaya and **Muni Puṇyavijaya**, who were of assistance to him in his studies, especially in his work with ancient **manuscripts** and their scripts. He began writing articles in Gujarati and Hindi for several journals.

While Jinavijaya was in Pune, he became acquainted with nationalist leaders there, including Lokamanya Tilak and the Jain nationalist Arjunlāl Seṭhī. At this time, Jinavijaya decided to leave the mendicant community in order to become more active in this movement. Mahātmā Gāndhī invited him to work in the archeological section of the Gujarat Vidyāpīṭh in Ahmedabad. During his eight years there, he studied German and met several German scholars of Indology. In 1928, at the invitation of **Hermann Jacobi**, Jinavijaya went to Germany and studied at the Universities of Bonn, Hamburg, and Leipzig, where he became proficient in Western research methods.

Jinavijaya returned to India at the end of 1929 and was arrested for his participation in Gāndhī's Salt March. During the time that he was in the Nasik jail, he came into contact with K. M. Munshi, which resulted in his association with Munshi's Bhāratīya Vidyā Bhavan after its establishment in 1938. Prior to this, in 1930, at the invitation of Bahadur Singh Singhi, a Calcutta businessman interested in Jain literature, Jinavijaya joined the faculty of Śāntiniketan (now Viśvabhāratī University), Bengal, which was founded by Rabindranath Tagore. Here he established the Jain Jñānapīṭh and initiated the Singhi Jain Granthamālā Series.

In the course of his career, Jinavijaya published a large number of texts, including important works on medieval Śvetāmbara history, and guided many students in their research. In 1952, he was appointed an honorary member of the German Oriental Society and, in 1961, he was honored by the Government of India with the title of Padmaśrī for his research and publication activities.

JINEŚVARASŪRI, ĀCĀRYA (11th century). Mendicant leader who was the pupil of Vardhamāna, the founder of the **Śvetāmbara Mūrtipūjaka Kharatara Gaccha**. He apparently was from a **Brahmin** family. It is said that in a debate at the court of King Durlabha of Patan, Gujarat, in 1024 C.E. he defeated Surācārya, a prominent temple-dwelling monk (**caityavāsī**) who had argued that it was proper for **mendicants** to live permanently at temple complexes and to own property. He was given the title Kharatara, "Extremely Sharp [in debate, or in conduct]," which subsequently became the name of the **mendicant lineage**.

JĪTMAL, MUNI. *See* JAYA, ĀCĀRYA.

JĪVA. Self, **soul**, or that which is sentient. A non-material substance (**dravya**) that is characterized by the quality (**guṇa**) of awareness or **consciousness** (caitanya). Other distinguishing qualities of the soul are energy (vīrya) and bliss (sukha). When viewed from the perspective of these qualities, the soul is regarded as eternal and unchanging because there is never a time when a soul is devoid of these qualities. However, from another perspective, the soul is constantly changing because its qualities are continuously undergoing modifications (pariṇāma), acquiring new modes (paryāya) and losing old modes. Although a soul is non-material, it is said to occupy a certain amount of space, expanding or contracting to correspond with the dimensions of its current physical body. Souls are individual and infinite in number. From beginningless time, all souls have been bound in the cycle of rebirth (**saṃsāra**) by a type of extremely subtle matter called **karma**, which either limits or defiles the qualities of the soul and which causes embodiment of the soul in birth after birth.

Some souls have been embodied only as the most rudimentary one-sensed life-form called **nigoda**. They have not begun to develop spiritually and have a type of false belief that is undifferentiated (avyakta mithyātva) with no tendency toward good or harmful actions. In some, for reasons that are not explained, there is a spiritual awakening, and false belief becomes differentiated (vyakta mithyātva) or assumes a certain form. These souls enter the path of spiritual development and are born in other life-forms. Eventually, some of these souls will attain liberation (**mokṣa**). Some souls have a quality called **bhavyatva** that renders them capable of attaining liberation. There are other souls, called **abhavyas**, that lack this quality and will remain in the cycle of rebirth forever. In Jainism, there is no Supreme Soul or Ultimate Reality (brahman) that has never been bound in saṃsāra, although disembodied perfected souls that have attained liberation (**siddhas**) may be called **God** (**deva**) or Supreme Soul (**paramātman**). *See also* ĀTMAN.

JĪVARĀJA, MUNI (ca. mid-16th to mid-17th centuries). One of the five principal reformers (pañca-munis) in the non-image-worshipping **Śvetāmbara** sectarian tradition that today is known as **Sthānakavāsī**. He probably was born in Surat, Gujarat, and lived sometime between 1524 and 1641. He broke with the **Loṅkā Gaccha** over a disagreement about their lax mendicant practices and support of temple worship. Some sources credit him with introducing the mouth cloth (**muhpattī**), whisk broom (**rajoharaṇa**), and other mendicant implements used by Sthānakavāsīs today. He may have selected the 32 Śvetāmbara scriptures (**Āgamas**) that have been accepted by all Sthānakavāsīs. However, some scholars associate these innovations with **Lavajī**.

JÑĀNA. Knowledge. It is the quality (**guṇa**) of the **soul** (**jīva**) that ascertains the details of an object. In cognition (upayoga), or the application of **consciousness** (caitanya), it operates in association with perception (**darśana**), the quality of the soul associated with an indistinct awareness of an object. Like other qualities of the soul, knowledge constantly undergoes changes or modifications (pariṇāma), acquiring new modes (paryāya) and losing old modes. These modes are expressed as five types of knowledge. Each is affected by a specific variety of obscuring (āvaraṇīya) **karma**, which is named in accordance with the type of knowledge that it obstructs. (1) Mati-jñāna is knowledge acquired through the senses, including the mind. All living beings, even the most elementary one-sensed beings (**ekendriya**), have some degree of sensory knowledge, experienced through the sense of touch. (2) Śruta-jñāna is knowledge associated with language and reasoning by interpreting words, writing, and gestures. All five-sensed beings with the ability to reason have some degree of this knowledge. (3) Avadhi-jñāna is extrasensory knowledge, or clairvoyance. It is inborn in heavenly beings (**devas**) and hell-beings (**nārakis**) and may be attained by humans through various **yogic** practices or spiritual disciplines. (4) Manaḥparyaya-jñāna is knowledge of the objects of another's mind, or telepathy. It is sometimes attained by humans in advanced states of spiritual development. (5) **Kevala-jñāna** is absolute or isolated knowledge, or omniscience. It is knowledge of all substances (**dravyas**) in all of their temporal modes (past, present, and future).

JÑĀNAMATI, ĀRYIKĀ (1934–). Digambara nun. She was born in the village of Tikaitanagara, Uttar Pradesh, and was named Mainā Devī. The eldest of 13 children, she was initiated in 1952 at the age of 18 as a **kṣullikā** by Ācārya Deśabhūṣaṇa at **Mahāvīrjī**, and was given the name Vīramatī. She was the first **woman** in this area to take initiation at this young age. In 1956, she was initiated as an **āryikā** at Madhorajapur, Rajasthan, by Ācārya Vīrasāgara, who gave her the name Āryikā Jñānamatī. Subsequently, her mother was initiated as a nun, and one brother and three sisters took the vows of a **brahmacārī**. Jñānamati studied logic and philosophy briefly with a **paṇḍit** in Jaipur, but she is mostly self-taught. She concentrated her research on the study and translation of cosmographical texts. In 1972, under her inspiration, the Digambara Jain Triloka Śodha Saṃsthāna (Institute of Cosmographical Research) was founded in Hastinapur, where she now spends most of her time due to health reasons. A large-scale model of **Jambūdvīpa** has been constructed here. She also has established a boarding school for boys here and a center that publishes the Vīra Jñānodaya Granthamālā series and the journal *Samyagjñāna*. Jñānamati is presently associated with the lineage of Sumatisāgara but effectively acts as an independent leader of a group that includes a number of her family members. In 1987, she became the first āryikā to initiate a male lay follower. A partial list of her writings may be found in her work, *Jaina Geography* (1985), and in Shāntā's *The Unknown Pilgrims*.

JÑĀNA-PAÑCAMĪ. Knowledge Fifth. A **Śvetāmbara festival** commemorating the day on which the Jain **scriptures (Āgama)** were first committed to writing. It takes place on the fifth day of the bright half of Kārtika (October/November). According to tradition, the Dvādaśāṅga-Sūtra ("Scripture in Twelve Parts") was completed on this day. Old **manuscripts** are displayed at **temples** and **laypeople** commission new copies of the sacred texts. Some Jains worship **Sarasvatī**, the **goddess** of learning, on this day. This festival is also known as Guru-Pañcamī (Teacher Fifth), Lābha-Pañcamī (Profit Fifth), and Saubhāgya-Pañcamī (Good-Fortune Fifth).

JÑĀN(A)SUNDAR(A), MUNI (1880–1955). Śvetāmbara Mūrtipūjaka mendicant leader and social organizer. He was born into a **Sthānakavāsī** family in a small village in Marwar, Rajasthan. After nine years of marriage, he took initiation as a Sthānakavāsī **monk** in 1906 and was given the name Sant Gayvarcand. His study of the texts led him to the conviction that image worship was the orthodox position, and so in 1916, he took a second initiation in Osian as Muni Jñānasundara from the **Tapā Gaccha** Muni Ratnavijaya (a disciple of Ācārya Dharmasūri). At Ratnavijaya's urging, he became a fully initiated monk (**saṃvegī sādhu**) in the **Upakeśa Gaccha**, which otherwise consisted of only a few **yatis**. He wrote several hundred stridently argumentative books and pamphlets in which he argued against the **Kharatara Gaccha**, Sthānakavāsī, and **Terāpanthī** versions of Jain history and practice, and promoted the Upakeśa Gaccha and the Tapā Gaccha. In 1943, the Mūrtipūjaka congregation of Jodhpur installed him as Ācārya Devaguptasūri, the last head of the Upakeśa Gaccha. He died in 1955 in Jodhpur. During his life he initiated only a handful of disciples, several of whom had previously been Sthānakavāsī and Śvetāmbara Terāpanthī monks. The last of these died in 1968.

JVĀLĀMĀLINĪ. A **goddess** who, according to most **Digambara** sources, is the **yakṣī** of Candraprabha, the eighth **Tīrthaṅkara** of this era. According to legend, in her previous life she was a princess named Kanakamālā. She was unhappy because of her husband's fondness for hunting. A goddess appeared to her and told her that she could become a goddess in her next life by worshipping the Tīrthaṅkaras, performing various **fasts**, and worshipping **Padmāvatī**, the **yakṣī** of the 23rd Tīrthaṅkara, **Pārśvanātha**. In medieval times, she was a popular goddess in Jain **tantra**, and is the subject of a tantric text, the *Jvālāmālinī Kalpa*, composed by Indranandī in the 10th century C.E. According to an account in this text, a **monk** named Helācārya (ca. mid-9th century) of the **Drāviḍa Saṅgha** began to worship her after she gave him an incantation to remove the influence of an evil spirit that was afflicting a female disciple named Kamalaśrī. The earliest **image** of Jvālāmālinī, dating from the 8th century, is from Aihole in Karnataka. A **temple** dedicated to this goddess was constructed at Javur in the Dharwar district of Karnataka in the 11th century by a monk of the **Yāpanīya** sect. She is the guardian deity of Simhanagadde (Narasimharajapura), the site of an important **maṭha** in Karnataka.

JYOTIṢKA DEVAS. A class of luminary gods (**devas**) associated with the sun, moon, planets, constellations, and certain scattered stars. They are characterized by their continuous movement around **Mount Meru**, which is located in the center of the occupied universe (**loka-ākāśa**).

– K –

KAḌUĀ GACCHA. A **Śvetāmbara Mūrtipūjaka** ascetic lineage whose members renounced the household life but did not take the five great mendicant vows (**mahāvratas**). It was founded by Kaḍuā Śāh (1438–1507), who originally was a lay member of the **A(ñ)cala Gaccha**. After reading a text on mendicant conduct, he realized that the mendicants he had met were domesticated monks (**yatis**) whose conduct did not correspond with rules outlined in the text. At the age of 19, he renounced the household life and accepted a variety of lifelong ascetic vows of **dietary restrictions** and of **celibacy** but continued to wear **layman**'s clothing. Instead of the traditional mendicant honorific title of **muni**, he took the title of saṃvarī. Ten years later, he became a leader (paṭṭadhara) who initiated other saṃvarīs. Like fully initiated mendicants (**saṃvegī sādhus**), these renunciants were itinerant except during the four-month rainy season period (**cāturmāsa**). They observed a code of conduct drawn up by Kaḍuā, which combined elements of idealized ascetic and lay behavior. The latest textual reference to this lineage dates from the 17th century, but there are reports that it still existed in Gujarat as late as the 1950s.

***KALPA SŪTRA*.** A **Śvetāmbara** text ascribed to **Bhadrabāhu**. It is composed in three sections. The first section contains biographies of the **Jinas** (Jinacaritra), all of which are modeled after the extensive narrative of the life of **Mahāvīra. Manuscripts** of the *Kalpa Sūtra* are often illustrated with these events. The second section contains lists called Sthavirāvalī, which enumerate the names of **mendicants** who were successors to Mahāvīra's chief disciples (**gaṇadharas**) in various mendicant lineages (gaṇas) and their branches (śākhās). The third section contains the rules for mendicant conduct to be observed during the four-month rainy season period (**cāturmāsa**). Portions of the *Kalpa Sūtra* are recited by Śvetāmbara mendicants as part of the observance of **Paryuṣaṇa**.

KALYĀṆAKA. An auspicious moment in the life of a **Tīrthaṅkara**. The five auspicious moments are conception (garbha), birth (janma), renunciation (vairāgya), enlightenment or omniscience (**kevala-jñāna**), and liberation (**mokṣa, nirvāṇa**). These events may be ritually reenacted, especially during **festivals**, such as **Mahāvīra Jayantī**, and during the consecration of a **temple**. In the **Śvetāmbara Mūrtipūjaka Kharatara Gaccha**, a sixth kalyāṇaka, the transfer of embryo, may be celebrated. Śvetāmbara **Terāpanthīs** do not celebrate the garbha kalyāṇaka.

KALYĀṆAVIJAYAGAṆI, PAṄNYĀSA. Śvetāmbara Mūrtipūjaka scholar-**monk** of the **Tapā Gaccha**. Born in 1887 in Rajasthan, he was initiated in 1906 in Jalora, Rajasthan. He was appointed to the rank of **gaṇi** in 1937 and to the rank of **paṅnyāsa** in 1974. He authored numerous books and articles in Gujarati and Hindi on the Jain **Āgamas**, grammar, logic, and history, and assisted **Muni Puṇyavijaya** in his work on Jain **manuscript** collections. In *Vīranirvāṇa Saṃvat aur Kālagaṇanā*, he disputed the date suggested by **Hermann Jacobi** for **Mahāvīra's nirvāṇa**. *Nibandha Nicaya* (1965) contains a collection of essays on a variety of topics, including Śvetāmbara **mendicant lineages**, **Digambara** literature, as well as Jain **images**, inscriptions, and **pilgrimage** sites. *Prabandha Pārijāta* (1966) contains essays on the *Niśitha-sūtra*, *Mahāniśitha-sūtra*, the *Paryuṣanā-kalpa-sūtra* and its **commentary**, grammatical literature, and ancient Jain pilgrimage sites. A list of his books has been published in *Śrī Kalyāṇa Kalikā* (1987).

KĀMADEVA. A category of heroic men who are not included in the 63 illustrious men (**śalākā-puruṣas**) in the **Universal History** texts and other Jain narratives. They are heroes with especially handsome bodies but they are different from the Hindu god Kāmadeva. In **Bharatakṣetra** (the part of the universe where we are said to live), 24 Kāmadevas are born in each progressive and regressive half-**cycle of time**. One lives during the time of each **Tīrthaṅkara**, and they always attain liberation (**mokṣa**) at the end of that life. Some individuals may be found under other categories. For example, **Śāntinātha**, Kunthunātha, and Aranātha are Kāmadevas as well as Tīrthaṅkaras. The 24 born in this era were **Bāhubali**, Prajāpati, Śrīdhara, Darśanabhadra, Prasenacandra, Candravarṇa, Agniyukta, Sanatkumāra, Vatsarāja, Kanakaprabha, Meghaprabha, Śāntinātha, Kunthunātha, Aranātha, Vijayarāja, Śrīcandra, Nalarāja, Hanumān, Balirāja, Vāsudeva, Pradyumna, Nāgakumāra, Jīvandhara, and **Jambū**.

KAMAṆḌALU. A gourd pot used by **Digambara mendicants** and advanced lay renunciants (**kṣullakas** and **ailakas**) to hold boiled water for toilet purposes.

KĀNJĪ SVĀMĪ (1889–1980). Jain reformer and founder of the **neo-Digambara Kānjī Svāmī Panth**. He was born into a **Sthānakavāsī**

family in a small village in the Kathiawar region of Gujarat and took initiation as a Sthānakavāsī **monk** in 1913. However, he was uninspired with the sacred **scriptures** until 1921 when he read the *Samayasāra* of **Kundakunda**. His faith in the Digambara tradition was further strengthened by the writings of **Paṇḍit Ṭoḍarmal** and **Śrīmad Rājacandra**. In 1934, in Songadh, Gujarat, he publicly renounced his mendicant vows and became a Digambara **layman**. He went to live in a house called "The Star of India," which became the birthplace of the Kānjī Svāmī Panth. He established a spiritual link with the tradition of Kundakunda in 1937 by declaring that in a previous life he had lived in **Mahāvideha** and was present when Kundakunda visited there to hear the preaching of **Tīrthaṅkara Sīmandhara Svāmī**. Kundakunda's writings on the nature of the innate pure **soul (ātman)** form the basis of Kānjī Svāmī's teachings. As a **celibate** layman, he traveled widely in India and also visited Kenya. He did not write any books, but his charismatic preachings have been preserved on recordings, which have been transcribed by his followers.

KĀNJĪ (SVĀMĪ) PANTH. A **neo-Digambara** sectarian tradition that follows the teachings of **Kānjī Svāmī**. This tradition began in Songadh, Gujarat, in 1934, when Kānjī Svāmī, who at the time was a **Sthānakavāsī monk**, publicly renounced his mendicant vows and became a **Digambara layman**. The "Star of India," a house on the outskirts of the city where Kānjī Svāmī went to live, is considered to be the birthplace of the panth. Devotees come here each year on his birthday to perform mental worship (bhāva **pūjā**).

Kundakunda's writings on the realization of the nature of the innate pure **soul (ātman)** form the basis of his teachings. As compared to others in the Digambara mystical tradition, Kānjī Svāmī has placed more emphasis on the higher level of truth (**niścaya naya**), but he does not totally reject the lower level of truth (**vyavahāra naya**). He did not write any books, but in his discourses (many of which were recorded) he focused on the nature of the soul as taught by Kundakunda. Although Kānjī Svāmī taught that rituals and meritorious activities were less important than the internal transformation of the soul, he did not reject the worship of **Tīrthaṅkara images**. However, the rituals are not as elaborate as in other Digambara sectarian traditions.

The panth's first building in its large complex at Songadh, the Digambara Svādhyāya Mandir, was consecrated in 1937. From here and its other center in Jaipur, Rajasthan, it has spread to other parts of India and abroad, becoming the most successful 20th-century Jain movement.

There are no **mendicant lineages** associated with the panth, but there are approximately 60 lower-order celibates, most of whom are **women**, who took **brahmacāriṇī** vows from Kānjī Svāmī. They are allowed to travel by mechanized transport and to own property. They have actively promoted the faith by training preachers and **paṇḍits**, establishing schools, and engaging in publishing activities. They have attracted followers from other Digambara sectarian traditions, from the Sthānakavāsī community, and from non-Jain communities as well. The movement also has attracted followers from the diaspora community, and temples have been established in Nairobi and London. Administration of the panth and its properties is handled by a board of trustees with a president who is elected every five years. **Campābahen Mātājī** assumed spiritual leadership of the panth in 1981 after the death of Kānjī Svāmī.

KAPADIA (KĀPAḌIYĀ), HĪRĀLĀL RASIKDĀS. **Śvetāmbara** scholar of Jainism. Born in Surat, Gujarat, he was educated in Bombay (now Mumbai) and received an M.A. in mathematics in 1918. From the early years of his career he was interested in reading Jain literature. When Ācārya Dharmasūri came to Bombay for the four-month rainy season period (**cāturmāsa**), Kapadia began to study Jain religion and literature with him while continuing to teach mathematics in college. He joined the Bhandarkar Oriental Research Institute, Pune, where he prepared a catalogue of the **manuscripts** in their collection. He edited a number of Jain texts, including *Anekāntajaya Patākā* (1940) and the ***Tattvārtha Sūtra*** with **commentaries** (1926). He also contributed to the field of Sanskrit, Prākrit, Apabhraṃśa, and Gujarati literature by publishing numerous journal articles. He is noted for his comprehensive study of the Jain **Āgamas** entitled *A History of the Canonical Literature of the Jainas* (1941).

KARMA. In Jainism, this term has two meanings. (1) Action or activity, in the sense of **karma-bhūmi** lands and **karmans**. (2) A type of extremely subtle matter (**pudgala**) that is attracted to the **soul (jīva)** by actions of body, speech, and mind. It is bound with the soul whenever actions are motivated by passions (**kaṣāyas**). It remains bound for a specific period of time. For part of this time, it remains dormant, until it comes to fruition and produces its effect, after which it drops away from the soul. From beginningless time, all souls have been bound in the cycle of rebirth (**saṃsāra**) by karma. Thus, there is no God, Supreme Soul, or Ultimate Reality (brahman) that has never been bound by karma although disembodied perfected souls that have attained liberation (**siddhas**) may be called God (**deva**) or Supreme Soul (**paramātman**). There is no supreme deity with the power to prevent karma from yielding its effects, and everyone experiences the effects of their own karma. Liberation (**mokṣa**) is attained by preventing the influx of new karma and by removing all previously bound karma from the soul.

There are eight main varieties of karmic matter and numerous sub-varieties, each of which produces a specific effect when it comes to fruition. Some varieties affect qualities (**guṇas**) of the soul and others are associated with embodiment and rebirth. Darśana-āvaraṇīya karma and jñāna-āvaraṇīya karma obscure the perception (**darśana**) and knowledge (**jñāna**) qualities of the soul and prevent the soul from experiencing omniscient knowledge (**kevala-jñāna**). Antarāya karma affects the energy (vīrya) quality of the soul, and it hinders one from giving things to others, from receiving things from others, and from enjoying food and material objects. Mohanīya karma affects the bliss (sukha) quality of the soul, causing delusion (moha) regarding the true nature of reality (**samyak-darśana**). It also generates passions (kaṣāyas) and emotions (**no-kaṣāyas**) and prevents one from observing proper conduct (samyak-cāritra). These four karmas are called destructive (ghātiyā) because they negatively affect the soul. A soul that has attained omniscience (kevala-jñāna) is devoid of these four destructive karmas. The other four main varieties of karma are called nondestructive (aghātiyā) because it is possible to attain right faith, right knowledge, and right conduct even though these karmas are still bound with the soul. They are associated with various aspects of embodiment. Āyu karma determines the maximum life span of the body and the state of existence into which a soul is born, either as a human, a heavenly being (**deva**), a hell-being (**nāraki**) or a plant or animal (**tiryañc**). Nāma karma causes the formation of the body, and gotra karma determines one's status, either high or low. Vedanīya karma causes pleasant and unpleasant feelings. An omniscient soul becomes devoid of these four karmas in the final moments of life when the body dies and the soul attains final liberation.

Karmic matter that is bound with the soul forms a karmic body (kārmaṇa-śarīra), which accompanies the soul in transmigration to its next state of existence. In general, it is thought that one's actions determine the state of one's rebirth. Good actions bind beneficial varieties of karma (puṇya prakṛtis) that causes rebirth in desirable states of existence. They include the varieties of life span and body-forming karmas that cause rebirth as a human being, a heavenly being, or a five-sensed animal with the capacity to reason, as well as the karmas associated with high status (ucca gotra karma) and pleasant feelings (sātā-vedanīya karma). Bad actions, especially those involving extreme intentional violence (**hiṃsā**), bind bad varieties of karma (pāpa prakṛtis) that cause rebirth in less desirable states of existence. They include varieties of life span and body-forming karmas that cause rebirth as a hell-being, or as a plant or animal without the capacity to reason, as well as the karmas associated with low status (nīca gotra karma) and unpleasant feelings (asātā-vedanīya karma). All varieties of destructive (ghātiyā) karmas also are included in this category because of their negative effects on the soul.

KARMA-BHŪMI. In Jain cosmography, a realm (bhūmi) of action (**karma**) where people must put forth effort in order to survive by engaging in agriculture and various occupational crafts. These are the continents of **Bharata-kṣetra**, Airāvata-kṣetra, and all lands of **Mahāvideha**, except for Devakuru and Uttarakuru, which are **bhoga-bhūmi** lands. Bharata-kṣetra and Airāvata-kṣetra are subject to the **cycle of time**, but in Mahāvideha time is not cyclical. There is a total of 15 karma-bhūmi lands: one set of three on the island-continent of **Jambūdvīpa**, two sets of three (i.e., six) on the island-continent of Dhātakīkhaṇḍa, and two sets of three (i.e., six) on the island-continent of Puṣkaravara. Because there is suffering in these lands, people are motivated to attain liberation (**mokṣa**). Therefore, **Tīrthaṅkaras** are born only in karma-bhūmi lands. Liberation is always possible for humans somewhere in one or more of the karma-bhūmi lands. *See also* MADHYA-LOKA.

KARMANS. Six daily activities recommended for **laypeople** in place of the **āvaśyakas** by some **Digambara** authors, such as **Jinasena**.

KĀRTIKA-PŪRṆIMĀ. The full moon day of Kārtika (October/November), approximately two weeks after **Dīvālī**, which marks the end of the four-month rainy season period (**cāturmāsa**). On this day, **mendicants** resume their travels. **Laypeople** are released from vows undertaken during this time, and they formally thank the mendicants for their sermons (**pravacana**). For **Śvetāmbaras**, this is an especially meritorious day for a **pilgrimage** to the top of **Mount Śatruñjaya**.

KAṢĀYA. Passion. A feeling of attraction (rāga) or aversion (dveṣa) to sense-objects. There are four types of passions: anger (krodha), pride (māna), deceitfulness (māyā), and greed (lobha). Each is generated in four degrees of intensity by varieties of conduct-deluding (cāritra-mohanīya) **karma**. Anantānubandhī kaṣāyas ("pursuers from the limitless past"), the strongest degree of passions, hinder the attainment of both right belief (**samyak-darśana**) and right conduct (samyak-cāritra). Lesser degrees of passions hinder the attainment of right conduct. Apratyākhyānāvaraṇa kaṣāyas ("obstructors of partial renunciation") hinder one from observing conduct associated with the lay vows (**aṇuvratas**). Pratyākhyānāvaraṇa kaṣāyas ("obstructers of complete renunciation") hinder one from observing conduct associated with the mendicant vows (**mahāvratas**). The weakest degree of passions, called saṃjvalana kaṣāyas ("smouldering"), cause lapses or carelessness in observing the mendicant vows and an unconscious attachment to life. Actions that are motivated by passions cause the binding of new karma with the **soul** (**jīva**). Therefore, in order to attain liberation (**mokṣa**) from the cycle of rebirth (**saṃsāra**), all passions must be eliminated, even in their weakest degree of intensity, by destroying all conduct-deluding karma that is bound with the soul. *See also* NO-KAṢĀYA.

KAṢĀYAPRĀBHṚTA*.** **Digambara** canonical text on Jain **karma** theory written in Jain Śaurasenī Prākrit. It was written by a **monk** named Guṇabhadra shortly after the completion of the ***Ṣaṭkhaṇḍāgama (ca. 2nd–3rd century C.E.). Tradition holds that this text is based on a small portion of ancient scriptures called the **Pūrvas** that had been preserved in the *Dṛṣṭivāda*. This expansive text focuses on one of eight main varieties of karmic matter, mohanīya **karma**, and the various passions (**kaṣāyas**) produced by it. There is one extant **commentary** on this text, the *Jayadhavalā*, which was begun by **Vīrasena** and was completed by his disciple **Jinasena** in 820 C.E. The text and commentary have been published along with a Hindi translation in 15 volumes (1942–1975).

KĀṢṬHĀ SAṄGHA. An extinct **Digambara mendicant lineage**. According to the *Darśanasāra*, written by Devasena of the **Mūla Saṅgha** at the beginning of the 10th century, the Kāṣṭhā Saṅgha was founded by Kumārasena in the 7th century at a village near Delhi. However, another source traces its origins to Loha I in the 5th century C.E. The first epigraphical evidence of its existence dates from the end of the 11th century. This group advocated the use of a cow-tail whisk broom by **mendicants** rather the traditional peacock-feather whisk broom (**piñchī**). Devasena criticized this group for what he considered to be their lax mendicant practices. It is not known when the tradition of itinerant naked **munis** in this **saṅgha** came to an end.

KAVI PANTH. A term that is sometimes used for the teachings of the mystic **Śrīmad Rājacandra**. Those who follow his teachings are called Kavi Panthīs.

KĀYOTSARGA. Mentally abandoning (utsarga) the body (kāya). Assuming a contemplative posture by remaining motionless for a period of time and concentrating the mind (**dhyāna**) on something other than the body. Although both seated and standing postures are described in the texts, it is most commonly understood as a specific type of standing posture. One stands erect, with legs slightly apart and arms hanging loosely at one's side, palms of the hand inward, and the fingers pointed straight at the ground, as depicted in the standing **images** of **Tīrthaṅkaras**. Kāyotsarga is one of six obligatory duties (**āvaśyakas**) of a **mendicant** and a recommended practice for a **layperson**. Temporarily abandoning the body is done as part of other rites, including attainment of equanimity (**sāmāyika**), confession (**pratikramaṇa**), mental worship (bhāva **pūjā**), and in various forms of **meditation**.

KEŚA-LOÑCA. The practice undertaken by **mendicants** of pulling out one's head and facial hair by hand. It signifies an attitude of indifference to the body and a willingness to endure the hardships of a mendicant life. Traditionally, during initiation into mendicancy, hair on the head was pulled out in five handfuls. Today, the head often is shaved prior to initiation, leaving a small tuft of hair on the crown of the head, which is pulled out during the initiation ceremony (**dīkṣā**). After initiation, both **monks** and **nuns** remove their hair by hand periodically, at least twice a year. In the **Digambara** community, this is performed in a public ceremony witnessed by **laypeople**.

KEVALA-JÑĀNA. Omniscience; perfect, absolute, isolated knowledge. It is knowledge of all substances (**dravyas**), including the Self or **soul** (**jīva**), in all of their possible modifications or modes (paryāya), including their temporal aspects (past, present, and future). It can be attained only by humans (and, according to **Digambaras**, only by males) who are living in **karma-bhūmi** realms in the third and fourth periods of the **cycle of time** when **Tīrthaṅkaras** are preaching. In order to attain omniscience, one first must have attained a proper view of reality (**samyak-darśana**) through the destruction of all darśana mohanīya **karma** and one must have eliminated all passions (**kaṣāyas**) and emotions (**no-kaṣāyas**) through the destruction of all cāritra mohanīya karma. When this passionless state has been attained, the energy quality of the soul automatically continues its destruction of the remaining destructive (ghātiyā) karmas, including all varieties of the obstructing (antarāya) karmas as well as the obscuring (āvaraṇīya) karmas that prevent the soul from realizing its own perfect knowledge. The person thereby becomes an omniscient-with-activity (sayoga **kevalin**) in the 13th stage of spiritual purity (**guṇasthāna**). Once it has been attained, this type of knowledge can never be lost, and one will attain liberation (**mokṣa**) at the end of life.

KEVALIN. A person who has attained omniscience (**kevala-jñāna**), self-knowledge, or direct knowledge of all substances (**dravyas**) in all of their possible modifications or modes (paryāya), including their temporal aspects (past, present, and future). The kevalin's **soul** (**jīva**) is isolated from (kevala), or devoid of, the varieties of **karma** that cause desires or passions (**kaṣāyas**), emotions (**no-kaṣāyas**), and imperfect conduct. Although a kevalin's perfect knowledge and perfect conduct are identical to that of a **Tīrthaṅkara**, a kevalin does not teach others the path of liberation. The state of the kevalin-with-activity (sayoga kevalin, the 13th **guṇasthāna**), where one has attained liberation (**mokṣa**) from the cycle of rebirth (**saṃsāra**) but still remains alive due to the natural life span of the body, is comparable to the jīvanmukta state in Hinduism. When life span is exhausted, just prior to the death of the body, the kevalin ends the activities of the body, speech, and mind, through a **meditational** state called śukla-**dhyāna**, becoming a kevalin-without-activity (ayoga kevalin, the 14th guṇasthāna). After remaining in this state for several moments, the soul, devoid of all karmic matter, rises to the top of the occupied universe (**loka-ākāśa**) to the siddha-loka, or īśat-prāgbhārā-bhūmi, and remains there forever in a disembodied state (**siddha**), experiencing its own inherent nature of infinite **consciousness** and bliss. There are differences between **Śvetāmbaras** and **Digambaras** regarding the nature of the body of a kevalin, but these are usually understood in the context of a Tīrthaṅkara.

KHARATARA GACCHA. A **Śvetāmbara Mūrtipūjaka mendicant lineage**. There are several stories associated with the formation of his lineage. According to one account, it was formed by Vardhamānasūri (d. 1031) who left his teacher, a temple-dwelling monk (**caityavāsī**), after a disagreement over lax mendicant conduct. He became the student of a learned **monk** named Udyotanasūri, who taught him the "true" Jain doctrine. The original name of this **gaccha** was Vidhimārga ("The Path of the [Proper] Method"), but it became known as Kharatara

("Extremely Sharp") after Vardhamāna's pupil **Jineśvarasūri** defeated a temple-dwelling monk named Sūra, in a debate in 1024 C.E. at the court of King Durlabha in Aṇahillavāḍa Paṭṭaṇa (Patan), the capital of medieval Gujarat. Other accounts associate its formation with Jinavallabhasūri. However, the sect emerges concretely with his successor, **Jinadattasūri**.

One of the distinctive features of those associated with this gaccha is their worship of four leading renouncers, collectively known as the **Dādāgurus**, who lived between the 11th and 17th centuries. They have advocated that the 11 stages of renunciation (**pratimās**) should not be adopted by **laypeople** any longer because the decline in strength has made it impossible to carefully observe more than the first four. In temple worship, laywomen of childbearing years are prohibited from anointing Tīrthaṅkara **images** with sandalwood paste. They celebrate six auspicious moments (**kalyāṇakas**) associated with the birth of Mahāvīra instead of the standard five, adding the transfer of the embryo from the womb of the **Brahmin woman** Devānandā to the womb of the **Kṣatriya** woman Triśalā.

Today, this is the third largest Mūrtipūjaka gaccha, and it is concentrated in Rajasthan and Mumbai. As of 1999, it was estimated that there were 229 **mendicants**, 20 **monks**, and 209 **nuns**. Because of the small number of monks, nuns in this gaccha are allowed to preach. There is no head mendicant leader who is the spokesman for the entire gaccha. Instead, authority is maintained by individual **ācāryas** at the level of sublineages (**samudāyas**). An identifying mendicant emblem is their alms bowls, which are black with a red stripe.

KNOWLEDGE. *See* JÑĀNA.

KṢATRIYA. A member of the occupational class of rulers and warriors in the ancient system of social organization (varṇa). According to the *Ādipurāṇa* of **Jinasena** (9th century), the Kṣatriya varṇa was the first occupational class established by **Ṛṣabḥa**, the first king of this era, prior to his renouncing the household life. He formed this varṇa in response to deteriorating social conditions to bring order to society. All **Tīrthaṅkaras** are born into a Kṣatriya family. *See also* CASTE.

KṢETRAPĀLA. Guardian of the Place. A non-liberated male guardian deity who protects **temple** precincts. His **image** is usually found near the door of the main temple. *See also* BHAIRAVA; BRAHMADEVA; NĀKOṚ(Ḍ)Ā BHAIRAVA; ŚĀNTIDEVĪ.

KṢULLAKA/KṢULLIKĀ. Literally, "junior." The title of a **Digambara** layman/laywoman who has attained the first level of the 11th stage of renunciation (**pratimā**). At initiation (**dīkṣā**), they formally take the vows of a layperson (**aṇuvratas**), which are interpreted more strictly than for an ordinary layperson, and agree to abide by the **guṇa-vratas**, **śikṣā-vratas**, and the pratimās. They observe strict **dietary restrictions**, do not eat after dark, are **celibate**, and renounce all household and business activities. They are given a new name, mendicant implements of a peacock-feather whisk broom (**piñchī**) and a water pot (**kamaṇḍalu**), and garments in accordance with their **gender**. Men are permitted to wear an undergarment and two outer garments and **women** wear a white sari. They live with a group of **mendicants** of the same gender and eat once a day at the home of a **layperson**, remaining seated and eating from a plate. They are allowed to cut their hair. *See also* VRATA.

KULAKARA. In **Universal History** texts and other Jain narratives, lawgivers or patriarchs who are born in **Bharata-kṣetra** (the part of the universe where we are said to live) in the third period (suṣamā-duṣamā kāla) of each progressive (utsarpiṇī) and regressive (avasarpiṇī) half-**cycle of time**. They initiate laws for maintaining order in society that are appropriate for societal conditions at their time. Their number varies in different sources (7, 10, or 14 in **Śvetāmbara** texts, and 14 or 16 in **Digambara** texts). In all narratives except the Digambara *Mahāpurāṇa*, Nābhi, the father of **Ṛṣabha**, is the last Kulakara of this era. In the *Mahāpurāṇa*, Ṛṣabha and his son **Bharata** are the last Kulakaras.

KUNDAKUNDA (ca. 2nd–3rd centuries C.E.). Digambara mendicant leader. It is thought that his original monastic name was Padmanandin. He was called Kundakunda after the place of his birth, a village located near today's boundary between the states of Karnataka and Andhra Pradesh. Although most scholars believe he flourished in the 2nd or 3rd centuries C.E., some have speculated that he lived after 750 C.E. Aside from his writings, what is known about Kundakunda is based on hagiographies dating from the 10th century. Some 84 texts called *Pāhuḍa* (Treatise) are ascribed to him, 16 of which have survived, although scholars have questioned the authorship of some of them. He is the author of some of the most influential works in the Digambara tradition. These include *Niyamasāra*, in which the obligatory ritual duties of a **mendicant** (**āvaśyakas**) are discussed; *Pañcāstikāya*, which describes the five basic elements of the universe; and *Pravacanasāra*, which may have been intended as a guide for new mendicants in conduct and spiritual practices. In his most important work, *Samayasāra*, Kundakunda describes the nature of the innate pure **soul** (**ātman**) and a person's mystical experience of it. In it, he employs a theory of reality as expressed in two levels of truth: the supreme or absolute standpoint (**niścaya naya**) and the worldly or conventional standpoint (**vyavahāra naya**). This work, together with an important **commentary** by Amṛtacandra (ca. 8th century C.E.) entitled *Ātmakhyāti*, influenced later Digambara authors, such as **Yogīndu**, **Tāraṇ Svāmī**, **Banārsīdās**, **Dyānatrāy**, **Ṭoḍarmal**, **Śrīmad Rājacandra**, and **Kānjī Svāmī**.

KŪṢMĀṆḌINĪ. In the **Digambara** tradition, the **goddess** who is the **yakṣī** of **Neminātha**. According to legend, in her previous life she was married to a **Brahmin** man who mistreated her. One day, she left home with her two children, and her husband went looking for her to repent for his behavior. Not realizing why he had come, she decided that it would be better to commit suicide. She and her children jumped off a cliff and they all died. Because of the good **karma** accumulated throughout her otherwise exemplary life, she was reborn as a yakṣī. Kūṣmāṇḍinī is the guardian deity of **Śravaṇa Beḷgoḷa**. She is represented in anthropomorphic form in several **temples** here, including the Cāmuṇḍarāya Basati on Candragiri. An image of Kūṣmāṇḍinī was installed at **Mūḍbidrī** when the **maṭha** of Śravaṇa Beḷgoḷa established a branch of itself there. According to some Digambara sources, **Ambikā** is the yakṣī of Neminātha.

– L –

LABDHISŪRI, ĀCĀRYA VIJAYA. *See* VIJAYALABDHISŪRI, ĀCĀRYA.

LANGUAGES. The disciples of **Mahāvīra** did not preach in Sanskrit, which was the language of learning and culture in ancient India, but in one of the vernacular Prākrit dialects spoken in the region of Magadha in eastern India. According to tradition, after a **Tīrthaṅkara** attains omniscience (**kevala-jñāna**), a divine sound (**divyadhvani**) emanates from his body. According to **Śvetāmbaras**, this sound took the form of Ardhamāgadhī, the language in which the Śvetāmbara **Āgamas** are written. The earliest **commentaries** on these texts were also written in Prākrit. The earliest extant **Digambara** texts, the ***Ṣaṭkhaṇḍāgama*** and the ***Kaṣāyaprābhṛta***, are written in Jain Śaurasenī, which is based on a Mahārāṣṭrī Prākrit dialect.

Around the 4th or 5th century C.E., Jains began to write texts on philosophy and logic in Sanskrit so that they would be accessible to a larger audience. The earliest Jain text written in Sanskrit is the ***Tattvārtha Sūtra*** of **Umāsvāti/Umāsvāmī**. **Siddhasena Divākara** was the first author to write in both Sanskrit and Prākrit, depending on his intended audience. **Haribhadra** wrote the earliest Sanskrit commentaries on the Śvetāmbara Āgamas, and the commentators that followed him also wrote in Sanskrit. A variety of works continued to be written in Prākrit, even though it had become archaic. Apparently there was resistance to translating the Śvetāmbara Āgamas into Sanskrit. According to legend, Siddhasena Divākara was expelled from the Jain community for 12 years for suggesting this. Some Jain texts were written in Apabhraṃśa, an artificial literary dialect used in the medieval period. In later times, a number of Jain texts and commentaries have been written in the vernacular languages of Gujarati, Hindi, Kannada, Marathi, Rajasthani, and Tamil.

LAVAJĪ or LAVAJĪ ṚṢI, MUNI (ca. 1609–1659). One of the five principal reformers (pañca-munis) in the non-image-worshipping **Śvetāmbara** sectarian tradition that today is known as **Sthānakavāsī**. Born in Surat, Gujarat, he broke with the **Loṅkā Gaccha** over a disagreement about their lax mendicant practices and support of temple worship. Although there is no evidence that he ever initiated himself by taking new mendicant vows, three **monks** who came after him formed a new lineage called Ḍhūṇḍiyā Gaccha, or "Seeker Tradition." This name relates to their search for suitable lodging after refusing to stay in buildings at temple precincts that were used by mendicants in various lineages of the Śvetāmbara image-worshipping (**Mūrtipūjaka**) tradition. Some credit him with introducing the mouth cloth (**muhpattī**), whisk broom (**rajoharaṇa**), and other mendicant implements used by Sthānakavāsīs today. Others, however, associate these innovations with **Jīvarāja**.

LAYPERSON. A Jain who has not been initiated into mendicancy and has not taken the five great vows (**mahāvratas**) of a **mendicant**. There are two terms that have been used for a layperson: **upāsaka/upāsikā** (literally, worshipper) and **śrāvaka/śrāvikā** (literally, listener). These two terms are also used in early Buddhist texts, but here śrāvaka is a designation for a mendicant, not a layperson. Although both of these terms are found in early inscriptions and in the **Śvetāmbara Āgamas**, śrāvaka is used in later texts. A number of texts called **śrāvakācāra** have been written detailing the ideal conduct of a layperson. In most cases, laypeople are married. They are engaged in an **occupation** and support various religious institutions and the mendicant community through gifting (**dāna**). Their primary concern is gaining merit (**puṇya**), which is associated with the well-being of their family in this life and a good rebirth in their next life.

Some laypeople choose to take a vow of lifelong **celibacy**, becoming a **brahmacārī** either at a young age prior to marriage or when they are older. In the **Digambara** community, a layperson may leave the household life and live as part of the mendicant community without taking the mendicant vows. Lay renunciants include brahmacārīs/brahmacāriṇīs (7th **pratimā**), who have taken a vow of lifelong celibacy, and **kṣullaka/kṣullikās** and **ailakas**, who have taken more stringent vows of renunciation (11th pratimā). Digambara nuns (**āryikās**) are technically advanced laywomen in the 11th pratimā. In the Śvetāmbara tradition, there was an ascetic lineage called the **Kaḍuā Gaccha** in which people renounced the household life and lived in an ascetic community without taking the mendicant vows. *See also* VRATA.

LAY VOWS. There are a total of 12 vows of restraint (**vratas**) that a **layperson** may take. They include the five lesser vows (**aṇuvratas**), which may also be called "minor vows" or "lay vows"; the three supplementary vows (**guṇa-vratas**); and the four vows of spiritual discipline (**śikṣā-vratas**). In taking these vows, one attains the second stage of renunciation for a layperson (vrata **pratimā**) and the fifth stage of spiritual purity (deśa-virata **guṇasthāna**).

LEŚYĀ. Karmic stain. A particular color that a **soul** (**jīva**) takes on that is indicative of its spiritual level. The souls of human beings may take on any of the six leśyās. Black, blue, and gray are indicative of lower stages of spiritual purity (**guṇasthāna**) associated with strong degrees of passions (**kaṣāyas**) and harmful actions. Yellow, lotus pink, and white are indicative of higher stages of spiritual purity associated with mild passions and actions that minimize harm. White is characteristic of those in the highest stages of the spiritual purity.

LEUMANN, ERNST (1859–1931). Philologist. Born in Berg, Switzerland, he studied Indo-European languages in Geneva, Zurich, Berlin, and Leipzig, where he received a Ph.D. in 1881 for his text edition and study of the **Śvetāmbara** *Aupapātika Sūtra*. In 1892, he edited the *Daśavaikālika Sūtra* and **commentary** (niryukti). He worked with **Georg Bühler** on the **manuscript** collection at the Royal Prussian State Library in Berlin. During the time that he was a professor at the University of Strasbourg, he was instrumental in obtaining both Śvetāmbara and **Digambara** manuscripts for the library that were not represented in the collection in Berlin. He was especially interested in the **āvaśyaka** texts and commentaries, which are a source of Jain narrative literature. These works became the focus of his research. He is known for his pioneering study *Übersicht über die Āvaśyaka-Literatur* (Hamburg, 1934). In 1919, he left Strasbourg and settled in Freiburg, where he remained until the end of his life.

LIBERATION. *See* MOKṢA; STRĪ-MOKṢA.

LOKA-ĀKĀŚA. Space having worlds; the inhabited or occupied universe. In Jain cosmography, the occupied universe is vast but finite and is surrounded by unoccupied space (aloka-ākāśa), which is infinite. The universe is without a beginning or end in time and was not created by a creator **god**. Early **Śvetāmbara** texts describe the shape of the occupied universe as expanded at the top and bottom and narrow in the middle. Since the 16th century, it frequently has been depicted in the shape of a giant man (loka-puruṣa). It is permeated by the substances (**dravyas**) of **souls** (**jīva**), matter (**pudgala**), motion (**dharma**), rest (**adharma**), space (ākāśa), and (according to some) time (kāla). One-sensed beings (**ekendriya**) can live in all parts of the occupied universe. Beings with more than one sense, including animals (**tiryañc**), humans, hell-beings (**nārakis**), and heavenly beings (**devas**), live only in the center portion of the occupied universe, in a cylindrically shaped area called the trasa-nāḍī. This part of the universe is divided into three realms. (1) The lower realm (**adho-loka**) is the abode of hell-beings and of certain demigods. (2) The middle realm (**madhya-loka**) is the abode of humans and animals and of certain demigods. (3) The upper realm (**ūrdhva-loka**) is the abode of one class of heavenly beings called **vaimānika devas**. The abode of disembodied liberated souls (**siddhas**) is located above the heavens at the very edge of the occupied universe. This region is called the siddha-loka, siddha-śilā, or the īśat-prāgbhārā-bhūmi (because of its slightly bent shape, like that of an inverted umbrella). *See also* BHARATA-KṢETRA; BHOGA-BHŪMI; JAMBŪDVĪPA; KARMA-BHŪMI; MAHĀVIDEHA.

LOṄKĀ (LOṄKĀ ŚĀH) (15th century). A reformer within the **Śvetāmbara** mendicant community, also known as Luṅkā or Lumpāka. Little is known about his life apart from hagiographic accounts. He was from a Rajasthani Osvāl family and was a court jeweler in Ahmedabad, Gujarat. As a copyist of Jain **manuscripts**, he had access to Jain **scriptures**. He noticed that the conduct of Śvetāmbara **mendicants** was not in accordance with the precepts outlined in the early texts. He did not find any references in these texts to image worship or to a sedentary lifestyle for the monastic community. Around 1450, he began his efforts to reform lax mendicant conduct and to convince **laypeople** not to finance **temple** construction or perform temple rituals. With the assistance of L. B. Bhansali, a Jain minister from Patan, he established a new ascetic tradition. He started living as an uninitiated ascetic and wrote the organizational rules for the **Loṅkā Gaccha**, which rejected image worship and advocated wandering (**vihāra**) and non-possession (**aparigraha**) for mendicants. He accepted the authority of 31 out of the 45 scriptures in the Śvetāmbara canon (**Āgama**). Although there are no fully initiated mendicants today who trace pupilage descent from him, his views inspired subsequent reformers to establish the non-image-worshipping Śvetāmbara sectarian tradition that today is known as **Sthānakavāsī**.

LOṄKĀ GACCHA. A **Śvetāmbara mendicant lineage** founded by Muni Bhāṇa, the first disciple of **Loṅkā Śāh**, who split with the **Tapā Gaccha** and initiated himself and 45 followers around 1475 C.E. by taking the five mendicant vows (**mahāvratas**). In accordance with the rules established by Loṅkā Śāh, they did not engage in any form of image worship, observed strict mendicant conduct with an itinerant lifestyle and non-possession (**aparigraha**), and initiated **mendicants** only from the merchant class (**Vaiśya** or Bania). In the century following the death of Loṅkā Śāh, this group split into several factions. Lax mendicant practices of sedentary quasi-mendicants (**yatis**) became the norm and support for image worship and temple-building activities reemerged. **Dharmasiṃha, Hara, Jīvarāja**, and **Lavajī**, four of the five principal reformers (pañca-munis) in the non-image-worshipping Śvetāmbara sectarian tradition that today is known as **Sthānakavāsī**, split from this group in the 17th century over these practices. There are no longer any fully initiated mendicants (**saṃvegī sādhus**) in this gaccha. As of 2003, there was one **yati**, but his status is the subject of debate since he reportedly took his vows from a **Mūrtipūjaka** monk. There are approximately 10,000 laypeople living in the area of Baroda who are associated with this gaccha.

– M –

MADHYA-LOKA. Middle realm. In Jain cosmography, the portion of the occupied universe (**loka-ākāśa**) located between the upper realm of the heavens (**ūrdhva-loka**) and the lower realm of the hells (**adho-loka**). It is the portion of the universe where animals (**tiryañc**) and humans reside. **Vyantara devas** also live in parts of the middle realm as do **jyotiṣka devas**, who occupy the sky, which is located above the earth and below the heavens. The madhya-loka contains a circular central island-continent called **Jambūdvīpa**, which is surrounded by an ocean. Beyond this, there are innumerable doughnut-shaped concentric island-continents, each surrounded by an ocean. Humans inhabit the innermost three island-continents: Jambūdvīpa, Dhātakīkhaṇḍa Dvīpa, and the inner half of Puṣkaravara Dvīpa, up to a mountain range called Mānuṣottara. Beyond this, only animals live on the other island-continents. The three island-continents inhabited by humans are subdivided into various lands or continents, which are separated by mountain ranges, containing a total of 35 continents. There is one set of seven continents located on Jambūdvīpa, two sets of seven continents (i.e., 14) on Dhātakīkhaṇḍa, and two sets of seven continents (i.e., 14) on Puṣkaravara. The names of each of the seven continents are identical in the five sets (**Bharata-kṣetra**, Haimavata, Hari, **Mahāvideha**, Ramyaka, Hairaṇyavata, and Airāvata-kṣetra), so there are five continents called Bharata-kṣetra, five called Airavata-kṣetra, and so forth.

MAHĀPADMA (PADMANĀBHA). The name of the first **Tīrthaṅkara** to be born in **Bharata-kṣetra** (the part of the universe where we are said to live) in the next progressive **cycle of time** (utsarpiṇī). *See also* ŚREṆIKA.

MAHĀPRAJÑA, ĀCĀRYA (MUNI NATHMAL) (1920–). The 10th and current mendicant leader of the **Śvetāmbara Terāpanthīs**. Born in Tamkor, a village in Rajasthan, at the age of 11 he was initiated as Muni Nathmal. In 1979, at the age of 59, he was appointed as successor-designate (yuvācārya) by **Ācārya Tulsī**. He was appointed **ācārya** in 1994 when Ācārya Tulsī renounced his position. Throughout his career, he worked closely with Ācārya Tulsī and has been active in the **Aṇuvrat movement** and in the establishment of **Jain Vishva Bharati**. He is noted for his contribution in editing the Terāpanthī version of the Śvetāmbara canonical **scriptures (Āgama)**, an ongoing project started in 1974. In 1975, he introduced a form of insight meditation called prekṣā-dhyāna** and in 1980 the "Science of Living" (jīvan vijñān), a guide to nonviolent living geared toward schools and universities. He was recognized for his dedication to nonviolence (**ahiṃsā**) and communal harmony with the Indira Gandhi Award for National Integration in 2002.

***MAHĀPURĀṆA*.** A **Digambara** text in the genre of Jain **Universal History**. This work of some 20,000 verses was begun by **Jinasena** (ca. 770–850 C.E.) and completed by his disciple Guṇabhadra. It contains the stories of the past, present, and future lives of the 63 exemplary men (**śalākā-puruṣas**) in this current descending **cycle of time** (avasarpiṇī), including the 24 **Tīrthaṅkaras**. The first part of this text, the *Ādipurāṇa*, contains 47 chapters. Jinasena wrote the first 42 chapters, and Guṇabhadra wrote the final five chapters. It contains the story of **Ṛṣabha**, the first universal emperor (**Cakravartin**) and the first Tīrthaṅkara of this era. It also contains accounts of the lives of Ṛṣabha's eldest sons, **Bharata** and **Bāhubali**. It describes how Ṛṣabha established order in society by initiating a system of kingship based on ethical conduct and by creating an occupational **caste** system (varṇa) and teaching the people agriculture and crafts. Through this narrative, elements of Hindu temple worship were incorporated into Digambara temple rituals, and the position of Digambara temple priests, called **Jaina Brahmins** or **Upādhyes**, was established. This text contains the earliest description of Jain secular life-cycle rites (**saṃskāras**), which were adapted from brahmanical models, as well as ceremonies marking approximately 40 other important events (kriyās) that may be celebrated in the course of one's life. The second part of this text, the *Uttarapurāṇa*, was written entirely by Guṇabhadra. Its 27 chapters contain the stories of the second through the 24th Tīrthaṅkaras of this era as well as the exemplary figures in the Jain religion associated with them. This work was completed in 897 C.E.

MAHĀSATĪ. A general designation for a **nun** in the **Sthānakavāsī** tradition. *See also* MENDICANT HIERARCHY.

MAHĀVIDEHA (VIDEHA). In Jain cosmography, one of seven continents located on the island-continents that are inhabited by humans. There are a total of five Videha continents: one on the island-continent of **Jambūdvīpa** and two each on the island-continents of Dhātakīkhaṇḍa and Puṣkaravara. Videha is divided into 32 regions that are realms of action (**karma-bhūmi**) and two regions in the center, named Devakuru and Uttarakuru, that are realms of enjoyment (**bhoga-bhūmi**). None of these regions is subject to the **cycle of time**. In the 32 karma-bhūmi regions, conditions are always suitable for **Tīrthaṅkaras** to be born and liberation (**mokṣa**) is always possible for a human born there. A minimum of four Tīrthaṅkaras, known as the Viharamāna (Wanderings Ones), preach on each of the Videha continents, or a total of 20 Tīrthaṅkaras on the five continents. Currently living in the Videha of Jambūdvīpa are four Tīrthaṅkaras named Bāhu, **Sīmandhara**, Subāhu, and Yugamandhara. At other times, there may be as many as 160 Tīrthaṅkaras in the Videhas (one in each of the 32 karma-bhūmi lands on the five Videhas). When conditions are suitable for Tīrthaṅkaras to be born in the other karma-bhūmi lands, there may be 170 Tīrthaṅkaras living at one time (32 in each of the five Videhas, totaling 160, and one in each of the five **Bharata-kṣetras** and one in each of the five Airāvata-kṣetras, totaling 10). *See also* MADHYA-LOKA.

MAHĀVIDYĀS. A group of 16 female **tantric** deities, called vidyādevīs, that are associated with magical incantations or spells (vidyās). As non-liberated deities, they are worshipped for their worldly powers. In early Jain texts, vidyās are described as occult powers, but by the 6th century they are described as **goddesses**. One of the earliest lists of vidyās is found in the *Paumacariya* (= *Padmacaritra*), a Jain *Rāmāyaṇa* of Vimalasūri (ca. 1st–5th centuries C.E.). A group of 16 vidyādevīs is found in the **Digambara** *Harivaṃśa Purāṇa* of Jinasena (late 8th century), while early **Śvetāmbara** texts usually listed four (Rohiṇī, Prajñapti, Gaurī, and Gāndhārī). By the 8th or 9th century, Śvetāmbaras had also adopted a list of 16. The final list of mahāvidyās includes the following names: (1) Rohiṇī, (2) Prajñapti, (3) Vajraśṛṅkhalā, (4) Vajrāṅkuśā or Kuliśāṅkuśā, (5) Apraticakrā or Cakreśvarī (Śvet.) and Jāmbūnadā (Dig.), (6) Naradattā or Puruṣadattā, (7) Kālī or Kālikā, (8) Mahākālī, (9) Gaurī, (10) Gāndhārī, (11) Sarvāstramahājvālā (Śvet.) and **Jvālāmālinī** (Dig.), (12) Mānavī, (13) Vairoṭyā (Śvet.) and Vairoṭī (Dig.), (14) Acchuptā (Śvet.) and Acyutā (Dig.), (15) Mānasī, and (16) Mahāmānasī. Some of the vidyādevīs are also found in lists of **yakṣīs**. Sculptures and paintings of some of the vidyādevīs are found on Śvetāmbara **temples** in western India, although representations of them as a group of 16 mahāvidyās are rare.

The earliest known representations of some are found on the **Mahāvīra** temple at Osian (Rajasthan) dating from the end of the 8th century. The 16 are found as a group on the ceiling of the **Śāntinātha** temple at Kumbharia (Banas Kantha district, northern Gujarat, 1077 C.E.), and at **Mount Ābū** on the ceilings of the Vimala Vasahī (2 sets, ca. 1150 and ca. 1185), Lūṇa Vasahī (1230 C.E.), and the Kharatara Vasahī (2 sets, ca. 1459). The only known representation of the mahāvidyās on a Digambara temple is on the facade of the Ādināth temple at Khajuraho dating from the late 11th century.

MAHĀVĪRA. The honorific title "Great Hero" of Vardhamāna Jñātṛputra, who was the 24th and last **Tīrthaṅkara** of this era. Although some Western scholars have viewed him as the founder of Jainism, it is now accepted by most scholars that an established Jain community already existed at the time of his birth. He was a contemporary of Gautama the **Buddha**. The dating of Mahāvīra has been the subject of scholarly debate. Most **Śvetāmbara** sources state that he lived between 599 B.C.E. and 527 B.C.E., but one says that he died in 467 B.C.E. According to **Digambaras**, he died in 510 B.C.E. In accordance with the revised later dating of the Buddha as proposed recently by some scholars, Mahāvīra's dates would be approximately 100 years after the earliest traditional dating.

Digambara and Śvetāmbara accounts of his life differ in certain respects. According to Śvetāmbaras, Mahāvīra was conceived in the womb of a **Brahmin woman** named Devānandā, the wife of Ṛṣabhadatta, who lived in Kuṇḍigrāma (near modern Patna in Bihar). When the god Śakra (**Indra**) realized that his parents were not **Kṣatriya**, as is always the case for a Tīrthaṅkara, he had the embryo transferred to the womb of Triśalā, the wife of King Siddhārtha, by the demigod **Harinegamesī**, who is the commander of Śakra's celestial army. Although Mahāvīra was uninterested in the household life, he had made a vow that he would not become a **mendicant** while his parents were still alive, and he honored his parents' wishes by marrying Princess Yaśodā. They had a daughter named Priyadarśanā. When he was 30, he renounced the household life and went to the forest alone where he discarded all possessions, including his clothing, and pulled out his hair in five handfuls (**keśa-loñca**). For 13 months, he wore a cloth given to him by the gods (deva-dūṣya) until one day it fell off by accident. From that time on, Mahāvīra practiced total **nudity**. He wandered on foot, begging for food, practicing severe penances, speaking little, **fasting** for long periods, and exposing himself to the elements. For six years, he was accompanied by **Makkhali Gosāla**, who later became the leader of the **Ājīvikas**.

At the age of 42, after 12-and-a-half years of asceticism, Mahāvīra attained omniscience (**kevala-jñāna**). After hearing him preach, 11 Brahmins became his chief disciples (**gaṇadharas**). For the next 30 years he traveled throughout northeast India, teaching the eternal truths of Jainism and showing others the path of salvation. He died at age 73 at **Pāvāpurī**, near Patna. It is said that at his death there were 14,000 monks, 36,000 **nuns**, 159,000 **laymen**, and 318,000 laywomen who were his followers.

Digambara accounts differ in the following respects. Mahāvīra was conceived directly by Triśalā, was never married, renounced prior to his parents' death, practiced total nudity and total silence after renunciation, and did not travel with Makkhali Gosāla.

MAHĀVĪRA-JAYANTĪ. Festival celebrating the birth of **Mahāvīra**. It takes place on the 13th day of the bright half of Caitra (March/April). In iconic traditions, images of auspicious objects seen by Triśalā in her dreams at the time of conception are displayed in **temples**. A couple, assuming the roles of **Indra** and Indrāṇī, reenacts the birth ceremony performed by the **gods (devas)** on **Mount Meru**. This is the only Jain holiday officially recognized by the government of India.

MAHĀVĪRJĪ. Digambara pilgrimage site in the Sawai Madhopur district east of Jaipur, Rajasthan. It is noted for a temple that houses an **image** of **Mahāvīra** that was found buried here. It is not known when this site was established, but there may have been a **temple** here by the 17th century.

MAHĀVRATAS. Five great vows of restraint that are taken during initiation into mendicancy (**dīkṣā**). They are the vows of non-harming (**ahiṃsā**), truthfulness (**satya**), taking only that which is given (**asteya**), **celibacy (brahmacarya)**, and non-possession (**aparigraha**). Although the categories of the vows for a **mendicant** are identical with the lesser vows (**aṇuvratas**) for a **layperson**, the mendicant vows are more restrictive in nature. Their purpose is to eliminate actions that harm other living beings, including those with only one sense (**ekendriya**), and that harm oneself by impeding spiritual progress. A person vows (1) not to perform prohibited actions oneself with body, mind, or speech (kṛta); (2) not to cause others to undertake such actions (kārita); and (3) not to approve of their performance (anumodana). *See also* CĀTUYĀMA-SAṂVARA; GUPTI; SAMITI; VRATA.

MAKKHALI GOSĀLA. An ascetic who became the leader of the **Ājīvikas** during the time of **Mahāvīra**. According to the account in the **Śvetāmbara** ***Bhagavatī Sūtra***, the two spent six years together prior to Mahāvīra's attaining omniscience (**kevala-jñāna**). Gosāla had heard of Mahāvīra's exceptional powers of prognostication and asked to become his disciple. Mahāvīra taught Gosāla how to perform the penance to acquire yogic bodily heat. Subsequently, Gosāla joined with the Ājīvika **mendicants** and proclaimed that he had attained omniscience and that he was the 24th and final **Tīrthaṅkara** of this era.

Some years later, after Mahāvīra had attained omniscience, the two met again when Mahāvīra came to Śrāvastī, where Gosāla was staying in the workshop of a potter **woman**. There was a series of verbal encounters, including a threat on Mahāvīra's life, which culminated with Gosāla incinerating two of Mahāvīra's mendicant followers with his yogic heat. He then directed his heat toward Mahāvīra, declaring that he would die from fever in six months. Mahāvīra directed this heat back toward Gosāla, who died shortly thereafter from its effects. However, Mahāvīra became ill from the force of this heat. The way in which he cured himself has been the subject of considerable controversy in recent years. He sent a disciple to obtain a medicinal substance called "kukkuṭa-māṃsa," which literally means "flesh of a chicken." Some scholars in India and abroad have taken this to mean that Mahāvīra consumed meat in order to cure himself. However, commentators interpret this phrase as the flesh of a fruit that is commonly used to treat dehydration.

In **Digambara** texts, there is no evidence that these two mendicant leaders ever traveled together or that such an encounter took place. Instead, Gosāla was a mendicant in the lineage of the 23rd Tīrthaṅkara, **Pārśvanātha**, and he wanted to become a chief disciple (**gaṇadhara**) of Mahāvīra. After being rejected, he established his own mendicant community and preached the "false doctrine" of the Ājīvikas. Because of this, he was reborn as a **nigoda**, the most elementary form of vegetable life.

MALLĪ/MALLINĀTHA. The 19th **Tīrthaṅkara** of this era. **Śvetāmbaras** believe that Mallī was female and that her birth as a **woman** was an extraordinary event (aścarya). According to Śvetāmbara narratives, in her previous life she was a **monk** named Mahābala. He was reborn as a woman because he was deceitful to his companions regarding his observation of lengthy **fasts**. Mallī rejected the offers of marriage of six kings, and encouraged them to renounce the world by placing rotting food in a gold statue that was a likeness of herself, thereby demonstrating the disgusting nature of the human body. **Digambaras** maintain that all Tīrthaṅkaras were male. They believe that Mallinātha was motivated to renounce when, upon seeing the city decorated for his wedding, he remembered his former life as a **mendicant**. Both agree that Mallī/Mallinātha was born in Mithilā, that s/he renounced the world prior to marriage, and that s/he attained liberation (**mokṣa**) on **Mount Sammeta**. There are no **images** depicting Mallī as a female that have been positively identified. There is a single image of a female ascetic seated in **meditation** that some have identified as Mallī, but it clearly shows a single braid of hair extending down her back, which would be uncharacteristic of a woman who has taken mendicant vows.

MĀLVAṆIĀ, DĀLSUKH (1910–2000). Śvetāmbara paṇḍit. Born in Sayla, Gujarat, he studied at Śāntiniketan (now Viśvabhāratī University), Bengal, which was founded by Rabindranath Tagore. He passed the Nyāyatīrtha examination in 1931 and was appointed lecturer at Banaras Hindu University, where he assisted **Paṇḍit Sukhlāl Saṅghavī** with his research. He became the director of the L. D. Institute of Indology in 1959. He was appointed visiting professor for Indian philosophy at the University of Toronto during 1968–1969. *Aspects of Jainology, vol. 3, Pt. Dalsukhbhai Malvania Felicitation Volume I* contains a bibliography of his works (pp. 14–29, in Hindi).

MĀNASTAMBHA. Literally, "Pride Pillar." A monolithic pillar, sometimes reaching 80 feet in height, erected in front of the main entrance to a **Digambara temple**, primarily in south India. The name is associated with an event in the life of **Indrabhūti Gautama**, the first chief disciple (**gaṇadhara**) of **Mahāvīra**. According to Digambara accounts, when Gautama entered the assembly hall (**samavasaraṇa**) and saw this pillar, his pride (māna) disappeared and he was able to understand Mahāvīra's teachings. The practice of erecting these pillars is quite ancient. Early representations are found on votive tablets (āyāgapaṭas) in **Mathurā** from the pre-Kuṣāṇa period (mid-2nd century B.C.E. through 1st century C.E.). Illustrated on these tablets are pillars surmounted by the wheel of law (dharmacakra), by a lion symbolizing Mahāvīra, and by an elephant symbolizing Ajitanātha, the second **Tīrthaṅkara** of this era. The earliest extant pillar is the Kahaon Pillar located in Uttar Pradesh, which is dated 460 C.E. Some mānastambhas are surmounted by an image of a Tīrthaṅkara facing in the four cardinal directions that is covered by an open-sided pavilion. Beginning in the 10th century, a seated image of a **yakṣa** or **yakṣī** associated with a specific Tīrthaṅkara was placed atop these pillars. The pillars themselves may be ornately decorated and their bases adorned with various figures. *See also* BRAHMADEVASTAMBHA.

MĀNATUṄGA. *See BHAKTĀMARA STOTRA.*

MANDIR MĀRGĪ. Literally, "followers of the temple-path." A term used primarily in Rajasthan for **Śvetāmbaras** who worship **images** of **Tīrthaṅkaras** in **temples** (mandirs). **Derāvāsī** and **Mūrtipūjaka** are other designations for this group of Śvetāmbaras.

MĀṆIBHADRA VĪR(A). One of 52 heroes, called Vīrs or Vīras, powerful non-liberated male deities that protect Jains and defeat the enemies of the Jain community. He is depicted with a boar's head and four arms, riding on an elephant. He is worshipped only by **Śvetāmbara** image-worshipping (**Mūrtipūjaka**) Jains of the **Tapā Gaccha**. He is the protector deity (**adhiṣṭhāyaka deva**) of the Tapā Gaccha. He intervenes in the worldly affairs of worshippers, especially when worshipped with fire (havan). He is said to be the reincarnation of Māṇekcandra, a 16th-century Jain **layman** who defended the practice of image worship against the followers of **Loṅkā Śāh**. In his next life, he was a Vīr who defeated a fierce **Bhairava** who had been invoked by opponents of the Tapā Gaccha. His worship may be a revival of the worship of the **yakṣa** Māṇibhadra, who was popular in northeastern India in ancient times. His principal shrines are at Magarvada and Aglor in north Gujarat and at Ujjain in Madhya Pradesh.

MANTRA. A sound, syllable, word, or phrase that is charged with special powers. When properly recited either vocally or mentally, it brings into reality auspicious things and protection for the person who recites it. In Jainism, the most frequently recited mantra is the **Namaskāra Mantra**. The sound **Oṃ** (or Auṁ) is another well-known mantra.

MANUSCRIPT LIBRARIES. The oldest manuscript libraries in India are those constructed at Jain temple complexes. Over the centuries, these bhaṇḍāras have been the repositories not only for valuable palm-leaf and paper manuscripts of Jain texts but for other classical Indian literature as well. Beginning in the 8th or 9th centuries, the production of manuscripts seems to have increased with the belief that **laypeople** can accrue merit (**puṇya**) by commissioning the copying of sacred texts. At this time, the **bhaṭṭārakas**, who managed **Digambara** temple/educational complexes (**maṭhas**), were instrumental in having libraries erected to house these manuscripts. The most famous among the Digambara manuscript libraries are those at Karanja (Akola) and at **Mūḍbidrī**. Likewise, **Śvetāmbaras** began building libraries at their temple sites. Broach, Cambay, and Patan are the sites of important Śvetāmbara manuscript libraries in Gujarat. A listing of the contents of these libraries compiled in 1383 is the oldest known Indian manuscript catalog. In Rajasthan, there are large collections of manuscripts at Bikaner and **Jaisalmer**.

Around the 17th century, Śvetāmbara manuscript libraries in the north began to be controlled by trustees from the lay community. Access to the libraries was difficult to obtain and often was limited to members of the sect associated with the library. Similar restrictions were enforced by the bhaṭṭārakas who controlled Digambara manuscript libraries. At many locations, manuscripts were brought out only on the days when the **scriptures** were worshipped (Śvet., **Jñāna-Pañcamī**; Dig, **Śruta-Pañcamī**). In the 1860s, the Indian government tried to catalog manuscript collections but this met with much resistance. This conservatism was prompted not only by fear of damage or loss of manuscripts, but also by the rule in some **mendicant lineages** that only **monks** were allowed to read the sacred texts after being given permission by their teachers.

By the end of the 19th century, the situation had begun to change, in part through the efforts of reformist mendicant leaders, such as **Ācārya Vijayadharmasūri**, **Ācārya Vijayarājendrasūri**, and **Ācārya Vijayavallabhasūri**, and Digambara lay scholars, such as **Hīrālāl Jain**, **Nāthūrām Premī**, and **A. N. Upādhye**. These individuals helped Western scholars gain access to manuscript libraries and encouraged the study of sacred texts and their reproduction in printed editions. Most of the important manuscript collections have now been cataloged by Jain mendicant and lay scholars. New libraries have been built where manuscripts are stored in steel cabinets to protect them from insects. Large collections of Jain manuscripts and printed texts are housed at the Abhaya Jain Library, Bikaner (established in the 1930s by **Agaracanda Nāhaṭa**), the Bhogīlāl Leherchand (B. L.) Institute of Indology, Delhi (established in 1980), the Hemacandrācārya Jñān Mandir, Patan (constructed in the 1930s to house collections scattered in the vicinity of Patan), the Lālbhāī Dālpatbhāī (L. D.) Institute of Indology, Ahmedabad (established by Kasturbhāī Lālbhāī in 1955 in association with **Muni Puṇyavijaya**), and the Mahāvīra Jain Ārādhana Kendra, Koba (near Ahmedabad) (established in 1980 under the inspiration of Ācārya Padmasāgarasūri).

MARUDEVĪ. The wife of Nābhi, one of the patriarchs (**kulakaras**) of this era, and the mother of **Ṛṣabha**, the first **Tīrthaṅkara** of this era. According to **Śvetāmbaras**, while she was on her way to hear Ṛṣabha preach his first sermon, she attained omniscience (**kevala-jñāna**) while riding on the back of an elephant. She died immediately, becoming the first person in this era to attain liberation (**mokṣa**). According to some Śvetāmbara narratives, prior to this birth, her **soul** (**jīva**) had been embodied only as the least developed form of vegetable life, called a **nigoda**, and thus she attained liberation in her first human birth. According to **Digambaras**, in her previous life Marudevī had been born as a **woman** on the continent of Pūrva-Videha. According to some Digambara sources, the first person to attain liberation was her son **Bāhubali**, and according to others, it was one of her grandsons named Anantavīrya, a son of the **Cakravartin Bharata**.

There is evidence that **images** of Marudevī have been worshipped at **Mount Śatruñjaya** since the 12th century C.E. when **Hemacandra** is reported to have visited her shrine. There are four images of Marudevī at Śatruñjaya today, three with her on the back of an elephant and one with the infant Ṛṣabha seated on her lap. The two with inscriptions are dated 1734 C.E. and 1836 C.E. There are also images of her seated on an elephant in the Ādināth temple at **Rāṇakpur**.

MARYĀDĀ MAHOTSAVA. **Festival** of Restraint that is observed by the entire **Śvetāmbara Terāpanthī** mendicant community and by representatives of various Terāpanthī lay communities throughout India. When it was established in 1864 by **Ācārya Jaya**, it was a ritual for **mendicants** only, but today it may attract some 50,000 pilgrims. It takes place for three or more days in January/February and celebrates the date that **Ācārya Bhikṣu** completed the rules of ascetic conduct. It is the only festival of the year where all mendicants (as far as possible) gather with the **ācārya** and recite a collective oath of loyalty to him. At this meeting, the ācārya organizes the mendicants into small groups (siṅghāṛs) who will travel together for the following year, decides on the residences of these groups for the four-month rainy season period (**cāturmāsa**), and decides where the groups will travel during the rest of the year.

MASTAKĀBHIṢEKA. Head-anointing ceremony of colossal **images** of **Bāhubali** that is held periodically by the **Digambara** community, approximately every 12 years. The most famous of these ceremonies is at the **pilgrimage** site of **Śravaṇa Beḷgoḷa**, where tens of thousands of Jains assemble to observe this rite. A scaffolding with a platform on top is erected behind the image, and yellow and red powder, sandalwood paste, milk, and pure water are poured over the image. The colors of these substances are symbolic of the stages of purification of Bāhubali's **soul** (**jīva**) as he progressed toward omniscience (**kevala-jñāna**). The liquid is poured from 1,008 pots by prominent members of the lay community who have bid for this privilege. This ceremony is performed periodically elsewhere in Karnataka, including Karkala, where an image of Bāhubali was erected in 1432, and Venur, where an image of Bāhubali was erected in 1604. Recently, images of Bāhubali have been erected at Bāhubalī Hill near the town of Kolhapur in southern Maharashtra and in north India near Delhi, and this ceremony is performed there as well.

MAṬHA. A Sanskrit term for a dwelling place for an ascetic (e.g., hut, cell) or a group of ascetics (e.g., **monastery**), or for a place of religious education. In the **Digambara** tradition, a maṭha is a complex of buildings that usually includes a **temple**, a **manuscript library**, temporary residences for **mendicants**, and buildings for housing and feeding visitors. It also includes a building that is the permanent residence of a **bhaṭṭāraka**, who is responsible for the administration of the site.

MATHURĀ. An ancient cultural and religious center in Uttar Pradesh. It is the site of the final liberation (**mokṣa**) of **Jambū**, the last person in this era to have attained omniscience (**kevala-jñāna**) and liberation. According to **Śvetāmbaras**, a council was convened here in the 4th century C.E. under the leadership of the Pontiff Skandila (300–343 C.E.) for a recitation of the Jain **Āgamas**. In the late 19th century, a number of Jain artifacts with inscriptions were discovered in archeological excavations at Kaṅkālī Ṭīlā in Mathurā dating to the pre-Kuṣāṇa and Kuṣāṇa periods (mid-2nd century B.C.E. through 3rd century C.E.). They include votive stone tablets called āyāgapaṭas donated by **lay** devotees that may have been placed on altars in enclosed areas at the base of a tree. The earliest of these depict various auspicious signs, such as the **svastika**, fish, and trees. Later there are tablets that show figures of **Tīrthaṅkaras**, either seated in **meditation** or standing in **kāyotsarga** posture, which remain the two iconic representations for Tīrthaṅkaras. Also found at Mathurā were the remains of a stūpa and depictions of stūpas, including a frieze containing a stūpa flanked by two seated Tīrthaṅkaras. A **temple** is mentioned in an inscription from the mid-2nd century C.E., and others mention **Arhat** shrines (devakula) and Arhat sanctuaries (āyatana). Over 170 Tīrthaṅkara **images** have been recovered here. On the pedestals of some are depictions of **monks** with a small piece of cloth draped over their left forearms to hide their **nudity**. Some scholars have identified them with the **Ardhaphālaka** and **Yāpanīya** monks that are mentioned in textual sources. **Mendicant lineages** in Mathurā inscriptions correspond with those named in the Śvetāmbara ***Kalpa Sūtra***. Inscriptions also include the names of male and female lay devotees who donated images at the urging of the monks (vācakas) and **nuns**, indicating that **mendicants** at Mathurā actively supported the construction of temples and the installation of images.

MEDITATION. Concentration of the mind upon a single object for a period of time, up to 48 minutes. **Dhyāna** is one of six internal austerities (**tapas**) that remove **karma** from the **soul** (**jīva**). In the classical works on meditation, there is a difference of opinion regarding who should engage in the various types of meditation. However, meditation was apparently not recommended for everyone because the commentators agree that a person who practices virtuous concentration must have attained a proper view of reality (**samyak-darśana**), or the fourth stage of spiritual purity (**guṇasthāna**). Some authors of the medieval texts on lay conduct (**śrāvakācāra**) treat this subject as belonging to mendicant conduct. Others have incorporated meditation on the syllables of the sacred **mantras**, meditation on powers possessed by the **Tīrthaṅkaras**, and meditation on the Tīrthaṅkara as a disembodied **Arhat** into the **caitya-vandana** ritual. In recent times, other types of meditational practices have been developed that are recommended for everyone. These include **prekṣā-dhyāna**, which was introduced by the **Śvetāmbara Terāpanthī Ācārya Mahāprajña**, and the Arhum Yoga system of meditation, which was introduced by the **Sthānakavāsī Ācārya Sushil Kumar**. *See also* ANUPREKṢĀ; BHĀVANĀ; KĀYOTSARGA.

MEHTA, RĀYCANDBHĀĪ. *See* RĀJACANDRA, ŚRĪMAD.

MENDICANT. A term used by some scholars for Jains who have renounced the household life and have taken the five great vows (**mahāvratas**). Ascetic and renouncer are other terms used in translation, although **laypeople** may also practice asceticism and take certain **lay vows** of renunciation. Among **Śvetāmbaras**, there are both male mendicants or **monks** (**sādhus**, **sants**, or **munis**) and female mendicants or **nuns** (**sādhvīs** or **mahāsatīs**). Śvetāmbara **Terāpanthīs** also have a class of "novice" mendicants (**samaṇ/samaṇī**) who are given special dispensations enabling them to travel abroad. Although few in number today, in the Śvetāmbara **Mūrtipūjaka** community there are men called **yatis** who take lesser vows of mendicant renunciation. To differentiate them from fully initiated mendicants (**saṃvegī sādhus**), yatis are sometimes called "quasi-mendicants." Among **Digambaras**, full initiation into mendicancy entails the renunciation of all clothing. Because **women** are not allowed to practice **nudity**, they take the mendicant vow of non-possession (**aparigraha**) in a modified form and technically are advanced **laywomen** in the 11th **pratimā**. However, both naked monks (**munis**) and clothed nuns (**āryikās**) are usually considered to be mendicants.

A person becomes a mendicant by requesting initiation (**dīkṣā**). The requirements for, and rituals associated with, initiation vary according to sectarian tradition. However, in all cases, it entails the removal of the hair on one's head by hand (**keśa-loñca**). Mendicants' responsibilities vary in accordance with their **gender** and with their rank and office in the **mendicant hierarchy**. However, all mendicants are expected to serve as exemplars of proper conduct for the lay community.

Mendicant practice is defined by a set of six daily obligatory rituals (**āvaśyakas**). In addition, they are guided by a number of rules of conduct that are designed to support their mendicant vows. These rules regulate daily activities, such as alms gathering, travel, and so forth. Today, instructions regarding mendicant conduct are usually transmitted orally. Because their vow of non-harming (**ahiṃsā**) includes one-sensed beings (**ekendriya**), mendicants do not cook their own food as doing so would harm both vegetable life and fire-bodied beings. Therefore, they obtain food from laypeople during alms-gathering rounds (Śvet., **gocarī**; Dig., **āhāra-dāna**). However, Jains do not believe that their mendicants live by begging. Giving food to a Jain mendicant is a form of religious gifting (**dāna**) by which a layperson accumulates merit (**puṇya**). Most mendicants practice some form of voluntary **fasting** in addition to fasts that may be prescribed as a penance for a lapse in conduct.

In most cases, mendicants remain in the mendicant lineage into which they were initiated. However, some request initiation into a new lineage. If this involves a change in sectarian tradition, it is customary to be given a second initiation and a new mendicant name. Although the mendicant vows are taken for life, a mendicant leader (**ācārya**) may decide that a mendicant must leave the community, either temporarily or permanently, if there has been a serious lapse in conduct. Occasionally, for personal reasons, a mendicant may leave the community and resume the life of a householder. Some of these individuals have remained **celibate** and others have married.

MENDICANT HIERARCHY. Historically, the Jain mendicant community has been organized hierarchically, and **mendicants** of higher rankings are ritually honored by those of lower rankings. Mendicant age (as measured from the time of initiation), **gender**, and appointment to official positions (padvīs) are determinants of hierarchy. A mendicant who holds an official position or office is senior to a mendicant who does not. A **monk** is always senior to a **nun** irrespective of mendicant age or office held.

In the mendicant community, there are a number of hierarchical positions. For example, within the **Śvetāmbara Mūrtipūjaka Tapā Gaccha**, a man who has taken initiation (**dīkṣā**) into a **mendicant lineage** is called a **sādhu**. If he does not hold any special position, he has the title of **muni**. A **gaṇin** is a monk who is responsible for a group of munis. Today, the office of **paṁnyāsa** (scholar) is essentially the same as the gaṇin. Previously, there was another supervisory post above this called pravartaka (promoter), which is seldom found today. Likewise, there are fewer **upādhyāyas** (preceptors) than in earlier times. The topmost position is the **ācārya** (teacher, mendicant leader). Within the Tapā Gaccha, there are a number of ācāryas, who are the leaders of individual groups of monks and nuns (**parivāras**). In the sublineages (**samudāyas**), there may be a chief mendicant leader, called a gacchādhipati, who supervises mendicants and subordinate ācāryas. However, there is no mendicant leader who supervises the entire Tapā Gaccha. Today, the only Mūrtipūjaka mendicant lineage that is headed by a single mendicant leader is the **A(ñ)cala Gaccha**. The **Sthānakavāsī Śramaṇa Saṅgha** and the entire Śvetāmbara **Terāpanthī** mendicant community are centrally organized, with only one ācārya.

In communities of female mendicants, there are fewer hierarchical positions. A nun who does not hold any special position has the title of **sādhvī**. Group leaders are called **guruṇī** and **pravartinī**, or among Śvetāmbara **Terāpanthīs**, **agragaṇyā** and **sādhvī pramukhā**. There are several other titles that may be used for Śvetāmbara mendicants. **Sant** and **mahāsatī** are often used by **Sthānakavāsīs** for a monk and nun, respectively.

Among **Digambaras**, muni is the general designation for a naked monk and **āryikā** is the title for a nun. Within the Digambara mendicant community there are men and **women** who are classified as "advanced householders" in the 11th **pratimā**. They have formally renounced the household life by taking the vows of a **kṣullaka/kṣullikā**. Men may take the more severe vows of an **ailaka**. These advanced householders, who live with a group of mendicants of the same gender, are junior to fully initiated munis and āryikās. At a later time, they may choose to take the vows of a fully initiated mendicant (**mahāvratas**).

In medieval times, there were many Śvetāmbara mendicants called **yatis** who lived a sedentary lifestyle and did not take the full vows of an itinerant mendicant. The leader of their mendicant lineages was called a **śrīpūjya**. There are now only a handful of yatis remaining in the Śvetāmbara Mūrtipūjaka community. Within the Digambara mendicant community, **bhaṭṭārakas** were the leaders of groups of mendicants who gave up the itinerant lifestyle and settled in one place. This office still exists, although bhaṭṭārakas no longer function as leaders of mendicant lineages.

MENDICANT LINEAGES. Historically, the Jain mendicant community was divided into a number of large groups descended from prominent teachers that were subdivided into smaller groupings. A number of terms are found for these groupings in early Jain texts, including the ***Kalpa Sūtra***, and in inscriptions at **Mathurā**. However, the precise meaning of the various organizational designations is unclear. **Gaṇa** ("troop") was the largest unit, which was comprised of kulas ("families"). Śākhās ("branches") referred to mendicant lineages that branched off from one teacher (**ācārya**). The term **gaccha** ("going" or "traveling together") has gradually replaced the designations of gaṇa and kula.

Gaccha is used today for the basic divisions or main mendicant lineages of the **Śvetāmbara Mūrtipūjaka** mendicant community. A sublineage within a gaccha is called a **samudāya**. A group of mendicants that travels together under the leadership of a single mendicant leader (ācārya) is called a **parivāra**. The term **sampradāya** is used by **Sthānakavāsīs** for the basic divisions or main mendicant lineages of their mendicant community.

Among **Digambaras**, **saṅgha** was the term used for the basic divisions, within which there were various subdivisions. For example, subdivisions of the **Mūla Saṅgha** included āmnāyas, anvayas, balis, gacchas, gaṇas, kulas, samudāyas, and vaṃśaṣ. Lists of mendicant lineages also mention various śākhās of several gaṇas that were named after a city or region (e.g., Delhi-Jaipur Śākhā of the Balātkāra Gaṇa).

MENDICANT VOWS. *See* MAHĀVRATAS.

MERIT. *See* PUṆYA.

MERU. *See* MOUNT MERU.

MOKṢA. Liberation of the **soul** (**jīva**) from embodiment in the cycle of rebirth (**saṃsāra**). From beginningless time, all souls have been bound in the cycle of rebirth by a type of extremely subtle matter called **karma**, which causes embodiment of the soul in birth after birth. In order to attain liberation, all karma must be removed from the soul. This is accomplished through one's personal efforts, not through the grace of a deity. Karma may be removed in various ways, including acts of physical and mental austerities such as **fasting** and **meditating**, and new karma may be prevented from binding by observing disciplined conduct as outlined in the various **lay vows** and in the mendicant vows (**mahāvratas**). Attaining right faith, or a proper view of reality, (**samyak-darśana**) is the first step toward liberation because all who have experienced it must attain liberation at some future time.

Liberation is attained in the same life in which one attains omniscience (**kevala-jñāna**). When the life span of the physical body has come to an end, the soul leaves the body and rises to the siddha-loka or īśat-prāgbhārā-bhūmi, which is located above the heavenly realms, at the very edge of the occupied universe (**loka-ākāśa**). The liberated soul, known as a **siddha**, remains individual and isolated from all other souls, forever free from suffering and embodiment. It eternally experiences its own nature of infinite **consciousness** and bliss.

Only human beings who are born in regions of action (**karma-bhūmis**) during suitable periods in the **cycle of time** can attain liberation. Heavenly beings (**devas**) cannot attain liberation from the heavenly realms. They must first be reborn as humans. **Śvetāmbaras** believe that it is possible for both men and **women** to attain liberation. **Digambaras** believe that women cannot attain liberation without being reborn as a man because of physical limitations inherent in a female-**gendered** body. Both believe that there are some souls, called **abhavya**, that lack the inherent capacity to ever attain liberation. Most souls, however, are **bhavya**, and have the inherent capacity to attain liberation called **bhavyatva**. In Jainism, there is no **God**, Supreme Soul, or Ultimate Reality (brahman) that has never been bound in saṃsāra, although souls that have attained liberation may be called God (**deva**) or Supreme Soul (**paramātman**). *See also* STRĪ-MOKṢA.

MONASTERY. A word used in translation for a building that serves as a temporary residence or dwelling-hall of those who have renounced the household life and have taken religious vows. These buildings are legally owned by the lay community. They include **upāśrayas** used by

Śvetāmbara Mūrtipūjaka mendicants and sthānakas used by **Sthānakavāsī** mendicants. A complex of buildings called a **maṭha** also may be translated as monastery.

MONK. A term used for indigenous categories of men who have renounced the household life and have taken the mendicant vows (**mahāvratas**) in either full or modified form. There are fully initiated monks, called **saṃvegī sādhus**, with the titles of **muni**, **sādhu**, or **sant**. In earlier times, they were known as "forest-dwelling" monks (**vanavāsī**). Prior to the 20th century, in the **Śvetāmbara Mūrtipūjaka** mendicant lineages (**gacchas**), there was a large number of "domesticated" monks called **yatis**, who were headed by an official called a **śrīpūjya**. In earlier times, they were known as "temple-dwelling" monks (**caityavāsī**). *See also* MENDICANT; MENDICANT HIERARCHY.

MOODABIDRI. *See* MŪḌBIDRĪ.

MOUNT ĀBŪ (DELVARA, DILWARA). Pilgrimage site near the village of Delvara in southern Rajasthan known for its ornate white marble temples. There are four **Śvetāmbara temples** on Mount Ābū. (1) Vimala Vasahī was erected in 1032 C.E. by Vimala Śāh, a minister to Bhīma I of the Caulukya dynasty. The **image** of **Ṛṣabha** installed at this time reportedly was found buried next to a temple dedicated to Arbuda, the tutelary **goddess** for whom the mountain is named. It is now located in a side niche of the temple. The image of Ṛṣabha currently in the inner sanctum was installed in 1322 C.E. following renovations to the temple. (2) Lūṇa Vasahī, dedicated to **Neminātha**, was erected in 1230 C.E. by Tejaḥpāla, a minister to Bhīma II. Both of these ornate white marble temples were badly damaged by Muslim invaders early in the 14th century and were repaired shortly thereafter. (3) Pittalahāra Vasahī, another white marble temple dedicated to Ṛṣabha, was built by Bhīma Shah in the 15th century. (4) Kharatara Vasahī, a sandstone temple dating from the 15th century, is dedicated to **Pārśvanātha**. There also is a small **Digambara** temple dedicated to **Mahāvīra** located here.

MOUNT AṢṬĀPADA. A legendary mountain where **Ṛṣabha** attained liberation (**mokṣa**). It often is identified with Mount Kailāsa in the Himalayas.

MOUNT GIRNĀR. Pilgrimage site near the town of Janagadh in eastern Gujarat. It is believed that **Neminātha** renounced the world and attained omniscience (**kevala-jñāna**) and liberation (**mokṣa**) here.

Digambaras also believe that the redaction of one of their sacred texts, the ***Ṣaṭkhaṇḍāgama***, took place at this site. Sixteen Jain **temples** have been built on a ledge halfway up the western side of the mountain. The earliest temple, dedicated to Neminātha, was constructed in 1128 C.E. by Sajjana, a minister under Jayasimha Siddharāja of Saurashtra. A three-shrined temple was erected in 1231 C.E. by Vastupāla, a minister to Bhīma II of the Caulukya dynasty.

MOUNT MERU. In Jain cosmography, the mountain that is located at the center of **Jambūdvīpa**, the innermost island-continent in the occupied universe (**loka-ākāśa**). When a **Tīrthaṅkara** is born, the gods (**Indras**) come to earth, take him to this mountain, and perform his birth ablutions (**abhiṣeka**) there. Jain **temples** may be surmounted by a tower that symbolizes Mount Meru, the axis mundi of the universe.

MOUNT SAMMETA. Pilgrimage site located on Paraśnāth Hill near the town of Madhuban, Jharkhand (formerly Bihar). It is believed that **Pārśvanātha** and 19 other **Tīrthaṅkaras** attained liberation (**mokṣa**) here. A **temple** containing a pair of footprints of Pārśva has been constructed on the summit of the hill and small shrines containing the footprint images (pādukās) of the other 19 Tīrthaṅkaras are constructed along the path to the summit. Because the **images** are not iconographic, both **Digambaras** and **Śvetāmbaras** worship in the same temples. In addition, there are several Śvetāmbara temples that have been constructed here in the 20th century.

MOUNT ŚATRUÑJAYA. The most important **pilgrimage** site for **Śvetāmbaras.** It is located near the town of Palitana in the Kathiawar district of Gujarat. It also is called Puṇḍarīka Mountain after a grandson and chief disciple (**gaṇadhara**) of **Ṛṣabha**, the first Tīrthaṅkara of this era, who is said to have attained liberation (**mokṣa**) here. According to traditional Śvetāmbara accounts, Śatruñjaya was the first pilgrimage site established in our current descending **cycle of time** (avasarpiṇī). Tradition holds that **Bharata**, the eldest son of Ṛṣabha, built the first **temple** at this site to house the **images** of Ṛṣabha and Puṇḍarīka. It is said that **Bāhubali**, Ṛṣabha's second son, erected the second temple here to house the image of **Marudevī**, Ṛṣabha's mother. It is believed that all of the Tīrthaṅkaras of this era except **Neminātha** preached here. Among the **mendicants** who are said to have attained liberation here are Rāma, Sītā, and the Pāṇḍava brothers along with their mother, Kuntī. The earliest inscription here is dated 1007 C.E. and is found on an image of Puṇḍarīka. Of the hundreds of temples erected over the centuries, the most important is the one dedicated to Ṛṣabha that was built in 1154 C.E. by Vāgbhaṭa, a minister of Kumārapāla of the Caulukya dynasty. It was rebuilt after being destroyed by a Muslim invasion in 1311 C.E. and has since been restored numerous times.

MṚGĀVATĪ, MAHATTARĀ (1926–1986). Śvetāmbara Mūrtipūjaka nun in the **Tapā Gaccha**. Born in Saradhara, near Rajkot, Gujarat, her father died when she was two and sometime later her brother and sister also died. When she was 13, **Ācārya Vijayavallabhasūri** initiated her as Sādhvī Mṛgāvatī and her mother also was initiated by him. She was one of the first Śvetāmbara Mūrtipūjaka nuns to be granted permission to be educated by **paṇḍits**, and she studied with **Paṇḍit Sukhlāl Saṅghavī** and **Paṇḍit Becardās Doshi**. Their work with Mahātmā Gāndhī in the nationalist movement influenced her thinking. She promoted the values of self-reliance through the establishment of cottage industries and the wearing of khādī and of social awareness by speaking out against the custom of dowry. An advocate of education for **women**, she established schools for women. She recommended that before young nuns were initiated, they should take a five-year curriculum to study the basic Jain texts as well as grammar, literature, and so forth with learned paṇḍits. Vijayavallabhasūri also broke with tradition when he allowed her to give public discourses. She raised money for various charitable causes. In memory of her teacher, she founded the Vijayavallabha Smāraka on G. T. Karnal Road near Delhi with a library, teaching facilities, and guest houses. The B. L. Institute of Indology, established in 1980 in memory of Bhogīlāl Leherchand (1883–1979), has been located at this complex since 1984. Several **temples** have been erected here, including Vijayavallabha Guru Samādhi Mandir, Bhagavān Vāsupūjya Mandir, **Padmāvatī** Mandir, and a memorial shrine to Mṛgāvatī. The Mahattarā Sādhvī Śrī Mṛgāvatī Foundation has been established in her memory.

MŪḌBIDRĪ (MUDBIDRE, MOODABIDRI). Small town in southwestern Karnataka that is a **pilgrimage** site for **Digambaras**. Eighteen Digambara **temples** have been built here. The largest, named Tribhuvana-Tilaka-Cūḍāmaṇi Basadi ("The Crest-Jewel of the Three Worlds Temple"), was erected in 1429 C.E. It is dedicated to Candraprabha, the eighth **Tīrthaṅkara** of this era. Another important temple, popularly known as Guru Basadi, dates from the 16th century. It replaces an 8th-century temple that housed an ancient stone **image** of

Pārśvanātha, which reportedly was discovered buried in a bamboo grove here. Mūḍbidrī is the seat of a **bhaṭṭāraka** known by the hereditary name of Cārukīrti. This is also the hereditary name of the bhaṭṭāraka at **Śravaṇa Beḷgoḷa**, reflecting the fact that the Mūḍbidrī seat was founded in the 13th century by Digambaras who had migrated from the Śravaṇa Beḷgoḷa area. At this time, they installed an image of **Kūṣmāṇḍinī** at Mūḍbidrī. This **goddess**, who is the **yakṣī** of **Neminātha**, is also the protector deity of Śravaṇa Beḷgoḷa. Mūḍbidrī is known for its valuable collection of **manuscripts**, including famous manuscript copies of the ***Ṣaṭkhaṇḍāgama*** and the ***Kaṣāyaprābhṛta*** dating from the 12th century.

MUHPATTĪ (MUHKHAVASTRIKĀ). A small rectangular piece of cloth that is placed in front of the mouth. This cloth is used by **Śvetāmbara mendicants** to prevent harm to one-sensed wind-bodied beings (vāyu-kāyika) by the sudden exhalation of warm breath from the mouth and to small insects by inhaling them. Śvetāmbara **Mūrtipūjaka** mendicants carry this cloth in their hands and place it in front of their mouths while preaching or reading aloud from sacred texts. **Sthānakavāsī** and **Terāpanthī** mendicants wear it tied in front of their mouths, securing it with strings looped over the ears, and they remove it while eating. **Laypeople** may hold a cloth in front of their mouths when performing certain rituals, such as **sāmāyika**. Mendicants with muhpattīs in their hands are represented on the bases of **Tīrthaṅkara images** from the Kuṣāṇa period at **Mathurā** (2nd–3rd centuries C.E.). The muhpattī is different from the cloth that a layperson ties over his or her mouth while performing image worship. The purpose of this cloth is to prevent a consecrated image from being defiled.

MUKHTĀR, JUGAL KIŚORE (1877–1968). Digambara scholar of Jainism. Born in Sarwara, Uttar Pradesh, he studied Sanskrit, Prākrit, Urdu, Persian, and Jain philosophy. He began editing the *Jain Gazette* in 1907. He worked as a solicitor (mukhtār) until 1914, when he began devoting his time to research and the publication of Jain texts. In 1929, he established Vīr Sevā Mandir (originally called Samantabhadra Āshram), a publishing house in Delhi. He was the founding editor of the periodical *Anekānta*. In addition to editing a number of Jain texts, Mukhtār is the author of several works, including *Jainagranthapraśasti-saṅgraha* (Delhi, 1954) and *Jain Sāhitya aur Itihās par Viśad Prakāś* (Calcutta, 1956). He also is known for his poetic composition "Merī Bhāvanā."

MŪLAGUṆAS. Basic restraints of a **layperson**. In **Digambara** texts, this term means not eating eight types of food: meat, alcohol, honey, and five kinds of figs. According to Digambaras, without observing these basic **dietary restrictions**, it is not possible for a layperson to attain the 11 stages of renunciation (**pratimās**). Although **Śvetāmbaras** may observe these dietary restrictions, in Śvetāmbara texts this term does not refer to this practice. Instead, it is a synonym for the five lay vows (**aṇuvratas**) or for non-harming (**ahiṃsā**). In both traditions, for **mendicants** these dietary restrictions are encompassed by their vow of non-harming.

MŪLA SAṄGHA. A **Digambara mendicant lineage** that is considered to be the original or root (mūla) group. This group was undivided from the time of **Indrabhūti Gautama** to the time of Arhadbali, who, according to some mendicant lineage lists, became the 32nd mendicant leader in the year 38 C.E. (i.e., 565 years after the **nirvāṇa** of **Mahāvīra**). During this time, at a large gathering of **mendicants**, it was noticed that factions had developed and the Mūla Saṅgha was reconstituted into four **saṅghas**: Deva, Nandī, Sena, and Siṃha Saṅghas. According to tradition, the first **ācārya** of the Nandī Saṅgha was Māghanandin, and Puṣpadanta and Bhūtabali, the authors of the ***Ṣaṭkhaṇḍāgama***, belonged to this mendicant lineage. The Nandī Saṅgha remained undivided through the time of **Kundakunda** and was divided into branches after the time of **Umāsvāmī**.

Beginning in the 5th or 6th centuries C.E. there are inscriptions mentioning the names of the numerous branches and subbranches of the original Mūla Saṅgha (āmnāyas, anvayas, gaṇas, saṅghas, etc.) and the senior **monks** belonging to them. One of the oldest and most important apparently was the Kundakunda-Anvaya, which is mentioned in the Merkara copper plates dated 466 C.E. Inscriptions referencing branches of the Mūla Saṅgha are located throughout south India as well as in Bengal, Bihar, Gujarat, Rajasthan, and Uttar Pradesh. The insignia of mendicants associated with these branches was a peacock-feather whisk broom (**piñchī**). Although the Mūla Saṅgha is mentioned in one 19th-century inscription at **Śravaṇa Beḷgoḷa**, it is unclear whether there were any itinerant naked monks (**munis**) associated with these lineages at this time. However, the munis who revived this tradition early in the 20th century traced their lineage to the Mūla Saṅgha. *See also* DRĀVIḌA SAṄGHA; KĀṢṬHĀ SAṄGHA.

MUNI. Literally, "silent one." A general designation for a Jain **monk** who does not hold any special office within a **mendicant lineage**. *See also* MENDICANT HIERARCHY.

MŪRTIPŪJAKA. Śvetāmbara sectarian tradition that venerates or worships (**pūjā**) **images** (mūrtis) of **Tīrthaṅkaras** in **temples**. This term came into use after the establishment of the non-image-worshipping **Sthānakavāsī** tradition between the mid-15th and the early 17th centuries C.E. **Laypeople** venerate images in temples and home shrines with material forms of worship (dravya pūjā) and with mental worship (bhāva pūjā). **Mendicants** perform only mental worship. Today, the mendicant community is divided into several **gacchas**, and the laypeople often are identified as followers of one of these gacchas. **Derāvāsī** and **Mandir Mārgī** are other designations for these Śvetāmbaras.

– N –

NĀHAṬA, AGARACANDA (1911–1983). Śvetāmbara scholar of Rajasthani and Hindi literature and history, and collector of manuscripts. Born in Bikaner, Rajasthan, into a wealthy merchant family, his formal education ended after fifth grade because no further schooling was available there. However, he always was interested in learning and was self-educated in his areas of specialization. When he was 17, he read an article about the Jain poet Samayasundara, which motivated him to begin reading manuscripts housed in Jain **manuscript libraries** in Bikaner. He soon discovered the vast amount of literature in the Rajasthani **language** and the state of decay of these valuable manuscripts. He began to acquire manuscripts, and he established the Abhaya Jain Library to house his valuable collection, which grew to some 60,000 manuscripts and 45,000 printed texts. He also founded the Saṅkaradān Nāhaṭa Art Museum, which contains his collection of thousands of old paintings and hundreds of **images** and rare coins. He wrote numerous books and articles on Jain history and literature, including the history of the **Kharatara Gaccha** and the **Dādāgurus**. **Paṇḍits** and **monks**, including **Muni Vinayasāgara**, came to Bikaner to study with him. He guided many scholars in their research and made it possible for Western scholars to obtain copies of manuscripts from Jain manuscript libraries.

NĀKOṚ(Ḍ)Ā BHAIRAV(A). A non-liberated guardian deity (**kṣetrapāla**) of a **Śvetāmbara** temple at Nakora, near Balotra in western Rajasthan, that houses an **image** of **Pārśvanātha**. He is the most popular guardian deity among Śvetāmbaras in most of Rajasthan. Some businessmen consider him to be a business partner and pledge a certain percentage of their yearly profits to him.

NAMASKĀRA MANTRA. An ancient Prākrit formula of homage to the five who are worthy of worship. Because these five have attained the highest stages of spiritual purity, they are considered supreme beings (**parameṣṭhin**). "Homage to the enlightened teachers (**Arhats**), homage to the liberated ones (**siddhas**), homage to the mendicant leaders (**ācāryas**), homage to the preceptors (**upādhyāyas**), homage to all mendicants in the world (**sādhus**). This is the fivefold homage that destroys all evil. And among all that is auspicious, it is the preeminent auspicious [statement]." ("ṇamo arahaṃtāṇaṃ, ṇamo siddhāṇaṃ, ṇamo āyariyāṇaṃ, ṇamo uvajjhāyāṇaṃ, ṇamo loe savva-sāhūṇaṃ, eso paṃca ṇamokkāro savva-pāvappaṇāsaṇo, maṃgalāṇaṃ ca savvesiṃ paḍhamaṃ havai maṃgalam.") This is the most frequently recited ritual formula in Jainism. It is believed to have special powers of protection, to give worldly success, to destroy **karma**, and to cure illnesses. Although this mantra is accepted by all Jains, there are some minor variations in versions accepted by different groups of **Śvetāmbaras**, and **Sthānakavāsīs** do not accept the second portion.

Like the **scriptures**, it is considered beginningless and to have been transmitted by the **Tīrthaṅkaras** to their **gaṇadharas**. However, from a historical perspective, its origins are not known. The Arhats and siddhas are invoked in an inscription of King Khāravela (ca. 150 B.C.E.). At the beginning of the Śvetāmbara ***Bhagavatī Sūtra*** there is a fivefold homage, but the Brāhmī script and the scriptures are invoked instead of mendicants. It appears at the beginning of the *Prajñāpanā Sūtra* (a Śvetāmbara Upāṅga text), but the commentators do not mention it, suggesting that they considered it to be an interpolation. It is found at the beginning of the **Digambara *Ṣaṭkhaṇḍāgama***, and in his **commentary Vīrasena** states that it was composed by **Puṣpadanta**. However, another text mentions that it was inserted here by Puṣpadanta. *See also* MANTRA.

NANDĪŚVARADVĪPA. In Jain cosmography, the eighth island-continent in the middle realm (**madhya-loka**). This land, which resembles the heavens and is inaccessible to humans, is visited by heavenly beings (**devas**) who travel there to worship the **Tīrthaṅkaras**. There are 52 eternally existing **temples** located here where the devas worship from the eighth through the 15th days of the bright half of the months of Kārttika (October/November), Phālguna (February/March), and Āṣāḍha (June/July). In north India, the island is represented as a circular plaque with four groups of 13 temples. In south India, the island is represented as a three-dimensional pyramid-shaped structure surrounded by 52 seated

images of the Tīrthaṅkaras. On the days when the devas are worshipping on Nandīśvaradvīpa, some Jains tend these plaques.

NANDYĀVARTA. *See* AṢṬAMAṄGALA.

NARAKA. Hell; the dwelling place of hell-beings (**nāraki**). *See* ADHO-LOKA.

NĀRAKI. Hell-being. One of four states of existence in the cycle of rebirth (**saṃsāra**). The life of a hell-being is characterized by physical and mental suffering in one of the seven hells (**narakas**) located below the earth in the **adho-loka**. One attains this birth from harmful actions performed in the previous life, especially those involving extreme violence (**hiṃsā**). When the predetermined life span of a hell-being is exhausted, its **soul** (**jīva**) is reborn again on earth, either as a human or a five-sensed animal (**tiryañc**).

NĀRĀYAṆA. *See* VĀSUDEVA.

NATHMAL, MUNI. *See* MAHĀPRAJÑA, ĀCĀRYA.

NAVADEVATĀ. Nine Divinities. A mystical diagram (**yantra**), typically in the shape of a lotus, that is used in **Digambara** rituals. This yantra symbolizes the teachings of the path of purification (mokṣa-mārga), which culminates in omniscience (**kevala-jñāna**) and liberation (**mokṣa**) from the cycle of rebirth (**saṃsāra**). It incorporates the five supreme beings (**parameṣṭhin**) who are honored in the **Namaskāra Mantra**. A figure representing the enlightened teachers (**Arhats**) is situated in the center, surrounded by eight petals containing figures representing disembodied liberated **souls** (**siddhas**) to the north, mendicant leaders (**ācāryas**) to the east, mendicant preceptors (**upādhyāyas**) to the south, and mendicants (**sādhus**) to the west. In the four intermediate directions are the image of a **Tīrthaṅkara**, a **temple**, the sacred wheel of law (dharmacakra), and the speech of the Tīrthaṅkaras as found in the **scriptures** (**śruta**). It is the most commonly used yantra in Jainism today. It is worshipped for the destruction of harmful **karmas** and for attaining prosperity and auspiciousness. **Śvetāmbaras** use a similar yantra called a **siddhacakra** or navapada in their rituals.

NAVAPADA. *See* SIDDHACAKRA.

NAVA TERĀPANTHĪ. *See* TERĀPANTHĪ (Śvet.).

NAYAVĀDA. Doctrine of philosophical viewpoints (naya). It allows for different estimates of reality by using different frames of reference. In Jainism, reality is understood to be multifaceted. It is impossible to express all aspects of reality simultaneously due to the limitations of human language. But a valid statement can be made about one aspect of reality at a time. Thus, a statement as viewed from a single aspect may be true, but it always is partial or limited. These standpoints serve as guides or insights into the different facets of reality and are complementary rather than mutually exclusive. As described in the ***Tattvārtha Sūtra*** (1.34–35), they are the common person's view (naigama), the generic view (saṃgraha), the practical view (vyavahāra), the linear view (ṛjusūtra), the literal view (śabdha), the etymological view (samabhirūḍha), and the actuality view (evambhūta). This is the classical interpretation of viewpoints. **Kundakunda** emphasized a two truths model of reality: the conventional point of view (**vyavahāra naya**) and the absolute point of view (**niścaya naya**). *See also* ANEKĀNTAVĀDA; SAPTA-BHAṄGI-NAYA; SYĀDVĀDA.

NEMINĀTHA (ARIṢṬANEMI). The 22nd **Tīrthaṅkara** of this era. According to Jain narratives, he lived in the area of Saurashtra some 84,000 years before the time of the 23rd Tīrthaṅkara, **Pārśvanātha**. His father, Samuḍravijaya, was the eldest brother of Vasudeva, the father of Vāsudeva Kṛṣṇa. While on the way to his marriage to **Rājīmati**, Nemi saw many animals penned up in enclosures. Upon learning that they were to be slaughtered for food at his wedding feast, Nemi realized that if he were the cause of their killing, there would be no happiness for him in the next life. Instead of marrying, he renounced the household life. He is said to have lived for one thousand years and to have attained liberation (**mokṣa**) at **Mount Girnār**.

NEO-DIGAMBARA. A term that is used in scholarly writing to define those who follow the teachings of **Kānjī Svāmī**. In general, rational and mystical aspects of Jainism are emphasized, including knowledge of the true nature of the innate pure **soul** (**ātman**), direct experience of the soul, and the absolute view of reality (**niścaya naya**). Ritual observances and institutionalized authority are de-emphasized, and **mendicants** are not usually accorded any special status.

NIGAṆṬHA. *See* NIRGRANTHA.

NIGODA. The most rudimentary form of vegetable life (vanaspati-kāya) in which an infinite number of **souls (jīvas)** live together in a submicroscopic common body, being born together and dying together, and breathing and taking nourishment together. Nigodas are said to pervade the entire occupied universe (**loka-ākāśa**). In the earthly realms, they inhabit the tissues of some plants, animals, and humans. Nigodas may be found in the tissues of root vegetables, such as potatoes, carrots, and radishes; in fleshy or seed-filled plants, such as figs; and in sweet or fermented substances, such as honey and liquor. To minimize the number of souls that may be harmed, Jain **mendicants** and some **laypeople** refrain from eating plants that contain nigodas.

There are some souls that have been embodied only as nigodas from beginningless time. They have not begun to develop spiritually and have a type of false belief that is undifferentiated (avyakta mithyātva) with no tendency toward good or harmful actions. In some, for reasons that are not explained, there is a spiritual awakening, and false belief becomes differentiated (vyakta mithyātva), or assumes a certain form. These souls enter the path of spiritual development and are born in other life-forms. There are some souls embodied as nigodas that previously were embodied in other life-forms. It is possible for a soul that has attained a human birth to be reborn as a nigoda in the next life.

NIRGRANTHA (Pkt., NIGAṆṬHA). Literally, without (nir) bonds or knots (grantha), the unattached ones, or those without possessions. The name used in earlier times for itinerant Jain **monks** and, by extension, the community of lay followers who supported them. This term also is found in Buddhist texts for **mendicants** who were followers of Nātaputta (Skt., Jñātṛputra), another name for **Mahāvīra**. The term used today, **Jaina**, or disciple of the **Jinas**, had come into use by the 9th century C.E.

NIRVĀṆA. *See* MOKṢA.

NIRYUKTI. *See* COMMENTARY.

NIŚCAYA NAYA. The nonconventional or absolute point of view in the two truths model of reality emphasized by **Kundakunda** and by those following him in the **Digambara** mystical tradition. It is contrasted with the conventional or worldly point of view (**vyavahāra naya**). The conventional and absolute points of view are most often employed in discussions of the sentient **soul (jīva)** and its relationship with everything that is non-soul, namely, the body and karmic matter.

From a conventional point of view, the cause of the bondage of the soul is **karma**, a form of subtle matter, which is the direct cause of a false view of reality (mithyātva), and of delusion (moha) and desire (**kaṣāya**). Liberation (**mokṣa**) is attained by removing all karmic matter from the soul. Here, there is an emphasis on the performance of austerities (**tapas**) in order to remove karmic matter from the soul.

From an absolute point of view, karma is not the direct cause of the soul's bondage. It is the lack of knowledge of the true nature of the Self, or the innate pure inner soul (**ātman**), as experienced by an omniscient being (**kevalin**) and by a liberated soul (**siddha**). This lack of knowledge is the cause of confusion (moha) regarding the nature of reality, including confusion regarding what is soul and what is non-soul, which results in desire for external objects. This desire causes transformations in subtle matter in the proximity of the soul into the different varieties of karma. It is the contiguity of karmic matter with the soul that causes the soul to bring about transformations in itself (upayoga) that are not innate to its true nature. Depending on the actions arising from these desires, there may be good transformations (śubha upayoga) that are conducive to auspicious rebirths or bad transformations (aśubha upayoga) that are conducive to inauspicious rebirths. However, a soul that has realized its true nature as pure knowledge and as isolated from, and unaffected by, all matter, including karmic matter, experiences pure transformations (śuddha upayoga) that do not give rise to desire. Thus, from the absolute point of view, it is the soul that binds itself in **saṃsāra**, and liberation is attained by knowledge of the Self. Here, there is an emphasis on **meditation (dhyāna)** to gain direct insight into the true nature of the soul.

A multifaceted view of reality (**anekāntavāda**), in which all views are equally valid when properly qualified in statements of assertion and negation, is different from a two truths model, in which niścaya naya is seen as a higher truth and vyavahāra naya is seen as a lower or provisional truth that should be discarded at some point. Later Digambara commentators elaborated and expanded on the ideas of Kundakunda. They were concerned with the status of the worldly level of truth and its inherent validity as a vehicle toward the higher level of truth, and by whom this worldly level of truth should be discarded.

Kundakunda's writings on niścaya naya, especially as expressed in his *Samayasāra*, have been a source of inspiration for those who followed him in Digambara mystical tradition, including **Yogīndu**, **Tāraṇ Svāmī** and the **Tāraṇ Svāmī Panth**, **Banārsīdās** and the **Adhyātma movement**, **Ṭoḍarmal** and the Digambara **Terāpanthīs**, and more recently in the 20th century **Śrīmad Rājacandra** and **Kānjī Svāmī**. Kundakunda's tendency to deny the worldly level of truth has been criticized by **Śvetāmbara** philosophers, such as **Yaśovijaya,** as a one-sided (ekānta) view of reality. *See also* NAYAVĀDA.

NISĪHI. A Prākrit expression meaning "it is abandoned." It is uttered when entering a Jain **temple**, indicating the intention to leave behind the outside, material world. It also is uttered before entering the inner sanctum and at the completion of external worship (dravya **pūjā**) before beginning internal worship (bhāva pūjā). *See also* AṢṬAKA PŪJĀ; AṢṬAPRAKĀRĪ PŪJĀ; PŪJĀ.

NIYAMASĀRA. *See* KUNDAKUNDA.

NO-KAṢĀYA. Subsidiary passion or emotion. Like passions (**kaṣāyas**) emotions are produced by varieties of conduct-deluding (cāritra-mohanīya) **karmas**. There are nine types of emotions: laughter (hāsya), pleasure in sense activity (rati), displeasure in sense activity (arati), sorrow (śoka), fear (bhaya), disgust (jugupsā), and sexual cravings (veda), including desire for **women** (puṃ-veda), desire for a men (strī-veda), and desire for both men and women (napuṃsaka-veda). In order to attain liberation (**mokṣa**) from the cycle of death and rebirth (**saṃsāra**), all of these emotions must be eliminated by destroying all conduct-deluding karma that is bound with the **soul** (**jīva**). *See also* GENDER.

NUDITY. The question of whether or not the mendicant vow (**mahāvrata**) of non-possession (**aparigraha**) entails the renunciation of all clothing led to a division of the Jain community in the early centuries of the common era into the two main sectarian traditions: the followers of white-clothed **mendicants** (**Śvetāmbaras**) and the followers of sky-clad **monks** (**Digambaras**).

When Śvetāmbaras take the aparigraha-vrata, they renounce mental attachment or feelings of possessiveness to all things, including clothing. The garments that Śvetāmbara monks and **nuns** wear are like the implements that assist them in carrying out a mendicant life, such as a whisk broom (**rajoharaṇa**) and alms bowls. According to Śvetāmbara sources, 22 of the 24 **Tīrthaṅkaras** wore clothing after renunciation. **Ṛṣabha** and **Mahāvīra**, the first and last Tīrthaṅkaras of this era, practiced nudity for most of their mendicant lives. At the time of renunciation, they were given a special cloth, called a deva-dūṣya, which they wore for approximately one year until it was accidentally lost. Today, all Śvetāmbara monks and nuns wear mendicant garments. However, during the time of Mahāvīra, monks had the option of practicing total nudity if they adopted a mode of mendicancy called **jina-kalpa**.

Digambaras believe that all Tīrthaṅkaras and all of their male mendicant followers practiced nudity. According to Digambaras, this vow entails the renunciation of all possessions, including clothing. In taking the mahāvratas, a Digambara monk (**muni**) renounces the wearing of all clothing and practices total nudity for the rest of his life. A Digambara nun (**āryikā**) takes the vow of non-possession in a modified form, and she wears a white sari. Therefore, she is classified as an advanced celibate **layperson** in the 11th **pratimā**. In spite of their strict interpretation of this mendicant vow, by the 13th or 14th century, under increasing pressure from Muslim rulers, many Digambara monks had abandoned the practice of total nudity. Some wore clothing in public but continued to practice nudity while inside the monastery (**maṭha**). By the mid-19th century, the lineages of naked Digambara monks had died out, although there are scattered reports of a few naked monks living in isolation. In the early 20th century, the tradition of nudity for Digambara munis was revived though the self-initiation of three men: **Ādisāgara**, **Śāntisāgara**, and **Śāntisāgara Chāṇī**.

NUN. A term used for indigenous categories of **women** who have renounced the household life and have taken the mendicant vows (**mahāvratas**). In the **Śvetāmbara** tradition, this includes women with the title of **sādhvī** or **mahāsatī**. In the **Digambara** tradition, it includes women with the title of **āryikā**, who have taken the mendicant vow of non-possession (**aparigraha**) in a modified form because they are not permitted to renounce the wearing of clothing and practice **nudity**. Among Śvetāmbara **Terāpanthīs**, there is a class of female renouncers called **samaṇīs** who take the five mahāvratas but are given special dispensation to observe more relaxed rules that enable them to travel abroad. They are usually called "novices."

According to traditional Śvetāmbara accounts, the number of nuns in the **mendicant lineages** of the **Tīrthaṅkaras**, including those of **Pārśvanātha** and **Mahāvīra**, are approximately twice the number of **monks**. Although these numbers are not historically verifiable, this ratio is reflected in the population statistics of the Śvetāmbara mendicant community today. In this respect, Jains probably differed from the other **śramaṇa** traditions, the Buddhists and the **Ājīvikas**, who also had established communities of female renunciants. The reason for the relatively large number of nuns is unknown. In earlier times, it may have been associated with a man having more than one wife. In modern times, the decision to renounce the household life may be associated with prohibitions on widow remarriage, restrictions that marriage impose upon a woman, educational opportunities, female relatives who have renounced, and the respect shown for Jain nuns.

Traditionally, only two types of women were forbidden to receive initiation: those who were recognized as being pregnant and those who were very young (under eight years of age) or who had a small child. A woman is initiated by a monk or a male mendicant leader (**ācārya**), and she becomes part of his mendicant lineage. Today, in most lineages, nuns live in small groups under the leadership of a senior nun. In texts discussing rules of mendicant conduct (Chedasūtras), special regulations are imposed upon nuns in order to safeguard their vow of **celibacy**. These include a prohibition against traveling alone and special restrictions on the alms they are allowed to accept and the places where they are allowed to stay.

In the **mendicant hierarchy**, a nun is subordinate to a monk, irrespective of their mendicant ages (as counted from time of initiation) or office held. There is no mention in lineage records of nuns being appointed to the seniormost position of ācārya. Among the Śvetāmbara Terāpanthīs, there is one nun with the title of pramukhā who is the head of all Terāpanthī nuns. However, she is subordinate to the single male ācārya who leads the entire Terāpanthī community. In recent times, a few nuns have been granted more autonomy. A **Sthānakavāsī** nun named **Sādhvī Candanā** was appointed ācārya, and she initiates nuns into her lineage. Also, a Digambara nun named **Āryikā Jñānamatī** has initiated her own lay disciples.

It is difficult to know about the general education of nuns in the past or the role they might have played in the religious education of the lay community. According to tradition, nuns and women in general were forbidden from studying the *Dṛṣṭivāda*, although knowledge of this text had become extinct prior to the redaction of the Śvetāmbara **Āgamas**. There are only a handful of references in the colophons of **manuscripts** to nuns studying sacred texts. However, there are inscriptions at **Mathurā** from the pre-Kuṣāṇa and Kuṣāṇa periods (mid-2nd century B.C.E. through 3rd century C.E.) that refer to disciples of female mendicants, and **Haribhadra** recognized Yākinī Mahattarā as his "spiritual mother."

Today, there are sectarian differences regarding the canonical texts that are accessible to nuns. **Sthānakavāsīs** and Śvetāmbara **Terāpanthīs** make no distinction between monks and nuns. In the Śvetāmbara

Mūrtipūjaka Tapā Gaccha, nuns are permitted to study only certain canonical texts and are forbidden access to the Chedasūtras, where the faults and punishments associated with mendicant conduct are recorded. In some mendicant lineages today, a nun is permitted to give public sermons (**pravacana**) and in others she may not. In some cases, this may be a matter of demographics. For example, in the **Kharatara Gaccha**, there are few monks, and nuns are permitted to preach. In the Tapā Gaccha, the number of monks is much greater, and it is not customary for nuns to preach.

In recent times, more emphasis has been placed on the education of nuns. **Sādhvī Mṛgāvatī** (1926–1986) was one of the first nuns in the Śvetāmbara tradition to be given permission to be educated by **paṇḍits**, and she was an advocate for the education of women. At the suggestion of **Ācārya Tulsī** a boarding school was established in 1948 at Ladnun for the education and training of young women who wanted to be initiated as Śvetāmbara Terāpanthī nuns.

NYĀYATĪRTHA, CAINSUKHDĀS JAIN (1899–1969). Digambara paṇḍit. Born in the village of Bhadva near Jaipur, Rajasthan, he attended Syādvāda Jain Mahāvidyālaya, **Banaras**, where he studied under Paṇḍit Ambādās Śāstrī. After passing the Nyāyatīrtha and Sāhityācārya examinations, he was appointed headmaster of Jain Vidyālaya, Kuchaman, in 1919. He became principal of the Digambara Jain Sanskrit College, Jaipur, in 1931, where he remained for 38 years. He trained a number of scholars and paṇḍits, including Dr. Kastūrcandra Kāsliwāl and Dr. Kamalcandra Sogānī. Nyāyatīrtha was editor of the periodicals *Jain Darśana*, *Jain Bandhu*, and *Vīr Vāṇī*, and the author of several works, including *Jain Darśanasāra*.

NYĀYAVIJAYA, MUNI (1890–1970). Śvetāmbara Mūrtipūjaka scholar-**monk** of the **Tapā Gaccha**. He was born in Mandal, Gujarat, and was named Narasiṃha. He studied in a Jain school established there in 1903 by Dharmavijaya (later, **Ācārya Vijayadharmasūri**) and then went to **Banaras** for advanced studies. In 1906, he and four other students who were disciples of Dharmavijaya were initiated by him in Calcutta. He is the author of some 17 books in Gujarati and 23 in Sanskrit, including *Adhyātmatattvāloka* and *Nyāyakusumāñjali*. For his work on logic and philosophy he was awarded the Nyāyaviśārada degree in 1910. In 1918, he wrote his most famous work, *Jaina Darśana*, which has been translated into English as *Jaina Philosophy and Religion*.

– O –

OCCUPATIONS. The contrast between the extreme ascetic poverty of Jain **mendicants** and the affluence of a number of their lay followers has been noted by scholars in recent times. While the focus of a mendicant's life is on liberation (**mokṣa**) from the cycle of rebirth (**saṃsāra**), the focus of a **layperson**'s life is on well-being, which includes auspiciousness, good fortune, welfare, health, gain, merit, prosperity, and wealth. Financial success is seen as a reward for past and present good deeds. For a layperson, the accumulation of wealth provides an opportunity of accumulating merit (**puṇya**) through religious gifting (**dāna**). If a person decides to renounce the household life, the greater the wealth, the greater is the virtue of renunciation. Historically, Jains often have been from **castes** associated with trading communities (**Vaiśya** or Bania). Lists of recommended occupations are found in medieval texts on lay conduct (**śrāvakācāra**). The **Śvetāmbara** lists mention trade, the practice of traditional medicine, (including astrology and divination), agriculture, artisanal crafts, animal husbandry, and service to a ruler. **Digambara** lists mention trade, clerical occupations, agriculture, artisanal crafts, and military occupations. Commerce is regulated by lists of forbidden occupations, which include trade in destructive articles, such as weapons, trade in timber, earning a livelihood from charcoal and so forth. Historically, more Jains have engaged in agriculture in south India than in the north, and trade has been the preferred occupation because it entails less harm (**hiṃsā**) than other ways of earning a livelihood. Military occupations should be understood in the context of occupational **caste**. While trade in weapons is forbidden for a businessman, a man who belongs to a caste that bears arms (**Kṣatriya**) may retain them if it is essential to his livelihood.

OGHĀ. *See* RAJOHARAṆA.

OḶĪ (Skt., AVALĪ). **Śvetāmbara festival** devoted to the worship of the **siddhacakra** observed primarily by **women** to ensure the health of their husbands. It takes place twice a year on the seventh through the 15th days of the bright half of Caitra (March/April) and Āśvina (September/October). On this series (avalī) of nine days, one of the nine petals (padas) of the siddhacakra is worshipped, and **mendicants** give sermons (**pravacana**) about the symbolism of each petal. The story of

King Śrīpāla, who was cured from leprosy by his wife's austerities, also is recited. Some undertake an **āyambil fast**, which entails eating only certain bland foods.

OṂ. A sacred syllable or **mantra** also written as Auṃ. In Jainism, this sound is associated with the epithet for those addressed in the **Namaskāra Mantra**. "A" is associated with **Arhats**, with liberated **souls (siddhas)** that are disembodied (aśarīra), and with mendicant leaders (**ācāryas**). "U" is associated with preceptors (**upādhyāyas**). "M" is associated with mendicants (**munis**).

– P –

PACCAKKHĀṆA. *See* PRATYĀKHYĀNA.

PADMANĀBHA. *See* MAHĀPADMA.

PADMĀVATĪ. A **goddess** who is the **yakṣī** of **Pārśvanātha**. She is the consort of **Dharaṇendra**, the king of the nāgakumāra gods, who is Pārśva's yakṣa. She may be identified by her hooded canopy. Her name is first found on sculptures in association with Pārśva around the 10th century C.E. In medieval times, she became the most popular goddess in Karnataka, where she was the lineage goddess (kuladevī) of several local ruling families. The **pilgrimage** site of **Hombuja** (Humcha), Karnataka, is popular among **Digambaras** because of a famous **image** of Padmāvatī located there. In medieval times, she was one of the goddesses that was worshipped in **tantric** rituals. *Bhairava Padmāvatī-kalpa,* composed by the Mallaṣeṇasūri in 1057 C.E. in Karnataka, is a Digambara tantric text that describes rituals for her worship.

PALITANA. *See* MOUNT ŚATRUÑJAYA.

PAÑCAKALYĀṆAKA. See KALYĀṆAKA.

PAÑCANAMASKĀRA MANTRA. *See* NAMASKĀRA MANTRA.

***PAÑCĀSTIKĀYA*.** *See* KUNDAKUNDA.

PAṆḌIT (PUNDIT). Literally, "learned one." Within the **Śvetāmbara Mūrtipūjaka** tradition, up until the early 19th century, the term paṇḍit was a level within the **mendicant hierarchy**, and was the equivalent of what is now a **paṅnyāsa**. In the **Digambara** tradition in former times, the term paṇḍit overlapped with pāṇḍe and referred to a lay ritual specialist under a **bhaṭṭāraka**. Today, paṇḍit is the term used for a scholar who is educated in the traditional manner and who has studied the religious texts of one or more of the Jain sectarian traditions. With the virtual disappearance of naked **monks** (**munis**) in the Digambara tradition in medieval times and the rejection of bhaṭṭārakas by segments of the Digambara community in north India in the 17th and 18th centuries, paṇḍits became the intellectual leaders, especially among the Digambara **Terāpanthīs**.

In the late 19th and early 20th centuries, a number of **educational institutions**, or pāṭhśālās, were established by the Śvetāmbara and Digambara lay communities. Some who attended these schools trained to become paṇḍits. They studied grammar, philosophy, and logic, took examinations, and were awarded Nyāyācārya, Nyāyatīrtha, Sāhityācārya, and Śāstrī degrees. Although the center of intellectual activity was **Banaras**, where the Śvetāmbara Yaśovijaya Jain Pāṭhśālā and the Digambara Syādvāda Jain Mahāvidyālaya had been established, paṇḍits taught in Jain educational institutions throughout India, and they trained both lay and mendicant scholars. Some were instrumental in movements to publish the Jain **scriptures** in printed form. In the latter half of the 20th century, there was a sharp decline in the number of Śvetāmbara and Digambara paṇḍits.

PĀÑJRĀPOḶ (PINJRAPOLE). Shelter for animals. In accordance with the principles of non-harming (**ahiṃsā**) and compassion for life (jīvadayā), Jains have built shelters where animals, including those that are sick, disabled, or economically useless, can live out their natural life span. Food is provided for them, and they may receive some medical care. Many of these animals are bought with funds set aside to save them from being slaughtered. In addition to shelters for cows and other domesticated animals, pāñjrāpoḷs often include a separate bird sanctuary. Although they are scattered throughout India, pāñjrāpoḷs are concentrated in Gujarat, with fewer in Rajasthan and Maharashtra. The antiquity of this institution is not known, but traveler accounts from the 16th century C.E. mention them. They are supported by merchants associations (mahājan), which may include Hindus as well as Jains. The Ahmedabad Pinjrapole Society has account books dating from 1758, and the Pāṭan Mahāman Pāñjrāpoḷ was started in the 1850s. **Śvetāmbara Terāpanthīs** reject the notion that pāñjrāpoḷs have any religious function and that donating to support them is a form of religious gifting (**dāna**) that results in the accumulation of merit (**puṇya**).

PAṄNYĀSA. Scholar. A title given today to learned **monks** in the **Śvetāmbara Mūrtipūjaka** community who are below the rank of **ācārya**. Today, this position may be combined with that of the **gaṇin**. *See also* MENDICANT HIERARCHY.

PARAMĀTMAN. The highest **soul** or Supreme Soul. A soul (**ātman**) that has attained liberation (**mokṣa**) from the cycle of rebirth (**saṃsāra**) through its own efforts. A synonym for a **siddha**. In Jainism, paramātman does not mean the Universal Soul or a soul that has never been bound in saṃsāra.

PARAMEṢṬHIN. Supreme divinity, one who is worthy of worship. In Jainism, there are five categories of supreme divinities: enlightened teachers (**Tīrthaṅkara** or **Arhat**), disembodied liberated **souls (siddha)**, mendicant leaders (**ācārya**), mendicant preceptors (**upādhyāya**), and **mendicants (sādhu)**.

PARIVĀR(A). Literally, "family." A term used by **Śvetāmbara Mūrtipūjakas** for a group of mendicants within a sublineage (**samudāya**) that follows one mendicant leader (**ācārya**). The parivār is named after the current ācārya. Within a parivār there are usually no more than two or three dozen **monks** and three or four dozen **nuns**. Parivārs may be subdivided into smaller temporary groups especially during the four-month rainy season period (**cāturmāsa**).

PĀRŚVANĀTHA (ca. 950–850 B.C.E.). The 23rd **Tīrthaṅkara** of this era, who according to tradition lived approximately 250 years prior to **Mahāvīra**. Born in **Banaras**, his parents were King Aśvasena and Queen Vāmā. According to **Śvetāmbaras**, he renounced the household life after marrying Prabhāvatī, but according to **Digambaras** he never married. After renunciation, he experienced various calamities, including a torrential rain caused by a demigod (asurakumāra) who had been his enemy in past lives. **Images** of Pārśva show him being sheltered from the downpour by a canopy formed from the expanded snake-hood of **Dharaṇendra**, king (**Indra**) of the nāgakumāra gods. He attained liberation (**mokṣa**) on **Mount Sammeta**.

The fourfold community (**saṅgha**) of **monks (sādhus)**, **nuns (sādhvīs)**, **laymen (śrāvakas)**, and laywomen (**śrāvikās**) that he established apparently flourished for hundreds of years. It is said that Mahāvīra's parents were followers of Pārśva. Śvetāmbara canonical texts contain passages in which **mendicant** disciples of Pārśva and those of Mahāvīra discuss differences in their mendicant praxis. Although many of Pārśva's disciples joined the mendicant community established by Mahāvīra, it is possible that some may have maintained their independence for quite some time. There are passages in Buddhist texts from the 5th century C.E. about mendicants in south India who observed the fourfold restraint (**cātuyāma-saṃvara**) associated with Pārśva.

Most scholars today accept the historicity of Pārśva. In accordance with the revised later dating of the **Buddha** and thus of his contemporary Mahāvīra as proposed recently by some scholars, Pārśva's dates would be approximately 100 years after the traditional dating.

PĀRŚVANĀTHA-JAYANTĪ. Festival celebrating the birth of **Pārśvanātha**. It falls on the 10th day of the dark half of the month of Pauṣa (December/January) and thus also is called Poṣ Tenth. **Images** are decorated with special ornamentations, and during evening worship a special 108-wick lamp may be used for the lamp ceremony (**āratī**). In the **Śvetāmbara** tradition, a **mendicant** recites the life story of Pārśvanātha. At this time, some observe a three-day **fast** known as Aṭhṭham.

PARYUṢAṆA. Rainy-Season **Festival**. Honoring the cultivation of religious restraints, this is the most important event in the **Śvetāmbara** ritual calendar. This eight-day festival begins either on the 12th or 13th day of the dark half of Śrāvaṇa (July/August). During this time, many Jains observe some form of voluntary **dietary restrictions**. They may vow to eat only once a day, or **fast** completely on the first and last days. Some spend the entire time in the company of **mendicants**, eating nothing and drinking only boiled water. In this way, for a short time, a **layperson**'s discipline becomes closer to that of a mendicant's. Mendicants give a daily sermon and recite the ***Kalpa Sūtra***. The auspicious moments of the conception and birth of **Mahāvīra** are celebrated by laypeople. The final day is the most sacred day of the year for Śvetāmbaras. Most fast and perform the annual ceremony of communal confession (**saṃvatsarī-pratikramaṇa**). *See also* DAŚA-LAKṢAṆA-PARVAN.

PAṬEL, AMBĀLĀL (DĀDĀ BHAGAVĀN) (1907–1988). A non-Jain **layman** who taught a syncretic blend of Jainism and Hinduism. The question of whether or not his teachings are part of Jainism remains a controversial issue. Born in Tarasali, a village near Baroda, into a Vaiṣṇava Pāṭidār family, he was raised in the village of Bhadran in central Gujarat. Shortly after the death of his two young children in 1928 and 1930, he became acquainted with the teachings of **Śrīmad Rājacandra** and with Jain philosophy. Together with this wife, he took a vow of lifelong **celibacy (brahmacarya)** in 1937. He claimed that in 1958 he had an experience of spontaneous self-realization in which he attained knowledge of the Self (ātma-jñāna). He stated that Dādā Bhagavān, the Lord for the Salvation of World, who exists in everyone in a latent form, becomes fully manifested in a person with knowledge of the Self (jñāni-puruṣa) and that such a person becomes a living instrument for Dādā Bhagavān. His followers believe that he could cause others to attain a proper view of reality (**samyak-darśana**), or to experience a sudden insight into the true nature of the Self. The first public performance of the rite of knowledge (jñāna vidhi), through which this insight is bestowed, took place in Bombay in 1968, and it attained its present form in 1983. Beginning in 1968, A. M. Paṭel taught his insights to others and referred to himself as the Jñāni, or the Self-realized Knower, who had directly experienced the difference between the self (puruṣa) and non-self (prakṛti).

A. M. Paṭel advocated the path of stepless acquisition of knowledge of the Self, known as the Akram Vijñān Mārg. It does not entail penances (**tapas**) or renunciation of the household life but offers a direct route to liberation (**mokṣa**) through the grace (kṛpā) of **Sīmandhara Svāmī**, a **Tīrthaṅkara** who is presently living on the continent of **Mahāvideha**, and who could be accessed through Paṭel, who served as his medium (nimitta). Paṭel's teachings emphasize the necessity of direct contact with a living Jñāni for the realization of the true nature of the Self, which cannot be attained through **scriptures** or **mendicants**. His followers believe that the devotees of the Jñāni and thus of Sīmandhara Svāmī will be reborn in not more than two lifetimes on Mahāvideha, where liberation is always possible.

The lay movement that grew out of his teachings, called the Akram Vijñān Mārg, first developed in Bombay and Baroda in the late 1960s and 1970 and spread throughout southern Gujarat and Maharashtra and among the Gujarati diaspora communities in East Africa, the United Kingdom, and North America. Most of the leaders of the movement are engineers, merchants, and medical doctors, and most of its followers in

India are members of the urban working classes. It includes a small group of celibate **laypeople** who are called āptaputras and āptaputrīs. Nīrubahen Amīn (born 1944) was instrumental in the development of this movement by formalizing the initiation ritual, creating **pūjā** rituals, promoting the construction of **temples** for the worship of Sīmandhara Svāmī, and publishing Paṭel's discourses under the title *Āptavāṇī* ("Words of Truth"). Worship includes the recitation of a modified version of the **Namaskāra Mantra**, which includes homage to Kṛṣṇa and Śiva, and the recitation of Nav Kalamo ("Nine Precepts"), a prayer to Dādā Bhagavān, which is said to contain the essence of all scriptures. In 1980, A. M. Paṭel agreed to the construction of a temple near Surat for the worship of images of Sīmandhara Svāmī, Kṛṣṇa, and Śiva, which was consecrated in 1993.

Shortly after the death of A. M. Paṭel in 1988, the movement split into two factions. One is led by Kanubhāī K. Paṭel, who was the person closest to A. M. Paṭel prior to 1978. Nīrubahen Amīn, the second chief disciple of A. M. Paṭel, is the leader of the other faction. She is the most popular leader of this movement today, especially in the diaspora. A complex called Sīmandhar City, where she resides, is being constructed in the village of Adalaj, near Ahmedabad, Gujarat. The Trimandir located here, which houses an image of Sīmandhara Svāmī in the central sanctum and images of Kṛṣṇa and Śiva in side sanctums, was dedicated in 2002. The followers of A. M. Paṭel publish two periodicals, *Akram Vijñān* and *Dādāvāṇī*.

PĀVĀPURĪ. Pilgrimage site near Patna, Bihar, where **Mahāvīra** attained liberation (**mokṣa**). A **temple** containing the footprint image (pādukās) of Mahāvīra is located here. Because the **image** is not iconographic, both **Digambaras** and **Śvetāmbaras** worship in the same temple. This site is a popular place to celebrate the anniversary of Mahāvīra's liberation (mokṣa), which coincides with the **festival** of **Dīvālī**.

PERCEPTION. *See* DARŚANA.

PILGRIMAGE. Journey to a sacred place (**tīrtha**) is called yātrā in Sanskrit. Pilgrimage has been a common practice throughout the history of Jainism for both **mendicants** and **laypeople**. Organizing and financing a large pilgrimage for those who cannot afford it is a way for wealthy and devout Jains to gain merit (**puṇya**). There are three categories of fixed sacred sites: (1) places where **Tīrthaṅkaras** attained final liberation (nirvāṇa-bhūmi), (2) places where **kevalins** attained final liberation (tīrtha-kṣetra), and (3) places where miraculous events in the lives of famous **monks** occurred (atiśāya-kṣetra). A place may become a temporary locus of pilgrimage while an eminent monk or **nun** is residing there. Monks and nuns are sometimes called "walking tīrthas." Laypeople go on pilgrimage to be in the presence of eminent mendicants, for the reverential sight of them **(darśana)** and to hear them preach, especially during the four-month rainy season period **(cāturmāsa)**. People also go on pilgrimages to sites where **images** of powerful non-liberated deities are located. *See also* HOMBUJA; JAISALMER; MAHĀVĪRJĪ; MOUNT ĀBŪ; MOUNT GIRNĀR; MOUNT SAMMETA; MOUNT ŚATRUÑJAYA; MŪḌBIDRĪ; PĀVĀPURĪ; RĀṆAKPUR; ŚAṄKHEŚVARA; ŚRAVAṆA BEḶGOḶA; TĀRAṄGĀ.

PIÑCHĪ. A small fan-shaped whisk broom used by **Digambara mendicants** and advanced lay renunciants (**kṣullakas/kṣullikās** and **ailakas**) to sweep the area before sitting or lying down to prevent harming insects and minute forms of life. It is made from naturally shed peacock tail feathers, which are attached to a short handle. *See also* RAJOHARAṆA.

PINJRAPOLE. *See* PĀÑJRĀPOḶ.

POṢADHA (POṢADHOPAVĀSA-VRATA). One of four vows of spiritual discipline of a **layperson (śikṣā-vratas)**. It is considered to be an extension of the ritual of attainment of equanimity **(sāmāyika)** from the minimum period of 48 minutes to 12 or 24 hours. During this time, a layperson becomes like a **mendicant**, and care must be taken not to harm any insects or minute forms of life. In addition to withdrawing from household activities, one vows to **fast** by abstaining from all food and water. Some observe this vow on a specific day each week, or on the four holy (parvan) days (the eighth and the 14th days of the moon's waxing and waning periods). More often, it is observed during **Paryuṣaṇa** (Śvet.) or **Daśa-Lakṣaṇa-Parvan** (Dig.), sometimes for one day, and sometimes for the entire period (eight days for **Śvetāmbaras**, 10 days for **Digambaras**). For lengthier observances, a layperson often stays in a dwelling-hall (**upāśraya**, sthānaka) with mendicants of the same **gender**. *See also* VRATA.

PRADAKṢIṆA. *See* CIRCUMAMBULATION.

PRASĀD, SĪTAL. *See* SĪTAL PRASĀD, BRAHMACĀRĪ.

PRATIKRAMAṆA. Confession of, and repentance for, faults that one has committed or for infractions of one's vows. It often is linked with an avowal of past transgressions (ālocanā). It is one of six obligatory duties (**āvaśyakas**) for a **mendicant** and a recommended practice for a **layperson**. There are different types of confession, which are based on the period of time to which the confession refers: (1) confession performed at nightfall covering the past day, (2) confession performed at dawn covering the past night, (3) confession covering the past half month, (4) the past four months, (5) and the past year. Mendicants perform all of these confessions. Some laypeople may perform this ritual on a daily basis but most do so less frequently. It is more common for laypeople to perform the evening confession during the four-month rainy season period (**cāturmāsa**), especially during **Paryuṣaṇa** (Śvet.) or **Daśa-Lakṣaṇa-Parvan** (Dig.). Most Jains participate in the annual ceremony of communal confession (Śvet., **saṃvatsarī-pratikramaṇa**; Dig., kṣamāpaṇā), which is performed on the final day of Paryuṣaṇa or Daśa-Lakṣaṇa-Parvan. It is performed in the presence of a mendicant, if possible, or sometimes in front of an **image** of a **Tīrthaṅkara**.

For each of these rituals, there are slight differences in the formulae, which end with the Prākrit phrase "tassa micchā me dukkaḍam," usually written as "micchāmi dukkaḍam" (Skt., "tasya mithyā me duṣkṛtam"). This has been translated is various ways: "May that fault have been done in vain" (i.e., have no effect; "May all my improper actions be inconsequential"; "My fault has been due to error"; or "May all my transgressions be forgiven"). One asks forgiveness from all living beings with this verse: "I ask pardon of all living beings, may all of them pardon me, may I have friendship with all beings and enmity with none." Confessional verses have been incorporated into other rites. For example, the formula for repentance for harm caused to all living beings is recited at the beginning of venerating images of the Tīrthaṅkaras (**caitya-vandana**).

PRATILEKHĀ (PRATILEKHANĀ). Inspection by **mendicants** of their clothing and implements, such as bedding, mouth cloth (**muhpattī**), whisk broom (**rajoharaṇa** or **piñchī**), alms bowls, and books, for any insects that might be trapped in them. If found, they are gently removed and deposited in a spot where they will not be harmed. This ritual is performed three times a day: after sunrise, in the late afternoon, and before sunset.

PRATIMĀS. Eleven stages of renunciation for a **layperson** whereby 12 **lay vows**, namely, the five **aṇuvratas**, the three **guṇa-vratas**, and the four **śikṣā-vratas**, are practiced with increasing rigor, culminating in a state just short of full mendicancy. (*See* appendix.)

PRATIVĀSUDEVA (PRATINĀRĀYAṆA, PRATIŚATRU). One of the five categories of the 63 illustrious men (**śalākā-puruṣas**) in **Universal History** texts and other Jain narratives. Each is a personification of the forces of evil and an enemy of one of the **Vāsudevas**. After being killed by a Vāsudeva, they are reborn in one of the hells. In **Bharata-kṣetra** (the part of the universe where we are said to live), nine Prativāsudevas are born in each progressive and regressive half-**cycle of time**. In this era, they were (1) Aśvagrīva, (2) Tāraka, (3) Meraka, (4) Madhukaiṭabha, (5) Niśumbha, (6) Bali, (7) Praharaṇa, (8) Rāvaṇa, and (9) Jarāsandha. See **Vāsudeva** for the Jain hero opposed by each Prativāsudeva.

PRATYĀKHYĀNA (Pkt. PACCAKKHĀṆA). A formal statement of intent to engage in a religious action for a specific period of time. It is one of the six obligatory duties (**āvaśyakas**) of a **mendicant** and is a recommended practice for a **layperson**. This vow usually is taken in front of the **image** of a **Tīrthaṅkara** or a mendicant during the performance of another rite. For example, during the evening confessional ritual (**pratikramaṇa**), a mendicant vows to renounce all food and water from sundown until 48 minutes after sunrise. It is often taken in the context of **fasting** or observing specific **dietary restrictions**. *See also* VRATA.

PRAVACANA (VYĀKHYĀNA). A spiritual discourse given by a **mendicant** or advanced **layperson**. During the eight months when mendicants travel regularly, they give sermons when requested by the laity, usually when they first arrive in a new town. During the four-month rainy season period (**cāturmāsa**) when mendicants do not travel, a sermon is given daily, usually by the seniormost mendicant of the group in residence. In this case, sermons may be a continuing series of lectures on one or two texts. Within most **Śvetāmbara Mūrtipūjaka mendicant lineages (gacchas)**, **nuns** are not allowed to preach. However, **sādhvīs** of the Mūrtipūjaka **A(ñ)cala Gaccha** and **Kharatara Gaccha**, as well as **Sthānakavāsī** and the Śvetāmbara **Terāpanthī** sādhvīs, are permitted to give sermons. **Digambara āryikās** and advanced laypeople also are permitted to preach. Sermons usually last for one or two periods of 48 minutes, which corresponds to the unit of time that a layperson may take the temporary vow of attaining inner tranquility (**sāmāyika**).

PRAVACANASĀRA. *See* KUNDAKUNDA.

PRAVARTINĪ. The title of a **nun** who has the authority over several small groups of nuns, each of which is headed by a **guruṇī**. Today, this is an honorary position in the **Śvetāmbara Mūrtipūjaka** community. In practice, it is the guruṇīs who have the decision-making authority for groups of nuns. This rank no longer exists among **Sthānakavāsīs**, and it has never existed among Śvetāmbara **Terāpanthīs** and **Digambaras**. *See also* MENDICANT HIERARCHY.

PREKṢĀ-DHYĀNA. Concentration of perception. A form of **meditation** introduced in 1975 by the **Śvetāmbara Terāpanthī Ācārya Mahāprajña**. It involves engaging the mind in the perception of the subtle, internal, innate phenomena of **consciousness** in order to purify the mind from emotions and the contamination of passions (**kaṣāyas**). This brings about equanimity, peacefulness, and well-being. Like Insight Meditation in Buddhism, the basic techniques are not founded on any specific theological beliefs and can be practiced by anyone, irrespective of faith. The meditation involves relaxation of the body and concentration on breathing, awareness of sensations of the body, and perception of psychic centers (cakras) and psychic colors (**leśyās**). However, another aspect of this meditation, concentration of thought, incorporates the teachings of Jainism. It includes repeated recitation of sacred utterances (**mantras**) and focused contemplation on one of the eternal truths of Jainism (**anuprekṣā**), such as impermanence or solitariness of existence. Writings about prekṣā dhyāna emphasize the scientific basis for relaxation techniques and autosuggestion that are used to reduce tensions and bring about physical and mental well-being.

PREMĪ, NĀTHŪRĀM (1881–1960). Digambara paṇḍit. Born in Devri, Madhya Pradesh, he was a teacher in Nagpur, Maharashtra. In 1901, he became the editor of the journal *Jain Mitra* in Bombay (now Mumbai). He also edited *Jaina Hitaiṣi* and *Jaina Grantha Ratnākara*. In 1912, he established the Hindi Grantha Ratnākara, the first publisher of Hindi books in western India. He was the general editor of the Māṇikachandra Digambara Jain Granthamālā series. Along with **Hīrālāl Jain** and **Ādināth Upādhye**, Premī was instrumental in the publication of the

Ṣaṭkhaṇḍāgama. He is the author of a number of books, including *Jain Sāhitya aur Itihās* (Bombay, 1956) and a series of monographs on various Jain authors.

PUDGALA. Matter. The non-sentient material substance (**dravya**), which is characterized by the qualities (**guṇas**) of color, taste, smell, and palpability. At its most basic level, matter is composed of indivisible units called "paramāṇus," often translated as "atoms." They join with other atoms, forming different types of aggregates (skandhas). Matter is classified into different categories in accordance with the grossness or subtleness of its aggregates. Earth, water, fire, air, sound, darkness, shade, light, and heat are all composed of different categories of matter. Other categories form various bodies. These include the gross physical body (audārika-śarīra) of animals and plants (**tiryañc**) and of humans, and the transformational body (vaikriya-śarīra) of heavenly beings (**devas**) and hell-beings (**nārakis**). The translocational body (āhāraka-śarīra), which may be formed by some advanced ascetics to travel to locations in the universe where a **Tīrthaṅkara** is currently preaching, is formed from more subtle aggregates of matter, as is the heat body (taijasa-śarīra), which maintains the vital temperature of an organism. The most subtle aggregates form a category of matter called **karma**, which binds with the **soul** (**jīva**), forming a karmic body (kārmaṇa-śarīra). The heat body and karmic body remain with the soul in its transmigration from life to life in the cycle of rebirth (**saṃsāra**) until liberation (**mokṣa**) is attained.

PŪJĀ. Honoring, worshipping. This term is used for ritual acts of honor or worship. Although all Jains worship the 24 **Tīrthaṅkaras**, there are differences in the rituals performed by Jains who follow the image-worshipping traditions and those who follow the non-image-worshipping traditions. There also are differences in rituals between **mendicants** and **laypeople**.

There are two basic types of ritual practices: external or material worship (dravya pūjā) and internal or mental worship (bhāva pūjā). Laity of image-worshipping traditions may perform rituals of external worship to **images** of Tīrthaṅkaras, to ancillary deities, such as **yakṣas/yaksīs**, and to images of deceased mendicant leaders. They may worship images in a home shrine or in a **temple**. In temple worship, there are daily rites of worship and more elaborate rites for special occasions. Among **Digambaras** in south India, a ritual specialist (**Jaina Brahmin**, **Upādhye**) performs some of the temple rituals on behalf of the laypeople. Mendicants, whose vows forbid them from possessing anything that could be offered, and laypeople both venerate the image of a Tīrthaṅkara by viewing it reverentially (**darśana**).

Internal or mental worship (bhāva pūjā) is performed by all Jains. In the image-worshipping traditions, this may be performed in front of an image of a Tīrthaṅkara. In non-image-worshipping traditions, mental worship is either performed at home or in a mendicant dwelling-hall (sthānaka). Mental worship may include singing hymns of praise to the Tīrthaṅkaras (**stavas** or stotras), the recitation of **mantras**, and **meditating** upon of the exemplary qualities of the Tīrthaṅkaras. *See also* ABHIṢEKA; AṢṬAKA PŪJĀ; AṢṬAPRAKĀRĪ PŪJĀ; MASTAKĀBHIṢEKA; MŪRTIPŪJAKA; SNĀTRA PŪJĀ.

PUJĀRĪ. A term used for a man who is employed as a ritual assistant in a **Śvetāmbara temple**. Although this term often is translated as temple-priest, in the Jain tradition pujārīs are regarded as temple servants. They prepare ingredients for worship, decorate and clean the **images** in the temple, and clean the temple precinct. Unlike priests in Hindu temples, they do not function as ritual mediators. They perform daily worship to a consecrated **Tīrthaṅkara** image only as a stand-in for absent Jains. They may assist laypeople in performing elaborate **pūjās** that are sponsored on special occasions. As part of their compensation, they receive the food that is offered to the Tīrthaṅkaras. Because Jains are forbidden from consuming this food, pujārīs are often from **Brahmin** or other high caste Hindu families. *See also* JAINA BRAHMIN; UPĀDHYE.

PŪJYAPĀDA. *See TATTVĀRTHA SŪTRA*.

PUNDIT. *See* PAṆḌIT.

PUṆYA. Merit. Actions that are beneficial or ethical and that cause a minimum of harm (**hiṃsā**) to other living beings bind varieties of **karmas** that cause well-being in this life (prosperity, health, and good fortune) and that cause rebirth in circumstances conducive to spiritual development. While mendicant practices focus on avoiding the binding of all karmic matter, lay practices focus on binding puṇya karmas and avoiding binding their opposite, non-meritorious (pāpa) karmas. Gifting (**dāna**) to worthy recipients by giving food and requisites to Jain **mendicants**, veneration of the Jinas (**vandana**), sponsoring **pilgrimages**, and the copying of sacred texts are examples of merit-making activities. Among image-worshipping traditions, sponsoring rituals and financing the construction and upkeep of temples are ways of accruing merit.

PUṆYAVIJAYA, MUNI (1895–1971). Śvetāmbara Mūrtipūjaka scholar-**monk** of the **Tapā Gaccha**. He was born in Kapadvanj, Gujarat, and was named Maṇilāl Doshi. He was educated in Bombay (now Mumbai). After the death of his father, both he and his mother decided to renounce the household life. In 1909, he was initiated by Muni Cāturvijaya, a disciple of Pravartaka Kāntivijaya and **Ācārya Vijayānandasūri**. A few days later his mother was initiated as Sādhvī Ratnaśrī. In addition to these learned monks, he had the guidance of Muni Haṁsavijaya and **Paṇḍit Sukhlāl Saṅghavī**.

The preservation of manuscripts in Jain **manuscript libraries** and the publication of Jain texts were the focus of his work. He and Muni Cāturvijaya edited the *Vasudevahiṇḍi* of Saṅghadāsa Gaṇin, a Jain version of the lost *Bṛhatkathākośa* of Guṇāḍhya, and the *Bṛhatkalpabhāṣya*. He and **Paṇḍit Dālsukh Mālvaṇiā** were the general editors for a critical edition of the Śvetāmbara canon, the Jaina Āgama Text series, that is being published by Mahāvīra Jaina Vidyālaya, Bombay (now Mumbai). He organized and catalogued the collections of manuscript libraries in several cities and prepared microfilms of rare manuscripts at **Jaisalmer**. His collection of some 10,000 manuscripts, which he donated to the L. D. Institute of Indology, Ahmedabad, and his publication of the *Catalogue of Palm-leaf Manuscripts in the Śāntinātha Jaina Bhaṇḍāra at Cambay* and the *Catalogue of Sanskrit and Prakrit Manuscripts in the Collections of Muni Puṇyavijayajī*, have been of great value to scholars, who have also benefited from his vast knowledge of Jain texts. He was honored by the Jain community with the title Āgama-Prabhākara ("Illuminator of the Sacred Texts"). A bibliography (in Hindi) of his works has been published in *Jñānāñjali* (Vadodara, Śrī Sāgara Gaccha Jain Upāśraya, 1969).

PŪRṆIMĀ GACCHA. Śvetāmbara Mūrtipūjaka mendicant lineage. It was established in either 1093 or 1103 C.E. by monks in the Candrakula, with Ācārya Candraprabhasūri as the first mendicant leader. It arose out of a long-standing dispute concerning whether the fortnightly performance of **pratikramaṇa** should be done on the 14th or 15th of the fortnight. While the majority of Śvetāmbara gacchas have maintained that the performance is properly on the 14th, the Pūrṇimā Gaccha argued that it should be observed on the days of the new moon and full moon (pūrṇimā). It also rejected the authority of the *Mahāniśītha Sūtra* and the performance of **upadhāna tapas** that is a central feature of this text. This **gaccha** produced many learned monks, and split into various subbranches. As of the late 20th century, seats of married **yatis** survived in Patan and Chanasma in north Gujarat.

PŪRVAS. A collection of 14 "ancient" texts in the Jain scriptural canon (**Āgama**), all of which are extinct. This term has been interpreted in several ways. A traditional view is that the chief disciples (**gaṇadharas**) of each **Tīrthaṅkara** compose these texts on the basis of the material that he taught to them first, which would constitute his oldest teachings. Historically, scholars have speculated that these texts contained some of the teachings of the 23rd Tīrthaṅkara, **Pārśvanātha**. These texts were never committed to writing and knowledge of them was gradually lost. **Śvetāmbaras** and **Digambaras** agree that **Bhadrabāhu I** (ca. 3rd century B.C.E.) was the last śrutakevalin, or person who knew all 14 Pūrvas. It is believed that portions of the Pūrvas were incorporated into the 12th **Aṅga**, the *Dṛṣṭivāda*, knowledge of which was also lost prior to the redaction of the Āgamas. The names and subject matter of the 14 Pūrvas have been preserved in extant Śvetāmbara and Digambara texts, although the authenticity of these accounts has been questioned by some scholars. Both Śvetāmbaras and Digambaras maintain that some of their canonical texts are based on portions of the Pūrvas.

PUṢPADANTA. *See ṢAṬKHAṆḌĀGAMA.*

– R –

RĀJACANDRA, ŚRĪMAD (1867–1901). Jain mystic and reformer. He was born in Vavania, Gujarat, and was named Rāycandbhāī Mehta (Raicandbhāī Mahetā). His father was from a Vaiṣṇava family, and his mother was a **Sthānakavāsī** Jain. When he was seven, he claimed to have attained memory of his previous births. He had extraordinary powers of concentration and memorization, which he displayed on occasion at public gatherings. He showed an early interest in religious matters, and by the age of 20 he had written on a variety of topics, including Jain philosophy. He was influenced by the writings of **Kundakunda** and other authors in the **Digambara** mystical tradition. His teachings emphasize the attainment of knowledge of the true nature of the innate inner **soul** (**ātman**) and experiencing its purity through **meditation**. Rājacandra criticized the sectarian nature of Jainism and its emphasis on rituals, but he did not reject image worship, viewing it as beneficial for those who were in the early stages of spirituality.

Although he was deeply devoted to his own spiritual development and that of his close followers, he never became a **mendicant**. Rājacandra was a jeweler by profession. Married at age 20, he was the father of three children. He believed that the householder's life was more arduous than that of a mendicant because of the inherent difficulties that it presented, and that it was appropriate for his own spiritual quest because it was brought about by his own **karma**. Toward the end of his life, after practicing severe austerities on a hill outside Idar in northern Gujarat, he declared to seven **Śvetāmbara monks** who had become his followers that he had attained direct knowledge of the inner soul. He died at the age of 34 in Rajkot, his body emaciated from the effects of **fasting** and illness.

During his short life, Rājacandra wrote more than two dozen books, including *Ātmasiddhi*, a summary of his views on Jainism that he wrote in one night in 1896. About 800 of his letters have been published, including three to Mohandās (Mahātmā) Gāndhī. In his autobiography, Gāndhī credits Rājacandra with restoring his faith in Hinduism. He advised Gāndhī to observe the duties and **dietary restrictions** ascribed to his merchant **caste**. His discussions of nonviolence (**ahiṃsā**) and compassion for all living beings influenced Gāndhī in his development of nonviolent means of resistance and his views on society. Following his death, a memorial shrine (samādhi mandir) was erected at Rajkot.

RĀJENDRASŪRI, ĀCĀRYA VIJAYA. *See* VIJAYARĀJENDRASŪRI, ĀCĀRYA.

RĀJĪMATI. Daughter of Ugrasena, King of **Mathurā**, who is known as Sutanu in the Hindu *Viṣṇu Purāṇa*. She decided to live a life of **celibacy** after **Neminātha** renounced the world just prior to their marriage. According to **Śvetāmbara** accounts, she rejected an offer of marriage by Nemi's younger brother, Rathanemi, and both took mendicant vows. She is considered to be an exemplar of moral conduct by vehemently rejecting the advances of Rathanemi during a chance encounter in a cave, where both had taken refuge in a rainstorm. Subsequently, they both attained liberation (**mokṣa**) along with Nemi at **Mount Girnār**. According to **Digambara** accounts, she took the vows of a **nun** (**āryikā**) and was reborn as a male god (**deva**) in the 16th heaven.

RAJOHARAṆA. A small whisk broom used by **Śvetāmbara mendicants** to sweep the area before sitting or lying down in order to avoid harming insects and minute forms of life. It is made of long strands of soft white wool that are attached to a short wooden handle. The handle is wrapped in a white cloth. Some **Mūrtipūjaka** mendicants first wrap the handle in a red cloth that is embroidered with the eight auspicious symbols (**aṣṭamaṅgala**). Some **laypeople** use a rajoharaṇa when performing certain rituals, such as **sāmāyika**. Mendicants with rajoharaṇas are represented on the bases of **Tīrthaṅkara images** from **Mathurā** (ca. 2nd century C.E.). Oghā is another name for this whisk broom. *See also* PIÑCHĪ.

RĀMACANDRASŪRI, ĀCĀRYA. *See* VIJAYARĀMACANDRASŪRI, ĀCĀRYA.

RĀṆAKPUR. In southern Rajasthan, the site of an ornate white marble **Śvetāmbara temple**, the Dharṇā Vihāra, commissioned by Dharṇā Śāh, a wealthy merchant and a minister to Rāṇā Kumbha. It was patterned after his dream of the assembly hall (**samavasaraṇa**) of **Ṛṣabha** located on the island-continent of **Nandīśvara**. Designed by a local architect named Depaka, construction was begun in 1391 C.E. The temple was consecrated in 1441 by Ācārya Somasundrasūri of the **Tapā Gaccha**. Although never completely finished, it was the largest Jain temple in premodern India with some 1,400 ornately carved columns and 108 subsidiary shrines. Although the Mughal emperor Akbar spared this temple from destruction, it eventually fell into decay. Extensive restoration undertaken by the Ānandjī Kālyanjī Trust was completed in 1944.

RATNACANDRA, MUNI (1879–1941). Śvetāmbara Sthānakavāsī scholar-**monk**. He was born in the village of Bharora in the Kathiawar region of Gujarat and was named Rājaśi Bhai Shah. At the age of 12, he began working with his brother in the family business and was married at 13. Three years later when his wife died in childbirth he left the household and began his study of Jain scriptures, philosophy, and logic with Gulābcandra of Limbdi. In 1896, he was initiated as Sant Ratnacandra. He wrote several books in Gujarati, including a work on Ardhamāgadhī grammar, and he taught **mendicants** Sanskrit, Prākrit, and the Jain **scriptures**. He was the editor of *An Illustrated Ardha-Māgadhī Dictionary* (1923) and wrote the Gujarati sections of this work. In his travels to Delhi and the Punjab, Ratnacandra noticed that the Ārya Samāj was well organized and thought that the Sthānakavāsī community would benefit from a similar organization. In 1934, he established the Sohan Jain Dharma Pracāraka Samiti (Missionary Society) in Amritsar, which later was moved to **Banaras** and renamed Pārśvanātha Mahāvidyāśrama. A collection of his articles has been published in *Ratna Gadya Mālikā*. A number of libraries and institutions have been established in his name.

RATNATRAYA. The Three Jewels. As stated in the opening verse of the *Tattvārtha Sūtra*, right faith (**samyak-darśana**) in the teachings of the omniscient **Jinas**, right knowledge (samyak-jñāna), and right conduct (samyak-cāritra) constitute the path to liberation (mokṣa-mārga). Another term for this triad is the Three Qualities (Guṇatraya).

REINCARNATION. *See* SAMSĀRA.

ṚṢABHA. The first **Tīrthaṅkara** of this era. He is also called Ādinātha, the First Lord. According to narrative accounts, Ṛṣabha was born near the end of the third period in the current regressive half-**cycle of time** (avasarpiṇī) when life was no longer idyllic. His father was Nābhi, one of the patriarchs (**kulakaras**) of this era, and his mother was **Marudevī**. He was appointed king by his father, and he organized the ruling class in society (**Kṣatriya** varṇa). Since people were transgressing the laws established by the earlier patriarchs, Ṛṣabha instituted further laws and punishments for their violations. He instructed the people about agriculture and various crafts and organized society into occupational **castes**. He taught the alphabets to his daughter Brāhmī and math to his daughter Sundarī. When he renounced the household life, he appointed his eldest son, **Bharata**, to succeed him as king, and he gave portions of his territory to his other sons, including **Bāhubali**. In a previous life, **Mahāvīra** was a grandson of Ṛṣabha named Marīci. According to the **Digambara** ***Mahāpurāṇa***, he and his son Bharata were the last patriarchs (kulakaras) of this era.

Śvetāmbaras believe that both Ṛṣabha and Mahāvīra practiced **nudity** for most of their **mendicant** lives. Śvetāmbaras and Digambaras agree that the mendicant followers of both Ṛṣabha and Mahāvīra observed the five great vows (**mahāvratas**). Ṛṣabha is said to have attained liberation (**mokṣa**) on **Mount Aṣṭāpada** (= Mount Kailāsa).

Ṛṣabha's symbol is the bull (Ṛṣabha means bull). Some think that he was worshipped in the Indus civilization where numerous seals with images of bulls have been found and also a nude image of a male standing in an erect posture similar to the meditative posture called **kāyotsarga**. Others have identified Ṛṣabha with the bull mentioned in vedic hymns (usually an epithet for Indra) or with a long-haired sage in *ūSI Veda* 10.136 (who is often associated with Śiva). In the Hindu *Bhāgavata-purāna*, Ṛṣabha is mentioned as a minor incarnation of the god Viṣṇu, which is indicative of his popularity in medieval times.

Unlike the other Tīrthaṅkaras, in early **images** Ṛṣabha is often depicted with locks of hair hanging on his shoulders. According to

Śvetāmbaras, he was asked by Śakra (**Indra**) not to remove the fifth handful of hair at the time of his renunciation. According to Digambaras, he removed his hair in five handfuls but it regrew later from performing austerities. *See also* KEŚA-LOÑCA.

– S –

SĀDHU. Literally, "virtuous man" or "one who has accomplished his goals." A general designation for a Jain **monk**. It is synonymous with **muni**, although this term is used more often for **Śvetāmbara** monks than for **Digambara** monks. *See also* MENDICANT HIERARCHY.

SĀDHVĪ. Literally, "virtuous **woman**" or "one who has accomplished her goals." A general designation for a **nun** in the **Śvetāmbara** tradition. *See also* MENDICANT HIERARCHY.

SĀDHVĪ PRAMUKHĀ. The title of the chief nun in the **Śvetāmbara Terāpanthī** tradition. She is subordinate to the male mendicant leader (**ācārya**), who is the head of the entire undivided mendicant community. She is responsible for making sure that the ācārya's decisions are implemented by **agragaṇyās**, who lead small groups of **nuns**. *See also* MENDICANT HIERARCHY.

SĀGARĀNANDASŪRI, ĀCĀRYA (1874–1950). Śvetāmbara Mūrtipūjaka Tapā Gaccha mendicant leader. Born in Kapadvanj, Gujarat, he and his elder brother Maṇilāl Gāndhī studied religious texts with relatives. After the initiation of his brother, he decided to renounce the household life. In 1890, over the objections of his in-laws, he was initiated as Muni Ānandasāgara by Muni Jhaverasāgara. In 1917, Ācārya Vimalakamalasūri installed him as Ācārya Sāgarānandasūri. He focused his activities on the preservation and publication of the Śvetāmbara **Āgamas**, and he established some 15 associations in cities like Udaipur and Surat for this purpose. Sāgarānandasūri had the 45 canonical texts inscribed on copper plates, which were deposited in the Āgama Mandir at Surat, and on marble slabs, which were deposited in the Āgama Mandir at Palitana. At a time when there was strong resistance to publishing the Āgamas among the more conservative members of the Śvetāmbara mendicant community, he edited the **manuscripts** with their traditional **commentaries** and published them in the Āgamodaya Samiti series and the

Śreṣṭhidevacandra Lālabhāī Jaina Pustakoddhāraka Phaṇḍa series. In all, he was responsible for the publication of some 87 titles in these two series. His efforts revived the study of the **scriptures** and their commentaries in India, and these scholarly editions have been instrumental in the research of Western scholars. For his work, he was known as Āgamoddhāraka ("The Restorer of the Scriptures").

ŚĀH, KAḌUĀ. *See* KAḌUĀ GACCHA.

ŚĀH, LOṄKĀ. *See* LOṄKĀ.

ŚAKRA. *See* INDRA.

ŚALĀKĀ-PURUṢAS. Illustrious men whose life stories are related in **Universal History** texts and other Jain narratives. Since the 9th century, there has been a standardized list of 63 śalākā-puruṣas who appear in each progressive and regressive half-**cycle of time** in **Bharata-kṣetra** (the part of the universe where we are said to live). These include 24 **Tīrthaṅkaras**, 12 **Cakravartins**, nine **Baladevas**, nine **Vāsudevas**, and nine **Prativāsudevas**. **Kulakaras** and **Kāmadevas** are also exemplary men, but they are not classified as śalākā-puruṣas.

SALLEKHANĀ. Religious death through **fasting**. As in other religious traditions of South Asia, the manner in which one dies is important in Jainism because one's mental state at the time of death could affect, positively or negatively, one's destiny in the next life. It is best to die in a calm mental state with a minimum of agitation and fear. In addition, those who live in accordance with the **lay vows** or the mendicant vows (**mahāvratas**) should try to avoid situations where the observance of them and of the daily obligatory rites (**āvaśyakas**) would be impossible. Therefore, under certain circumstances, when the spiritual benefits of dying would most likely outweigh any spiritual benefits that could be gained by maintaining the body, a person may choose to take the vow of sallekhanā, which entails a gradual withdrawal of food and liquids.

In observing sallekhanā, which means "thinning out" or "scouring out," there are external manifestations in emaciation of the body and internal manifestations in destroying **karma** bound with the **soul** (**jīva**), thereby reducing passions (**kaṣāyas**), which negatively affect concentration on spiritual matters. Jain commentators have emphasized that sallekhanā is not suicide because there are no passions associated with it and it is not done secretly. If possible, it is carried out with the guidance of a **mendicant**.

For a **layperson** today, this vow may be taken in the final stages of a terminal illness or when death is imminent. In the case of a mendicant, the reasons for undertaking this vow may include other factors associated with terminal illness or old age, such as blindness or the inability to walk, that would make it impossible to properly observe the mendicant vows. For example, a **Digambara monk (muni)** might choose to take this vow if he is no longer able to walk to a layperson's home to eat, to stand while eating, or to see well enough to inspect each handful of food. Fasting until death, which is called saṃthāra ("deathbed") by **Śvetāmbaras**, is not as common in the Śvetāmbara mendicant community, although in recent times it has been observed by some **Sthānakavāsī** and **Terāpanthī nuns**. Historically, there were several other reasons for observing this vow, including famine when appropriate food was impossible to obtain, and other calamities, such as warfare.

Originally, sallekhanā may have been undertaken only by mendicants. In the earliest texts, such as the ***Ācārāṅga Sūtra***, this practice is mentioned in the context of heroic monks whose physical or mental capacities had not declined and who performed this ritual in solitude without the guidance of a preceptor. Fasting until death is mentioned more frequently in inscriptions in the south, especially at **Śravaṇa Beḷgoḷa** in Karnataka. From the 7th to the 10th centuries, hundreds of memorials (niṣidhi) were erected here honoring mendicants whose lives ended in this manner, and from the 10th through the 15th centuries memorials were erected for laypeople. After the 12th century, this practice became less common and is seldom mentioned in inscriptions after the 15th century.

SAMAIYA PANTH. *See* TĀRAṆ SVĀMĪ PANTH.

SAMAṆ/SAMAṆĪ. The title of an intermediary class of novice **mendicants** in the **Śvetāmbara Terāpanthī** tradition established by **Ācārya Tulsī** in 1980. They take the five mendicant vows (**mahāvratas**) but are given special dispensation to use modern means of mechanized transport and communication, to travel abroad, and to eat food prepared especially for them. They do not wear a mouth cloth (**muhpattī**) over their mouths. Instead, they hold a small cloth in their hands and place it in front of their mouths while speaking. One can be a samaṇ or a samaṇī permanently, or one can later become a **sādhu** or a **sādhvī** with the permission of the **ācārya**.

SAMANTABHADRA (ca. 5th century C.E.). Digambara mendicant leader and logician. He is the author of the *Āptamīmāṃsā*, also called the *Devāgama Stotra*, a philosophical work of 114 verses written in stotra style. In discussing the subject of whether an omniscient being (**kevalin**) is a valid source of knowledge, he examines the nature of the **Tīrthaṅkara** and establishes that his authority rests on his perfect conduct (samyak-cāritra), on his teachings, and on an absence of passions (**kaṣāyas**). He uses the technique of **syādvāda** in his argumentation to establish the omniscience (**kevala-jñāna**) of the Tīrthaṅkara and to examine claims made by Buddhists for the **Buddha** and by theists for their God. Important **commentaries** on this work include the *Aṣṭaśatī* of **Akalaṅka** (8th century C.E.) and the *Aṣṭasahasrī* of Vidyānanda (9th century C.E.). He also wrote the *Svayambhū Stotra*, a hymn in praise of the 24 Tīrthaṅkaras, beginning with the first (**Ṛṣabha**), who here is called Svayambhū ("Self-existent"). The earliest Digambara work on lay conduct (**śrāvakācāra**), the *Ratnakaraṇḍa*, was authored by him.

SAMANTABHADRA, MUNI (1891–1988). Digambara monk. He was born in Karmole, near Solapur, Maharashtra, and was named Devcand Kāstūrcand Śāh. In 1911, a year after entering Wilson College in Bombay (now Mumbai), he heard Arjunlāl Seṭhī speak in Sangali. Along with several other students, he decided to participate in Arjunalāl's independence activities in Jaipur. When his friend Motīcand Jain was sentenced to death by the British, Devcand decided to dedicate his life to nonviolence (**ahiṃsā**).

After receiving a B.A. in 1917, he began studying the works of **Kundakunda** with **Bhaṭṭāraka** Vīrasena. At this time, he became interested in establishing boarding schools (gurukulas) for elementary and high school students. These schools became the focus of his activities for the rest of his life. He established two boarding schools in Karanja (Akola), Maharashtra: Mahāvīra Brahmacaryāśram in 1918 and Kuṅkubāī Jain Śrāvikāśram for **women**. In 1934, he established Bāhubalī Brahmacaryāśram at Kumbhoj (Kolhapur), Maharashtra.

It was during this time that he took **lay vows** of renunciation. In 1925, he took the vows of a **brahmacārī** and, in 1933, he was initiated as a **kṣullaka** by **Ācārya Śāntisāgara**. In 1952, at the age of 61, he took the vows of a naked **muni** at Bāhubalī (Kumbhoj) from Muni Vardhamānasāgara, a disciple of Ācārya Śāntisāgara. The first monk initiated by him in 1959, Muni Āryanandī, became the head of Pārśvanātha Jain Gurukula, which was founded in 1962 in Ellora. He died at Bāhubalī at the age of 97, where a footprint shrine (pādukā) has been erected in his memory.

SAMAVASARAṆA. Holy assembly hall where a **Tīrthaṅkara** preaches. Tradition holds that it is constructed by the gods soon after a Tīrthaṅkara attains omniscience (**kevala-jñāna**). In the center of this circular structure, there is a three-tiered dais with a jeweled lion throne where the Tīrthaṅkara sits, simultaneously facing all four directions. The area where the congregation gathers to listen to the Tīrthaṅkara's religious discourse encircles this. **Mendicants** assemble inside the first wall, along with the gods (**devas**). Animals assemble inside the second and third walls. In the environs of the assembly hall, there is no hostility or jealousy, and there is freedom from disease and any unpleasant sights characteristic of the profane world. The samavasaraṇa is an important feature of Jain art. Large-scale representations of this structure may be constructed at temple complexes, especially at important **pilgrimage** sites.

SAMAYASĀRA. *See* KUNDAKUNDA.

SĀMĀYIKA. This term is used in two contexts. (1) According to the **Śvetāmbara** ***Ācārāṅga Sūtra***, a single great vow of restraint called sāmāyika-cāritra was taken by **Mahāvīra** when he renounced the household life. It entails avoiding all harmful actions. According to the Digambara *Mūlācāra*, a vow of restraint called sāmāyika-saṃyama, which consists of refraining from all harmful actions, was taught by 22 of the 24 **Tīrthaṅkaras,** excepting the first and last, who teach the five **mahāvratas.** During initiation today, **mendicants** vow to observe sāmāyika at all times by constantly being aware of their actions and attentive to their mendicant vows (mahāvratas). (2) A ritual in which one strives to attain equanimity or tranquility of mind by the detachment of the senses from external objects; becoming one with the Self and attaining pure self-awareness. It is one of six obligatory duties (**āvaśyakas**) of a mendicant and one of the **śikṣā-vratas** of a **layperson**.

A layperson who takes a vow to practice this ritual three times a day (as mendicants do) attains the third **pratimā**. The recitations and ritualized gestures accompanying this rite vary in the different Jain traditions. In all cases, one vows to renounce all harmful actions and to remain in **meditation** for a period of 48 minutes. During this time, a layperson becomes like a mendicant, and extreme care is taken to avoid harming any insects or minute forms of life. Thus, a layperson, like a mendicant, carefully inspects the area before sitting, and some **Śvetāmbara** laypeople clean the area with a whisk broom (**rajoharaṇa**). A layperson may spend this time meditating, repeating a **mantra**, or listening to a sermon by a mendicant. Some recite from ritual manuals composed by mendicants called *Sāmāyika Sūtras*, which incorporate other rites, such as praising the 24 **Tīrthaṅkaras** (caturviṃśati-stava), veneration of mendicants (guru-**vandana**), and confession (**pratikramaṇa**). *See also* ČĀTUYĀMA-SAṂVARA; VRATA.

SĀMĀYIKA-VRATA. One of four vows of spiritual discipline of a layperson (**śikṣā-vratas**). One agrees to perform the ritual of attainment of equanimity (**sāmāyika**) on a regular basis. When performed once a day, it usually is done at sunset after the household activities are over. *See also* VRATA.

SAMITI. A set of five rules of conduct for a **mendicant** that entails extreme care in performing daily activities. (1) Care in walking (īryā-samiti) involves walking slowly and inspecting the path to avoid stepping on minute life-forms. (2) Care in speaking (bhāṣā-samiti) involves speaking only when necessary and being mindful about what one says. (3) Care in accepting alms (eṣaṇā-samiti) entails accepting only boiled water and food suitable for a mendicant and consuming it without enjoyment. (4) Care in picking things up and putting them down (ādāna-nikṣepaṇa-samiti) avoids harming minute life-forms. (5) Care in performing excretory functions (utsarga-samiti) entails selecting a place for toilet purposes that is free of living beings. By carefully observing these rules, the potential for harming living beings, even those with only one sense (**ekendriya**), is greatly reduced.

SAMMETA ŚIKHARA. *See* MOUNT SAMMETA.

SAMPRADĀYA. The term used by **Sthānakavāsīs** for **mendicant lineages** within their mendicant community. Today, the community is divided into 26 groups. Within the Northern tradition, or non-Gujarati **mendicants**, there are 13 independent groups who trace their lineage to Mūlacandra, one of Dharmadāsa's 22 leading **monks**. These groups are not headed by a chosen mendicant leader (**ācārya**) but by the monk with the highest monastic age. His main decisions must agree with those of the leader of the lay community (saṅghapati), a position that often is hereditary. Within the Central tradition, or Gujarati mendicants, there are 12 independent groups and also the centrally organized **Śramaṇa Saṅgha**. Each of these groups is headed by a chosen mendicant leader (ācārya). As of 1999, it was estimated that there were 3,223 Sthānakavāsī mendicants (533 monks and 2,690 **nuns**): 1,160 in the independent Northern tradition, 967 in the independent Central tradition, and 1,096 in the Śramaṇa Saṅgha. *See also* MENDICANT LINEAGES.

SAṂSĀRA. Literally, "wandering around," the cycle (of life). The term is used for the cycle of life, death, and rebirth. It is contrasted with its opposite, liberation from rebirth (**mokṣa**). From beginningless time, all **souls (jīvas)** have been bound in the cycle of rebirth by a type of extremely subtle matter called **karma**, which affects the qualities (**guṇas**) of the soul, and which causes embodiment of the soul in a series of rebirths. Until all karma has been removed from the soul, when the life span of the body comes to an end and the body dies, the soul will be born again in another body. One's destiny in the next life is determined when a specific type of karma, called life span (āyu) karma, is bound with the soul. Depending on the subvariety of this karma that is bound, rebirth will be in one of four states of existence: as a human being, a heavenly being (**deva**), a hell-being (**nāraki**), or as a plant or animal (**tiryañc**). In general, meritorious actions lead to an auspicious rebirth as a heavenly being, human being, or a five-sensed animal, and bad actions, especially those involving extreme volitional violence (**hiṃsā**), lead to an inauspicious rebirth as a hell-being or as a lower form of animal or plant life. At the time of **death**, the soul, housed in a subtle karmic body, leaves its gross physical body and within a few moments arrives at its locus of rebirth, where a new body is formed. In Jainism, rebirth is virtually instantaneous, and there is no intermediate state of existence like the bardo existence in Buddhism or the realm of the ancestors called the Pitṛ Loka in Hinduism. In Jainism, there is no **God**, Supreme Soul, or Ultimate Reality (brahman) that has never been bound in saṃsāra, although souls that have attained liberation may be called God (**deva**) or Supreme Soul (**paramātman**).

SAṂSKĀRA. A rite of consecration that serves as a rite of passage into a new status or phase of life. These rites of passage were first incorporated into a religious framework in the **Digambara** ***Ādipurāṇa*** by **Jinasena** (ca. 770–850 C.E.). The 16 Hindu saṃskāras were incorporated into this work as part of a list of 53 kriyās (actions). The portion of the kriyās that pertain to the householder lists a series of 23 rites that culminate in renunciation of the household life (equivalent to the 11th **pratimā**) and initiation into mendicancy (**dīkṣā**). These rites include the five essential elements of Hindu ritual: the presence of a deity, a priest to perform the ceremony, the use of **mantras**, ritual offerings, and sacred fire. However, the manner in which these rituals are performed is not identical with Hindu rituals nor is the symbolism of these five elements. For example, the three fires are sacred because of their contact with divine bodies during the cremation of the **Tīrthaṅkaras**, **gaṇadharas**, and **kevalins**. The mantras used are different (e.g., taking refuge in the Three Jewels, or **Ratnatraya**), and violence (**hiṃsā**) is reduced by restricting offerings to the Jinas to plants or dairy products. At a later time, **Śvetāmbaras** observed a series of 16 saṃskāras that are described in the *Ācāra-Dinakara* of Vardhamāna (1411 C.E.). The first 11 are associated with conception, birth, name giving, food giving, ear piercing, and the tonsure ceremony. The final five are associated with studentship, marriage, taking **lay vows**, and death. Which saṃskāras are performed today is a matter of custom, varying in different families and in different regions. For example, both Digambara and Śvetāmbara saṃskāras include an upanayana ceremony in which a boy is given a sacred thread with three strands representative of the Three Jewels. However, today this saṃskāra is observed only by some Digambaras living in south India. The ceremonies performed during each of the saṃskāras differ according to sectarian tradition and by region.

SAṂTHĀRA. In the **Śvetāmbara** tradition, the term used today for a voluntary religious death through fasting. *See* SALLEKHANĀ.

SAMUDĀYA. Literally, "those with the same origin" or "co-arising." A term used today by **Śvetāmbara Mūrtipūjakas** for an independent mendicant sublineage within a **gaccha**. Samudāyas are named after the deceased founding mendicant leader (**ācārya**), although people sometimes refer to the samudāya by the name of the current head. In general, each is headed by a chief teacher (gacchādhipati) who presides over other **mendicants**, including subordinate ācāryas. Samudāyas are further subdivided into **parivārs**. Geography, demographics, and the rise of charismatic leaders are factors in the formation of new samudāyas. *See also* MENDICANT LINEAGES.

SAṂVATSARĪ-PRATIKRAMAṆA. Annual ceremony of communal confession performed by **Śvetāmbaras**. It takes place on the final day of **Paryuṣaṇa**, either on the fourth or fifth day of the bright half of Bhādrapada (August/September). Most Śvetāmbaras **fast** on this day, and in the evening gather in the local **temple** or meditation hall (sthānaka), where they confess their transgressions with the words "tassa micchā me dukkaḍam," usually written as "micchāmi dukkaḍam," (Skt., "tasya mithyā me duṣkṛtam"). This has been translated in various ways: "May that fault have been done in vain" (i.e., have no effect); "May all my improper actions be inconsequential"; "My fault has been due to error"; or "May all my transgressions be forgiven." Forgiveness is asked of all living beings: "I ask pardon of all living beings; may all of them pardon me. May I have a friendly relationship with all beings, and unfriendly with none." At this time, Jains exchange requests for forgiveness with their relatives and friends, either in person or by telephone or mail. It is similar to the ceremony of kṣamāpaṇā, which is performed by **Digambaras** during **Daśa-Lakṣaṇa-Parvan**. *See also* PRATIKRAMAṆA.

SAṂVEGĪ SĀDHU. A **mendicant** who is focused on emancipation (**mokṣa**). A term for a **Śvetāmbara Mūrtipūjaka** mendicant who observes an itinerant lifestyle, performs the obligatory daily mendicant rituals (**āvaśyakas**), and does not own any property. Historically, their predecessors were groups of forest-dwelling monks (**vanavāsīs**) who criticized the practices of sedentary temple-dwelling monks (**caityavāsīs**). In all of the Mūrtipūjaka mendicant lineages (**gacchas**), there have been times when the sedentary mendicants, who in later times were known as **yatis**, have outnumbered the saṃvegī sādhus, and there have been repeated efforts to reform these lax mendicant practices. Mendicants who had been initiated as yatis could become saṃvegī sādhus in a ceremony called kriyoddhāra, literally, reform (uddhāra) of the rites (kriyā). It has been reported that some 500 **Tapā Gaccha monks** performed this rite in 1525. Reform efforts continued in the 17th century, with a meeting of saṃvegī sādhus headed by **Mahopādhyāya Yaśovijaya** where a proclamation was issued listing 42 principles of proper mendicant conduct.

It is estimated that by the mid-19th century there were only several dozen saṃvegī sādhus and no mendicant leaders (**ācāryas**). At this time, with the support of influential members of the lay community, several monks undertook a campaign to reform lax mendicant practices. The followers of **Ācārya Vijayavallabhasūri** began to wear yellow garments, instead of the traditional white mendicant garments, so that they could be distinguished from the yatis. Other reformist monks included Paṅnyāsa Maṇivijayagaṇi (1796–1879), his disciple Muni Buddhivijaya (also known by his **Sthānakavāsī** mendicant name of

Buṭerāyjī), and Buddhivijaya's disciple **Ācārya Vijayānandasūri** (also known by his Sthānakavāsī mendicant name of Ātmārāmjī). As a result of their efforts, there was a sharp increase in the number of saṃvegī sādhus in the Mūrtipūjaka community, mostly within the Tapā Gaccha, and a decline in the number of yatis. As of 1999, it was estimated that there was a total of 6,843 saṃvegī mendicants in the various Śvetāmbara lineages. There are a few yatis remaining in the **Kharatara Gaccha** and the **Upakeśa Gaccha**.

SAMYAK-DARŚANA. Proper view of reality, proper insight, or right faith. Faith in the teachings of the **Tīrthaṅkaras** and belief in the categories of truths (**tattvas**). In order to attain this state of spiritual purity, also called samyaktva, a **soul** (**jīva**) must have a quality called **bhavyatva** and be embodied in a life-form with five senses, as either a heavenly being (**deva**), hell-being (**nāraki**), human, or five-sensed animal (**tiryañc**) with the ability to reason.

This quality of bhavyatva may be activated by encountering appropriate external conditions, such as seeing a Tīrthaṅkara or viewing his **image**, by hearing the teachings of a Tīrthaṅkara, or by remembering one's past lives. Attaining samyak-darśana is not restricted to the periods in the **cycle of time** when liberation (**mokṣa**) is possible (the third and fourth periods). **Śvetāmbaras** and **Digambaras** agree that both males and females can attain samyak-darśana. In attaining samyak-darśana, the soul's energy (vīrya) is directed away from a state of delusion or a false view of reality (mithyātva) and for a short time it suppresses the operation of the variety of **karma** that causes this delusion (darśana-mohanīya karma). The soul thereby experiences a proper view of reality for the first time, attaining the fourth stage of spiritual purity (**guṇasthāna**). Soon, the soul will fall back into a state of delusion (first guṇasthāna) when these karmas begin their operation again. However, eventually the soul will have the energy to destroy all reality-deluding karma and it will never fall lower than the fourth guṇasthāna. Such a soul will never again be reborn as a female or in inauspicious states of rebirth (hell-being or animal). Attaining proper insight is of great significance because all souls that experience it must attain liberation at some future time. Right faith is one of the Three Jewels (**Ratnatraya**) in Jainism.

SĀṆḌESARĀ, BHOGILĀL. **Śvetāmbara** scholar of history, and the literature and history of Gujarat. Born in 1917 in Patan and educated there, he studied Sanskrit, Prākrit, Apabhraṃśa, and old Gujarati. From 1951 to 1975 he was professor of Gujarati at the M. S. University of

Baroda and director of the Oriental Research Institute from 1958 to 1975. His works include a critical edition and translation of the ***Uttarādhyayana Sūtra*** with a **commentary** in old Gujarati, *Jain Āgama Sāhitya Gujarata* (a study of Gujarat as described in Jain Āgamic literature), and *Literary Circle of Mahāmātya Vastupāla and Its Contribution to Sanskrit Literature*. He also studied art and sculpture of India and has written on the archeological remains of Jagannatha Puri and Orissa. *Pradakṣinā* contains an account of his extensive travels.

SAṄGHA. Community. This term is used in several ways in Jainism. (1) The fourfold community (caturvidha-saṅgha) of Jain **monks (sādhus)**, **nuns (sādhvīs)**, laymen (**śrāvakas**), and laywomen (**śrāvikās**). This also is called the complete saṅgha (sakala saṅgha). (2) The community of **mendicants** (sādhu-, or sādhu-sādhvī saṅgha). (3) A neighborhood or citywide congregation of Jain **laypeople**. (4) A term used by **Digambaras** for the basic unit of their **mendicant lineages** (e.g., **Mūla Saṅgha**). (5) A term used by **Sthānakavāsīs** for several of their mendicant lineages, including the centrally organized **Śramaṇa Saṅgha**.

SAṄGH(A)VĪ, SUKHLĀL(JĪ) (1880–1978). Śvetāmbara paṇḍit. Born in Limbdi, Gujarat, he lost his eyesight at the age of 17 due to smallpox. However, with the help of readers, he learned Sanskrit and Prākrit and memorized many verses from Jain texts. Between 1903 and 1907, he studied philosophy and logic at Yaśovijaya Jain Pāṭhśālā, **Banaras**. After passing the Nyāyācārya examination in 1912, he continued to teach at Jain pāṭhśālās, where his students included **Muni Jinavijaya**, Muni Lalitvijaya, and **Muni Puṇyavijaya**. For a time, he worked in the nationalist movement with Mahātmā Gāndhī and lived at Kocharab Ashram, Ahmedabad, and Satyāgraha Ashram, Sabarmati. In 1921, Saṅghavī began editing and translating the *Sanmati-prakaraṇa* of **Siddhasena Divākara**, a project that took some nine years to complete. He was appointed professor of Jain **scriptures** at Banaras Hindu University in 1933, retiring in 1944. In 1947, he became honorary professor at B. J. Vidya Bhavan, Ahmedabad, and was awarded an honorary D.Litt. from Gujarat University in 1953. In the course of his career, he edited and translated more than 30 works on Jain philosophy and logic. His discourse on the **soul**, the world, and god delivered in the Sayajirao Memorial Lecture Series has been translated as *Indian Philosophy* (1977) and his collected papers have been published in a book entitled *Darśan ane Cintan*. He also wrote an autobiography called *Mārum Jīvanvṛtta*. With an award received from the Government of India, Saṅghavī formed the Jñānodaya Trust for the study of Indian philosophy and religion. The Paṇḍit Śrī Sukhlāljī Sanmān Samiti was founded in his honor.

ŚAṄKHEŚVARA. Small town in north Gujarat that is an important regional **pilgrimage** site for **Śvetāmbaras**. The earliest reference to this site dates from 1099. There is an old Śvetāmbara **temple** here with a famous **image** of **Pārśvanātha**. Due the power of the **Yakṣa Dharaṇendra** and the **Yakṣī Padmāvatī**, the tutelary deities of Pārśvanātha enshrined here, it is believed that obstacles will be removed and there will be great wealth for those who worship here. A number of new temples have been built at this site. It is a favorite place to observe a three-day **fast** known as Aṭhṭham, which is performed in conjunction with **Pārśvanātha-Jayantī**.

SANT. A general designation for a Jain **monk** in the **Sthānakavāsī** tradition. *See also* MENDICANT HIERARCHY.

SANTBĀL, MUNI (1893–1982). Śvetāmbara Sthānakavāsī scholar-**monk**. He was born in Tol, Gujarat, and was named Śivalāl. He was initiated by Muni Jñānacandra, who had persuaded the Mahārāja of Morabi to lift a prohibition against initiation (**dīkṣā**) of Jain **mendicants**. He was given the name Muni Saubhāgyacandra although he was commonly known as Santbāl. He studied various branches of Jain learning and translated several **Āgamas** into Gujarati. Having expressed certain views that were not in keeping with the mendicant social order, he was excommunicated from the **saṅgha**. However, he adhered to the mendicant lifestyle and traveled only on foot. He was influenced by the Gandhian movement and engaged in various projects, including village education, cottage industries, and animal protection.

ŚĀNTIDEVĪ. In the **Śvetāmbara Mūrtipūjaka** tradition, a non-liberated female deity who is responsible for maintaining peace (śānti) and safety of the **temple**. Her **image** is usually located beneath the main image in the inner sanctum of the temple.

ŚĀNTINĀTHA. The 16th **Tīrthaṅkara** of this era. In part, because of the power of his name to bring about peace (śānti) when chanted, his worship has become popular. There are many hymns of praise (**stava**) dedicated to him.

ŚĀNTISĀGARA, ĀCĀRYA (1873–1955). One of three mendicant leaders who revived the **Digambara** tradition of naked **monks** (**munis**) in the 20th century. He was born in northern Karnataka and was named Sāt Gouḍa. Influenced by the writings of **Kundakunda**, he wanted to take initiation as a Digambara monk. However, his parents were opposed to this, and the lineages of naked ascetics had come to an end in earlier times. Eventually, he initiated himself as an **ailaka** in front of an **image** of **Neminātha**. In 1920, at the age of 47, he took the vows of a Digambara muni in Yarnal in the presence of **Bhaṭṭāraka** Devendrakīrti. By discarding his loincloth and pulling out his hair in front of the lay community assembled there for an image-installation ceremony, he revived the ancient tradition of naked monks in that area. Śāntisāgara was actively engaged in reestablishing the tradition of fully initiated Digambara munis. He was instrumental in the publication of the ***Ṣaṭkhaṇḍāgama***, and he supported the Jain community's efforts in prohibiting the unrestricted access of Hindus to Jain temples after the enactment of the Temple Entry Bill in 1948. *See also* ĀDISĀGARA; ŚĀNTISĀGARA (CHĀṆĪ).

ŚĀNTISĀGARA (CHĀṆĪ), ĀCĀRYA (1888–1944). One of three mendicant leaders who revived the **Digambara** tradition of naked **monks** (**munis**) in the 20th century. He was born in the village of Chani, near Udaipur, Rajasthan, and was named Kevaladās Jain. At age 15, he joined the family business but was always interested in studying religious texts. In 1919, at **Mount Sammeta** before the **image** of **Pārśvanātha**, he took the vows of a **brahmacārī**. In 1922, at Kesariyaji he initiated himself as a **kṣullaka** in front of an image of **Ṛṣabha** and took the name Śāntisāgara. In 1923, at the age of 35, while staying in Sagavada he initiated himself as a naked Digambara muni in front of an image of Ṛṣabha, pulling out his hair and discarding his clothing while reciting the **Namaskāra Mantra**. The following year in Indore, he initiated his first **ailaka** disciple and, in 1925, in Hatapipalya he initiated his first monk, Muni Sūryasāgara. Śāntisāgara Chāṇī was appointed **ācārya** in 1926 by the Jain community of Giridiha. In 1933, he and the other ācārya named Śāntisāgara, who was from south India (Dakṣina), both stayed with their **saṅghas** in Byavara, near Jaipur, Rajasthan, for the four-month rainy season period (**cāturmāsa**). Here, their followers met on many occasions and Śāntisāgara (Chāṇī) presided over the Diamond Jubilee celebration for Śāntisāgara (Dakṣiṇa). By the time of his death, there were four or five Digambara ācāryas in north India and almost 50 monks. *See also* ĀDISĀGARA; ŚĀNTISĀGARA.

ŚĀNTIVIJAYASŪRI, ĀCĀRYA. *See* VIJAYAŚĀNTISŪRI, ĀCĀRYA.

SAPTA-BHAṄGI-NAYA. The formulation of sevenfold predication. In Jainism, reality is understood to be multifaceted. It is impossible to express all aspects of reality simultaneously due to the limitations of human language. But a valid statement can be made about one aspect of reality at a time. Thus, a statement as viewed from a single aspect may be true, but it always is partial or limited. Employing the doctrine of qualified assertion (**syādvāda**), a series of seven statements can be made about any object. The formulation of sevenfold predication includes statements of affirmation, negation, and indescribability: (1) in some respects it is (syād asti eva), (2) in some respects, it is not (syād nāsti eva), (3) in some respects, it is and it is not (syād asti-nāsti eva), (4) in some respects, it is inexpressible (syād avaktavyaḥ eva). The final three assertions are combinations of these: (5) in some respects it is, and it is inexpressible, (6) in some respects it is not, and it is inexpressible, and (7) in some respects it is, and it is not, and it is inexpressible. Taken together as a whole, these statements are a proper expression of reality. This sophisticated system of argumentation is employed in philosophical discourse and is not used by Jains in day-to-day conversations. For example, in discussing the nature of the **soul** (**jīva**), which is a substance (**dravya**), one may say that a soul is eternal from the perspective of its qualities (**guṇas**). One may say that a soul is non-eternal from the perspective of its modes (paryāya). This formulation may have been developed by Mallavādin (ca. 4th century C.E.).

SARASVATĪ. Goddess of learning. Because she presides over the teachings (**śruta**) of the **Tīrthaṅkaras**, she also is known as Śrutadevatā. She is mentioned in several early Jain texts, including the **Śvetāmbara** ***Bhagavatī Sūtra.*** An **image** of Sarasvatī from the Kaṅkālī Ṭīlā at **Mathurā** dated 132 C.E. is the oldest extant image of her in any tradition. She holds a text in her right hand and is depicted in a squatting posture, called the "cow-milking pose" (godohikāsana), in which **Mahāvīra** attained enlightenment (**kevala-jñāna**). Her worship as an independent deity apparently was quite popular because when the **Āgamika Gaccha** was established in the 12th century, they specifically rejected her worship. In medieval times, worship of her in a **tantric** form known as Vāgīśvarī became popular. Sarasvatī is still worshipped today, especially on **Jñāna-Pañcamī** by Śvetāmbaras and on **Śruta-Pañcamī** by **Digambaras.**

ŚARĪRA. Body. *See* PUDGALA.

ŚĀSANADEVATĀ. A pair of non-liberated male and female deities who are attendants of a **Tīrthaṅkara** and are protectors of his teachings (śāsana). They are first mentioned in the Jain *Harivaṃśa-purāṇa* (783 C.E.), where they are described as having the ability to pacify malevolent powers. According to tradition, the god **Indra** appoints one **yakṣa** and one **yakṣī** to serve as the śāsanadevatās for each of the Tīrthaṅkaras.

ŚĀSTRĪ, KAILAŚCANDRA (1903–1987). Digambara paṇḍit. Born in Nihtaur, Uttar Pradesh, he attended Syādvāda Jain Mahāvidyālaya at **Banaras** and Māṇikacandra Digambara Jain Parīkṣālaya at Bombay (now Mumbai). He passed his Śāstrī examination in 1923 and received his Nyāyatīrtha degree in 1931. He was the principal of Syādvāda Jain Mahāvidyālaya from 1927 until his retirement in 1972. Kailaścandra Sāstrī translated a number of texts into Hindi and wrote several works, including *Jain Dharma, Jain Nyāya,* and *Ṣaṭprarūpanā-sūtra.*

ŚĀSTRĪ, PHŪLCANDRA (PHOOLCHANDRA) SIDDHĀNTA (1901–1991). Digambara paṇḍit. Born in Silavan, a village near Lalitpur, Uttar Pradesh, he was a protege of **Gaṇeśprasād Varṇī**. He taught at Syādvāda Jain Mahāvidyālaya, **Banaras**, and was director of the Varṇī Research Institute. He also was a social activist in both the Digambara community and the Indian National Congress. He was instrumental in reducing the tensions between the Samaiyā **caste**, who were members of the **Tāraṇ Svāmī Panth**, and his own Parvār caste, who were Digambara **Terāpanthīs**. In 1941, he was jailed for his activities in the nationalist movement. Phūlcandra edited and translated into Hindi a number of classical texts, including the ***Ṣaṭkhaṇḍāgama***, *Mahābandha*, and ***Kaṣāyaprābhṛta***. He authored eight books, including *Varṇa, jāti aur dharma* (Banaras, 1963) and *Jaipur (Khāniyā) Tattvacarcā* (Jaipur, 1967). He was awarded the title of Siddhāntācārya in 1962.

SATĪ. Virtuous **woman**. A term for a woman who is venerated for her virtues, especially for remaining firm in the vow of **celibacy** (**brahmacāriṇī**), in marriage vows, or for her resolve to renounce the household life. In Hinduism, a satī is a widow who accompanies her husband into death by ritual suicide on his funeral pyre. However, in Jainism, such a woman is not considered virtuous. The names and the number of satīs vary. The *Pañcapratikramaṇa Sūtra* of the **Śvetāmbara Mūrtipūjakas** lists 47 names, although 16 is a common number. In one

Śvetāmbara hymn, the 16 satīs venerated are Brāhmī, **Candanā**, **Rājīmati**, Draupadi, Kausalyā, Mṛgāvatī, Sulasā, Sītā, Subhadrā, Śivā, Kuntī, Damayantī, Puṣpacūlā, Prabhāvatī, Padmāvatī, and Sundarī. Brāhmī and Sundarī, the daughters of **Ṛṣabha** and his two wives, Sumāṅgalā and Sundanā, respectively, were the first women to become **nuns (sādhvīs)** in his era. Mṛgāvatī, the wife of King Śatānīka of Kosambī who had saved the kingdom, her son's life, and her chastity after the death of her husband, became a nun under Candanā. Śivā, Prabhāvatī, and Padmāvatī were sisters of Mṛgāvatī who also became nuns under Candanā during the time of **Mahāvīra**. Subhadrā, who had proved the purity of her intentions when she removed an object from the eye of a **monk**, also became a nun under Candanā. Kuntī, Draupadī, and Damayantī are virtuous women in the Jain *Mahābharatas* and Kausalyā and Sītā in the Jain *Rāmāyaṇas*. Satīs are venerated by reciting their names in hymns of praise (**stavan**), which bestows auspiciousness on the worshipper.

ṢAṬKHAṆḌĀGAMA. "Scripture in Six Parts." **Digambara** canonical text on Jain **karma** theory written in Jain Śaurasenī Prākrit. It is the oldest Digambara sacred text and may have been the first written **scripture** of the Jains. According to tradition, this work is based on the oral teachings of a **monk** named Dharasena. According to tradition, he flourished 683 years after **Mahāvīra**'s liberation (**mokṣa**) or 137 C.E. He had memorized a small portion of ancient scriptures called the **Pūrvas** that had been preserved in the 12th **Aṅga**, the *Dṛṣṭivāda*. Concerned that all of this knowledge would soon be lost, he summoned two monks, Puṣpadanta and Bhūtabali, to his retreat on **Mount Girnār**. He told them what he remembered of these texts, and they committed these teachings to writing. *Mahābandha* (or *Mahādhavalā*), the sixth book, discusses the binding (bandha) of karma with the **soul (jīva)**. The *Dhavalā* is the only extant **commentary** on the first five books. It was completed by **Vīrasena** in 816 C.E. It is not known how widely circulated these works might have been in earlier times.

By the beginning of the 20th century, there was only a single extant palm-leaf manuscript of the text and commentary that had been copied around 1100 C.E., which was housed in a **manuscript library** at **Mūḍbidrī**, Karnataka. In the 18th century, **Paṇḍit Ṭoḍarmal** reported that no one had access to this manuscript. It could only be viewed reverentially (**darśana**) since no one in the current world age was capable of understanding it. In the 19th century, a wealthy merchant raised money to have this manuscript, which was written in old Kannada script, copied into Devanāgarī script. When this was completed in 1922, authorities at Mūḍbidrī refused to allow it to be published. However, a second copy had been made at the same time that had been secretly taken from Mūḍbidrī. A group of **paṇḍits** headed by **Hīrālāl Jain** and **Ādināth Upādhye** began editing this manuscript for publication. The first five books of the *Ṣaṭkaṇḍāgama* and the *Dhavalā* commentary have been published along with a Hindi translation in 16 volumes (1939–1959). The *Mahābandha* is published separately in 7 volumes (1947–1958).

ŚATRUÑJAYA. *See* MOUNT ŚATRUÑJAYA.

SATYA. Truthfulness or refraining from lying. The satya-**vrata** is the second of five mendicant vows (**mahāvratas**) and lay vows (**aṇuvratas**). For a **layperson**, lying is understood to be an untruth that is uttered for one's own benefit, out of passion or hatred. Truthfulness includes honesty in business practices and refraining from speech that would hurt others. There is no infraction of this lay vow if one utters a false statement in order to avoid potential harm to another living being. A **mendicant** vows never to utter any untrue statement whatsoever. In this case, potential harm can be avoided only through silence.

SAUDHARMA BṚHAT TAPĀ GACCHA. *See* TRISTUTI GACCHA.

SAYOGA KEVALIN. Kevalin with activity.

SCHUBRING, WALTHER (1881–1969). Indologist and scholar of Prākrit **languages**. Born in Lübeck, Germany, he studied with **Ernst Leumann** at the University of Strasbourg. He received a Ph.D. in 1904 for his critical edition and German translation of the *Bṛhatkalpa Sūtra* (English translation, *Indian Antiquary*, 1910). While employed as a librarian at the Royal Prussian State Library in Berlin from 1904 to 1920, he prepared a descriptive catalogue of the 1,127 **manuscripts** that had been acquired since **Albrecht Weber**'s 1892 catalogue (Leipzig, 1944). In 1920, he was appointed to the chair of Indology at the University of Hamburg, where he remained until his retirement in 1950. He is noted for his work on **Śvetāmbara** canonical literature. His *Wörte Mahāvīras* (Göttingen, 1926) is a translation of selected passages primarily from the ***Ācārāṅga Sūtra*** and ***Sūtrakṛtāṅga Sūtra***. With the publication of *Die Lehre der Jainas nach alten Quellen dargestellt* (1934), translated as *The Doctrine of the Jainas* (Delhi, 1962), Schubring became the first Western scholar to give a comprehensive survey of the Jains based entirely on the ancient

Śvetāmbara Prākrit texts. He also prepared text editions and translations of several chap'ers of the *Mahāniśītha Sūtra*. A bibliography of his writings has been published in *Jain Journal* (4.3, 1970).

SCRIPTURAL COMMENTARY. *See* COMMENTARY.

SCRIPTURE. A body of writings considered to be sacred or authoritative. The terms scripture and canon are problematic in Jainism because there is not a single list of texts accepted as sacred scripture by all sectarian traditions. There also are different opinions regarding the types of knowledge that should be considered as authoritative. For details, see "The Jain Scriptures," pp. xix–xxvi. *See also* ĀGAMA; AṄGA; AṄGABĀHYA; PŪRVAS; SIDDHĀNTA; ŚRUTA.

SHAH, UMĀKANT P. (1915–1988). Indologist and art historian. Born into a Vaiṣṇava family in Baroda, he studied Sanskrit, English, and epigraphy at the University of Bombay and received an M.A. in 1936 and a Ph.D. in 1953 for his thesis *Elements of Jaina Iconography*. He joined the Oriental Institute of M. S. University of Baroda in 1954 as deputy director and retired in 1975. He was head of the Rāmāyaṇa Department at the Oriental Institute and was general editor of the critical edition of the *Uttarakāṇḍa* of Vālmīki's *Rāmāyaṇa*. He was a trustee of the L. D. Institute of Indology, Ahmedabad, and the B. L. Research Institute, Delhi. He was one of the first scholars in India to specialize in the study of Jain art and iconography, especially the art of Gujarat. His monograph on the Akota bronzes, which were discovered in Baroda in 1951–1952, demonstrated that western India had its own school of bronze sculpture parallel to the medieval Chola bronzes from south India and the Pāla bronzes from Bengal and Bihar. Shah's extensive study of illustrated Jain **manuscripts** led to the publication of *Treasures of Jaina Bhandars* (1978). His research on Jain iconography culminated in the publication of *Jaina Rūpa Maṇḍana* (1987). *Studies in Jaina Art and Iconography and Allied Subjects in Honour of Dr. U. P. Shah* (1995) contains a bibliography of his works.

SIDDHA. Literally, "one who has accomplished his goals." A term for a **soul** that has attained liberation **(mokṣa)** from the cycle of rebirth **(saṃsāra)**. Devoid of a body, it experiences its own true nature of infinite **consciousness** and bliss. It dwells forever in the siddha-loka, or īśat-prāgbhārā-bhūmi, which is located just above the heavenly realms, at the very top of the occupied universe **(loka-ākāśa)**. Supreme Soul **(paramātman)** and God **(deva)** are other terms for a liberated soul.

SIDDHACAKRA. Circle of Perfection, also called navapada (Nine Petals). A mystical diagram (**yantra**), typically in the shape of a lotus, that is used in **Śvetāmbara** rituals. It symbolizes the teachings of the path of purification (mokṣa-mārga), which culminates in omniscience (**kevala-jñāna**) and liberation (**mokṣa**). It incorporates the five supreme beings (**parameṣṭhin**), who are honored in the **Namaskāra Mantra**, and the four essentials of liberation (**mokṣa**). A figure representing the enlightened teachers (**Arhats**) is situated in the center, surrounded by eight petals containing figures representing disembodied liberated **souls (siddhas)** to the north, mendicant leaders (**ācāryas**) to the east, mendicant preceptors (**upādhyāyas**) to the south, and mendicants (**sādhus**) to the west. In place of these figures, phrases of homage from the Namaskāra Mantra may be used. In the four intermediate directions are words honoring right asceticism (samyak-**tapas**) and the Three Jewels (**Ratnatraya**) of right faith (**samyak-darśana**), right knowledge (samyak-jñāna), and right conduct (samyak-cāritra). More elaborate forms of this yantra may include surrounding concentric circles with various mantras, the 16 **mahāvidyās**, and the **yakṣa/yakṣīs** of the various **Tīrthaṅkaras**. It is the most commonly used yantra in Jainism today. It is worshipped for the destruction of harmful **karmas** and for attaining prosperity and auspiciousness. It is the focus of worship during the Śvetāmbara festival of **Oḷī**. **Digambaras** use a similar yantra called **navadevatā** in their rituals.

SIDDHĀNTA. Doctrine. A term used by Jains for their sacred texts. It often is translated as "**scripture**" or "canon." It is used more frequently by **Digambaras** as a collective term for their scriptural canon. **Śvetāmbaras** tend to use the term **Āgama** for the **Pūrvas** and for the **Aṅga** and **Aṅgabāhya** texts. For a listing of the individual texts, see "The Jain Scriptures" (pp. xix–xxvi).

SIDDHASENA DIVĀKARA (4th or 5th century C.E.). Logician who is claimed by both the **Digambara** and **Śvetāmbara** traditions. Some have speculated that he may have been associated with an extinct sect called **Yāpanīya**. According to traditional 12th-century biographies, Siddhasena was a **Brahmin** who was proud of his learning. His defeat in a debate with a Jain **monk** prompted his conversion to Jainism. It is said that he was attached to the court of the legendary king Vikramāditya, who gave him his epithet Divākara (Sun). Regarding his scholarship, he wrote two pioneering logic texts, the *Nyāyāvatāra* and the *Sanmati-tarka-prakaraṇa*. These works advanced the doctrine of manifold aspects (**anekāntavāda**) and qualified assertion (**syādvāda**), making his the first works on logic in which arguments were articulated in Jain terms. He thereby gave Jains tools to use in formal debates with their opponents. He was banished from the mendicant community for 12 years after suggesting that the Jain **scriptures** be translated from the Prākrit **language** Ardhamāgadhī into Sanskrit.

ŚIKṢĀ-VRATAS. Four vows of spiritual discipline that a **layperson** may undertake for a limited period of time. In taking one of these vows, a person agrees to engage in a specific ritual activity on a regular basis (e.g., daily, weekly). *See also* DĀNA-VRATA; DEŚĀVAKĀŚIKA-VRATA; POṢADHOPAVĀSA-VRATA; SĀMĀYIKA-VRATA; VRATA.

SĪMANDHARA SVĀMĪ. One of four **Tīrthaṅkaras** who, according to tradition, is currently living on the continent of **Mahāvideha** on the island-continent of **Jambūdvīpa**. There are references to him in the **Śvetāmbara** *Vasudevahiṇḍi* (4th century C.E.) and in early **Digambara** purāṇas. It is believed that certain advanced ascetics have benefited from his teachings. For example, it is said that the Digambara **Kundakunda** visited Sīmandhara's assembly (**samavasaraṇa**) on the continent of Mahāvideha by means of a special translocational body (aharaka-śarīra) to resolve doubts about the sacred teachings, and that the Śvetāmbara **Abhayadevasūri** was inspired by Sīmandhara's knowledge when composing his scriptural **commentaries**. Sīmandhara Svāmī's **image** is worshipped in a number of **temples** today, primarily by Śvetāmbaras and by followers of the Digambara **Kānjī Svāmī Panth**.

SĪTAL PRASĀD, BRAHMACĀRĪ (1879–1941). Digambara ascetic-scholar. Born into an Agarvāl family in Lucknow, after his education in Sanskrit, English, and Jain doctrine, he worked as a jeweler in Calcutta and later as a government bureaucrat in Lucknow. After the death of his wife, mother, and younger brother within eight days during the plague in 1904, he resigned from government service and devoted the rest of his life to the study and propagation of Jainism. While living in Bombay (now Mumbai) from 1904 to 1909, he began editing the periodicals *Jain Gazette*, *Jain Mitra*, and *Jain Vīr*. In 1910, Sītal Prasād took the vows of a **brahmacārī** from **Ailaka** Pannālāl in Solapur.

Over the next several decades, he produced Hindi paraphrases (ṭīkā) on the *Niyamasāra*, *Pañcāstikāya*, *Pravacanasāra*, and *Samayasāra* of **Kundakunda**, the *Samayasāra Kalaśa* of Amṛtacandra, the *Yogasāra* of **Yogīndu**, and the *Svayambhū Stotra* of **Samantabhadra**. He also wrote a study of the *Mokṣamārgaprakāśaka* by **Paṇḍit Ṭoḍarmal**. He prepared editions and Hindi versions of nine of **Tāraṇ Svāmī**'s 14 texts. He authored a number of books, including *Jainism: A Key to True Happiness* (Jaipur, 1951) and *Jainadharma Prakāśa* (Bijanaura, 1939). After studying Buddhism in Sri Lanka (Ceylon) and Burma (Myamar), he wrote *A Comparative Study of Jainism and Buddhism* in 1932. He was associated with the Digambara Jain Mahāsabhā and was one of the founders of the Digambara Jain Pariṣad. Sītal Prasād also served as the head of Syādvāda Jain Mahāvidyālaya, **Banaras**.

SNĀTRA PŪJĀ. A ceremony of ritual bathing of the **image** of a **Tīrthaṅkara**. It is a reenactment of the bathing of the infant Tīrthaṅkara by the **Indras** during the birth ceremony performed by the gods (**devas**) on **Mount Meru**.

SOUL. *See* ĀTMAN; JĪVA; PARAMĀTMAN; SIDDHA.

SPIRITUAL LIBERATION OF WOMEN. *See* STRĪ-MOKṢA.

ŚRAMAṆA. Literally, one who practices religious exertions. A non-Brahmanical **mendicant**, especially one of the **Ājīvika**, Buddhist, or Jain traditions. A collective term of reference for all of the non-vedic or heterodox religions and their associated systems of philosophy that existed in the Ganges Valley around the time of the **Buddha** and **Mahāvīra**.

ŚRAMAṆA SAṄGHA. A centrally organized **Sthānakavāsī mendicant lineage**. It was founded in 1952 in Sadari, Rajasthan, by an assembly of 32 mendicant leaders (**ācāryas**), in an attempt to unite all Sthānakavāsī mendicant lineages. The original 22 founding traditions are under the command of a single ācārya for the purposes of initiation and excommunication. For other matters, the various lineages have tended to operate independently. This unification has been only partially successful, as some senior **mendicants** have broken away and have reestablished their own independent groups and others continued to maintain their independence. Their first ācārya was Ātmārām (born 1882, initiated 1894, died 1962), and the current ācārya is Dr. Śiv Muni (born 1942, initiated 1972, ācārya 1999).

ŚRĀVAKA/ŚRĀVIKĀ. Literally, "listener." A Jain **layman**/laywoman. A synonym for **upāsaka/upāsikā**.

ŚRĀVAKĀCĀRA. Proper conduct (ācāra) for a **layperson** (**śrāvaka**). A term that is used for treatises that describe proper lay conduct. In his study of the śrāvakācāra texts composed in Sanskrit and Prākrit from the 5th through the 17th centuries entitled *Jaina Yoga*, R. Williams lists over 40 works. All describe the conduct of the ideal layperson and thus are prescriptive in nature. Except for a layman named **Āśādhara** (Dig., 13th century), all of the authors were **monks**. Topics discussed include a proper view of reality (**samyak-darśana**), the 12 **lay vows**, the 11 stages of renunciation for a layperson (**pratimās**), the obligatory duties (**āvaśyakas**), worship (**pūjā**), moral faults or sacrilegious acts (**āśātanās**), **pilgrimage**, austerities (**tapas**), **meditation** (**dhyāna**), life-cycle rituals (**saṃskāras**, kriyās), contemplations or meditations (**anuprekṣās**, **bhāvanās**), **dietary restrictions**, recommended **occupations**, religious gifting (**dāna**), religious death through fasting (**sallekhanā**), and the qualities of an ideal layperson (śrāvaka-guṇas).

ŚRAVAṆA BEḶGOḶA. **Pilgrimage** site near the town of Śravaṇa Beḷgoḷa, Karnataka, encompassing two hills, Indragiri and Candragiri, colloquially called Big Hill and Little Hill, respectively. The earliest inscription, dated 600 C.E., is located on Candragiri. It mentions a migration from the north under the leadership of **Ācārya Bhadrabāhu** at the time of a severe famine. From the 7th to the 10th centuries, hundreds of memorials (niṣidhi) were erected on this hill in the form of commemorative stones, pillars, **images**, and **temples** honoring **mendicants** who undertook a religious death through fasting (**sallekhanā**). Beginning in the 10th century, memorials also were erected for **laypeople** who performed sallekhanā. People also come here to worship the 57-foot image of **Bāhubali** standing erect in meditative posture (**kāyotsarga**) with creepers entwining his arms and legs. Situated on the summit of Indragiri, this image, which also is known as Gommaṭa Svāmī or Gommaṭeśvara, was commissioned in 981 C.E. by Cāmuṇḍarāya, a general of a king in the Gaṅga dynasty. Thousands of people come here to perform an elaborate head-anointing ceremony (**mastakābhiṣeka**) for this image, which takes place approximately every 12 years. **Kūṣmāṇḍinī**, the **yakṣī** of the 22nd **Tīrthaṅkara Neminātha**, is the protector deity of Śravaṇa Beḷgoḷa.

ŚREṆIKA. King of Magadha and a contemporary of **Mahāvīra**. His capital at Rājagṛha became an important center for Mahāvīra's assembly. He was imprisoned by his eldest son and subsequently took his own life to save his son from the karmic consequences of killing his own father. According to both **Śvetāmbara** and **Digambara** accounts, because of harmful actions committed earlier in his life, he acquired the variety of **karma** that causes rebirth as a hell-being (**nāraki**). Mahāvīra predicted that after his sojourn in hell Śreṇika will be born as **Mahāpadma** (alt. Padmanābha), the first Tīrthaṅkara in **Bharata-kṣetra** (the part of the universe where we are said to live) in the next progressive **cycle of time** (utsarpiṇī). His story is often cited as an example of the karmic rule that one's destiny in the next life cannot be changed after life span (āyu) karma has been bound.

ŚRĪPŪJYA. The title of a leader in the **Śvetāmbara Mūrtipūjaka** mendicant community who was the head of a group of quasi-mendicants known as **yatis**, whose vows were less stringent than those of a fully initiated mendicant (**saṃvegī sādhu**). At installation, a śrīpūjya was given various insignia associated with royalty, including a mace and fly whisk. He sat on a throne that was affixed to the floor of the mendicant dwelling-hall (**upāśraya**) that was his permanent residence and the seat or headquarters for his lineage of yatis. He rode in a palanquin and was shaded by umbrellas. Many wore elaborate shawls, which were donated by wealthy **laypeople**. They often owned personal property, including land with **temples** and dwelling-halls, which they passed on to their self-appointed successors. Some were closely associated with the courts of Rajput and Muslim rulers and served as royal preceptors. At the beginning of the 20th century, when the majority of Mūrtipūjaka **mendicants** were yatis rather than full-fledged saṃvegī sādhus, there were 12 śrīpūjya lineages in the **Tapā Gaccha** with a chief who had his seat in Jaipur. Since there are no longer any yatis in the Tapā Gaccha, these lineages have disappeared and the subdivisions that exist today are lineages of the saṃvegī sādhus. Although today there are only a few yatis remaining in the **Kharatara Gaccha** in Rajasthan who are associated with the seats in Bikaner, thrones of the śrīpūjyas are still found in some of the older upāśrayas. A **bhaṭṭāraka** is the counterpart of a śrīpūjya in the **Digambara** mendicant community.

ŚRUTA. Literally, "that which has been heard." In Jainism, this term is used in several ways. It is roughly equivalent to "**scripture**" in the same sense that śruti is used in Hinduism for the totality of revealed truth contained in the Vedas. It is sometimes used for the texts containing the orally transmitted teachings of the **Tīrthaṅkaras**. In Jain philosophical texts, it means any spoken or written symbol. A deity who protects the teachings of a Tīrthaṅkara is known as a śrutadevatā or a **śāsanadevatā**. *See also* SARASVATĪ.

ŚRUTA-PAÑCAMĪ. Scripture Fifth. A **Digambara festival** commemorating the day on which the orally transmitted teachings (**śruta**) of the Jain **scriptures** were first committed to writing. It takes place on the fifth day of the bright half of Jyeṣṭha (May/June). According to tradition, the ***Ṣaṭkhaṇḍāgama*** ("Scripture in Six Parts") was completed on this day. Old **manuscripts** are displayed at **temples** and **laypeople** commission new copies of the sacred texts. Some Jains worship **Sarasvatī**, the **goddess** of learning, on this day.

STAVA(N). A devotional hymn or hymn of praise addressed to a **Tīrthaṅkara** that may be sung during daily rites of worship (**pūjā**) or on special occasions, such as **fast**-breaking and weddings. There are three hymns preserved in both the **Śvetāmbara** and **Digambara** traditions that date from canonical times. The Śakra-Stava, which is believed to have been recited by **Indra** (= Śakra), praises the exemplary qualities of the Tīrthaṅkaras. The Nāma-Jina-Stava, or Caturviṁśati-Stava, invokes the names of the 24 Tīrthaṅkaras of this era. The Śruta-Stava praises the Holy Law (**Dharma**) preserved in the sacred texts (**Śruta**) as taught by the Tīrthaṅkaras, including those living today in **Mahāvideha**. Stavan is the term that is commonly used for hymns composed in vernacular **languages**, such as Gujarati and Hindi.

The singing of stava(n) is done singly as an offering to the Tīrthaṅkaras and as a form of **meditation**. It also may be done in a group, or maṇḍal, where the singers practice and perform publicly at formal pūjās and at events, such as fast-breaking and weddings. The majority of maṇḍals today are composed of **women** singers.

STHĀNAK(A)VĀSĪ. One of two non-image-worshipping **Śvetāmbara** sectarian traditions. The name is derived from the practice of their **mendicants** staying in special dwelling-halls (sthānakas) that were not part of a temple complex. Tradition holds that the Sthānakavāsī tradition originated with a 15th-century reformer named **Loṅkā Śāh**, although no fully initiated mendicants today trace their descent to him. They trace their origins to one or more of the five principal reformers (pañca-munis) who broke away from various branches of **Loṅkā Gaccha** in the 17th century. Although the name Sthānakavāsī is found in a 17th-century text, it was not commonly used to identify these **mendicant lineages** and their lay followers collectively until early in the 20th century.

Sthānakavāsīs reject the veneration of **images** in both material form (dravya **pūjā**) and mental form (bhāva pūjā). However, both mendicants and **laypeople** perform mental worship (bhāva pūjā) to the

Tīrthaṅkaras through **meditation** (**dhyāna**) in mendicant dwelling-halls. They also engage in study of the **scriptures** (svādhyāya) and in acts of austerities (**tapas**), such as **fasting**. Members of the lay community venerate living mendicants as symbols of the Jain ideals of non-harming (**ahiṃsā**) and restraint. They perform merit-making activities, such as religious gifting (**dāna**) through support of their mendicants and by compassionately helping humans and animals. Their mendicants may be identified by the practice of wearing a white rectangular cloth over their mouths (**muhpattī**), which is always worn except when eating. *See also* MŪRTIPŪJAKA; TERĀPANTHĪ (Śvet.).

STHĀPANĀCĀRYA. Literally, "the established ācārya." A ritual object representative of the **mendicant hierarchy** used by **Śvetāmbara Mūrtipūjaka mendicants**. It consists of four sticks of wood that are bound together and splayed out in the shape of an hourglass. Five chowrie shells wrapped in a cloth are placed on this stand. The shells represent the five supreme lords (**parameṣṭhins**), namely, the enlightened teachers (**Arhats** or **Tīrthaṅkaras**), disembodied liberated **souls** (**siddhas**), past and present mendicant leaders (**ācāryas**) in the **mendicant's lineage**, mendicant preceptors (**upādhyāyas**), and all mendicants (**sādhus**). It is placed before a mendicant as a witness when performing certain rites alone, such as confession (**pratikramaṇa**), veneration of the mendicant teacher (guru-vandana), and the inspection of the requisites (**pratilekhanā**), or when giving a sermon (**pravacana**). It is a physical symbol that mendicants are never alone but are in the presence of the mendicant community.

STHAVIRA. Elder. **Monks** who were leaders of the mendicant community after the time of **Mahāvīra**. The elders are differentiated from the mendicant leaders who came after them by their knowledge of the teachings contained in ancient texts called **Pūrvas**. According to **Śvetāmbaras**, the first elder was **Jambū**, who was a disciple of **Gaṇadhara Sudharman**. Vajra, who had knowledge of 10 Pūrvas, was the last sthavira. After his death, knowledge of these texts was completely lost. **Hemacandra** wrote a narrative of the lives of the sthaviras entitled *Pariśiṣṭsaparvan* ("The Appendix"), a sequel to the *Triṣaṣṭi-śalākāpuruṣacaritra* ("The Lives of Sixty-Three Illustrious Persons").

STHAVIRA-KALPA. A mode of mendicant life like that of the elders (**sthaviras**) or leaders of the early mendicant communities. During the time of **Mahāvīra**, there were two modes of life that a **monk** could follow. Monks who followed this mode lived in organized mendicant communities and were supervised by a mendicant leader (**ācārya**) in matters like confession. For **nuns**, this was the only mode of mendicant life. However, a monk could choose a more austere life as a **jina-kalpa** monk. With the death of **Jambū**, which took place 64 years after the death of Mahāvīra, the sthavira-kalpa became the only permissible mode of mendicancy.

STHŪLABHADRA (ca. 3rd century B.C.E.). According to both **Śvetāmbara** and **Digambara** accounts, Sthūlabhadra was an elder (**sthavira**) who was a pupil of **Ācārya Bhadrabāhu**, the fifth elder in the lineage beginning with **Jambū**. According to Śvetāmbaras, he presided over an assembly of **mendicants**, called the First Council. They had gathered at Pāṭaliputra (now Patna) after a famine that had caused the scattering of the mendicant community in order to recite what they remembered of the Jain **Āgamas**. It was discovered that no one present there had memorized the 12th book called the *Dṛṣṭivāda*, which contained the teachings of earlier texts called the **Pūrvas**. Sthūlabhadra went to Nepal to learn these texts from **Bhadrabāhu**. Although Bhadrabāhu eventually taught all 14 Pūrvas to Sthūlabhadra, he forbade him from reciting certain portions of two of them out of his displeasure at Sthūlabhadra's inappropriate use of his magical powers. According to Digambaras, Sthūlabhadra was living in the region of Avantī when a famine caused the scattering of the mendicant community. He and two other ācāryas went to Sindh, but they still had difficulty obtaining alms. So they adopted the lax mendicant practice of using a half piece of cloth (**ardhaphālaka**) to cover their **nudity** when on food-gathering rounds. After the famine was over and the mendicant community was reunited, Sthūlabhadra gave up this lax conduct and returned to the practice of nudity. Śvetāmbaras and Digambaras agree that after the time of Sthūlabhadra only 10 Pūrvas were known.

STRĪ-MOKṢA (STRĪ-NIRVĀṆA). Spiritual liberation of **women**. The subject of biological gender, particularly the nature of the female body, has occupied an important place in debates regarding the spiritual liberation of women. **Digambaras** have maintained that a woman cannot attain liberation (**mokṣa**) from the cycle of rebirth (**saṃsāra**) without being reborn as a man. **Śvetāmbaras** have maintained that **gender** is not a factor in the attainment of liberation.

One would expect that the mendicant authors of these two traditions would express different views regarding the nature of the female-gendered body, but this is not the case. These authors agree that a female body has certain biological characteristics that make it inferior to a male body. Menstruation is seen as the source of injury (**hiṃsā**) to submicroscopic lives, and female genital organs are said to be a breeding ground for minute forms of life. They both maintain that a female is subject to mental distraction due to incessant sexual desire and she must cover her body to shield herself from the glances of men. They agree that females are incapable of experiencing the most extreme forms of unwholesome volitions and therefore they cannot be reborn into the lowest (seventh) hell (**naraka**). Digambaras maintain that those who cannot fall to the lowest hell cannot rise to the highest heaven, nor can they attain the realm of liberated **souls** beyond the highest heaven (siddha-loka). Śvetāmbaras do not agree with this parallel argument, nor do they accept the Digambara argument that the biological deficiencies mentioned above preclude the attainment of liberation.

The focus of this debate is over the wearing of clothing, which is of importance to male renunciants for the legitimization of their own mendicant practices, because Digambara **monks** (**munis**) practice total **nudity** and Śvetāmbara monks wear mendicant garments. Digambaras maintain that a person who takes the mendicant vow (**mahāvrata**) of non-possession (**aparigraha**) must renounce all clothing. They understand clothing to be possessions and the wearing of them to be indicative of residual shame and sexual desire. Because a woman is not allowed to practice nudity, it is impossible for her to attain the highest spiritual goal. Śvetāmbaras believe that in taking this vow, a **mendicant** must give up all mental attachments, including all attachment to clothing. They believe that mendicant garments are a necessary support for mendicant life, like the whisk broom (**piñchī**) that is carried by naked Digambara munis. Therefore, a woman's anatomy does not prevent her from observing the highest precepts of mendicancy, and spiritual liberation is possible for both men and women. And according to the Śvetāmbara ***Kalpa Sūtra***, twice as many **nuns** (1,400) as monks (700) attained liberation during the time of **Mahāvīra**. Śvetāmbaras believe that **Marudevī**, the mother of the first **Tīrthaṅkara**, **Ṛṣabha**, was the first person to attain liberation in our current **cycle of time**, and that **Mallī**, the 19th Tīrthaṅkara, was a woman.

SUDHARMAN. One of the 11 chief disciples (**gaṇadharas**) of **Mahāvīra**. Since he had not attained omniscience (**kevala-jñāna**) during Mahāvīra's lifetime, he could still lead the mendicant community. He became the sole leader of the mendicant community and custodian of the sacred **scriptures** after **Indrabhūti Gautama** attained omniscience at the time of Mahāvīra's liberation (**mokṣa**). He attained omniscience and liberation 13 years after Indrabhūti Gautama at 100 years of age. With the exception of the **Upakeśa Gaccha**, all **Śvetāmbara mendicant lineages** that exist today trace their descent from him. **Images** of him are worshipped in a number of Śvetāmbara temples.

ŚŪDRA. A member of the occupational class of craftsmen and laborers in the ancient system of social organization (varṇa). According to the *Ādipurāṇa* of **Jinasena**, the varṇa system was established by **Ṛṣabha**, the first king of this era, prior to his renouncing the household life in order to establish order in society. Although there is no evidence in early Jain texts of restriction by **caste** for initiation into mendicancy, Jinasena states that Śūdras are not permitted to receive mendicant initiation (**dīkṣā**). However, members of the Śūdra class could observe most Jain life-cycle rites (**saṃskāras**), but not the sacred-thread ceremony, and they could take lay vows of renunciation (**pratimās**), including the vows of an **ailaka**. At certain times in history, Śūdras were not permitted to enter Jain **temples**, but this practice has come to an end. The Constitution of the Republic of India, adopted in 1950, states that it is illegal to discriminate against anyone based on their caste status.

ŚUKLA-DHYĀNA. See DHYĀNA.

SŪRI. A title meaning "learned man" that is appended to the name of a **Śvetāmbara Mūrtipūjaka ācārya** at the time of his installation.

SUSHIL KUMAR (SUŚĪLKUMĀR), ĀCĀRYA (1926–1994). Śvetāmbara Sthānakavāsī mendicant leader. Born into a **Brahmin** family in the village of Shikopur (Haryana), he left home at seven to become a disciple of a Jain **monk** named Chotelāl, and was initiated in 1941 at the age of 15. He is noted for his development of the Arhum Yoga system of **meditation** and for promoting harmony among religious traditions and within the Jain community itself. He encouraged nonviolent resolutions to conflicts and was active in promoting **vegetarianism**, animal welfare, and environmental concerns.

In 1975, he traveled by air to the United States, ignoring the prohibition against the use of mechanized conveyance. In 1983, he established a religious center called Siddhachalam in Blairstown, New Jersey. It is the headquarters for the World Fellowship of Religions, which he founded in the 1950s to promote unity and understanding among world religions, and for the International Mahavir Jain Mission, which he established in 1978 to spread the teachings of Jainism. This organization has been affiliated with the United Nations since 1992 as a non-governmental organization (NGO). He participated in a number of international conferences, including the 1993 World Parliament of Religions, the 1992 Earth Summit at Rio de Janeiro, Brazil, and the 1993 Global Forum in Kyoto, Japan.

SŪTRAKṚTĀṄGA SŪTRA. The second **Aṅga** in the **Śvetāmbara** scriptural canon (**Āgama**). It is divided into two books. Based on linguistic and metrical evidence, scholars believe that Book One contains some of the oldest portions of the extant canon. These books contain lectures on various circumstances in which a **mendicant** might go astray. Views of heretical teachers who advocated fatalism (niyativāda), agnosticism (ajñānavāda), nonaction (akriyāvāda), eternalism, and annihilationism are also discussed. These all are rejected as one-sided (ekānta) views of reality and are seen as inferior to the multifaceted view (**anekāntavāda**) expounded by Jain teachers. There also are lectures on the various hardships of mendicant life and the tortures experienced in the hells.

SVASTIKA (SWASTIKA). From the Sanskrit words su + asti + ka, meaning a marker of goodness. It is represented as a cross with each of its four arms at a right angle, turned in a clockwise direction. It symbolizes the four states of existence in the cycle of rebirth, namely, heavenly beings (**deva**), hell-beings (**nāraki**), animals (**tiryañc**), and human beings. It also symbolizes the fourfold Jain community of **monks (sādhu)**, **nuns** (sādhvī), **laymen** (**śrāvaka**), and laywomen (**śrāvikā**). From early times, it has been one of the eight auspicious symbols (**aṣṭamaṅgala**) in Jainism. It is found on votive tablets (āyāgapaṭas) from the Kuṣāṇa period at **Mathurā** (2nd–3rd centuries C.E.), and is the emblem of Supārśvanātha, the seventh **Tīrthaṅkara** of this era. In spite of its negative connotations after its appropriation by the Nazi Party in Germany, this symbol is still widely used in Hinduism, Buddhism, and Jainism.

ŚVETĀMBARA. White-clad. One of the two main Jain sectarian traditions that exist today. The name is derived from the practice of their **mendicants** of wearing simple white (śveta) cotton garments (ambara). Today, the community is divided into the **Mūrtipūjakas**, who venerate **images** of **Tīrthaṅkaras**, and the **Sthānakavāsīs** and **Terāpanthīs**, who do not worship images but venerate Tīrthaṅkaras through mental worship (bhāva **pūjā**). Historically, Śvetāmbaras have lived primarily in Gujarat, Rajasthan, and the Punjab. *See also* DIGAMBARA.

SYĀDVĀDA. Doctrine of qualified assertion. It is used in a formal system of philosophical argumentation to describe the multifaceted nature of reality (**anekāntavāda**). Jains maintain that a statement is correct only when it is qualified by the Sanskrit indeclinable "syāt," which means "it may be" or "it might be." In this context, it is often translated as "in some respect." When combined with the Sanskrit emphatic particle "eva," an assertion is made, qualified by the phrase "in this particular respect." This particular respect is associated with four specific factors: a specific being or object (sva-dravya), a specific location (sva-kṣetra), a specific time (sva-kāla), and a specific state (sva-bhāva). It excludes all other locations, times, and so forth. In this way, it is possible to make a specific assertion about any substance (**dravya**) and still leave room for other possible assertions. By using this formulation in the system of sevenfold predication (**saptabhaṅgi-naya**), the limitations of human language can be overcome, and an object can be described in all of its possible aspects or modes.

– T –

TANTRA. Rites of worship focusing on the use of verbal spells (**mantras**) and mystical diagrams (**yantras**). Although mantras are sometimes used to invoke **Tīrthaṅkaras**, often they are used to summon various non-liberated deities, who still have the power to intervene in worldly matters on behalf of their worshippers. In Jainism, these rites rarely involve elaborate forms of **meditation** or visualization, nor do they include forbidden substances, such as meat and wine, that are used in some Hindu and Buddhist tantric rituals. Because these rituals are effective only in the realm of rebirth (**saṃsāra**), in Jainism there is no full-scale tantric tradition that serves as a path of liberation (mokṣa-mārga). In medieval times, the worship of **goddesses** such as **Jvālāmālinī**, **Padmāvatī**, and of **Sarasvatī** as Vāgīśvarī in tantric rituals became popular.

TAPĀ GACCHA. A **Śvetāmbara Mūrtipūjaka mendicant lineage**. It was founded in Chitor (southern Rajasthan) by Jagaccandrasūri in 1228 C.E., who split from the Vaṭa ("Figtree") Gaccha in a disagreement over lax mendicant practices. After seeing the intensity of his austerities (**tapas**), King Jaitrasiṃha of Chitor gave him the epithet Tapā ("Asceticism"). His successor Devendrasūri wrote a number of important works on ritual, lay conduct (**śrāvakācāra**), and **karma** theory. In the 16th and 17th centuries, the Tapā Gaccha broke into a number of different independent and semi-independent groups, most of which consisted of **yatis** and **śrīpūjyas**. Starting in the mid-19th century, there was a reform movement among the **monks**, with growing lay support, including Maṇivijaya (1796–1879) and his disciple Buṭeyarāyjī (also known as Buddhivijaya), **Ācārya Sāgarānandasūri**, and **Ācārya Buddhisāgarasūri**. This resulted in the almost total disappearance of yatis from this gaccha. In the 20th century, this reform has been accompanied by a very significant growth in the number of monks in this mendicant lineage.

Today, the Tapā Gaccha is the largest of the Mūrtipūjaka mendicant lineages. Approximately 85–90 percent of all Mūrtipūjaka **mendicants** belong to this gaccha. There is a common understanding that the contemporary Tapā Gaccha consists of 18 **samudāyas**, although different sources disagree on the names and boundaries between them. In most samudāyas of the Tapā Gaccha, **nuns** are not allowed to preach or to read certain **Āgama** texts, including the Chedasūtras, which discuss mendicant conduct. In 1999, it was estimated that there were 6,027 mendicants, 1,349 monks and 4,678 nuns, in the Tapā Gaccha. An identifying mendicant emblem is their alms bowls, which are red with a black stripe.

TAPAS. An act of austerity, asceticism, or self-discipline that is thought to produce bodily heat (tapas), which burns away accumulated **karma**. Austerities may be external or internal. For **laypeople** today, external austerities almost always entail some sort of **fasting**, either abstention from food, or limiting the type or quantity of food. Lists of six external austerities in texts on lay conduct (**śrāvakācāra**) include fasting, eating a partial meal, limiting one's choice of food, abstaining from delicacies, avoiding temptations, and mortification of the body by heat, cold, etc. The list of six internal austerities includes confession (**pratikramaṇa**), respect for **mendicants** (or, for mendicants, respect for elders in their **mendicant lineage**), rendering service to mendicants, studying the scriptures (svādhyāya), abandoning the body (**kāyotsarga**), and **meditation (dhyāna)**. Similar lists are found in texts on mendicant conduct.

TĀRAṄGĀ. Pilgrimage site on a hill in northern Gujarat. It is famous for the many Jain **mendicants** who attained liberation (**mokṣa**) here. A **Śvetāmbara temple** dedicated to Ajitanātha, the second **Tīrthaṅkara** of this era, was erected here in 1164 C.E. by King Kumārapāla of the Caulukya dynasty. There also is a **Digambara** temple dedicated to **Mallinātha** here.

TĀRAṆ SVĀMĪ (1448–1515). Digambara scholar-**monk** and reformer, also known by the name Jin Tāraṇ Taraṇ. He was born in the village of

Puṣpāvatī, which has been identified with the contemporary village of Bilhari near Katni in the Jabalpur District of Madhya Pradesh. His given name is not known, but his father's name was Gaṛhā Sāha and he was of the Parvār **caste**. Between the ages of 11 and 21, he is said to have studied various Jain scriptures, and he spent the next nine years in various spiritual pursuits. Having never married, at age 30 he took the vows of a **brahmacārī**. Thirty years later, at the age of 60, he renounced all clothing and became a Digambara **muni**. He died approximately six years later.

He opposed the worship of all **images**, including those of the **Tīrthaṅkaras**. Some accounts of his life emphasize his associations with the Digambara mystical tradition of **Kundakunda**, his efforts at reform of ritual practices, and his criticism of the institution of the **bhaṭṭārakas**. He is said to have attracted many disciples from various social backgrounds, including lower castes. Some were from Jain families, and others were non-Jains, including Muslims. The community of his followers is known as the **Tāraṇ Svāmī Panth**.

Tāraṇ Svāmī is credited with writing 14 texts, although some scholars have questioned his authorship of two of them. His best-known works are *Mālārohaṇa*, *Paṇḍita Pūjā*, and *Kamala Battīsī,* which are 32-verse compositions that emphasize the Three Jewels (**Ratnatraya**) of right faith, right knowledge, and right conduct, respectively. *Jñānasamuccayasāra*, *Upadeśaśuddhasāra*, and *Tribaṅgīsāra* discuss Digambara philosophy and metaphysics. Written in a mixture of Sanskrit, Prākrit, Apabhraṃśa, and Bundelkhandi Hindi, his works are difficult to understand, and there are no known **commentaries** on them.

TĀRAṆ SVĀMĪ PANTH (SAMAIYA PANTH). A **Digambara** sectarian tradition that follows the teachings of **Tāraṇ Svāmī**. A follower of these teachings is known as a Tāraṇ Svāmī Panthī. Books containing the writings of Taraṇ Svāmī, **Kundakunda**, and other authors in the Digambara mystical tradition are worshipped on the altars of their **temples**, but the **images** of **Tīrthaṅkaras** are not worshipped. It has also been called the Samaiya Panth because its followers worship the Samaya, or sacred books. Members of the Tāraṇ Panth are found in six merchant **castes** from the cultural area in central India known as Bundelkhand. Those belonging to the Samaiyā, Dosakhe, and Gulālāre castes were from image-worshipping Jain communities, and those belonging to the Asethi, Ayodhyāvāsī, and Cārnagar castes were from Hindu communities. These six communities have traditionally practiced religious rituals together and began intermarrying in 1927. Estimates of the size of the community range from 20,000 to 100,000.

There are approximately 130 temples for this panth, which are concentrated in Madhya Pradesh, extending into southern Uttar Pradesh and northwestern Maharashtra. Their exteriors are similar to Digambara **Terāpanthī** temples in the region, but inside there are altars, often three in number, symbolizing the focus of Digambara ritual on god (**deva**), teacher (guru), and religion (**dharma**). Books are placed on these altars, which are ornamented with various auspicious symbols, such as **svastikas**, full pots, elephants, and divine musicians. The worship ceremony includes recitations from Tāraṇ Svāmī's works and the singing of hymns. It may also include a sermon by a local lay intellectual, known as bhāījī or pāṇḍe, or by a visiting Digambara Terāpanthī **paṇḍit**. The worship concludes with a lamp ceremony (**āratī**) in which platters of lighted candles are offered to the **scriptures**.

There are four main **pilgrimage** sites for this panth, the most important of which is called Nisaījī ("Honored Memorial"). It is the place on Betwa River near the village of Malhargarh where Tāraṇ Svāmī died and where he spent his final years with his disciples, who also have been commemorated here with memorials (samādhis). It is the site of an annual three-day fair in February/March, and many members of the panth have the first tonsure of their children performed here. At Semarkheri, near Sironj in the Vidisha District, where he is said to have renounced the world, a shrine has been built and there are caves nearby where he reportedly meditated. Bilhari, near Katni in the Jabalpur District, is where Tāraṇ Svāmī was born and Ṣukha, near Pathariya in the Damoh District, is where he preached.

TATTVA. That which exists or is real; truths as taught by the omniscient **Tīrthaṅkaras**. These include (1) sentient entities or **souls** (**jīva**), (2) non-sentient entities (ajīva), (3) influx of **karma** to the soul (āsrava), (4) bondage of karma with the soul (bandha), (5) stopping the influx of karma (saṃvara), (6) falling away of karma from the soul (nirjarā), and (7) liberation (**mokṣa**) of the soul from karmic bondage in the cycle of rebirth (**saṃsāra**). Some sources list two additional tattvas: inauspicious varieties of karma (pāpa prakṛtis), and auspicious varieties of karma (puṇya prakṛtis). A person who has attained proper insight (**samyak-darśana**) accepts the tattvas as a matter of faith.

TATTVĀRTHA SŪTRA/TATTVĀRTHĀDIGAMA SŪTRA. An influential Jain text in which the canonical teachings are organized into a system of philosophy for the first time. It is the first Jain work to be written in Sanskrit and in the terse aphoristic sūtra style traditionally employed in brahmanical writings. The author's choice of **language** and sūtra style facilitated discussions between Jains and proponents of other schools of philosophy. It was written sometime between the 2nd and 5th centuries C.E. by a **monk** named **Umāsvāti/Umāsvāmī**. It is one of the few texts that is accepted as authoritative by both **Śvetāmbaras** and **Digambaras**. The sectarian affiliation of the author of the *Tattvārtha Sūtra* and the dating of this text have been the subject of much debate. It is probable that its author lived prior to the time when the disagreement over mendicant **nudity** had caused a total separation of the Digambara and Śvetāmbara mendicant communities.

The Jain view of the nature of reality is described in approximately 350 sūtras organized by topic into 10 chapters: (1) the path of salvation (mokṣa-mārga) and cognition, (2) nature of the **soul (jīva)**, (3) the lower worlds (**adho-loka**) and human abodes (**madhya-loka**), (4) celestial abodes (**ūrdhva-loka**), (5) insentient substances (**dravyas**), (6) karmic influx (āsrava), (7) vows (**vratas**) and morality, (8) karmic bondage (bandha), (9) inhibiting (saṃvara) and wearing off (nirjarā) of **karma**, and (10) omniscience (**kevala-jñāna**) and liberation (**mokṣa**). There have been numerous **commentaries** written on this text. The most important Digambara commentaries include Devanandi's (= Pūjyapāda's) *Sarvārthasiddhi* (6th century), **Akalaṅka's** *Rājavārtika* (8th century), and Vidyānanda's *Ślokavārttika* (9th century). The most important Śvetāmbara commentaries include one written by Umāsvāti, which Śvetāmbaras classify as an autocommentary (*Svopajña-bhāṣya*), and one that was written by Siddhasenagaṇi (= Gandhahastin) in the 8th century.

TEMPLE. For image-worshipping Jains, the temple is the center of public worship. According to tradition, the worship of **images** of **Tīrthaṅkaras** in temples is beginningless in time. On the island-continent of **Nandīśvaradvīpa**, which is inaccessible to humans, there are 52 eternally existing temples where the gods (**devas**) come to worship. On **Jambūdvīpa** (our location of the universe) in the current era, it is said that the first temples were constructed by the Universal Emperor (**Cakravartin**) **Bharata** on **Mount Śatruñjaya** to house the images of his father, **Ṛṣabha**, and of Puṇḍarīka, a grandson of Ṛṣabha. Temples are mentioned in two early **Śvetāmbara** canonical sources. In the *Rājapraśnīya*, there is mention of the worship of a **Jina** image (pratimā) in a Jina temple by a multitude of gods. In the *Jñātṛdharmakathāḥ*, there is an account of Princess Draupadī worshipping a Jina image in a Jina temple. However, in the narratives of Mahāvīra's life, there is no evidence that he stayed in the precincts of Jain temples, although like the **Buddha** he stayed in **yakṣa** caityas.

Inscriptions provide the earliest historical evidence for the existence of Tīrthaṅkara images and temples that would have housed them. An inscription found in the Hāthīgumphā cave on Udayagiri Hill outside of Bhubaneswar, Orissa, which has been dated to the late 1st century B.C.E. or the early 1st century C.E., states that in the 12th year of his reign Mahāmeghavāhana King Khāravela of the Chedi dynasty "brought Kāliṅga Jina that had been taken away by King Nanda" back to his capital. This image would have dated from the 4th century B.C.E. because the Nanda dynasty was ruling Magadha from their capital at Pāṭaliputra (Patna, Bihar) when Alexander the Great entered northwestern India (327 B.C.E.). Given its importance, it is possible that it may have been housed in a royal temple. There also is evidence of temple worship at **Mathurā** in inscriptions dating from the pre-Kuṣāṇa and Kuṣāṇa periods (mid-2nd century B.C.E. through 3rd century C.E.). A temple is mentioned in an inscription of the mid-2nd century B.C.E. and another in an inscription from just before the time of Kaniṣka. Other inscriptions mention **Arhat** shrines (devakula) and Arhat sanctuaries (āyatana). These inscriptions indicate that patronage of Jain temples and shrines came from a wide variety of social classes. By the 3rd to 4th centuries C.E. there is also ample evidence of rock-hewn cave temples.

Although the architectural style varies according to tradition and region, the Jain temple is representative of the **samavasaraṇa**, the assembly hall in which the Tīrthaṅkara preaches after attaining omniscience. Jain temples may be surmounted by a tower that symbolizes **Mount Meru**, the axis mundi of the universe. In south India, a freestanding pillar called a **mānastambha** is often erected in front of Jain temples. However, in some cities like Delhi and Jaipur, Jain temples are indistinguishable from the buildings that surround them.

TERĀPANTHĪ (Dig.). Followers of the Terāpanth, one of the two main **Digambara** sectarian traditions in north India today, including Madhya Pradesh, northern Maharashtra, Rajasthan, and Uttar Pradesh. In addition to rejecting the authority of the **bhaṭṭārakas**, Terāpanthīs rejected certain temple rituals that they believe are non-Jain in origin. In their temples, they worship **images of Tīrthaṅkaras** but not images of nonliberated deities, such as **kṣetrapālas** and **yakṣa/yakṣīs**. Out of concern for the principle of non-harming (**ahiṃsā**), when performing material worship (dravya **pūjā**), substances are not used that are thought to contain life or that would attract insects, such as flowers, fruits, sandalwood paste, sweets, and dairy products. Only dry substances are used, including unbroken nonviable grains of rice, almonds, cloves, dates, and dry coconuts. They worship while standing rather than while seated, and out of concern for fire-bodied beings (tejo-kāyikas), the lamp ceremony (**āratī**) is not performed.

This division of the Digambara lay community began with the **Adhyātma movement** in Agra and other north Indian cities in the mid-17th century. There are several stories about the origins of this group that mention a wealthy **layman** named Amrā Bhauṅsā Godīkā and his son Jodhrāj who lived in Sanganer when Narendrakīrti was the bhaṭṭāraka of Amer from 1634 to 1665. In all versions, local laymen who were acquainted with the Adhyātma teachings disapproved of the authority and style of the bhaṭṭārakas. There was a division of the Digambara community and the establishment of a new temple with a congregation that identified itself as the Terāpanth, which means either The Path (panth) of Thirteen (teraḥ) or Your (terā) Path. Thirteen has been associated with 13 laymen from the Adhyātma movement who built the new temple, 13 principles of disagreement with the bhaṭṭāraka, or 13 aspects of Digambara ritual culture that they had abandoned. "Your Path" is associated with a proclamation by Jodhrāj to the **Jina** that the other sects (panths) are deluded, but the Terāpanth is yours (terā).

The Terāpanth grew rapidly with the disillusionment of the lay community with the conduct of local bhaṭṭārakas. When Jai Singh (1688–1743), the king of Amer, established his new capital city of Jaipur in 1727, separate temples were built by the **Bīsapanthīs** and Terāpanthīs. Having rejected the authority of the bhaṭṭārakas, lay intellectuals or **paṇḍits**, including **Paṇḍit Ṭoḍarmal**, became leaders of the Terāpanth and provided the intellectual foundation for the growth of the community. However, the Terāpanthīs were actively opposed by the bhaṭṭārakas and their lay followers, who continued to hold large festivals at which thousands of images were consecrated and to exert influence at royal courts.

After the death of Ṭoḍarmal in the mid-18th century, the animosity between the Bīsapanthīs and Terāpanthīs in Jaipur began to decrease. In the 1770s, Ṭoḍarmal's younger son Gumānīrām established a stricter set of ritual rules for his followers, who formed a group known as the Gumān Panth, although their preferred name is Śuddha Terāpanth Āmnāya ("The Pure Terāpanth Tradition"). It is often considered to be a branch of the Terāpanthīs, and it does not have a significant following outside of Jaipur.

The main Terāpanthī tradition subsequently spread throughout northern India. In Jaipur today, the majority of Digambaras are Bīsapanthīs, who in Jaipur are usually from the Khaṇḍelvāl **caste**, while the Terāpanthīs elsewhere are usually from the Agarvāl caste. However, the Terāpanthī became the dominant Digambara sectarian tradition in large parts of central India. The Bīsapanthī-Terāpanthī division does not exist in Karnataka, southern Maharashtra, or Tamil Nadu. With the decline of bhaṭṭārakas in the 20th century, the revival of the institution of naked **munis** who do not identify themselves as Bīsapanthī or Terāpanthī, and the adoption of many Terāpanthī ritual practices by Bīsapanthīs in north India, the differences between these two sectarian traditions have been lessened. Recently, there has been a division in the Terāpanthī community. Some Terāpanthīs have accepted the teachings of **Kānjī Svāmī** and are associated with the **Kānjī Svāmī Panth**.

TERĀPANTHĪ (Śvet.). Followers of the Terāpanth, one of the two non-image-worshipping **Śvetāmbara** sectarian traditions. It was founded in 1760 when a **Sthānakavāsī monk** named Muni Bhīkhanjī (later called **Ācārya Bhikṣu**) and four other monks split with their mendicant leader (**ācārya**) over disagreements about mendicant conduct and about the efficacy of meritorious activities undertaken by the lay community. This name is interpreted in two ways: (1) Path of Thirteen (terah), signifying the 13 monks who were the first followers of Ācārya Bhikṣu, or (2) Your (terā) Path, which is the 13-fold path of **Mahāvīra**, including the five mendicant vows (**mahāvratas**), the five comportments (**samitis**), and the three restraints (**guptis**). The majority of the Terāpanthīs are from Rajasthani merchant families of the Bīsā Osvāl **caste**, who are part of the Mārvāṛī community. They reject the veneration of **images** in both material form (dravya **pūjā**) and mental form (bhāva pūjā). However, both **mendicants** and **laypeople** perform mental worship (bhāva pūjā) through **meditation** (**dhyāna**). They also engage in study of the scriptures (svādhyāya) and in acts of austerity (**tapas**), such as **fasting**. Members of the lay community venerate living mendicants as symbols of the Jain ideals of non-harming (**ahiṃsā**) and restraint. An identifying emblem of their mendicant community is a rectangular cloth tied over their mouths (**muhpattī**), which is always worn except when eating.

Unlike other Jain mendicant communities, there has always been only one mendicant lineage with a single leader (ācārya), who is chosen by his predecessor. The present leader is **Ācārya Mahāprajña**, and his chosen successor is Yuvācārya Mahāśramaṇa (b. 1962). There is an annual gathering of the mendicant community, called **maryādā mahotsava**, where a collective oath to the ācārya is recited. Unlike other Śvetāmbara mendicants, they do not stay in mendicant dwelling-halls (**upāśrayas** or sthānakas). They stay in the homes of their lay followers, although recently in large cities they have begun to stay in community assembly houses (sabhābhavans). Originally social activism and meritorious community activities were discouraged. However, over the last 75 years, non-harming and moral conduct in society have been actively promoted through various means, including the establishment of the **Aṇuvrat movement** by **Ācārya Tulsī** in 1949. In 1980, he introduced a new category of mendicants, intermediate between laypeople and **monks** and **nuns** (**sādhus** and **sādhvīs**), called **samaṇ/samaṇī**, who are permitted to use mechanized transport, to travel abroad, and to use money. Following this, a few monks split with Ācārya Tulsī, and some of them formed a group called the Navā Terāpanth. To date, they have not attracted many mendicant or lay followers. In 1999, there were a total of 688 mendicants in the main Terāpanthī tradition, 145 sādhus and 543 sādhvīs, and a total of 23 mendicants who are separate from this tradition.

THREE JEWELS. *See* RATNATRAYA.

ṬĪKĀ. *See* COMMENTARY.

TĪRTHA. Ford or crossing-place. This term has two meanings in Jainism. (1) It is used for sacred places. This may include Jain **temples**, Jain **pilgrimage** sites, and places where Jain **mendicants** are present. In Hinduism, this term is associated with fords at rivers, but no Jain pilgrimage site is sacred because of its association with water. Sanctity is associated with auspicious events at these sites, especially the birth, renunciation, omniscience (**kevala-jñāna**), or liberation (**mokṣa**) of a **Tīrthaṅkara**. Some pilgrimage sites are associated with miraculous events in the life of a mendicant or where there is an especially powerful **image** of a tutelary deity. Jain mendicants are sometimes called "walking tīrthas," and their presence renders a site temporarily sacred. (2) It denotes the fourfold Jain community of **monks** (**sādhu**), **nuns** (**sādhvī**), **laymen** (**śrāvaka**), and laywomen (**śrāvikā**).

TĪRTHAṄKARA. Maker of a Ford (**tīrtha**). An epithet used by Jains for a human being who has attained omniscience (**kevala-jñāna**) through his own efforts and who teaches others the path to liberation (mokṣa-mārga), thereby establishing a ford (tīrtha) across the river of rebirth (**saṃsāra**). A Tīrthaṅkara establishes the fourfold Jain community (tīrtha) of **monks (sādhu)**, **nuns (sādhvī)**, **laymen** (**śrāvaka**), and laywomen (**śrāvikā**). In early Buddhist texts, this term (Pāli, titthiya) also was used for teachers of other non-Buddhist schools. Tīrthaṅkaras are born in various locations in the middle realm (**madhya-loka**) inhabited by humans where conditions are neither extremely good nor extremely bad, so that people will be motivated to follow their teachings. Our location of the universe, known as **Bharata-kṣetra**, is subject to changing conditions in progressive and regressive half-**cycles of time**. Here, 24 Tīrthaṅkaras are born in succession during the third and fourth periods of every half-cycle of time. Because these cycles are eternal, there has been an infinite number of Tīrthaṅkaras living here in the past, and there will be an infinite number in the future as well. In this era, **Ṛṣabha** was the first Tīrthaṅkara to be born here and **Mahāvīra** was the last. Approximately three years after the death of Mahāvīra, the fifth period of time began. Thus, Tīrthaṅkaras cannot be born here at this time, and therefore it is not possible for anyone born here to attain liberation. However, there are continents located elsewhere, such as **Mahāvideha**, that are not subject to cyclical time where conditions are always suitable for the birth of Tīrthaṅkaras and there are always Tīrthaṅkaras preaching. Thus, liberation is always possible in some location of the universe.

The career of each Tīrthaṅkara is essentially the same. At the time of conception, their mothers experience auspicious dreams. They are born into a family of the ruling class (**Kṣatriya** varṇa). They are reminded of their destinies as great spiritual teachers by the gods (**devas**), who tell them that it is time to renounce the household life. All Tīrthaṅkaras are born with a body that is able to withstand the most severe physical and mental austerities, which they undertake to eliminate **karma** from their **soul (jīva)** that has accumulated over innumerable lives. After attaining enlightenment, which is defined as omniscient or isolated knowledge (**kevala-jñāna**), they preach their first sermon by uttering a special divine sound (**divyadhvani**) while seated in an assembly hall (**samavasaraṇa**) constructed for them by the gods. They attract a community of mendicant followers, which is headed by a group of chief disciples (**gaṇadharas**). On the basis of these teachings, the gaṇadharas compile the Jain sacred texts (**Āgamas**). After some time, their life spans come to an end and they die after performing special meditations (**dhyāna**) to bring to an end all activity of the body, speech, and mind. Free from all karmic matter, their souls instantaneously rise to the siddha-loka, or īśat-prāgbhārā-bhūmi, which is located just above the heavenly realms at the very top of the occupied universe (**loka-ākāśa**).

Their souls remain there forever, disembodied and isolated from all other liberated souls (**siddhas**), experiencing pure **consciousness** and bliss. The five auspicious moments (**kalyāṇakas**) in the life of a Tīrthaṅkara, namely, conception, birth, renunciation, omniscience, and liberation, are celebrated by Jains on special occasions.

Tīrthaṅkaras have not made a resolution in a past life to help other beings attain enlightenment, like the Bodhisattvas in Buddhism. Nor are they manifestations of a Supreme God on earth, like the avatāras in Hinduism. They are not the creators of the universe, which is eternal and uncreated. They are human beings who preach the eternal truths of Jainism. Although they are known as "Supreme Souls" (**paramātman**) because of their achievements, their souls do not become omnipresent or universal after attaining liberation. They remain separate and isolated from all other souls. They do not interact with other souls, either non-liberated souls in saṃsāra or other liberated souls in the siddha-loka. They do not respond to the prayers of worshippers, although non-liberated deities, such as the **yakṣas/yakṣīs** associated with them, can intervene in worldly matters.

There are several differences in beliefs about Tīrthaṅkaras in the **Digambara** and **Śvetāmbara** traditions. Digambaras maintain that all Tīrthaṅkaras are conceived in the womb of a Kṣatriya **woman**, are born as males, and practice **nudity** after renunciation. According to Śvetāmbaras, **Mallī**, the 19th Tīrthaṅkara of this era, was a woman. Only **Ṛṣabha** and **Mahāvīra**, the first and last Tīrthaṅkaras of this era, practiced nudity, and the soul of Mahāvīra was conceived in the womb of a **Brahmin** woman and transferred to the womb of a Kṣatriya woman.

There also are differences between Śvetāmbaras and Digambaras regarding the nature of the body of an omniscient being (**kevalin**), including the body of a Tīrthaṅkara. According to Śvetāmbaras, after one becomes a kevalin, the skin and blood are as white as milk, eating and evacuation of food are invisible, and hair does not grow. However, a kevalin still experiences bodily afflictions and illnesses and unpleasant feelings, including hunger. He still eats to nourish his body, although there is no desire associated with eating. Digambaras view the body as a supreme (Śramaṇa) body, which is like pure crystal and lacks the fundamental physical constituents of a normal human body, like blood and so forth. He does not suffer from afflictions and illnesses or any unpleasant feelings, including hunger. He does not eat to nourish his body. Instead, his body is nourished by a special type of extremely subtle matter that is automatically absorbed. Digambaras believe that the Tīrthaṅkara is totally withdrawn from the world and that his "preaching" in the samavasaraṇa consists of a sacred sound that automatically emanates from his body. The different understanding of the nature of the Tīrthaṅkara is reflected in the iconographic features of the **images** in the two sectarian traditions. For a listing of the 24 Tīrthaṅkaras of this era, see the appendix. *See also* JINA; MAHĀPADMA; NEMINĀTHA; PĀRŚVANĀTHA; ŚĀNTINĀTHA; SĪMANDHARA.

TIRYAÑC. Literally, "moving horizontally," an animal or plant. One of four states of existence into which a **soul (jīva)** may be reborn. Living beings are subdivided into the different classes according to mobility and the number of senses. The most elementary life-forms are one-sensed beings (**ekendriya**), which experience the world through the sense of touch. They are also called sthāvara because they are incapable of moving on their own. This category includes all types of vegetable life (vanaspati-kāya), including the **nigoda**, and also single-sensed organisms with the elements themselves as their bodies. Life-forms with more than one sense are called trasa because they can move on their own. Various types of worms and insects comprise the two-, three-, and four-sensed categories. Five-sensed animals are divided into those with the capacity to reason (saṃjñī) and those lacking this capacity (asaṃjñī). Because **mendicants** must avoid harming all living beings, there are detailed discussions in early Jain texts about all forms of life, including the various one-sensed beings.

ṬOḌARMAL, PAṆḌIT (fl. first half of the 18th century). Digambara lay teacher and leader of the Digambara **Terāpanthī** sectarian tradition. Born in Jaipur into a Khaṇḍelvāl family who were followers of the Digambara Terāpanth, he was a learned scholar who knew Sanskrit, Prākrit, and probably also Kannada. He frequently lectured at the Dīvān Badhīcandjī Sāh temple, the most important Terāpanthī **temple** in Jaipur. Through his lectures and his writings, he established the intellectual foundation for the Terāpanthī tradition. He wrote Hindi **commentaries** on a number of important Digambara philosophical works, including Guṇabhadra's *Ātmānuśāsana* and Nemicandra's *Gommaṭasāra*, *Labdhisāra*, *Kṣapakasāra*, and *Trilokasāra*. Ṭoḍarmal wrote the first of his independent works, the *Rahasyapūrṇa Ciṭṭhī* ("Spiritual Letter"), in 1754. In it, he answers questions that had been posed by some members of the **Adhyātma movement** and discusses the nature of the **soul (jīva)** in each of the 14 stages of spiritual purity (**guṇasthānas**).

At the time of his death, Ṭoḍarmal was writing his most famous work, the *Mokṣamārgaprakāśaka*, in which he discusses the concept of wrong faith (mithyātva). This includes following Hindu, Muslim, or **Śvetāmbara** Jain traditions, and the worship of non-liberated deities, such as **kṣetrapālas** and **yakṣa/yakṣīs**. He also criticizes those who follow "false gurus," or the **bhaṭṭārakas**. This work is the most influential text of the Terāpanthī tradition and is very popular among Digambaras today.

After his death in the mid-18th century, his younger son Gumānīrām became a leader of the Terāpanthī community. In the 1770s, he established a stricter set of ritual rules for his followers, who became known as the Gumān Panth, although they prefer to be called the Śuddha Terāpanth Āmnāya ("The Pure Terāpanth Tradition").

TRISTUTI GACCHA (BṚHAT SAUDHARMA TAPĀ GACCHA). A **Śvetāmbara Mūrtipūjaka mendicant lineage**. The historical origins of this lineage may be traced to a branch of quasi-mendicants (**yatis**) in the Vijaya branch of the **Tapā Gaccha** that reformed itself in the late 19th century through the efforts of **Ācārya Vijayarājendrasūri**. The **mendicants** in this lineage then broke with the rest of the Tapā Gaccha over matters of mendicant praxis. At the time of its reform, they adopted from a past tradition the practice of not worshipping protector deities (**kṣetrapālas**) or **Sarasvatī**, the **goddess** of learning (śrutadevatā). They also adopted the related practice of omitting three hymns (tristuti) to the goddess of learning from their ritual of confession (**pratikramaṇa**). Because of an important difference in their ritual calendars, it is unlikely that this lineage is a remnant of the ancient ("Prācīna") Tristuti Gaccha (also called the **Āgamika Gaccha**), which became extinct after the 17th century. The Āgamika Gaccha followed the **Pūrṇimā Gaccha** in performing pratikramaṇa on the full and new moon days. The contemporary Tristuti Gaccha follows the Tapā Gaccha in performing pratikramaṇa on the 14th of each fortnight. As of 1999, it was estimated that there were approximately 190 mendicants in this lineage, 49 **sādhus** and 141 **sādhvīs**.

TULSĪ, ĀCĀRYA (1914–1997). Ninth mendicant leader of the **Śvetāmbara Terāpanthī** tradition. He was born in Ladnun, Rajasthan, into an Osvāl Jain family and was initiated into mendicancy in 1924. He was named successor-designate (yuvācārya) by Ācārya Kālūrām in 1936 and became **ācārya** this same year at the age of 22. He was interested in actively promoting nonviolence (**ahiṃsā**) and moral conduct in society at large. In this regard, Tulsī introduced the **Aṇuvrat movement** in

1949, the Communal Harmony Movement in 1954, and the New Turn movement (naya mod) in 1960. At his suggestion, a boarding school was established in 1948 at Ladnun for the education and training of young **women** who wanted to be initiated as **nuns**. His interest in promoting education that incorporated spiritual and moral values was reflected in the establishment of the **Jain Vishva Bharati Institute** at Ladnun 1970. In 1980, he introduced a new category of novice mendicants called **samaṇ/samaṇī**, who are permitted to use mechanized transport and to travel abroad to visit the diaspora community. For his contributions in strengthening the unity of India through the Aṇuvrat movement, Tulsī received the Indira Gandhi National Unity Award in 1993. He voluntarily renounced his position as leader of the Terāpanthī community in 1994 when he appointed his successor-designate, Yuvācārya **Mahāprajña**, as ācārya. He was the first Terāpanthī ācārya to be given the title gaṇādhipati, "Supreme Leader of the Order." Under his leadership, the mendicant community grew rapidly. Tulsī performed more initiations than any other Terāpanthī ācārya. He encouraged the interpretation of Jainism in light of contemporary society and modern scientific knowledge.

– U –

UMĀSVĀTI/UMĀSVĀMĪ (ca. 2nd–5th centuries C.E.). Mendicant-scholar and author of the ***Tattvārtha Sūtra*** (also known as the ***Tattvārthādigama Sūtra***), which is accepted as authoritative by all Jain traditions. The sectarian affiliation and the dates of this author have been the subject of much debate. It is probable that he lived prior to the time when the disagreement over mendicant **nudity** had caused a total separation of the **Digambara** and **Śvetāmbara** mendicant communities. Śvetāmbaras know him as Umāsvāti. Almost nothing is known about his life, but it is thought that he came from a **Brahmin** family. Śvetāmbaras traditionally have attributed many other works to him, but only a few are known today, including the *Praśamarati-prakaraṇa* and an autocommentary (*Svopajña-bhāṣya*) on the *Tattvārtha Sūtra*. Digambaras believe that the sūtra and its earliest **commentary** were written by different authors. The author of the sūtra is called Umāsvāmī by many contemporary Digambaras. This name appears in some mendicant lineage lists as a pupil of **Kundakunda**. According to Digambaras, another name for this author was Gṛddhapiccha ("One Who Uses a Vulture Feather [**piñchī**]").

UNIVERSAL HISTORY. A term used by Western scholars for works containing the Jain legendary history of the world. They contain the stories of the lives of the 63 illustrious men who are born during each progressive and regressive half-**cycle of time**. The *Triṣaṣṭiśalākā-puruṣacaritra,* or the life stories (caritra) of 63 (triṣaṣṭi) illustrious men (**salākā-puruṣas**), composed by the **Śvetāmbara** author **Hemacandra**, and the ***Mahāpurāṇa***, composed by the **Digambara** authors **Jinasena** and Guṇabhadra, contain the life stories of the illustrious men who were born in **Bharata-kṣetra** (the part of the universe where we are said to live) during the current era. The life stories of some of the individual heroes also are related in the Śvetāmbara canonical texts and **commentaries**, in the Jain *Mahābhāratas* and *Rāmāyaṇas*, and in various Jain purāṇas.

UPADHĀNA TAPAS. A communal austerity of **fasting**, **meditation**, and devotion practiced by some members of the **Śvetāmbara Mūrtipūjaka** community. This austerity is described in the 7th-century *Mahāniśītha Sūtra*. For an extended period of time (35 or 47 days), a **layperson** goes to a mendicant dwelling-hall (**upāśraya**) and observes many of the mendicant restraints. This includes a series of fasts, twice-daily rites of confession (**pratikramaṇa**), various rites of worship, and the study of certain texts, including the **Namaskāra Mantra** and sections of the *Pratikramaṇa Sūtra*. Because of its length, most participants are **women**.

UPĀDHYĀYA. Preceptor. (1) A **monk** who is appointed to teach the sacred **scriptures** to junior monks. Among **Digambaras**, this rank no longer exists. (2) The name of a **caste** of temple priests that officiate in Digambara **temples** in south India, although the name **Upādhye** is more commonly used. *See also* MENDICANT HIERARCHY.

UPĀDHYE. A **caste** of **Digambara Jains** in south India whose men serve as hereditary priests in Digambara **temples** in the south. *See also* INDRA; JAINA BRAHMIN.

UPĀDHYE, ĀDINĀTH (1906–1975). Digambara scholar of Jainism and the Prākrit and Apabhraṃśa **languages**. Born in Sadalga, Karnataka, he received an M.A. (1930) and a D.Litt. (1939) from the University of Bombay, where he specialized in the Sanskrit and Prākrit languages. He was professor of Prākrit languages at Rājarām College, Kolhapur, Maharashtra, for 32 years until his retirement in 1962. He served as dean of the Faculty of Arts at Śivājī University, Kolhapur, from 1962 to

1971, and was head of the Department of Jainology and Prākrits at the University of Mysore from 1971 to 1975. Upādhye is noted for his learned introductions to classical Jain texts that he critically edited and translated. He collaborated with **Hīrālāl Jain** in editing the ***Ṣaṭkhaṇḍāgama***. The *Bibliography of the Works of Dr. A. N. Upādhye* (Jīvarāja Jain Granthamālā, Sholapur, 1977) contains a listing of his writings.

UPAKEŚA GACCHA. Śvetāmbara Mūrtipūjaka mendicant lineage. This **gaccha** is unique in that it claims descent not from **Mahāvīra**, but from the **saṅgha** founded by **Pārśvanātha**. The earliest historical reference to this lineage is from the 10th century C.E. The lineage claimed a special relationship with the Osvāl **caste**, the city of Osian (Upakeśapura) in Marwar, and the goddess Sacciyā or Saccikā. Sacciyā was the patron deity of the lineage, the Osvāl caste, and Osian. In medieval times, it was one of the most influential **caityavāsī** lineages. It followed the custom otherwise seen only in Digambara **bhaṭṭāraka** lineages of assigning a set of hereditary or rotating names to the heads of the lineage. At first, the rotation involved five names, Ratnaprabhasūri, Yakṣadevasūri, Kakkasūri, Devaguptasūri, and Siddhasūri, but in medieval times the rotation was reduced to just the last three. In 1315 C.E., one Kakkasūri of the gaccha inspired the **layman** Desala to restore the main **temple** on **Mount Śatruñjaya**. The last **śrīpūjya** of this lineage was a Siddhasūri, who died in the early 20th century. In the first half of the 20th century, **yatis** of this lineage had seats in several towns in Marwar. In 1916, the former **Sthānakavāsī** monk Gayvarcand took re-initiation as the Upakeśa Gaccha monk **Muni Jñānsundar** and established a lineage of fully initiated mendicants (**saṃvegī sādhus**). He was installed as the final **ācārya** of the lineage as Devaguptasūri in **1943** in Jodhpur. While he had several disciples, this short-lived saṃvegī portion of the lineage died with him in 1955. As of 1998, the lineage consisted of one celibate yati who resided in Bikaner and Bombay.

UPĀSAKA/UPĀSIKĀ. Literally, "worshipper." (1) A Jain **layman**/laywoman. A synonym for **śrāvaka/śrāvikā**. (2) In the **Śvetāmbara Terāpanthī** tradition, a title given to a man/woman who is in the first year of study at the boarding school for aspiring **monks** and **nuns** at Ladnun.

UPĀŚRAYA. A dwelling-hall located in the vicinity of a **temple** where Jain **mendicants** stay for a short time during their travels (**vihāra**) or for the four-month rainy season period (**cāturmāsa**). There usually is a large main room where **laypeople** gather to hear mendicants give sermons (**pravacana**). Laypeople may also come here to perform **fasts**, such as the **upadhāna tapas** or rituals such as **poṣadha** that involve temporarily abandoning household activities. In the past, upāśrāyas were under the control of **śrīpūjyas** but today they are maintained by the local lay community.

UPAVĀSA. *See* FAST.

ŪRDHVA-LOKA. Upper realm. In Jain cosmography, the portion of the occupied universe (**loka-ākāśa**) that is the realm of one class of heavenly beings called **vaimānika devas**. It is comprised of a series of heavens, 26 (Śvet.) or 39 (Dig.), located one above the other. In the lower heavens (12 or 16), heavenly beings have different ranks with a chief, who has the title of **Indra**. Those born in the highest group of heavens have already attained proper insight (**samyak-darśana**) and will attain liberation (**mokṣa**) within two human births. Those born in the highest heaven, Sarvārthasiddhi, will attain liberation in their next human birth. After completing their lives in the heavens, all **souls** (**jīvas**) are born in the middle realm (**madhya-loka**). In their next birth, they cannot be born as a heavenly being (deva) or as a hell-being (**nāraki**). Liberation cannot be attained directly from the heavenly realms.

UTSARPIṆĪ. Progressive half of the **cycle of time.**

UTTARĀDHYAYANA SŪTRA. "Book of Later Instructions." One of the Mūlasūtra texts in the **Aṅgabāhya** portion of the **Śvetāmbara** scriptural canon (**Āgama**). It is said to be the last sermon preached by **Mahāvīra**. However, scholars believe that these 36 lectures on a wide variety of subjects were composed by numerous authors over an extended period of time. Some lectures deal with mendicant conduct and the hardships of mendicant life and others provide details about **karma** and the nature of the living (**jīva**) and nonliving (ajīva) substances (**dravyas**). Included here is a discussion between Keśi, a **monk** in the lineage of **Pārśvanātha**, and **Indrabhūti Gautama**, one of Mahāvīra's chief disciples (**gaṇadharas**). The story of the renunciation of **Neminātha** is also narrated here.

UTTARAPURĀṆA. *See MAHĀPURĀṆA.*

– V –

VAIMĀNIKA DEVAS. A class of gods or heavenly beings (**devas**) that are endowed with a celestial vehicle (vimāna). They live in the various heavenly realms in the **ūrdhva-loka**, which is located above the middle or earthly realms (**madhya-loka**) of the occupied universe (**loka-ākāśa**). There are two categories of vaimānika devas. The ones that reside in the lower of these heavenly realms, the Kalpa Heavens, are called kalpopapanna devas. Some of the **souls** (**jīvas**) that are reborn as heavenly beings here have previously attained proper insight (**samyak-darśana**) while others have a false view of reality (mithyātva). The ones that reside in higher heavens are called kalpātīta devas. All souls that are reborn as heavenly beings here have previously attained proper insight, and they will attain liberation (**mokṣa**) within two or three births. Those that are reborn as heavenly beings in the highest heaven, Sarvārthasiddhi, will attain liberation in their next rebirth as a human.

VAIŚYA. A member of the occupational class of merchants and agriculturalists in the ancient system of social organization (varṇa). According to the *Ādipurāṇa* of **Jinasena** (9th century), this varṇa was established by **Ṛṣabha**, the first king of this era, prior to his renouncing the household life. Historically, many Jain families have been engaged in business occupations that entail a minimum of violence (**hiṃsā**). *See also* CASTE.

VALLABHASŪRI, ĀCĀRYA VIJAYA. *See* VIJAYAVALLABHASŪRI, ĀCĀRYA.

VANAVĀSĪ. Forest-dweller. A term used for **mendicants** who practiced an itinerant lifestyle, staying for a short time in temporary dwellings except during the four-month rainy season period (**cāturmāsa**). Although they sometimes stayed in secluded places, the term refers to observing more stringent rules of mendicant conduct practiced by the disciples of **Mahāvīra**, who often stayed in the forest near villages. Vanavāsī mendicants viewed as lax the conduct of **caityavāsī** mendicants, who lived a sedentary life in temple complexes. In the **Śvetāmbara** community, these itinerant mendicants who observed strict mendicant conduct came to be known as **saṃvegī sādhus**.

VANDANA. Veneration of those who are worthy of respect. It is one of six obligatory duties (**āvaśyakas**) of a **mendicant** and a recommended practice for a **layperson**. Both image-worshipping and non-image-worshipping traditions venerate the **Tīrthaṅkaras** (deva-vandana) by the recitation of the "Hymn of Praise to the Twenty-Four" (caturviṃśati-stava), and they venerate mendicants and mendicant leaders (**ācāryas**) of their sectarian tradition (guru-vandana). Mendicants and laypeople of image-worshipping traditions also perform a ritual venerating the **images** of Tīrthaṅkaras (**caitya-vandana**). *See also* PŪJĀ.

VĀRĀṆASĪ. *See* BANARAS.

VARDHAMĀNA STHĀNAKAVĀSĪ JAIN ŚRAMAṆA SAṄGHA. *See* ŚRAMAṆA SAṄGHA.

VARṆA. *See* CASTE.

VARṆĪ, GAṆEŚPRASĀD (1874–1961). **Digambara paṇḍit** and renunciant. Born in Hansera, Uttar Pradesh, he was employed as a teacher in various village schools. After the death of his father, he devoted more time to the study of philosophy and logic and passed the Nyāyācarya examination. Recognizing the need for **educational institutions** devoted to the study of Jainism, he was active in the establishment of Syādvāda Jain Mahāvidyālaya at **Banaras** in 1905 and later the Ganesh Digambara Jain Sanskrit Vidyālaya at Sagar. He also was instrumental in the incorporation of Jain studies in the curriculum of Banaras Hindu University. In 1944, he took the lay vow renouncing household activities (10th **pratimā**) and, in 1947, he became a **kṣullaka** (11th pratimā), receiving the honorific title of Varṇī. He wrote an autobiography entitled *Merī jīvana gāthā* (Banaras, 1949). On his deathbed at the age of 87, he took the vows of a Digambara **muni**.

VĀSAKṢEPA (VĀSKEP). A mixture of sandalwood, saffron, and camphor powder that is believed to have protective powers. It is used by **Śvetāmbara Mūrtipūjakas** for a variety of ritual purposes. It is empowered through the recitation of sacred formulas (**mantras**) by a **mendicant**. Some **monks** and **nuns** sprinkle it on the crown of a **layperson**'s head as part of their blessing. Some laypeople keep the powder given to them by a mendicant in their homes. They may sprinkle it on the right big toe of a mendicant while performing guru-**vandana**.

VĀSUDEVA (NĀRĀYAṆA). One of the five categories of the 63 illustrious men (**śalākā-puruṣas**) in **Universal History** texts and other Jain narratives. They are the younger half brothers of the **Baladevas**, having the same father and different mothers. Like the Baladevas, they are Half-Cakravartins, with half the status and power of full universal emperors (**Cakravartins**). In **Bharata-kṣetra** (the part of the universe where we are said to live), nine Vāsudevas are born in each progressive and regressive half-**cycle of time**. In this era, they were (1) Tripṛṣṭa, (2) Dvipṛṣṭa, (3) Svayaṃbhū, (4) Puruṣottama, (5) Puruṣasiṃha, (6) Puruṣapuṇḍrīka, (7) Datta (Puruṣadatta), (8) Nārāyaṇa or Lakṣmaṇa (in Jain narratives, it is Lakṣmaṇa, not Rāma, who kills Rāvaṇa), and (9) Kṛṣṇa. They engage in war and kill their enemies, the **Prativāsudevas**, because of which they always are reborn in their next life as hell-beings (**nārakis**). However, after this, some may be reborn as **Tīrthaṅkaras**. For example, Kṛṣṇa, although now in the third hell, will be reborn as a Tīrthaṅkara in his next life. See Prativāsudeva for the corresponding enemy of each Vāsudeva.

VEDA. Sexual cravings. *See* GENDER; NO-KAṢĀYA.

VEGETARIANISM. *See* DIETARY RESTRICTIONS.

VIDEHA. *See* MAHĀVIDEHA.

VIDYĀDEVĪS. *See* MAHĀVIDYĀS.

VIDYĀNANDA, ĀCĀRYA (1925–). **Digambara** mendicant leader. He was born in the town of Shedaval, Karnataka, into an **Upādhye** family and was named Surendra. After finishing his schooling, he worked in a factory and later became involved in India's struggle for independence. He was threatened with jail in 1942 for his participation in the Quit India Movement, but he was able to escape. After returning to Shedaval he became ill. He made a resolution that if he was cured, he would take the vows of a **brahmacārī** and devote his life to the service of religion. Thus in 1946, at the age of 21, he was initiated as a **kṣullaka** by Ācārya Mahāvīrakīrti and was given the name Pārśvakīrti. During the years that he was a kṣullaka, he traveled extensively throughout India, including Bengal and Rajasthan. While he was in north India, he learned Hindi and, in 1960, he wrote *Viśvadharma kī Rūparekhā* ("Outline of Universal Dharma"), in which he discussed gifting (**dāna**) and worship (**pūjā**). In 1963, during **cāturmāsa** in Delhi, he was initiated as a naked

muni by Ācārya Deśabhūṣaṇa and was given the name Vidyānanda. In 1970, he made a **pilgrimage** of some 70 days to the Himalayas, including Bhadranath. He was the first Digambara muni to have visited this area in modern times. He was appointed **ācārya** in 1987 by the community in Delhi. Vidyānanda was instrumental in the establishment of Kundakunda Bharati in Delhi in 1987 for the study of the Digambara **scriptures** and Prākrit **languages**.

VIDYĀSĀGARA, ĀCĀRYA (1946–). Digambara mendicant leader. He was born in Sadalga, in the Belgaum District of Karnataka, and was named Vidyādhar Mallappa. When he was nine, he met **Ācārya Śāntisāgara** and soon became inclined toward renunciation. At the age of 20, he went to Jaipur and took the vows of a **brahmacārī** from Ācārya Deśabhuṣaṇa. In 1968, at age 22, he took the vows of a Digambara **muni** from Ācārya Jñānasāgara in Ajmer, Rajasthan. Jñānasāgara appointed him **ācārya** at Nasirabad (Ajmer) in 1972 before taking the vow of **sallekhanā**. Subsequently, his parents, two younger brothers, and two sisters took vows of initiation. He established the Vidyāsāgar Research Institute, Jabalpur, Madhya Pradesh, and several **educational centers** for new **mendicants**. Vidyāsāgara has translated many Digambara texts into Hindi and has written a number of poetical works, including *Mūk Māṭī*, which has been translated into many languages. He also has been very active in the cow protection movement. He inspired the formation of a lay organization based in Delhi called Ahiṃsā Army, which works for a total ban on the slaughter of cows in India. Vidyāsāgara heads the largest group of Digambara renunciants, many of them highly educated. As of 1999, it was estimated that there were 195 mendicants in his group (62 **munis**, 10 **ailakas**, 9 **kṣullakas**, and 114 **āryikās**) in addition to some 50 **brahmacārīs** and 150 brahmacāriṇīs.

VIHĀRA. Literally, wandering or roaming about. The term used by Jains for the travels of their **mendicants**. An itinerant lifestyle is considered the proper mode of mendicant conduct except during the four-month rainy season period (**cāturmāsa**), although mendicants may be given special dispensation to stay in one location on account of illness. Mendicants travel from place to place on foot, but they do not wander aimlessly. They know in advance where they are traveling and the purpose for their journey, and they may be accompanied by **laypeople** for portions of their journey. The itinerary for some groups of mendicants may be tentatively planned several years in advance.

VIJAYADHARMASŪRI, ĀCĀRYA (1868–1922). Śvetāmbara Mūrtipūjaka Tapā Gaccha mendicant leader. He was born in Mahuva, Kathiawar, Gujarat, and was named Mūla Candra. In 1887, he was initiated as Muni Dharmavijaya by Muni Vṛddhicandra. His interests were focused on promoting education, publishing Jain texts, and encouraging collaboration between Indian and Western scholars of Jainism. He founded the Yaśovijaya Jain Pāṭhśālā in Mandal, Gujarat, in 1902, which he moved to **Banaras** the following year. This was the first Jain school to be established in this city renowned for its traditional scholarship. To promote the publication of Jain literature, he founded the Yaśovijaya Jaina Granthamālā series in 1904, which later was moved to Bhavnagar. He is noted for his work on a text edition of **Hemacandra**'s *Yogaśāstra* and for his publication of Old Gujarati literature.

For a number of years, Vijayadharmasūri corresponded with scholars of Jainism in Europe, providing them with **manuscripts**, clarifying passages in texts, and assisting them when they came to India. Under his auspices, the first Jain Literary Conference was held in Jodhpur, Rajasthan, in 1914, where **Hermann Jacobi** and scholars of Jainism from India met with influential members of the Jain community to discuss the preservation and publication of Jain texts. This same year he met the Italian scholar L. P. Tessitori, who wrote a biography on him.

After his death, a memorial temple (samādhi mandir) was erected in Shivpuri and, in 1924, the Vīra-Tattva-Prakāśaka Mandal, which he had established in Bombay (now Mumbai) in 1920, was moved there. Headed by his disciple Muni Vidyāvijaya, this college prepared students for examinations in Jain history, literature, philosophy, and logic. Some of his disciples became scholars in their own right, including Muni Maṅgalavijaya, Ācārya Vijayaindrasūri, and **Ācārya Vijayavallabhasūri.**

VIJAYALABDHISŪRĪ, ĀCĀRYA (1884–1961). Śvetāmbara Mūrtipūjaka Tapā Gaccha mendicant leader. He was born in the village of Balshasan, near Ahmedabad, Gujarat, and was named Lālcand Ugarcand. He was motivated to renounce the household life after hearing the preaching of Muni Kamalavijaya. He requested initiation when he was 14 but was told to wait until he was older. In 1903, at the age of 19, he left home without telling his family and went to the village of Boru where Kamalavijaya initiated him as Muni Labdhivijaya. He began studying grammar, philosophy, and logic and soon attracted a number of disciples. Labdhivijaya traveled extensively in the Punjab, debating leaders of the Ārya Samāj on the subject of image worship and preaching nonviolence (**ahiṃsā**) and **vegetarianism** to non-Jain communities. He argued against proposed laws that would have prohibited child initiation. In 1924, the community at Chani installed him as Ācārya Vijayalabdhisūri. He is noted for his reconstruction of the text of the *Nyāyāgamānusāriṇī* of Mallavādin (5th or 6th century C.E.), a work on Jain logic that survived only in Siṃha Nandi's **commentary**, a task that spanned some 14 years. A bibliography of his works has been published in *Jain Journal* (7.2, October 1972).

VIJAYĀNANDASŪRI, ĀCĀRYA (1837–1896). Śvetāmbara Mūrtipūjaka Tapā Gaccha mendicant leader. He was born in Lahara, Punjab, into a Brahmakṣatriya family. While attending school he came into contact with **Sthānakavāsī monks** and, in 1853, he was initiated as Sant Ātmārāmjī. His study of the scriptures led him to the conviction that image worship was the orthodox position, and so in 1876 in Ahmedabad he took a second initiation as Muni Ānandavijaya from Muni Buddhivijaya (Buṭerāyajī, 1807–1882), who also had previously been a Sthānakavāsī monk. In 1886, the Mūrtipūjaka congregation of Palitana installed him as Ācārya Vijayānandasūri.

Vijayānandasūri was invited to be a delegate at the World's Parliament of Religions in Chicago in 1893. Because his vows prohibited travel by mechanized conveyance, he appointed **Vīrcand Rāghavjī Gāndhī** to represent the Jain community. Based on questions that he had received from the organizers of the Parliament, Vijayānandasūri wrote a book for the occasion entitled *The Chicago-Prashnottar or Questions and Answers on Jainism for the Parliament of Religions Held at Chicago U.S.A. in 1893* (Agra, 1918).

Vijayānandasūri was influential in reviving the tradition of fully initiated monks (**saṃvegī sādhus**). He persuaded many Sthānakavāsīs in the Punjab to join the image-worshipping (**Mūrtipūjaka**) tradition and encouraged the construction and renovation of **temples**. Roughly one-fourth of the current **samudāyas** within the Tapā Gaccha, comprising over 400 of the **mendicants** in the **gaccha**, trace their origins back to him. Following his death, a memorial temple (samādhi mandir) was erected in Gujranwala, Punjab.

VIJAYARĀJENDRASŪRI, ĀCĀRYA (1827–1906). Śvetāmbara Mūrtipūjaka mendicant leader in the **Tristuti Gaccha**. He was born in Bharatpur, Rajasthan, and was named Ratnarāj Pārak. Ratnarāj decided to become a disciple of **Yati** Pramodavijaya after hearing him preach. In 1846, Hemavijaya initiated him as Yati Ratnavijaya. Pramodavijaya arranged for him to study grammar, philosophy, and logic with

Sāgaracandra. While in Udaipur, he was appointed to the rank of **paṅnyāsa** by **Śrīpūjya** Devendrasūri, who asked him to instruct his disciple Dhīravijaya. When Devendrasūri died, Dhīravijaya was installed as śrīpūjya and was given the name Dharaṇendravijaya. In 1866, while staying in the city of Ghanerav, Ratnavijaya had a disagreement with Dharaṇendravijaya over what possessions were necessary for a mendicant, and he left, taking with him like-minded yatis. He went to the city of Ahora, where Pramodavijaya was staying. The community there installed him as śrīpūjya in 1867, giving him the name Vijayarājendrasūri, and a local official presented him with the insignia of the office. In 1869, he left the śrīpūjya insignia in a **Pārśvanātha** temple and accepted the five great vows (**mahāvratas**) of a fully initiated monk (**saṃvegī sādhu**).

Vijayarājendrasūri encouraged others to take the full mendicant vows, and he initiated 33 **sādhus**. He and his followers, who had broken with the rest of the Tapā Gaccha over matters of mendicant praxis, adopted from a past tradition the practice of not worshipping protector deities (**kṣetrapālas**) or **Sarasvatī**, the goddess of learning (śrutadevatā). Having adopted the related practice of omitting three hyms (tristuti) to the goddess of learning from their ritual of confession, (**pratikramaṇa**), this mendicant group became known as the **Tristuti Gaccha** or the Bṛhat Saudharma Tapā Gaccha.

Vijayarājendrasūri was instrumental in the restoration of Jain **temples** and the installation of **images of Tīrthaṅkaras**. He advocated the publication of the **Āgamas** and their study by **monks**. In 1889, at the age of 63, he began to compile a Jain encyclopedia, *Abhidhānarājendrakośa*, a seven-volume work of some 9,200 pages, which he completed 14 years later in 1903. It contains approximately 60,000 Ardhamāgadhī Prākrit words and their etymologies, their Sanskrit equivalents, and extensive quotations from the Āgamas and **commentaries**. He also wrote vernacular commentaries on the Āgamas and composed collections of hymns. Following his death, a memorial temple (samādhi mandir) was constructed at Mohanakheda, Madhya Pradesh. A bibliography of his works (in Hindi) has been published in *Rājendrasūri Smāraka Grantha* (1956).

VĪJAYARĀMACANDRASŪRI, ĀCĀRYA (1896–1991). Śvetāmbara Mūrtipūjaka Tapā Gaccha mendicant leader. Born in a village near Baroda, Gujarat, he took mendicant initiation in 1913 as Muni Rāmacandravijaya from Ācārya Premsūri in the lineage of **Ātmārāmjī**. He was appointed **ācārya** in Bombay (now Mumbai) in 1936. His preaching emphasized the path of liberation (mokṣa-mārga) and the importance of renunciation in following a spiritual life. He insisted on strict monastic practices and criticized many of his contemporaries for laxity in their compromises with modernity and scientific innovations. He stressed a literalist reading of texts on mendicant praxis and refused to compromise with other Tapā Gaccha mendicant leaders over calendrical issues associated with the observance of sacred days (parvans). For this reason, his mendicant sublineage (**samudāya**) may observe important **festivals**, such as **Paryuṣaṇa**, on different days from the majority of the Tapā Gaccha. In his 78 years as a **monk** and 55 years as an ācārya, he became seniormost in the Tapā Gaccha in terms of longevity. He initiated some 250 monks and 500 **nuns**. His samudāya split after his death, and as of 1999 there were three branches headed by individual ācāryas.

VIJAYAŚĀNTISŪRI, ĀCĀRYA (1889–1943). Śvetāmbara Mūrtipūjaka Tapā Gaccha mendicant leader. Born in Manadar, Rajasthan, into a family of the Raika (Rabāri) **caste**, he was named Sagtojī. The Rabāri are semi-nomadic pastoralists concentrated in Gujarat and Rajasthan who breed camels and sheep, are vegetarian, do not offer blood sacrifice, and have a tradition of ascetic renouncers in the Śaiva and Jain traditions. He followed in a tradition of low-caste (Ahir/Raika/Rabāri) Jain **monks** that included Muni Dharmavijaya and Muni Tīrthavijaya.

It is said that when Sagtojī was eight, he was out herding animals when one of them became ill. His father's younger brother, who had become a Jain monk, passed by and offered to help if he agreed to become a **mendicant**. Thus, he went to live with the mendicant community and, in 1904, Muni Tīrthavijaya initiated him as Muni Śāntivijaya. He was noted for practicing severe austerities and reportedly received spiritual assistance from various deities, including **Sarasvatī**. There are numerous accounts of his miraculous powers, including causing rain to fall, increasing the quantity of food, and making prognostications, including the time of his own death. At his urging, many **temples** were constructed, and he endeavored to free the Jain **pilgrimage** site of Kesariyaji from the control of the **Brahmins**. He spent his later years observing a lifestyle that is uncharacteristic of a Jain monk. He lived alone in a cave near the top of **Mount Ābū** and did not travel from place to place. Instead of going on alms-gathering rounds (**gocarī**), he received food from his devotees, and he did not perform the regular ascetic rites of Jain monastic life. Even though he had taken initiation in the Tapā Gaccha, he declared that he was not a member of a specific **mendicant lineage**. The only two **nuns** that he initiated both joined the **Kharatara Gaccha**. A temple complex at Mandoli (Jalore) dedicated to him has become a popular **pilgrimage** site.

VIJAYAVALLABHASŪRI, ĀCĀRYA (1879–1954). Śvetāmbara Mūrtipūjaka Tapā Gaccha mendicant leader. He was born in Baroda and was named Chaganbhāī. After losing his parents at an early age, he was influenced by the teachings of **Ācārya Vijayānandasūri**, who had come to Baroda in 1885. The following year in Rāṇakpur the **ācārya**'s disciple, Muni Harṣavijaya, initiated him as Muni Vallabhavijaya. He was dedicated to social reform, participated in the nationalist movement, and inspired others to take mendicant initiation (**dīkṣā**). He promoted modern education, and a number of schools were founded in his name. In 1915, he established the Mahāvīra Jain Vidyālaya in Bombay (now Mumbai), which presently has seven branches in other cities, including Ahmedabad and Pune. He traveled and preached for many years in the Punjab, and after independence helped to relocate Jain refugees from the West Punjab. Descended from him is a mendicant sublineage called the Vallabha Samudāya, whose fully initiated mendicants (**saṃvegī sādhus**) originally wore saffron-colored robes to distinguish themselves from the white-robed **yatis**. More recently, his samudāya has been active in preaching to tribal and low-caste people in Gujarat.

VINAYASĀGARA (1929–). Śvetāmbara Mūrtipūjaka scholar-**monk** in the **Kharatara Gaccha**. Born in Jodhpur into an Osvāl Jain family, he was named Bastīmal Jhābak. After his initiation in 1940 by Ācārya Jinamaṇisāgarasūri, he studied with **Agaracanda Nāhaṭa** and Bhanvarlāl Nāhaṭa in Bikaner, Rajasthan, who taught him to read Sanskrit, Prākrit, Apabhraṃśa, and old Gujarati, Hindi, and Rajasthani. He enrolled in Mahārāja Sanskrit College in 1950 and was awarded a Sāhityācārya degree in 1951 and the title of Sāhitya Mahopādhyāya in 1960. The focus of his life was on research and on bringing to light old Jain **manuscripts** by publishing text editions and translations.

In 1956, in Ajmer Vinayasāgara left the mendicant community after a disagreement on the emphasis placed on the performance of rituals. Although he returned to the household life and married in 1962, his interest in research on Jainism and publishing Jain literature has continued. During the 1960s he opened the Jain Printing Press in Quota, Rajasthan, and was director of the Rajasthan Oriental Research Institute, Jodhpur. In the early 1990s, he taught at the B. L. Institute of Indology, Delhi. Vinayasāgara has edited and authored a number of works, including histories of mendicant leaders (**ācāryas**) in the **Kharatara Gaccha**. A bibliography of his works has been published in *Mahopādhyāya Vinayasāgara: Jīva, Sāhitya, aura ācārya* (Jaipur, 1999).

VĪRA-NIRVĀṆA. *See* DĪVĀLĪ.

VĪRASENA. *See* COMMENTARY; JINASENA; *KAṢĀYAPRĀBHṚTA*; *ṢAṬKHAṆḌĀGAMA*.

VĪSĀPANTHĪ or **VIŚVAPANTHĪ.** *See* BĪSAPANTHĪ.

VRATA. A formal statement of an intent to refrain from a specific activity. There are different vows of restraint for **mendicants** and **laypeople**. The five great vows (**mahāvratas**), also called the mendicant vows, are taken during initiation (**dīkṣā**) into mendicancy. Laypeople have the option of taking 12 **lay vows**: the five lesser vows (**aṇuvratas**), the three supplementary vows (**guṇa-vratas**), and the four vows of spiritual discipline (**śikṣā-vratas**). These vows are lifelong and are irreversible. The **sallekhanā**-vrata, or the vow to undertake a religious death through fasting, is a supplementary vow that may be taken by both mendicants and laypeople. People may take this vow informally in advance by resolving that they intend to undertake a ritual fast until death when the end of life is near. The term vrata is also used as a general term for a Hindu **fast**. *See also* PRATYĀKHYĀNA.

VṚTTI. *See* COMMENTARY.

***VYĀKHYĀPRAJÑAPTI SŪTRA*.** "Proclamation of Explanations." The fifth **Aṅga** in the **Śvetāmbara** scriptural canon (**Āgama**). *See BHAGAVATĪ SŪTRA*.

VYANTARAVĀSĪ DEVAS. A class of peripatetic gods or heavenly beings (**devas**) who are born in the middle realm of the universe (**madhya-loka**) on continents inaccessible to humans. They may visit our location of the universe on occasion. There are eight classes of these deities, which also are found in Hinduism: kinnara, kiṃpuruṣa, mahoraga, gandharva, **yakṣa**, rākṣasa, bhūta, and piśāca.

VYAVAHĀRA NAYA. The conventional or worldly point of view in the two truths model of reality emphasized by **Kundakunda** and by the authors following him in the **Digambara** mystical tradition. It is contrasted with the nonconventional or absolute point of view (**niścaya naya**). The conventional and absolute points of view are most often employed in discussions of the sentient **soul (jīva)** and its relationship with everything that is non-soul, namely, the body and **karmic** matter.

– W –

WEBER, ALBRECHT (1825–1901). Indologist. Born in Breslau (now Wroclaw, Poland), he studied Sanskrit at Bonn, Berlin, and Breslau Universities, receiving a Ph.D. in 1846. He was appointed professor of Sanskrit at the University of Berlin in 1856, where he remained until his death. Weber prepared a descriptive catalogue of the **manuscripts** sent by **Georg Bühler** to the Royal Prussian State Library in Berlin (1892). The **Śvetāmbara** canonical manuscripts in this collection formed the basis for his study "Über die heiligen Schriften der Jaina" (*Indische Studien* 16 and 17, 1883–1885), translated as "Weber's Sacred Literature of the Jains" by H. W. Smyth in *Indian Antiquary* 17–21 (1888–1892). His translation of the *Śatruñjaya Māhātmya* (1858) has been published in English in *Indian Antiquary*, beginning in volume 2 (1873).

WOMEN. The portrayal of women by mendicant authors of early Jain texts is similar to that found in brahmanical and Buddhist texts. These texts are representative of a general Indian social and cultural environment, including negative ideas about womanhood. Being born as a female is considered to be indicative of negative habits in one's previous life, such as cheating and crookedness (māyā). It is also indicative of a false view of reality (mithyātva) in one's previous life because those who have attained a proper view of reality (**samyak-darśana**) must be reborn as a male. However, being born as a female does not prevent the attainment of samyak-darśana, because this is possible for all five-sensed beings with the ability to reason. A woman is seen as a dangerous temptress and an ever-present threat to a **monk**'s vow of **celibacy (brahmacarya-vrata)**. Monks are warned to avoid all contact with women because they will try to seduce them and lure them back into a household life. Nevertheless, when **Mahāvīra** established his community of followers, he included **nuns**, unlike Gautama the **Buddha** who did so reluctantly some five years after his enlightenment. Some women are portrayed in a positive light in the narratives, such as **Rājīmati** who resisted unwanted advances. The mothers of the

Tīrthaṅkaras and other virtuous women (**mahāsatīs**) serve as exemplars of proper conduct for women.

The general duties of a Jain **laywoman** are dependent on the Indian environment and are similar to those of Hindu and Buddhist laywomen. A woman's physical chastity is equated with her spiritual purity. She should be faithful to her husband and concerned for the well-being of her family. Women ensure the reproduction of the Jain community through marriage and religious teaching of their children. They are associated with religious gifting (**dāna**) in the home by feeding Jain **mendicants**. A woman must observe strict **dietary restrictions** in order for mendicants to accept food from her, which she carefully prepares in accordance with the rules governing mendicant alms-gathering (**āhāra-dāna**, **gocarī**). Women tend to **fast** more often than men. Fasting is a public display of a woman's chastity and religiosity, and it enhances the reputation of her family in the community. It is also more common for women to perform daily worship (**pūjā**) in the **temple** than it is for men. Men often are associated with public forms of religious gifting. However, inscriptional evidence from **Mathurā** indicates that early in the common era women donated **images** at the urging of nuns, and later inscriptions from Tamil Nadu also mention a number of donations by women. *See also* STRĪ-MOKṢA.

– Y –

YAKṢA/YAKṢĪ (YAKṢIṆĪ). In Jainism, a pair of male and female deities who are attendants of a **Tīrthaṅkara** and are the protectors of his teachings (**śāsanadevatās**). According to tradition, the god **Indra** appoints a yakṣa and yakṣī to serve as the śāsanadevatās for each of the Tīrthaṅkaras. In ancient India, yakṣas were popular cult figures among those who were not involved with the vedic sacrificial cult, and both the **Buddha** and **Mahāvīra** frequently stayed in yakṣa shrines during their travels. According to **U. P. Shah**, the earliest iconographic representation of a yakṣa/yakṣī pair is found on an **image** of **Ṛṣabha** from the Akota bronze hoard (ca. 550 C.E.). The earliest pair to be represented was a potbellied Kubera-like yakṣa named Sarvānabhūti or Yakṣeśvara and a yakṣī named **Ambikā**. In earlier times, these two were the tutelary deities for all of the Tīrthaṅkaras. They were followed by **Dharaṇendra** and **Padmāvatī**. By the 10th century, there was an individual pair of deities with unique names and iconographic features for each of the 24 Tīrthaṅkaras. Recently, Sonya Quintanilla has identified the two figures flanking a Tīrthaṅkara on an āyāgapaṭas at **Mathurā** (ca. 1st century C.E.) as śāsanadevatās. She believes that the yakṣa-yakṣī association with a specific Jina may have begun at this time.

Because these deities have not attained liberation (**mokṣa**), they can be worshipped for worldly gains. There is evidence that by the 10th century, some were becoming important deities in their own right. These include the yakṣīs Cakreśvarī (associated with Ṛṣabha), **Jvālāmālinī** (in the **Digambara** tradition, associated with Candraprabha, the eighth Tīrthaṅkara of this era), Ambikā or **Kūṣmāṇḍinī** (associated with **Neminātha**), Padmāvatī (associated with **Pārśvanātha**), and the Yakṣa **Brahmadeva** (associated with Śītala, the 10th Tīrthaṅkara of this era). *See also* BRAHMADEVASTAMBHA.

YANTRA. A mystical diagram, usually symmetrical, used in worship and ritual activities. In Jainism, they typically have concentric circles, which may incorporate the diagram of a lotus and be surrounded by squares. They contain the names of the **Tīrthaṅkaras**, the words of the **Namaskāra Mantra**, or seed syllables (bīja mantras) sacred to guardian deities (**śāsanadevatās**). Although there is evidence of more than 40 yantras, only a few are used in rituals today, including the Gaṇadharavalaya (representing the **Pūrvas** and **Aṅgas**), Kalikuṇḍadaṇḍa, **Navadevatā**, Ṛṣimaṇḍala, and **Siddhacakra** yantras. In the **Digambara** tradition, rituals using yantras were conducted by advanced **laymen** (**kṣullakas** or **bhaṭṭārakas**) and in the **Śvetāmbara Mūrtipūjaka** tradition by **yatis** and **śrīpūjyas**. Fully initiated mendicants (**saṃvegī sādhus**) could recite the mantras but could not conduct the rituals or participate in them.

YĀPANĪYA. An early **mendicant lineage** that combined features from the **Digambara** and **Śvetāmbara** traditions. There is no independent historical evidence about the origins of this group. Digambaras have maintained that they were an offshoot of Śvetāmbaras while Śvetāmbaras claim the opposite. Some scholars believe that the **monks** depicted on the āyāgapaṭas (votive tablets) and the bases of **Tīrthaṅkara images** at **Mathurā** during the pre-Kuṣāṇa and Kuṣāṇa periods (mid-2nd century B.C.E. through 3rd century C.E.) with a small piece of cloth (**ardhaphālaka**) draped over their forearms to hide their **nudity** are associated with this lineage. They may have modified the Digambara practice of total nudity for monks by using a single piece of cloth when traveling in populated areas. They recognized the authenticity of certain Śvetāmbara scriptures and supported two doctrines acceptable to Śvetāmbaras: that **women** can attain liberation (**strī-mokṣa**) and that an omniscient (**kevalin**) being partakes of food.

Yāpanīyas are mentioned in numerous inscriptions from the 5th through the 14th centuries, primarily in Karnataka. Although few of their works have survived, both Digambara and Śvetāmbara authors have discussed their views, and **Haribhadra** quotes a long passage from a text called the *Yāpanīya-tantra*. Two extant works have been identified as Yāpanīya: *Strīnirvāṇaprakaraṇa*, on women attaining liberation, and *Kevalibhukiprakaraṇa*, on the taking of food by an omniscient being. Both were written with auto**commentaries** by Ācārya Śākaṭāyana (ca. 814–867 C.E.). There has been speculation that some early authors, such as **Siddhasena Divākara**, may have been Yāpanīya, and that certain Digambara works, such as the *Mūlācāra* of Vaṭṭakera and the *Bhagavatī-Ārādhanā*, may have been written by Yāpanīyas.

This mendicant lineage had a community of lay followers who apparently were quite affluent. They built a number of **temples** in northern Karnataka (in the present-day Belgaum, Dharwar, and Gulburga districts) and installed images of Tīrthaṅkaras that were unclothed, like those in Digambara temples. They apparently became extinct sometime in the 15th century. It is likely that their **mendicants** may have gradually merged with the Digambara mendicant communities in south India.

YAŚOVIJAYA, MAHOPĀDHYĀYA (1624–1688). Śvetāmbara Mūrtipūjaka Tapā Gaccha preceptor (upādhyāya). Born in Kanoda, Gujarat, he studied various branches of brahmanical learning in **Banaras**, focusing on the techniques of New Logic (navya-nyāya). He studied the writings of the **Banārsīdās** and was familiar with the doctrines of the **Digambara Adhyātma movement**, which he refuted. He wrote more than a hundred works in Sanskrit, Prākrit, Gujarati, and Rajasthani on a variety of topics. He is highly respected for his difficult works on logic, such as *Jainatarkabhāṣa*, *Jñānabindu*, and *Nyāyāloka*. He wrote a polemical work entitled *Ādhyātmikamatakhaṇḍa* in which he defends Śvetāmbara doctrinal views on the nature of an omniscient being (**kevalin**) and the ability of **women** to attain liberation (**strī-mokṣa**). He also wrote an important **commentary** on *Dharma-saṃgraha*, a work on lay conduct (**śrāvakācāra**) written by Mānavijaya in 1681, in which he rejects non-Jain elements that had been incorporated into the writings of certain of his predecessors. In his later years, under the influence of the writings of the mystic-poet **Ānandghan**, he wrote *Jñānasāra*, which discusses the mystical nature of the inner **soul** (**ātman**). He is often described as a reformer and standardizer of Jain practice.

YATI. A **Śvetāmbara mendicant** whose vows of initiation are less stringent than those of a full mendicant. Historically, their predecessors were groups of temple-dwelling monks (**caityavāsīs**). Although in medieval times this term was synonymous with **sādhu**, it later was used more restrictively for those **monks** who could possess property, reside in one place, sleep in beds, wear shoes, cut their hair and shave, and travel by mechanized transport. Most did not perform all of the obligatory daily mendicant rituals (**āvaśyakas**). As they increased in number, yatis were organized as separate domesticated branches within the existing mendicant lineages (**gacchas**). Commonly known as gorjīs (from guru), these quasi-mendicants were of two types: worldly (saṃsārī) yatis, who were married; and renunciant (tyāgī) yatis, who were single and practiced **celibacy**. Only a renunciant yati could become a **śrīpūjya**, the leader of a lineage of yatis.

Yatis performed temple rituals for money, especially those with magical or tantric elements (**mantras** and **yantras**), and specialized in astrology and traditional medicine (āyurveda). They also worshipped the **goddess** in both Jain and Hindu manifestations. Yatis served as administrators and clerics, managing the **temples** and their associated schools, **manuscript libraries**, and lands. Some also served as lineage gurus who maintained records of births, marriages, and deaths within Jain castes. Some were closely associated with the courts of Rajput and Muslim rulers.

In most Śvetāmbara **Mūrtipūjaka** mendicant lineages there have been times when yatis have outnumbered itinerant mendicants who observed stricter vows (**saṃvegī sādhus**), and there have been repeated efforts to reform these lax mendicant practices. It has been estimated that in the 19th century there were only a few dozen saṃvegī sādhus and no mendicant leaders (**ācāryas**) in the various Mūrtipūjaka gacchas. In the latter half of the 19th century, as a result of the reform efforts of a small group of mendicants and influential **laypeople**, the number of yatis began to decrease, and there was a sharp increase in the number of saṃvegī sādhus, mostly within the **Tapā Gaccha**. The followers of **Ācārya Vijayavallabhasūri** began to wear yellow garments, instead of the traditional white mendicant garments, so that they could be distinguished from the yatis. Other reformist monks included Paṅnyāsa Maṇivijayagaṇi (1796–1879), his disciple Muni Buddhivijaya (also known by his **Sthānakavāsī** mendicant name of Buṭerāyjī), and Buddhivijaya's disciple **Ācārya Vijayānandasūri** (also known by his Sthānakavāsī mendicant name of Ātmārāmjī).

There have been no yatis in the Tapā Gaccha since the mid-1950s.

There are a few yatis still remaining in the **Kharatara Gaccha** in Rajasthan, but they are no longer influential in the community. Property that belonged to the yatis is now owned by local lay Jain organizations that are responsible for the administration of the temple complexes.

YOGA. In Jainism, yoga has several meanings. (1) **Meditation**, mental concentration, and associated practices as described in Jain yoga texts by authors like **Haribhadra**. (2) Spiritual discipline associated with proper lay and mendicant conduct, as described in **Hemacandra**'s *Yogaśāstra*. (3) As a technical term in Jain **karma** theory, yoga means movement or vibration of the **soul (jīva)** and activity of the body, speech, and mind. Thus, an omniscient being (**kevalin**) in the 13th **guṇasthāna** is called a kevalin-with-activity (sayoga kevalin). Yoga causes the influx of karmic matter to the soul, and passions (**kaṣāyas**) cause the bondage of karma with the soul.

YOGĪNDU (fl. 6th–10th centuries C.E.). Author in the **Digambara** mystical tradition also known as Joindu, Jogicandra, Yogīndra, and Yogendra. Nothing is known about his life and his dating is uncertain. Scholars believe that he flourished sometime after **Kundakunda** and Pūjyapāda and prior to **Hemacandra** (11th century). Although nine works have traditionally been attributed to him, he is accepted as the author of two extant works, *Paramātmaprakāśa* and *Yogasāra*. Both are written in Apabhraṃśa in the dohā metre. In these works, he discusses the nature of the outer **soul** (bahirātman), inner soul (antarātman), and the Supreme Soul (**paramātman**), which he also calls Brahman, **Buddha**, Hari, Hara, and Śiva. Like Kundakunda, he discusses the nature of the soul and karmic bondage from the conventional point of view (**vyavahāra naya**) and the absolute point of view (**niścaya naya**). Yogīndu describes the mystical experience of the realization of the true nature of soul through **meditation**. Like other authors in the Digambara mystical tradition, his works influenced authors in the **Adhyātma movement** and the Digambara **Terāpanthī** tradition.

Appendix

THE FOURTEEN GUṆASTHĀNAS

To attain liberation from rebirth (mokṣa), a soul (jīva) must be free of all karma, which in Jainism is a type of extremely subtle matter. Jain spiritual practices, which emphasize non-harming (ahiṃsā) and non-possession (aparigraha), provide a mechanism for preventing the influx of karmic matter to the soul. Other activities, such as fasting and meditation, destroy karmic matter previously bound with the soul. Central to this process is reducing the strength of, and eventually eliminating, all deluding (mohanīya) karmas because they give rise to passions (kaṣāyas), which cause karmic matter to bind with the soul. The progression of the soul from a state of delusion to a state of omniscience (kevala-jñāna) and final liberation is delineated in the 14 stages of spiritual progress or purification, which are envisioned as rungs on a ladder.

1. Mithyādṛṣṭi. The lowest state, in which a soul suffers from delusion or wrong views (mithyā-darśana) and the strongest degree of passions (anantānubandhī-kaṣāyas).
2. Sāsvādana. A transitional state attained momentarily when falling from a higher state to that of mithyādṛṣṭi.
3. Samyak-mithyātva. A transitional state attained momentarily when going from the first to the fourth stage or the fourth to the first stage.
4. Samyak-dṛṣṭi. The state of having a proper view of reality (samyak-darśana). All who attain this state will, in some life, proceed to the higher stages of purification and ultimately attain liberation (mokṣa).
5. Deśa-virata. The state in which non-restraint (avirati) is partially overcome, allowing one to take the lay vows (aṇuvratas).
6. Sarva-virata. The state in which non-restraint (avirati) is totally overcome, allowing one to take the mendicant vows (mahāvratas). However, there is still carelessness in observing these vows. This state is also called Pramatta-virata.

7. Apramatta-virata. The state of observing the mendicant vows without carelessness.
8. Apūrva-karaṇa.
9. Anivṛtti-karaṇa.
10. Sūkṣma-sāmparāya. In these three states attained in meditation, one either suppresses or eliminates the most subtle forms of passions (kaṣāyas) and subsidiary passions or emotions (no-kaṣāyas).
11. Upaśānta-moha. The state attained temporarily when all passions (kaṣāyas) in 8–10 are temporarily suppressed. From here, the soul must fall again to a lower state. Further progress is possible only for those who have eliminated all passions.
12. Kṣīṇa-moha. The state attained for a short period of time when all passions are eliminated through the destruction of all mohanīya karmas. In this stage, the remaining three varieties of destructive karmas are eliminated. These include all knowledge-obscuring (jñānāvaraṇīya) karmas, perception-obscuring (darśanāvaraṇīya) karmas, and obstructing (antarāya) karmas. The soul will not fall into any of the lower states. It proceeds to the 13th guṇasthāna.
13. Sayoga kevalin. The state of omniscience (kevala-jñāna) attained when all four varieties of destructive (ghātiyā) karmas have been eliminated. The soul remains embodied with activity (sayoga) due to the force of lifespan (āyu) karma. This is the state of the embodied soul of the Arhat, Kevalin, Jina, or Tīrthaṅkara.
14. Ayoga kevalin. Omniscience without activity. A momentary state attained just prior to the death of the body in which all activity of body, speech, and mind have been stopped through a meditation called śukladhyāna. Death occurs when the four varieties of nondestructive (aghātiyā) karmas that determine life span (āyu), embodiment (nāma), status (gotra), and feelings (vedanīya) have been exhausted or expelled from the soul.

Mokṣa. The state of the liberated, perfected, disembodied soul (siddha), which is permanently free of all karmic matter. At the death of the body, the soul rises instantaneously to the top of the universe and dwells eternally in the siddha-loka or the īśat-prāgbhārā-bhūmi, experiencing its own innate perfected nature of infinite consciousness and bliss.

THE ELEVEN PRATIMĀS

Pratimās are a series of vows that constitute 11 stages of renunciation for a layperson. They are enumerated in both Śvetāmbara and Digambara texts on lay conduct (śrāvakācāra), but there is some variation in the names and ordering. This list is based on Digambara texts. For variations, see R. Williams, *Jaina Yoga*, pp. 172–181.

According to Digambaras, the basic restraints (mūla-guṇas) of not consuming eight types of food is observed prior to attaining the first pratimā.

1. Darśana-pratimā. Right views. Those who have right views accept the Tīrthaṅkaras as the supreme objects of worship, the Jain Āgamas as sacred scripture, and Jain mendicants as the proper teachers of Dharma.
2. Vrata-pratimā. Taking the 12 lay vows (śrāvaka-vratas).
3. Sāmāyika-pratimā. Practicing the ritual of sāmāyika three times a day (the minimum for a mendicant), at dawn, noon, and sunset. Mūrtipūjaka Jains also must perform pūjā daily before the morning meal.
4. Poṣadha-pratimā. Fasting and abstaining from normal business or household activities on the four parvan (holy) days, the eighth and the 14th days of the moon's waxing and waning periods.
5. Sacittatyāga-pratimā. Abandoning foods that are normally allowed for a layperson. The items vary from list to list but may include green leafy vegetables, roots and tubers, uncooked grains or pulses, as well as unboiled water and salty liquids. (In some Śvetāmbara texts, this is listed after the brahmacarya-pratimā.)
6. Rātribhakta-pratimā or Kāyotsarga-pratimā. Continence by day.
7. Brahmacarya-pratimā. Absolute continence.
8. Ārambhatyāga-pratimā. Abandoning the performance of normal household and business activities, but retaining an advisory role.
9. Parigrahatyāga-pratimā. Abandoning possessions, or formally disposing of one's property.
10. Anumatityāga-pratimā. Abandoning the overseeing of household activities and the advisory role in business.
11. Uddiṣṭatyāga-pratimā. Abandoning specially prepared food and shelter and living in a place of residence for mendicants and traveling with them. For Digambaras, this stage is twofold:
    a. kṣullaka, a male who is permitted to wear three pieces of clothing (an under garment and two outer garments) or kṣullikā, a female who wears a white sari;
    b. aikala, a male who wears only a loincloth.

THE JAIN FESTIVAL CALENDAR

MAHĀVĪRA-JAYANTĪ. Commemorates the birth of Mahāvīra. Thirteenth day of the bright half of Caitra (March/April).

AKṢAYA-TṚTĪYĀ. Undying Third. Commemorates the first occasion in the current descending cycle of time when alms were given a mendicant. Third day of the bright half of Vaiśākha (April/May).

ŚRUTA-PAÑCAMĪ. Scripture Fifth (Digambara). Commemorates the day on which the Jain scriptures (śruta) were first committed to writing. Fifth day of the bright half of Jyeṣṭha (May/June).

PARYUṢAṆA. Rainy-Season Festival (Śvetāmbara). Honoring the cultivation of religious restraints. Eight-day festival beginning on either the 12th or 13th day of the dark half of Śrāvaṇa (July/August).

DAŚA-LAKṢAṆA-PARVAN. Festival of Ten Virtues (Digambara). Honoring the cultivation of religious restraints. Ten-day festival beginning on the fifth day of the bright half of Bhādrapada (August/September).

DĪVĀLĪ (DĪPĀVALĪ). Festival of Lights. Commemorates the day on which Mahāvīra attained final liberation. Fifteenth day of the dark half of Āśvina (September/October).

OḶĪ (AVALĪ). Śvetāmbara festival devoted to the worship of the siddhacakra observed primarily by women to ensure the health of their husbands. Twice a year on the seventh through the 15th days of the bright half of Caitra (March/April) and Āśvina (September/October).

JÑĀNA-PAÑCAMĪ. Knowledge Fifth (Śvetāmbara). Commemorates the day on which the Jain scriptures were first committed to writing. Fifth day of the bright half of Kārtika (October/November).

KĀRTIKA-PŪRṆIMĀ. The full moon day of Kārtika (October/November), approximately two weeks after Dīvālī, which marks the end of the four-month rainy season period (cāturmāsa).

PĀRŚVANĀTHA-JAYANTĪ. Commemorates the birth of Pārśvanātha. Tenth day of the dark half of Pauṣa (December/January), and thus also is called Poṣ Tenth.

TĪRTHAṄKARAS' COGNIZANCES

	NAME	COGNIZANCE (Śvet.)	COGNIZANCE (Dig.)
1	Ṛṣabha (Ādinātha)	Bull	Bull
2	Ajita	Elephant	Elephant
3	Saṃbhava	Horse	Horse
4	Abhinandana	Monkey	Monkey
5	Sumati	Krauñca-bird	Krauñca-bird
6	Padmaprabha	Red lotus	Red lotus
7	Supārśva	Svastika	Nandyāvarta or Svastika
8	Candraprabha	Crescent moon	Crescent moon
9	Puṣpadanta (Suvidhi)	Makara (crocodile)	Crocodile or Crab
10	Śītala	Śrīvatsa	Svastika or Wishing-tree
11	Śreyāṃśa	Rhinoceros	Rhinoceros
12	Vāsupūjya	Buffalo	Buffalo
13	Vimala	Boar	Boar
14	Ananta	Falcon	Bear
15	Dharma	Vajra (thunderbolt)	Vajra (thunderbolt)
16	Śānti	Deer	Deer
17	Kunthu	Goat	Goat
18	Ara	Nandyāvarta	Fish, Flower
19	Malli	Kailaśa (water pot)	Kailaśa (water pot)
20	Munisuvrata	Tortoise	Tortoise
21	Nami	Blue lotus	Blue lotus
22	Nemi	Conch	Conch
23	Pārśva	Snake (cobra)	Snake (cobra)
24	Mahāvīra	Lion	Lion

TĪRTHAṄKARAS' YAKṢAS

	NAME	YAKṢA (Śvet.)	YAKṢA (Dig.)	YAKṢA (TP)*
1	Ṛṣabha (Ādinātha)	Gomukha	Gomukha	Govadana
2	Ajita	Mahāyakṣa	Mahāyakṣa	Mahāyakṣa
3	Saṃbhava	Trimukha	Trimukha	Trimukha
4	Abhinandana	Yakṣanāyaka	Yakṣeśvara	Yakṣeśvara
5	Sumati	Tumbaru	Tumbaru	Tumburava
6	Padmaprabha	Kusuma	Kusuma	Mātaṅga
7	Supārśva	Mātaṅga	Varanandī	Vijaya
8	Candraprabha	Vijaya	Śyāma	Ajita
9	Puṣpadanta (Suvidhi)	Ajita	Ajita	Brahma
10	Śītala	Brahma	Brahma	Brahmeśvara
11	Śreyāṃśa	Yakṣet	Iśvara	Kumāra
12	Vāsupūjya	Kumāra	Kumāra	Ṣaṇmukha
13	Vimala	Ṣaṇmukha	Ṣaṇmukha	Pātāla
14	Ananta	Pātāla	Pātāla	Kinnara
15	Dharma	Kinnara	Kinnara	Kiṃpuruṣa
16	Śānti	Garuḍa	Kiṃpuruṣa	Garuḍa
17	Kunthu	Gandharva	Gandharva	Gandharva
18	Ara	Yakṣendra	Khendra	Kubera
19	Malli	Kubera	Kubera	Varuṇa
20	Munisuvrata	Varuṇa	Varuṇa	Bhṛkuṭi
21	Nami	Bhṛkuṭi	Bhṛkuṭi	Gomedha
22	Nemi	Gomedha	Gomedha	Pārśva
23	Pārśva	Pārśva or Dharaṇendra	Pārśva	Mātaṅga
24	Mahāvīra	Mātaṅga	Mātaṅga	Guhmaka

***TP = Yakṣas according to *Tiloyapaṇṇatti* of Yativṛṣabha (Dig.)**

TĪRTHAṄKARAS' YAKṢĪS

	NAME	YAKṢĪ (Śvet.)	YAKṢĪ (Dig.)	YAKṢĪ (TP)*
1	Ṛṣabha (Ādinātha)	Cakreśvarī	Cakreśvarī	Cakreśvarī
2	Ajita	Ajitā	Rohiṇī	Rohiṇī
3	Saṃbhava	Duritāri	Prajñapti	Prajñapti
4	Abhinandana	Kālikā	Vajraśṁkhalā	Vajraśṁkhalā
5	Sumati	Mahākālī	Puruṣadattā	Vajrāṅkuśā
6	Padmaprabha	Acyutā	Manovegā	Apraticakreśvarī
7	Supārśva	Śāntā	Kālī	Puruṣadatta
8	Candraprabha	Bhṛkuṭi	Jvālāmālinī	Manovegā
9	Puṣpadanta (Suvidhi)	Sutārā	Mahākālikā	Kālī
10	Śītala	Aśokā	Mānavī	Jvālāmālinī
11	Śreyāṃśa	Mānavī	Gaurī	Mahākālī
12	Vāsupūjya	Caṇḍā, Candrā	Gāndhārī	Gaurī
13	Vimala	Viditā	Vairoṭī, Vairoṭyā	Gāndhārī
14	Ananta	Aṅkuśā	Anantamatī	Vairoṭī
15	Dharma	Kandarpā	Mānasī	Anantamatī
16	Śānti	Nirvāṇī	Mahāmānasī	Mānasī
17	Kunthu	Balā	Vijayā	Mahāmānasī
18	Ara	Dhāriṇī	Ajitā	Jayā
19	Malli	Dharaṇapriyā, Vairoṭyā	Aparajitā	Vijayā
20	Munisuvrata	Naradattā	Bahurūpiṇī	Aparājitā
21	Nami	Gāndhārī	Cāmuṇḍī	Bahurūpiṇī
22	Nemi	Ambikā	Ambikā	Kūṣmāṇḍinī
23	Pārśva	Padmāvatī	Padmāvatī	Padmā
24	Mahāvīra	Siddhāyikā	Siddhayikā	Siddhayinī

*TP = Yakṣīs according to *Tiloyapaṇṇatti* of Yativṛṣabha (Dig.)

TĪRTHAṄKARAS' BIRTH AND NIRVĀṆA SITES

	NAME	PLACE OF BIRTH	PLACE OF NIRVĀṆA
1	Ṛṣabha (Ādinātha)	Ayodhyā	Mt. Aṣṭāpada (= Mt. Kailāsa)
2	Ajita	Ayodhyā	Mt. Sammeda (= Pārasnātha Hill)
3	Saṃbhava	Śrāvastī	Mt. Sammeda
4	Abhinandana	Ayodhyā	Mt. Sammeda
5	Sumati	Ayodhyā	Mt. Sammeda
6	Padmaprabha	Kauśāmbī	Mt. Sammeda
7	Supārśva	Kāśī (= Vārāṇasī)	Mt. Sammeda
8	Candraprabha	Candrapurī	Mt. Sammeda
9	Puṣpadanta (Suvidhi)	Kākandī	Mt. Sammeda
10	Śītala	Bhadrikāpurī	Mt. Sammeda
11	Śreyāṃśa	Siṃhapurī	Mt. Sammeda
12	Vāsupūjya	Campāpurī	Campāpurī
13	Vimala	Kāmpilya	Mt. Sammeda
14	Ananta	Ayodhyā	Mt. Sammeda
15	Dharma	Ratnapurī	Mt. Sammeda
16	Śānti	Hastināpura	Mt. Sammeda
17	Kunthu	Hastināpura	Mt. Sammeda
18	Ara	Hastināpura	Mt. Sammeda
19	Malli	Mithilāpurī	Mt. Sammeda
20	Munisuvrata	Kuśagranagara	Mt. Sammeda
21	Nami	Mithilāpurī	Mt. Sammeda
22	Nemi	Śaurīpura or Dvārakā	Mt. Girnār
23	Pārśva	Kāśī	Mt. Sammeda
24	Mahāvīra	Kuṇḍagrāma	Pāvāpurī

Bibliography

INTRODUCTION

In preparing this bibliography, it is striking to see the advances that have been made in research on Jainism over the last 15 years. Prior to the publication of the *Jaina Path of Purification* by Padmanabh S. Jaini in 1979, the few survey works that were available to an English-speaking audience presented Jainism in a critical light. Mrs. Sinclair Stevenson's *The Heart of Jainism*, published in 1915 and recently reprinted in India, viewed Jainism through the lens of a Christian missionary, concluding that the heart of Jainism was empty because it lacked the saving grace of Jesus. Jain literature was described by Maurice Winternitz as being "dry-as-dust" and "seldom instinct with that general human interest which so many Buddhist texts possess." In an article entitled "The Jains and the Western Scholar" published in 1976, P. S. Jaini commented that "western scholars have been attracted to Jaina studies for various reasons, but almost none of them have been motivated by a passionate interest in Jainism as a whole and for its own sake." He noted that only three or four scholars had ever visited the Jain community in India and none had visited the Digambaras.

Although there are relatively few scholars who work in the area of Jain studies, the number of books and articles published recently reflects a growing international academic interest in all aspects of this religious tradition. Many of these scholars have spent time in India with both the Śvetāmbara and Digambara communities learning about their traditions and practices. It is now possible for an English reader to get a more comprehensive view of the history of Jainism, of its doctrines, of its sectarian traditions, of the practices of its mendicant and lay communities, of its literature, of its rituals, and of its art. There are now English translations of traditional biographies, of narratives, and of hymns of praise that challenge the view of Jain literature as dry and stereotyped.

In this bibliography I have used, with slight modifications, the categories found in Bruce M. Sullivan's *Historical Dictionary of Hinduism*, volume 13 in this series. It was difficult to decide how to classify many works that could be listed under more than one category. Each work is listed only once in the category that seemed to be the most appropriate except for several entries in the section entitled "The Study of Jainism." I would encourage the reader to scan the entire bibliography for the variety of works that is available and to look in related areas to find articles of interest. Because of the large number of conference volumes, collected papers volumes, and festschrifts published recently that are not thematic, I have added a section entitled "Collections of Articles on Various Topics." The individual essays within these volumes are not listed separately by category elsewhere in the bibliography. I would urge the reader to consult these volumes for articles of interest to them.

With the emergence of Jainism as a world religion, chapters on Jainism now are found in many survey texts on world religions. I have listed only a few of these. Most encyclopedias include an entry on Jainism, but I have not listed them here. Most of the works in the bibliography are written in English. I have included only a few of the works on Jainism that are written in French and German and none that are written in Japanese. There also is a vast literature on Jainism written in Hindi, Gujarati, and Kannada that has not been included here. The names of some of the scholars who authored these works are listed in the dictionary, and with the availability of electronic records of library holdings such as WorldCat it should be possible for readers to locate their books.

I would like to draw the reader's attention to several works in the bibliography. In the section "Art, Architecture, and Iconography," Jain and Fisher's *Jain Iconography* contains photographs of temple worship, Jain mendicants, as well as iconography. In the section "Sacred Places," Titze's *Jainism: A Pictorial Guide to the Religion of Non-Violence* and Vaid's *Teerth Darshan* contain photographs and descriptions of Jain pilgrimage sites. These works provide useful illustrations for entries in this dictionary. The most up-to-date survey text on Jainism is the second edition of *The Jains* by Paul Dundas.

The following are English-language journals devoted to Jainism that are listed on WorldCat: *Jain Digest*, *Jain Journal*, *Jain Jyoti* (1974–1989), *Jain Spirit*, *The Jaina Gazette*, *Jinamanjari*, and *The Voice of Ahimsa* (1951–1967). *Ahiṁsā Times* (www.jainsamaj.org) and *Jain Voice* (www.jainheritagecentres.com) are Internet-based Jain periodicals. The Centre of Jaina Studies was established in 2004 at the School of Oriental and African Studies (SOAS), University of London, to promote the study of Jain religion and culture. Recent publications on Jainism are posted on their website (www.soas.ac.uk/jainastudies).

CONTENTS

SURVEY AND INTRODUCTORY WORKS

Basham, A. L. *History and Doctrines of the Ājīvikas*. London: Luzac, 1951; reprint, Delhi: Motilal Banarsidass, 1981.

———. "The Basic Doctrines of Jainism" and "Jain Philosophy and Political Thought," chapters 3 and 4 in *Sources of Indian Tradition*, ed. Ainslie T. Embree, vol. 1, second ed., pp. 49–92. New York: Columbia University Press, 1988.

Caillat, Colette. "Jainism," in *The Encyclopedia of Religion*, ed. Mircea Eliade. Reprinted in *The Religious Traditions of Asia*, ed. Joseph M. Kitagawa, pp. 97–109. New York: Macmillan, 1989.

Dundas, Paul. *The Jains*. London: Routledge, 1992; second ed., 2002.

———. "Jainism," in *The Cambridge Illustrated History of Religions*, ed. John Bowker, pp. 56–63. Cambridge: Cambridge University Press, 2002.

Folkert, Kendall W. "The Jainas," in *A Reader's Guide to the Great Religions*, ed. Charles J. Adams, second ed., pp. 231–246. New York: The Free Press, and London: Collier Macmillan, 1977.

———. "Jainism," in *A Handbook of Living Religions*, ed. John R. Hinnells, second rev. ed., pp. 340–368. Revised and expanded by John E. Cort. Oxford: Blackwell, 1996; paperback ed., London: Penguin Books, 1997.

Glasenapp, Helmuth von. *Der Jainismus: eine indische Erlösungsreligion: nach den Quellen dargestellt*. Berlin: Alf Häger, 1925. Trans. Shridhar B. Shrotri as *Jainism: An Indian Religion of Salvation*. Delhi: Motilal Banarsidass, 1996.

Gopalan, S. *Outlines of Jainism*. New York: Halstead Press, 1973.

Jaini, Padmanabh S. *The Jaina Path of Purification*. Berkeley: University of California Press, 1979; rev. ed., New Delhi: Motilal Banarsidass, 1998.

Nyayavijayaji, Muni. *Jaina Philosophy and Religion*, trans. Nagin J. Shah. Delhi: Motilal Banarsidass, 1998.

Padhi, Bibhu, and Minakshi Padhi. "Jainism," in *Indian Philosophy and Religion: A Reader's Guide*, pp. 63–95. Jefferson, N.C.: McFarland, 1990.

Schubring, Walther. *The Doctrine of the Jainas: Described after the Old Sources*, trans. Wolfgang Buerlen, 1962; second rev. ed., Delhi: Motilal Banarsidass, 2000.

Shah, Natubhai. *Jainism: The World of Conquerors*, 2 vols. Brighton: Sussex Academic Press, 1998.

COLLECTIONS OF ESSAYS ON VARIOUS TOPICS

Alsdorf, Ludwig. *Kleine Schriften*, 2 vols., ed. A. Wezler. Glasenapp-Stiftung 10 and Nachtragsband Glasenapp-Stiftung 35. Wiesbaden: Franz Steiner, 1974 and 1998.

Balbir, Nalini, and Joachim K. Bautze, eds. *Festschrift Klaus Bruhn*. Reinbek: Verlag für Orientalistische Fachpublikationen, and Hamburg: Drucke and Kopie, 1994.

Balbir, Nalini, and Colette Caillat, eds. *Indologica Taurinensia* 11 (Jaina Canonical and Narrative Literature: International Symposium, Strasbourg, 16–19 June 1981), 1983.

Balcerowicz, Piotr, and Marek Mejor, eds. *Essays in Jaina Philosophy and Religion*. Warsaw Indological Studies, vol. 2, 2002. Delhi: Motilal Banarsidass, 2003.

Bhattacharyya, N. N., ed. *Jainism and Prakrit in Ancient and Medieval India: Essays for Prof. Jagdish Chandra Jain*. New Delhi: Manohar, 1994.

Bruhn, Klaus, and Albrecht Wezler. *Studien zum Jainismus und Buddhismus: Gedenkschrift für Ludwig Alsdorf*. Wiesbaden: Franz Steiner, 1981.

Caillat, Colette, ed. *Middle Indo-Aryan and Jaina Studies* (Panels of the 7th World Sanskrit Conference, vol. 6–7). Leiden: E. J. Brill, 1991.

Carrithers, Michael, and Caroline Humphrey. *The Assembly of Listeners: Jains in Society*. Cambridge: Cambridge University Press, 1991.

Cort, John E., ed. *Open Boundaries: Jain Communities and Cultures in Indian History*. Albany: State University of New York Press, 1998.

Dhaky, M. A., and Sagarmal Jain, eds. *Aspects of Jainology, vol. 2: Pt. Bechardas Doshi Commemoration Volume*. Varanasi: P. V. Research Institute, 1987.

———. *Aspects of Jainology, vol. 3: Pt. Dalsukhbhai Malvania Felicitation vol. 1*. Varanasi: P. V. Research Institute, 1991.

Flügel, Peter, ed. *Doctrines and Dialogues: Studies in Jain History and Culture*. London: Routledge Curzon, forthcoming.

Folkert, Kendall W. *Scripture and Community: Collected Essays on the Jains*, ed. John E. Cort. Atlanta: Scholars Press, 1993.

Jacobi, Hermann. *Kleine Schriften*, ed. B. Kölver. Glasenapp-Stiftung 4.2. Wiesbaden: Franz Steiner, 1970.

Jain, J. B., ed. *Nirgrantha: Festschrift for Muni Jambūvijayajī*. Ahmedabad: Sharadaben Chimanbhai Educational Research Centre, forthcoming.

Jain, Jagdish Chandra. *Studies in Early Jainism: Selected Research Articles*. New Delhi: Navrang, 1992.

Jain, Sagarmal, and Shriprakash Pandey. *Jainism in a Global Perspective: A Compilation of the Papers Presented at the Parliament of World's Religions, Chicago (U.S.A.), 1993*. Varanasi: Pārśvanātha Vidyāpīṭha, 1998.

Jain, Surender K., ed. *Glimpses of Jainism*. Delhi: Motilal Banarsidass, 1997.

Jain, V. P., ed. *Proceedings of the International Seminar on Umāsvāti and His Works* (January 4–6, 1999). Delhi: Bhogilal Leherchand Institute of Indology, forthcoming.

Jaini, Padmanabh S. *Collected Papers on Jaina Studies*. Delhi: Motilal Banarsidass, 2000.

———. *Collected Papers on Buddhist Studies*. Delhi: Motilal Banarsidass, 2001.

Kalghatgi, T. G., ed. *Jainism and Karnatak Culture*. Dharwar: Karnatak University, 1977.

Krause, Charlotte. *German Jain Śrāvikā, Dr. Charlotte Krause: Her Life and Literature*, vol. 1. Comp. H. Banthia and L. Soni, ed. S. Pandey. Varanasi: Pārśvanātha Vidyāpīṭha, 1999.

Kulkarni, V. M. *Studies in Jain Literature: The Collected Papers Contributed by Prof. V. M. Kulkarni*, ed. J. B. Shah. Ahmedabad: Shresthi Kasturbhai Lalbhai Smarak Nidhi, 2001.

Lalwani, Ganesh, ed. *Jainthology: An Anthology of Articles Selected from* Jain Journal *of Last 25 Years*. Calcutta: Jain Bhawan, 1991.

Leumann, Ernst. *Kleine Schriften*, ed. Nalini Balbir. Glasenapp-Stiftung 37. Stuttgart: Franz Steiner, 1998.

Norman, K. R. *Collected Papers*, 7 vols. Oxford: Pali Text Society, 1990–2001.

O'Connell, J. T., ed. *Jain Doctrine and Practice: Academic Perspectives*. Toronto: University of Toronto, 2000.

Qvarnström, Olle, ed. *Jainism and Early Buddhism: Essays in Honor of Padmanabh S. Jaini*. Fremont, Calif.: Asian Humanities Press, 2003.

Raghavan, V., et al., eds. *The Adyar Library Bulletin* 38 (1974, Mahāvīra Jayanti volume).

Rangarajan, Haripriya, et al., eds. *Jainism: Art, Architecture, Literature, and Philosophy*. Delhi: Sharada Publishing House, 2001.

Sangave, Vilas Adinath. *Facets of Jainology: Selected Research Papers on Jain Society, Religion, and Culture*. Mumbai: Popular Prakashan, 2001.

Schubring, Walther. *Kleine Schriften*, ed. K. Bruhn. Glasenapp-Stiftung 13. Wiesbaden: Franz Steiner, 1977.

Singhi, N. K., ed. *Ideal, Ideology, and Practice: Studies in Jainism*. Jaipur: Printwell Publishers, 1987.

Skoog, Kim, ed. *Philosophy East and West* 50.3 (July 2000, special issue on Jainism).

Smet, Rudy, and Kenji Watanabe, eds. *Jain Studies in Honour of Jozef Deleu*. Tokyo: Hon-no-tomosha, 1993.

Soni, J., ed. *Vasanthagauravam: Essays in Jainism Felicitating Professor M. D. Vasantha Raj*. Mumbai: Vakils, Feffer, and Simons, 2001.

Tessitori, Luigi Pio. *Studi Giainici*. Udine: Societá Indologica "Luigi Pio Tessitori," 2000.

Upadhye, Adinath N. *Upadhye: Papers*. Mysore: University of Mysore, 1983.

Upadhye, Adinath N., et al., eds. *Mahāvīra and His Teachings*. Bombay: Bhagavān Mahāvīra 2500th Nirvāṇa Mahotsava Samiti, 1977.

Wagle, N. K., and Olle Qvarnström, eds. *Approaches to Jaina Studies: Philosophy, Logic, Rituals, and Symbols*. Toronto: University of Toronto, Centre for South Asian Studies, 1999.

TEXTS IN TRANSLATION

Balcerowicz, Piotr, ed. and trans. *Jaina Epistemology in Historical Perspective: Critical Edition and English Translation of Logical-Epistemological Treatises* Nyāyāvatāra, Nyāyāvatara-vivṛti, *and* Nyāvāvatara-tippana. Stuttgart: Franz Steiner, 2001.

Banerjee, Satya Rajan, ed. *Mahāmahopādhyāya Satis Chandra Vidyābhūṣaṇa's* Nyāyāvatāra: *The Earliest Work on Pure Logic by Siddhasena Divākara*. (Incorporates S. C. Vidyābhūṣaṇa's edition and translation of the *Nyāyāvatāra* published in 1909 in Calcutta.) Calcutta: Sanskrit Book Depot, 1981.

Barnett, L. D., trans. *The* Antagaḍa-dasāo *and* Aṇuttarovavāiya-dasāo. Oriental Translation Fund New Series, vol. 27. London: Royal Asiatic Society, 1907.

Bhargava, Dayanand, ed. and trans. Jaina-Tarkabhāṣa *of Yaśovijaya*. Delhi: Motilal Banarsidass, 1973.

Bhattacharya, Harisatya, trans. Pramānanayatattvalokālaṅkāra *of Vādi Devasūri*. Bombay: Jain Sahitya Vikas Mandal, 1967.

Bhogāvat, Premrāj, and Prem Bhaṇḍārī, eds. *Bhaktāmara*, English trans. Himmatt Sinha Sarupria. Jaipur: Samyagjñān Pracārak Maṇḍal, 1975.

Bollee, Willem, and Jayandra Soni. *Mahāvīra's Words by Walther Schubring* (trans. from the German with added material). Ahmedabad: L. D. Institute of Indology, 2004.

Bossche, Frank van den. "Jain Arguments against Vedānta Monistic Idealism: A Translation of the *Parabrahmotthāpanasthala of Bhuvanasundra Sūri.*" *Journal of Indian Philosophy* 25 (1997): 337–374.

———. "Jain Arguments against Nyāya Theism: A Translation of the Īśvarotthāpaka Section of Guṇaratna's *Tarka-Rahasya-Dīpikā.*" *Journal of Indian Philosophy* 26 (1998): 1–26.

Caillat, Colette. "The Offering of Distics (Dohāpāhuḍa) Translated from Apabhraṃśa with Critical Notes." *Sambodhi* 5.2–3 (July–October 1976): 175–199.

Chakravarti, A., trans. Pañcāstikāyasāra: *The Building of the Cosmos by Kundakundacharya*. The Sacred Books of the Jainas, vol. 3. Arrah: Central Jain Publishing House, 1920.

Dharmaraja, M. K., trans. Samayasāra *of Śrī Kundakunda*. Varanasi: Bhāratīya Jñānapīṭha, 1950.

———. *Kundakunda*'s Barasanuvekkha: *Twelve Contemplations*. New Delhi: Kundakunda Bharati, 2003.

Dixit, K. K., trans. *The* Yogabindu *of Ācārya Haribhadrasūri*. L. D. Series no. 10. Ahmedabad: L. D. Institute of Indology, 1968.

———. Yogadṛṣṭisamuccaya *and* Yogaviṃśikā *of Ācārya Ḥaribhadrasūri*. L. D. Series no. 27. Ahmedabad: L. D. Institute of Indology, 1970.

Faddegon, B., ed. and trans. *The* Pravacanasāra *of Kundakunda Ācārya*. Jaina Literature Society Series, vol. 1. Cambridge: Cambridge University Press, 1935.

Ghoshal, Sarat Chandra, trans. *Dravya-Saṃgraha*. The Sacred Books of the Jainas, vol. 1. Arrah, 1917; reprint, New Delhi: Today & Tomorrow's Printers and Publishers, 1990.

———. *Parīkṣāmukham*. The Sacred Books of the Jainas, vol. 11. Calcutta: Metropolitan Printing & Publishing House, 1940; reprint, New Delhi: Today & Tomorrow's Printers & Publishers, 1990.

Gopani, Amritlal, trans. Jñānasāra *of Yaśovijaya*. Bombay: Jaina Sahitya Vikasa Mandala, 1986.

Gore, N. A., ed. and trans. *The* Uvāsagadasāo: *The Seventh Aṅga of the Jain Canon*. Poona Oriental Series, no. 87. Poona: Oriental Book Agency, 1953.

Goswami, S. K. L., trans. *Victory of Discipline* (translation of *Jaya Anuśāsana*, selected verses from the writings of Jayācārya), ed. Muni Mahendra Kumar. Ladnun: Jain Vishva Bharati, 1981.

Goya, D. K., trans. *The Path to Enlightenment*: Svayambhu Stotra. New Delhi: Radiant Publishers, 2000.

Hoernle, A. F. Rudolf, ed. and trans. *The* Uvāsagadasāo *or The Religious Profession of an Uvāsaga Expounded in Ten Lectures being The Seventh Aṅga of the Jains*, Bibliotheca Indica Series, vol. 105. Calcutta: Asiatic Society, 1885.

Jacobi, Hermann, trans. *Jaina Sūtras*, pt. 1 (translation of the *Ācārāṅga-sūtra* and the *Kalpa-sūtra*). Oxford: Oxford University Press, 1884; reprint, Delhi: Motilal Banarsidass, 1989.

———. *Jaina Sūtras*, pt. 2 (translation of the *Uttarādhyayana-sūtra* and the *Sūtrakṛtāṅga-sūtra*). Oxford: Oxford University Press, 1895; reprint, Delhi: Motilal Banarsidass, 1989.

Jain, Champat Rai, trans. *The Householder's Dharma:* Ratna-karanda-śravakācāra *of Samanta Bhadra Acharya*. Arrah: Central Jain Publishing House, 1917; reprint, Meerut: Veer Mirvan Bharati, 1975.

Jain, Jagdish P. "Sadhak," ed. *Spiritual Enlightenment*: Paramatma Prakash *by Sri Yogindu Deva* (revised 1915 trans. of Rickhab Dass Jain and commentary by A. N. Upadhye). New Delhi: Radiant Publishers, 2000.

———. *Spiritual Insights:* Ishtopadesh *and* Samadhi Shatak *by Acarya Pujyapada Svami* (reprint of the translation of Champat Rai Jain and Raoji Nemchand Shah). New Delhi: Radiant Publishers, 2000.

Jain, N. L. *Biology in Jaina Treatise on Reals: English Translation with Notes on Chapter Two of* Tattvārtha-Rāja-Vārtika *of Akalaṅka*. Varanasi: Pārśvanātha Vidyāpīṭha, and Chennai: Śri Digambar Jain Samāj, 1998.

———. *Jaina Karmology: English Translation with Notes on Chapter Eight of* Tattvārtha-Rāja-Vārtika *of Akalaṅka*. Varanasi: Pārśvanātha Vidyāpīṭha, 1998.

Jain, S. A. *Reality: English Translation of Shri Pujyapada's* Sarvarthasiddhi. Calcutta: Vīra Śāsana Sangha, 1960; reprint, Madras: Jwalamalini Trust, 1992.

Jaini, J. L., trans. *Tattvārthādhigama Sūtra*. Assisted by Brahmachari Sital Prasad. The Sacred Books of the Jainas, vol. 2. Arrah: Central Jaina Publishing House, 1920; reprint, New Delhi: Today & Tomorrow's Printers and Publishers, 1990.

———. Gommatsara Jiva-Kanda *of Nemicandra*. Assisted by Brahmachari Sital Prasad. The Sacred Books of the Jainas, vol. 5. Lucknow: Central Jaina Publishing House, 1927; reprint, New Delhi: Today & Tomorrow's Printers & Publishers, 1990.

———. Gommatsara Karma-Kanda *of Nemicandra*, 2 vols. Assisted by Brahmachari Sital Prasad. The Sacred Books of the Jainas, vols. 6 and 10. Lucknow: Central Jaina Publishing House, 1927, 1937; reprint, New Delhi: Today & Tomorrow's Printers & Publishers, 1990.

———. *Atmanushasana*. Assisted by Brahmachari Sital Prasad. The Sacred Books of the Jainas, vol. 7. Lucknow: Central Jaina Publishing House, 1928; reprint, New Delhi: Today & Tomorrow's Printers & Publishers, 1991.

———. *Samayasara*. Assisted by Brahmachari Sital Prasad. The Sacred Books of the Jainas, vol. 8. Lucknow: Central Jaina Publishing House, 1930; reprint, New Delhi: Today & Tomorrow's Printers and Publishers, 1990.

Jaini, Padmanabh S., trans. *Amṛtacandrasūri*'s Laghutattvasphoṭa. L. D. Series no. 62. Ahmedabad: L. D. Institute of Indology, 1978.

Kapadia, Hiralal Rasikdas, trans. *Bhaktāmara-kalyāṇamandira-namiūṇa-stotra-trayam*, ed. Hermann Jacobi (includes English trans. of Mānatuṅgasūri's *Bhaktāmara Stotra* and *Namiūṇa Stotra*, and Siddhasena Divākara's *Kalyāṇamandir Stotra*). Surat: Sheth Devchand Lalbhai Jain Pustakoddhar Fund Series, no. 79, 1932.

Kumar, Muni Mahendra, trans. *Āyāro* (*Ācārāṅga Sūtra*). New Delhi: Today and Tomorrow's Printers & Publishers, 1981.

Lalwani, K. C., trans. *Bhagavatī Sūtra*, 4 vols. Text and trans. of śatakas 1–11. Calcutta: Jain Bhawan, 1973–1985.

———. *Daśavaikālika Sūtra*. Delhi: Motilal Banarsidass, 1973.

———. *Kalpa Sūtra*. Delhi: Motilal Banarsidass, 1979.

Modi, M. C., trans. *The* Antagaḍa-dasāo *and the* Aṇuttarovavāia-dasāo: *The Eighth and Ninth Aṅgas of the Jain Canon*. Ahmedabad: Gurjar Granth Ratna Karyalay, 1932.

Mookerjee, Satkari, trans. Pramāṇamīmāṃsā *of Hemacandra*. Varanasi: Tara Publications, 1970.

Nirvāṇa Sāgara, Muni, trans. Pratikramaṇa Sūtra *with Explanation*. 2 vols. Koba, Gujarat: Shree Arunoday Foundation, 1997.

Qvarnström, Olle. *The Yogaśāstra of Hemacandra: A Twelfth Century Handbook of Śvetāmbara Jainism*. Harvard Oriental Series 60. Cambridge, Mass.: Department of Sanskrit and Indian Studies, Harvard University, 2002.

Prasad, Ajit, trans. *Purushartha-Siddhyupaya*. The Sacred Books of the Jainas, vol. 4. Lucknow: Central Jaina Publishing House, 1933; reprint, New Delhi: Today & Tomorrow's Printers and Publishers, 1990.

Rajacandra, Shrimad. *Atma-Siddhi* (*Self-Realisation*), trans. D. C. Mehta. Bombay: Bharatiya Vidya Bhavan, 1976.

Rājayaśasūri, Ācārya Vijaya, ed. *Bhaktāmara Darśana*, trans. K. Srinivasan. Broach: Sri Jain Dharma Fund Pedhi, 1997.

Sain, Uggar, ed. and trans. Niyamasara: *The Perfect Law*. Assisted by Brahmachari Sital Prasad. The Sacred Books of the Jainas, vol. 9. Lucknow: Central Jaina Publishing House, 1931; reprint, New Delhi: Today & Tomorrow's Printers and Publishers, 1990.

Sanghavi, Sukhlal, and Bechardās Doshi, ed. and trans. *Siddhasena Divākara*'s Sanmati Tarka. With a critical introduction and an original commentary by Sukhlāl Saṅghavi and Bechardās Doshi. English trans. by A. B. Athavle and A. S. Gopani. Bombay: S. Doshi and B. Modi, Shri Jain Shwetambar Education Board, 1939; reprint, Ahmedabad: L. D. Institute of Indology, 2000.

Shastri, Yajneshwar, ed. and trans. *Ācārya Ūmāsvāti Vācaka's* Praśamrati-prakaraṇa. L. D. Series no. 107. Ahmedabad: L. D. Institute of Indology, 1989.

Solomon, Esther A., trans. *Gaṇadharavāda*. Ahmedabad: Gujarat Vidya Sabha, 1966.

Surānā, Śrīcand "Saras," ed. Illustrated Agama Publication Series is publishing the Śvetāmbara Āgamas accepted by the Sthānakavāsīs with English translation. Unless noted below, all are published by Padma Prakashan, Delhi. The following have been published to date: *Sacitra* Uttarādhyayana Sūtra/*Illustrated* Uttarādhyayana Sūtra (Agra: Diwakar Prakashan, 1992), *Sacitra* Antakṛddaśā Sūtra (1993), *Sacitra* Daśavaikālika Sūtra (1997), *Sacitra* Jñātādharmakathāṅga Sūtra (2 vols., 1997), *Sacitra* Ācārāṅga Sūtra (2 vols., 1999), *Sacitra* Anuyogadvara Sūtra (2001), *Sacitra* Upāsakadasā Sūtra *and* Anuttaraupapātikadaśā Sūtra (2001), *Sacitra* Rāyapaseṇiya Sūtra (2002), *Sacitra* Aupapātika Sūtra (2003), *Sacitra* Nirayāvalika Sūtra and Vipāka Sūtra (2003), *Sacitra* Kalpa Sūtra, *Sacitra* Śrī Nandī Sūtra.

———. *Sacitra* Bhaktāmara Stotra/Bhaktamar Stotra *Illustrated.* With English trans. by Surendra Bothara, fifth ed. Agra: Diwakar Prakashan, and Jaipur: Prakrit Bharati Academy, 1996.

———. *Illustrated Namokara Mahamantra.* With English trans. by Surendra Bothara. Agra: Diwakar Prakashan, 1998.

Tatia, Nathmal, trans. *That Which Is* (*Tattvārtha Sūtra*). San Francisco: Harper Collins, 1994.

Thomas, F. W. *The Flower-Spray of the Quodammodo Doctrine* (trans. of *Syādvādamañjarī* of Malliṣeṇa). Berlin: Akademie-Verlag, 1960.

Tulsi, Acarya. *Jaina-Siddhānta-Dīpakā.* Trans. Satkari Mukherjee as *Illuminator of Jaina Tenets.* Ladnun: Jain Vishva Bharati, 1985.

Upadhye, Adinath N., ed. *Siddhasena Divākara*'s Nyāyāvatāra *and Other Works* (S. C. Vidyabhusan trans. of *Nyāyāvatāra* and Mohanlal Desai trans. of The *Naya Karṇikā* of Upādhyāya Vinayavijaya). Bombay: Jain Sāhitya Vikāsa Maṇḍala, 1971.

Upadhye, Adinath N., ed. and trans. *Pravacanasāra.* Agas: Śrīmad Rājacandra Jaina Śāstramālā, 1964.

Vidyabhushana, Satish Chandra, trans. Nyāyāvatāra: *The Earliest Jaina Work on Pure Logic.* Arrah: Central Jaina Publishing House, 1915.

Vaidya, N. V., trans. *Nāyādhammakahāo* (trans. of chapters 4–8, 9, and 16). Poona: N. V. Vaidya, n.d., ca. 1930s).

Vaidya, P. L., trans. *The* Uvasagadasāo: *The Seventh Aṅga of the Jain Canon.* Poona: P. L. Vaidya, 1930.

Vinayasagar, Mahopadhyay, ed. and trans. *Kalpasūtra,* second ed. English trans. Mukund Lath. Jaipur: Prakrit Bharati Academy, 1984.

———. *Isibhasiyaim Suttaim* (Rishibhashit Sutra). English trans. Kalanath Shastri and Dinesh Chandra Sharma. Jaipur: Prakrit Bharati Academy, 1988.

Wiles, Royce. "The *Nirayāvaliyāsuyakkhandha* and Its Commentary by Śrīcandra: Critical Edition, Translation, and Notes." Ph.D. dissertation. Australian National University, 2000.

Zydenbos, Robert J. *Mokṣa in Jainism according to Umāsvāti* (trans. of the 10th chapter of the *Tattvārtha Sūtra*). Wiesbaden: Franz Steiner, 1983.

Studies of Texts and Modern Commentaries

Alsdorf, Ludwig. "What Were the Contents of the *Dṛṣṭivāda*?" in *German Scholars on India*, vol. 1, pp. 1–5. Varanasi: Chowkhambha Sanskrit Series Office, 1973.

Balcerowicz, Piotr. "Two Siddhasenas and the Authorship of the *Nyāyāvatāra* and the *Sanmati-tarka-prakaraṇa*." *Journal of Indian Philosophy* 29 (2001): 351–378.

Banerjee, Satya Ranjan. "Siddhasena Divākara and His *Nyāyāvatāra*." *Jain Journal* 32.4 (April 1998): 93–114.

———. "Chronological Development of Jain Literature." *Jain Journal* 35.4 (April 2001): 206–231.

Bollee, Willem B. "Āyāranga 2.16 and Sūyagada 1.16." *Journal of Indian Philosophy* 18 (1990): 29–52.

———. "Notes on Diseases in the Canon of the Śvetāmbaras." Traditional South Asian Medicine 7 (2003): 69–110.

Bronkhorst, Johannes. "On the Chronology of the *Tattvārtha Sūtra* and Some Early Commentaries." *Wiener Zeitschrift für die Kunde Südasiens* 29 (1985): 155–184.

Caillat, Colette. "Interpolations in a Jaina Pamphlet or Emergence of One More Āturapratyākhyāna." *Wiener Zeitschrift für die Kunde Südasiens* 36 (1992): 35–44.

Cakravarti, A. *Jaina Literature in Tamil*. New Delhi: Bhāratīya Jñānapīṭha, 1974.

Deleu, Jozef. Viyāhapannatti (Bhagavaī)*: The Fifth Aṅga of the Jaina Canon*. Brugge: De Tempel, Tempelhof, 1970; reprint, Delhi: Motilal Banarsidass 1996.

———. "A Further Inquiry into the Nucleus of the Viyāhapannatti." *Indologica Taurinensia* 14 (1987–1988, Professor Colette Caillat Felicitation Volume): 169–179.

Deleu, Jozef, and Walther Schubring, ed. and trans. *Studien zum* Mahānisīha (English trans. of chapters 1–3, German trans. of chapters 4–5). Hamburg: Cram, De Gruyter, 1963.

Deo, Shantaram B. *Jaina Canonical Literature: An Appraisal*. Mysore: Department of Jainology and Prakrits, University of Mysore, 1981.

Dundas, Paul. "Somnolent Sūtras: Scriptural Commentary in Śvetāmbara Jainism." *Journal of Indian Philosophy* 24 (1996): 73–101.

Ghatage, A. M. "The Daśavaikālika Niryukti." *Indian Historical Quarterly* 11 (1935): 627–639.

Hanaki, Taiken. Aṇuogaddārāiṃ (Anuyogadvāra-sūtra): *A Critical Study*. Vaishali: Research Institute of Prakrit, Jainology, and Ahiṃsā, 1970.

Hardy, Friedhelm. "Creative Corruption: Some Comments on Apabhraṃśa Literature, Particularly Yogīndu," in *Studies in South Asian Devotional Literature*, ed. Alan W. Entwistle and Francoise Mallison, pp. 3–15. New Delhi: Manohar, and Paris: L'École Francaise d'Extreme Orient, 1994.

Jain, Campat Rai. *The Jaina Law*. Madras: Jain Mission Society, 1926.

Jain, G. R. *Cosmology Old and New Being A Modern Commentary on the Fifth Chapter of* Tattvārthādhigama Sūtra. Delhi: Bhāratīya Jñānapīṭha, 1975.

Jain, Jagdish Chandra. *History of Prakrit Literature from 500 B.C. to 1800 A.D.* Varanasi: Chowkhamba Vidya Bhawan, 1961.

Jain, Sagarmal. Rishibhashit *A Study*, trans. Surendra Bothara. Jaipur: Prakrit Bharati Academy, 1988.

Jaini, J. L. *Jaina Law*. Arrah: Central Jaina Publishing House, 1916.

Jhaveri, Mohanlal Bhagwandas. *Comparative and Critical Study of Mantraśāstra* (introduction to the *Śrī Bhairava Padmāvatī Kalpa* by Malliṣeṇasūri). Ahmedabad: Sarabhai Manilal Nawab, 1944.

Kapadia, Hiralal Rasikdas. "The Jaina Commentaries." *Annals of the Bhandarkar Oriental Research Institute* 16 (1934–1935): 292–312.

———. *A History of the Canonical Literature of the Jainas*. Surat: H. R. Kapadia, 1941; reprint, Ahmedabad: Sharadaben Chimanbhai Educational Research Centre, 2000.

Kumar, Muni Mahendra, and K. C. Lalwani. *Āgama and Tripiṭaka: A Comparative Study: A Critical Study of Jaina and Buddhist Canonical Literature*. New Delhi: Today & Tomorrow's Printers and Publishers, 1986.

Law, Bimala Churn. *Some Jaina Canonical Sūtras*. Bombay: Royal Asiatic Society, 1949.

Mehta, Mohanlal, and K. Rishabh Chandra, comp. *Prakrit Proper Names*, 2 vols. (Compiled from Śvetāmbara canonical texts and Prakrit commentaries.) L. D. Series nos. 28 and 37. Ahmedabad: L. D. Institute of Indology, 1970 and 1972.

Ohira, Suzuko. "Problems of the Pūrva." *Jain Journal* 15 (1980): 41–55.

———. *A Study of the* Tattvārthasūtra *with Bhāṣya*. L. D. Series no. 86. Ahmedabad: L. D. Institute of Indology, 1982.

———. *A Study of the* Bhagavatīsūtra*: A Chronological Analysis*. Ahmedabad: Prakrit Text Society, 1994.

Sanghavi, Sukhlal. *Pt. Sukhlāljī's Commentary on* Tattvārtha Sūtra *of Vācaka Umāsvāti*, trans. K. K. Dixit. L. D. Series no. 44. Ahmedabad: L. D. Institute of Indology, 1974.

Sen, A. C. *A Critical Introduction to the* Paṇhāvagaraṇāim, *the Tenth Aṅga of the Jaina Canon*. Würzburg: Bachdruckerei R. Mayr, 1936.

Shah, Nagin J. *Samantabhadra*'s Āptamīmāmsā: *Critique of an Authority*. Ahmedabad: Jagruti Dilip Shah, 1999.

Shah, Nagin. J., and M. Sen, eds. *Concept of Pratikramaṇa* (an Abridged Version of Pt. Sukhlalji's introduction to *Pañca Pratikramaṇa*). Ahmedabad: Jagruti Dilip Sheth, 1993.

Sikdar, Jogendra C. *Studies in the* Bhagavatīsūtra. Mazaffarpur: Research Institute of Prakrit, Jainology, and Ahimsa, 1964.

Upadhye, Adinath N. "Joindu and His Apabhraṃśa Works." *Annals of the Bhandarkar Oriental Research Institute* 12.2 (1931): 132–163.

Upadhye, Adinath N., ed. and trans. *Śrī Yōgīndudeva's* Paramātmaprakāśa: *An Apabhraṃśa Work on Jaina Mysticism*. English introduction, pp. 1–92. Bombay: Sheth Manilal Revashankar Jhaveri, 1937.

———. *Siddhasena Divākara's* Nyāyāvatāra. Bombay: Jaina Sāhitya Vikāsa Maṇḍala, 1971.

Winternitz, Maurice. *A History of Indian Literature, vol. 2: Buddhist and Jaina Literature*, trans. V. Srinivasa Sarma; rev. ed., Delhi: Motilal Banarsidass, 1983; reprint 1988.

HISTORY AND HISTORICAL DEVELOPMENT

Balbir, Nalini. "Jain-Buddhist Dialogue: Material from the Pāli Scriptures." *Journal of the Pali Text Society* 26 (2000): 1–42.

Banerjee, Satya Ṛanjan. "Jainism through the Ages." *Jain Journal* 19.4 (April 1995): 129–166.

Banks, Marcus. "Views of Jain History," in *Anthropologists in a Wider World*, ed. Paul Dresch, Wendy James, and D. Parkin, pp. 187–204. New York: Berghahn Books, 2000.

Bronkhorst, J. "The Buddha and the Jainas Reconsidered." *Asiatische Studien/Études Asiatiques* 1995: 330–350.

———. "The Riddle of the Jainas and Ājīvikas in Early Buddhist Literature." *Journal of Indian Philosophy* 28 (2000): 511–529.

Carrithers, Michael. "Jainism and Buddhism as Enduring Historical Streams." *Journal of the Anthropological Society of Oxford* 21 (1990): 141–163.

Champalakshmi, R. "Religious Conflict in the Tamil Country: A Re-Appraisal of Epigraphic Evidence." *Journal of the Epigraphic Society of India* 5 (1978): 69–81.

Chatterjee, Asim Kumar. *A Comprehensive History of Jainism*, 2 vols. (vol. 1, From the Earliest Beginnings to A.D. 1000; vol. 2, A. D. 1000–1600). Calcutta: Firma KLM, 1978. Second rev. ed., New Delhi: Munshiram Manoharlal, 2000.

Cort, John E. "Genres of Jain History." *Journal of Indian Philosophy* 23 (1995): 469–506.

———. "The Jain Knowledge Warehouses: Libraries in Traditional India." *Journal of the American Oriental Society* 115 (1995): 77–87.

———. "A Tale of Two Cities: On the Origins of Digambara Sectarianism," in *Essays in Honour of Dr. Rajendra Joshi*, ed. Lawrence A. Babb, Varsha Joshi, and Michael W. Meister. Jaipur: Rawat Publications, forthcoming.

Dhaky, M. A. "Umāsvāti in Epigraphical and Literary Tradition," in *Śrī Nāgābhinandanam: Dr. M. S. Nagaraja Rao Festschrift*, vol. 2, ed. L. K. Srinivasan and S. Nagaraju, pp. 505–522. Bangalore: M. S. Nagaraja Rao Felicitation Committee, 1995.

Dixit, K. K. *Early Jainism*. L. D. Series no. 64. Ahmedabad: L. D. Institute of Indology, 1978.

Dundas, Paul. "The Laicisation of the Bondless Doctrine: A New Study of the Development of Early Jainism." *Journal of Indian Philosophy* 25 (1997): 495–516.

———. "Jain Perceptions of Islam in the Early Modern Period." *Indo-Iranian Journal* 42 (1999): 35–46.

———. "Conversion to Jainism: Historical Perspectives," in *Religious Conversion in South Asia*, ed. Rowena Robinson and Sathianathan Clarke, pp. 125–148. New Delhi: Oxford University Press, 2003.

———. *Sudharman's Heirs: History, Scripture, and Authority in a Medieval Jain Sect*, forthcoming.

Epigraphia Carnatica, 6 vols., rev. ed. (Includes English trans. of inscriptions.) Vol. 1, Coorg District (1972); vol. 2, Śravaṇa Beḷgoḷa (1973); vols. 3–5, Mysore (1973–1975); vol. 6, Mandya District (1977). Mysore: Institute of Kannada Studies, University of Mysore.

Findly, Ellison. "Jahāngīr's Vow of Non-Violence." *Journal of the American Oriental Society* 107.2 (1987): 245–256.

Flügel, Peter. "Protestant und Post-Protestantische Jaina Reformbewegungen: Zur Geschichte und Organisation der Sthānakavāsī I." *Berliner Indologische Studien* 13–14 (2000): 37–103.

———. "Protestant und Post-Protestantische Jaina Reformbewegungen: Zur Geschichte und Organisation der Sthānakavāsī II." *Berliner Indologische Studien* 15–17 (2003): 149–240.

Gombrich, Richard. "The Buddhists and the Jains: A Reply to Professor Bronkhorst." *Asiatische Studien/Études Asiatiques* 48 (1994): 1069–1095.

Granoff, Phyllis. "Tales of Broken Limbs and Bleeding Wounds: A Study of Some Hindu and Jain Responses to Muslim Iconoclasm." *East and West* 41 (1991): 189–205.

Jain, Bhag Chandra. *Jainism in Buddhist Literature*. Nagpur: Alok Prakashan, 1972.

Jain, Jyoti Prasad. *The Jaina Sources of the History of Ancient India (100 B.C.–A. D. 900)*. Delhi: Munshi Ram Manohar Lal, 1964.

Jain, Kailash Chand. *Jainism in Rajasthan*. Sholapur: Jaina Saṃskṛti Saṃrakshaka Sangha, 1963.

———. *Lord Mahāvīra and His Times*. Delhi: Motilal Banarsidass, 1974.

Janert, Klaus L., ed. *Heinrich Lüder's Mathurā Inscriptions: Unpublished Papers*. Göttingen: Vandenhoeck & Ruprecht, 1961.

Jawaharlal, G. *Jainism in Andhra As Depicted in Inscriptions*. Jaipur: Prakrit Bharati Academy, 1994.

Lüders, H. *A List of Brahmi Inscriptions from the Earliest Times to about A. D. 400 with the Exception of Those of Asoka: Appendix to Epigraphia Indica and Record of the Archaelogical Survey of India*, vol. 10 (contains Jain inscriptions from Kaṅkālī Ṭīlā at Mathurā). Calcutta: Superintendent Government Printing, 1912.

Mukherjee, Bikash. *Religious Centres of North India: Buddhist, Jaina, and Brahmanical Based on Archaeological and Literary Sources*. New Delhi: Ramanand Vidya Bhawan, 1993.

Nagarajaiah, Hampa. *Jaina Corpus of Koppala Inscriptions X-Rayed*. Bangalore: Ankita Pustaka, 1999.

———. *A History of the Rāṣṭrakūṭas of Maḷkhēḍ and Jainism*. Bangalore: Ankita Pustaka, 2000.

Norman, K. R. "When Did the Buddha and the Jina Die?" in *Prācyaśikṣāsuhāsinī: Seventh-fifth Anniversary Celebration Volume of the Department of Ancient Indian History and Culture*, ed. Samaresh Bandyopadhyay, pp. 460–470. Calcutta: University of Calcutta, 1999. Reprinted in *Collected Papers*, K. R. Norman, vol. 7, pp. 130–144. Oxford: Pali Text Society, 2001.

———. "Early Buddhism and Jainism: A Comparison." *Memoirs of the Chūō Academic Research Institute* 28 (1999): 3–30.

Ohira, Suzuko. "The 24 Buddhas and the 24 Tīrthaṅkaras." *Jain Journal* 29.1 (July 1994): 9–22.

Saletore, Bhasker Anand. *Medieval Jainism*. Bombay: Karnatak Publishing House, 1938.

Sharma, Krishna Gopal. *Early Jaina Inscriptions of Rajasthan*. New Delhi: Navrang, 1993.

Sharma, S. R. *Jainism and Karnatak Culture*. Dharwar: N. S. Kamalapur, 1940.

Shastri, Hariprasada Gangasankara. *A Historical and Cultural Study of the Inscriptions of Gujarat: From the Earliest Times to the End of the Caulukya Period (circa 1300 A.D.)*. Ahmedabad: B. J. Institute of Learning and Research, 1989.

Singh, Ram Bhushan Prasad. *Jainism in Early Medieval Karnataka*. Delhi: Motilal Banarsidass, 1975.

Somani, Ram Vallabh. "History of Kharatargaccha." *Jain Journal* 27.1 (July 1992): 33–52.

Tiwari, Binod Kumar. *History of Jainism in Bihar*. Gurgaon: The Academic Press, 1996.

Upadhye, Adinath N. "Yāpanīya Saṅgha: A Jaina Sect." *Journal of the University of Bombay* 1.6 (1933): 224–231.

Williams, R. "Haribhadra." *Bulletin of the School of Oriental and African Studies* 28 (1965): 101–111.

Zydenbos, Robert J. "Jainism Endangered: The View of the Medieval Kannada Poet Brahmaśiva," in *"Minorities" on Themselves*, ed. Hugh van Skyhawk, pp. 174–187. Heidelberg: South Asia Institute, University of Heidelberg, 1985.

RELIGIOUS THOUGHT

Philosophy and Logic

Alsdorf, Ludwig. "Nikṣepa—a Jaina Contribution to Scholastic Methodology." *Journal of the Oriental Institute of Baroda* 22 (1973): 455–463.

Balcerowicz, Piotr. "Taxonomic Approach to *dṛṣṭāntābhāsa* in *Nyāya-bindu* and in Siddarṣigaṇi's *Nyāyāvatāra-vivṛti*—Dharmakīrti's Typology and the Jaina Criticism Thereof," in *Dharmakīrti's Thought and Its Impact on Indian and Tibetan Philosophy*, ed. Shoryu Katsura, pp. 1–16. Vienna: Österreichische Akademie der Wissenschaften, Beiträge zur Kultur-und Geistesgeschichte Asiens, Nr. 32, 1999.

———. "The Logical Structure of the *Naya* Method of the Jainas." *Journal of Indian Philosophy* 29 (2001): 379–403.

Bhaskar, Bhagchandra Jain. *Jainism in Buddhist Literature*. Nagpur: Alok Prakashan, 1972.

Bhatt, B. "Vyavahāra and Niścayanaya in Kundakunda's Works." *Zeitschrift der Deutschen Morgenländischen Gesellschaft* (supplement, 1974): 279–291.

———. *The Canonical Nikṣepa: Studies in Jain Dialectics*. Leiden: E. J. Brill, 1978.

Bhattacharyya, Narendra Nath. *Jain Philosophy: Historical Outline*, second rev. ed. New Delhi: Munshiram Manoharlal, 1999.

Bollee, W. B. "Adda or the Oldest Extant Dispute between Jains and Heretics (Sūyagaḍa 2.6) Part Two." *Journal of Indian Philosophy* 27 (1999): 411–437. (Part One in *Nirgrantha: Festschrift for Muni Jambūvijayajī*, ed. J. B. Jain. Ahmedabad: Sharadaben Chimanbhai Educational Research Centre, forthcoming.)

Bossche, Frank van den. "Existence and Non-Existence in Haribhadra Sūri's *Anekāntajayapatākā*." *Journal of Indian Philosophy* 23 (1995): 429–468.

Bothera, Pushpa. "An Introduction to Jaina Logicians and Their Logic." *Jain Journal* 5.1 (July 1970): 15–19.

———. *The Jaina Theory of Perception*. Delhi: Motilal Banarsidass, 1976.

Bronkhorst, Johannes. "Abhidharma and Jainism," in *Abhidharma and Indian Thought: Essays in Honor of Professor Doctor Junsho Kata*, pp. 598–581 (reverse pagination). Tokyo: 2000.

Chapple, Christopher Key. "Monist (Ekatva) and Pluralist (Anekanta) Discourse in Indian Traditions," in *East-West Encounters in Philosophy and Religion*, eds. Ninian Smart and B. Srinivasa Murthy, pp. 120–129. Long Beach, Calif.: Long Beach Publications, 1996.

Dixit, K. K. *Jaina Ontology*. L. D. Series no. 31. Ahmedabad: L. D. Institute of Indology, 1971.

Granoff, Phyllis. "Refutation as Commentary: Medieval Jain Arguments against Sāṃkhya." *Asiatische Studien/Études Asiatiques* 53.3 (1999): 579–591.

Jain, Sagarmal, and Shriprakash Pandey, eds. *Multi-Dimensional Application of Anekāntavāda*. Varanasi: Pārśvanātha Vidyāpīṭha, and Ahmedabad: Navin Institute for Self-Development, 1999.

Johnson, W. J. "The Religious Function of Jaina Philosophy: *Anekāntavāda* Reconsidered." *Religion* 25 (1995): 41–50.

Mahāprajña, Yuvācārya. *New Dimensions in Jaina Logic*. New Delhi: Today and Tomorrow's Printers and Publishers, 1984.

Marathe, M. P., M. A. Kelkar, and P. P. Gokhale, eds. *Studies in Jainism*. Poona: Indian Philosophical Quarterly Publications, 1984.

Matilal, Bimal K. *The Central Philosophy of Jainism* (*Anekānta-Vāda*). L. D. Series no. 79. Ahmedabad: L. D. Institute of Indology, 1981.

Mehta, Mohan Lal. *Outlines of Jaina Philosophy: The Essentials of Jaina Ontology, Epistemology, and Ethics*. Bangalore: Jain Mission Society, 1954.

Mookerjee, Satkari. *The Jaina Philosophy of Non-Absolutism: A Critical Study of Anekāntavāda*. Calcutta: Bharati Mahāvidyālaya, 1944; second ed., Delhi: Motilal Banarsidass, 1978.

Padmarajiah, Y. J. *A Comparative Study of Jaina Theories of Reality and Knowledge*. Bombay: Jaina Sāhitya Vikāsa Maṇḍala, 1963.

Prasad, Brahmachari Sital. *A Comparative Study of Jainism and Buddhism*. Madras: Jain Mission Society, 1934; second ed., Delhi: Satguru Publications, 1982.

Pungaliya, U. K. *Philosophy and Spirituality of Śrīmad Rajchandra*. Jaipur: Prakrit Bharati Academy, and Pune: Sanmati Teerth, 1996.

Qvarnström, Olle. "Dharma in Jainism: Some Preliminary Remarks." *Journal of Indian Philosophy* (forthcoming).

Sanghavi, Sukhlal. *Advanced Studies in Indian Logic and Metaphysics*. Reprint, Calcutta: K. L. Mukhopadhyaya, 1961.

Shah, Nagin J. *Akalaṅkas's Criticism of Dharmakīrti's Philosophy: A Study*. L. D. Series no. 11. Ahmedabad: L. D. Institute of Indology, 1967.

———, ed. *Jaina Theory of Multiple Facets of Reality and Truth* (*Anekāntavāda*). Delhi: Motilal Banarsidass and Bhogilal Leherchand Institute of Indology, 2000.

Shastri, Indra Chandra. *Jaina Epistemology*. Varanasi: P. V. Research Institute, 1990.

Sikdar, Jogendra C. *Theory of Reality in Jaina Philosophy*. Varanasi: P. V. Research Institute, 1991.

Soni, Jayandra. "Dravya, Guṇa and Paryāya in Jaina Thought." *Journal of Indian Philosophy* 19 (1991): 75–88.

———. *Aspects of Jaina Philosophy*. Madras: Research Foundation for Jainology, 1996.

———. "Philosophical Significance of the Jaina Theory of Manifoldness." *Studien zur Interkulturellen Philosophie* 7 (1997): 277–287.

Tatia, Nathmal. *Studies in Jaina Philosophy*. Varanasi: P. V. Research Institute, 1951.

Tripathi, R. K. "The Concept of Avaktavya in Jainism." *Philosophy East and West* 18 (1968): 187–193.

Zydenbos, Robert J. "Jaina Influence in the Formation of Dvaitavedānta." *Jain Journal* 25.3 (January 1991): 103–118.

———. "On the Jaina Background of Dvaitavedānta." *Journal of Indian Philosophy* 19 (1991): 249–271.

Karma Theory

Bauer, Jerome H. "Karma and Control: The Prodigious and the Auspicious in Śvetāmbara Jaina Canonical Mythology." Ph.D. dissertation, University of Pennsylvania, 1998.

Chapple, Christopher Key. "Karma and the Path of Purification," in *Karma: Rhythmic Return to Harmony*, ed. V. Hanson, R. Stewart, and S. Nicholson, pp. 255–266. Wheaton, Ill.: Quest Books, 1990.

Glasenapp, Helmuth von. *Doctrine of Karman in Jain Philosophy*, trans. G. Barry Gifford. Bombay: The Trustees, Bai Vijibai Jivanlal Panalal Charity Fund, 1942; reprint, Varanasi: P. V. Research Institute, 1991.

Granoff, Phyllis. "Cures and Karma: Attitudes towards Healing in Medieval Jainism," in *Self, Soul, and the Body in Religious Experience*, ed. Al Baumgarten, pp. 218–256. Leiden: E. J. Brill, 1998.

Jain, L. C. *The Tao of Jaina Sciences*. Delhi: Arihant International, 1992.

Jain, N. L. *Scientific Contents in Prākṛta Canons*. Varanasi: Pārśvanātha Vidyāpīṭha, 1996.

Jain, Navinchandra. *Contributions of Jainism to Ayurveda*. Pune: Chakor Publications, 1991.

Johnson, W. J. *Harmless Souls: Karmic Bondage and Religious Change in Early Jainism with Special Reference to Umāsvāti and Kundakunda*. Delhi: Motilal Banarsidass, 1995.

Kalghatgi, T. G. "Karma in Jaina Thought," in *The Dimensions of Karma*, ed. S. S. Rama Rao Pappu, pp. 94–117. Delhi: Chanakya Publications, 1987.

Mardia, K. V. *The Scientific Foundations of Jainism*, second rev. ed. Delhi: Motilal Banarsidass, 1996.

Sikdar, J. C. *Jaina Biology*. L. D. Series no. 111. Ahmedabad· L. D. Institute of Indology, 1974.

———. *Concept of Matter in Jaina Philosophy*. Varanasi: P. V. Research Institute, 1987.

Wiley, Kristi L. "*Aghātiyā Karmas*: Agents of Embodiment in Jainism." Ph.D. dissertation, University of California, Berkeley, 2000.

Zaveri, J. S. *Microcosmology: Atom in Jain Philosophy and Modern Science*, second rev. ed. Ladnun: Jain Vishva Bharati, 1991.

Zaveri, J. S., and Muni Mahendra Kumar. *Neuroscience and Karma*. Ladnun: Jain Vishva Bharati, 1992.

Zwilling, L., and M. J. Sweet. "'Like a City Ablaze': The Third Sex and the Creation of Sexuality in Jain Religious Literature." *Journal of the History of Sexuality* 6 (1996): 359–384.

Spiritual Liberation, Tantra, and Yoga

Bhatt, B. "The Concept of the Self and Liberation in Early Jaina Āgamas," in *Self and Consciousnes: Indian Interpretation*, pp. 132–172. Rome, 1989.

Brónkhorst, J. *The Two Traditions of Meditation in Ancient India*, second ed. Delhi: Motilal Banarsidass, 1993.

Bruhn, Klaus. "Soteriology in Early Jainism," in *Hinduismus und Buddhismus: Festschrift für Ulrich Schneider*, ed. H. Falk, pp. 60–86. Freiburg: Hedwig Falk, 1987.

Chapple, Christopher Key. "Life Force in Jainism and Yoga," in *The Meaning of Life in the World Religions*, ed. Joseph Runzo and Nancy M. Martin, pp. 137–152. Oxford: Oneworld Publications, 2000.

———. *Haribhadra's Array of Views on Yoga*. Albany: State University of New York Press, forthcoming.

Desai, S. M. *Haribhadra's Yoga Works and Psychosynthesis*. L. D. Series no. 94. Ahmedabad: L. D. Institute of Indology, 1983.

Dundas, Paul. "Food and Freedom: The Jaina Sectarian Debate on the Nature of the Kevalin." *Religion* 15 (1985): 161–198.

Jain, S. C. *Structure and Functions of Soul in Jainism*. Delhi: Bhāratīya Jñānapīṭha, 1978.

Jaini, Padmanabh S. *Gender and Salvation: Jaina Debates on the Spiritual Liberation of Women*. Berkeley: University of California Press, 1991.

———. "Umāsvāti on the Quality of Sukha." *Journal of Indian Philosophy* 31 (2003): 643–664.

Joshi, L. M. *Facets of Jaina Religiousness in Comparative Light*. L. D. Series no. 85. Ahmedabad: L. D. Institute of Indology, 1981.

Mahāprajña, Yuvācārya. *Preksha Dhyana: Theory and Practice*. Ladnun: Jain Vishva Bharati, 1987.

Qvarnström, Olle. "Jain Tantra: Divinatory and Meditative Practices in the 12th Century *Yogaśāstra* of Hemacandra," in *Tantra in Practice*, ed. David G. White, pp. 595–604. Princeton, N.J.: Princeton University Press, 2000.

———. "Bhavyatva and Abhavyatva: A Forgotten Ājīvika Doctrine?" in *Svensk Religionshistorisk Arskrift*, forthcoming.

———. "Losing One's Mind and Becoming Enlightened: Some Remarks on the Concept of Yoga in Śvetāmbara Jainism and Its Relation to the Nāth Siddha Tradition," in *Yoga: Tradition and Interreligious Perspectives*, ed. I. Whicher. London: Routledge Curzon, forthcoming.

Sastri, Muni Suvrat. *Jain Yoga in Light of the* Yogabindu*: An Analytical Study*. Delhi: Nirmal Publications, 1995.

Singh, Ramjee. *The Jaina Concept of Omniscience*. L. D. Series no. 43. Ahmedabad: L. D. Institute of Indology, 1974.

Sogani, Kamal Chand. "The Concept of Samyagdarśana in Jainism." *Journal of the Oriental Institute of Baroda* 14.2 (1964): 171–181.

———. "Fundamentals of Jaina Mysticism." *Vishveshvaranand Indological Journal* 3.2 (September 1965): 255–272.

Tatia, Nathmal. *Jaina Meditation: Citta Samādhi, Jaina-Yoga*. Ladnun: Jain Vishva Bharati, 1986.

Yandell, Keith. "Persons (Real and Alleged) in Enlightenment Traditions: A Partial Look at Jainism and Buddhism." *International Journal for Philosophy of Religion* 42 (1997): 23–39.

Ethics

Bhargava, Dayanand. *Jaina Ethics*. Delhi: Motilal Banarsidass, 1968.

Chapple, Christopher Key. "Pushing the Boundaries of Personal Ethics: The Practice of Jaina Vows," in *Ethics in World Religions*, ed. Joseph Runzo and Nancy Martin, pp. 197–218. Oxford: Oneworld, 2001.

Dixit, K. K. "The Evolution of the Jaina Treatment of Ethical Problems." *Sambodhi* 2.1 (1973): 19–36.

———. "The Problems of Ethics and Karma Doctrine as Treated in the *Bhagavatī Sūtra*." *Sambodhi* 2.3 (October 1973): 1–13.

Heim (Hibbets), Maria R. *Theories of the Gift in South Asia: Hindu, Buddhist, and Jain Reflections on Dāna*. New York: Routledge, forthcoming.

Hibbets (Heim), Maria R. "Saving Them from Yourself: An Inquiry into the South Asian Gift of Fearlessness." *Journal of Religious Ethics* 27.3 (Fall 1999): 437–462.

Laughlin, Jack C. "Jain Monasticism in 'An Age without Eminence': Religious Gifting and the Acquisition and Transfer of Merit." *Asiatische Studien/Études Asiatiques* 55 (2001): 321–348.

Sogani, Kamal Chand. *Ethical Doctrines in Jainism*. Sholapur: Jaina Saṃskṛti Saṃrakshaka Sangha, 1967.

Nonviolence and Ecology

Chapple, Christopher Key. "Noninjury to Animals: Jaina and Buddhist Perspectives," in *Animal Sacrifices: Religious Perspectives on the Use of Animals in Science*, ed. Tom Regan, pp. 213–236. Philadelphia: Temple University Press, 1986.

———. *Nonviolence to Animals, Earth, and Self in Asian Traditions*. Albany: State University of New York Press, 1993.

———. "Contemporary Jaina and Hindu Responses to the Ecological Crisis," in *An Ecology of the Spirit: Religious Reflection and Environmental Consciousness*, ed. Michael Barnes, pp. 209–220. Lanham, Md.: University Press of America, 1994.

———. "Jainism and Nonviolence," in *Subverting Hatred: The Challenge of Nonviolence in Religious Traditions*, ed. Daniel L. Smith-Christopher, pp. 13–24. Cambridge, Mass.: Boston Research Center for the 21st Century, 1998, and Maryknoll, N.Y.: Orbis Books, 2000.

———. "Jainism and Buddhism," in *A Companion to Environmental Philosophy*, ed. Dale Jamieson, pp. 52–69. Oxford: Blackwell, 2001.

———. "The Living Cosmos of Jainism: A Traditional Science Grounded in Environmental Ethics." *Daedalus: Journal of the American Academy of Arts and Sciences* 130.4 (2001): 207–224.

———. "Jainism and Ecology," in *When Worlds Converge: What Science and Religion Tell Us about the Story of the Universe and Our Place in It*, ed. Clifford N. Matthews, Mary Evelyn Tucker, and Philip Hefner, pp. 283–292. Chicago: Open Court, 2002.

———. "Contemporary Hindu and Jaina Responses to the Ecological Crisis," in *Worldviews, Religion, and the Environment: A Global Anthology*, ed. Richard C. Foltz, pp. 113–119. Belmont, Calif.: Thomson Wadsworth, 2003.

———, ed. *Jainism and Ecology: Nonviolence in the Web of Life*. Religions of the World and Ecology Series, ed. Mary Evelyn Tucker and John Grim. Cambridge, Mass.: Harvard University Press, 2002.

Granoff, Phyllis. "The Violence of Non-Violence: A Study of Some Jain Responses to Non-Jain Religious Practices." *Journal of the International Association of Buddhist Studies* 15 (1992): 1–43.

Singhvi, L. M. *The Jain Declaration on Nature*. Cincinnati: Federation of Jain Associations in North America, 1990.

Zydenbos, Robert J. "Jainism as the Religion of Non-Violence," in *Violence Denied: Violence, Non-Violence and the Rationalization of Violence in South Asian Cultural History*, ed. J. E. M. Houben and K. R. van Kooij. Leiden: E. J. Brill, 1999.

PRACTICES, RITUALS, AND POPULAR BELIEFS

Babb, Lawrence A. "Giving and Giving Up: The Eightfold Worship among the Śvetāmbara Mūrtipūjak Jains." *Journal of Anthropological Research* 44 (1988): 67–86.

———. "Monks and Miracles: Religious Symbols and Images of Origin among Osvāl Jains." *Journal of Asian Studies* 52 (1993): 3–21.

———. *Absent Lord: Ascetics and Kings in a Jain Ritual Culture*. Berkeley: University of California Press, 1996.

Balbir, Nalini. "La fascination jaina pour l'alchimie." *Journal of the European Ayurvedic Society* 2 (1992): 134–150.

———. "Polémiques autour du 'voile buccal' des laïcs: la contribution de Vardhamānasūri." *Bulletin d'Études Indiennes* 17–18 (1999–2000): 113–152.

Bilimoria, P. "A Report from India: The Jaina Ethic of Voluntary Death." *Bioethics* 6 (1992): 331–355.

Caillat, Colette. "Fasting unto Death according to Jaina Tradition." *Acta Orientalia* 38 (1977): 43–66.

Carrithers, Michael. "On Polytropy: Or the Natural Condition of Spiritual Cosmopolitanism in India: The Digambar Jain Case." *Modern Asian Studies* 34.4 (2000): 831–861.

Cort, John E. "Mūrtipūjā in Śvetāmbar Jain Temples," in *Religion in India*, ed. T. N. Mandan, pp. 212–223. Delhi: Oxford University Press, 1991.

———. "Two Ideals of the Śvetāmbara Mūrtipūjak Jain Layman." *Journal of Indian Philosophy* 19 (1991): 391–420.

———. "Śvetāmbar Mūrtipūjak Jain Scripture in a Performative Context," in *Texts in Context: Traditional Hermeneutics in South Asia*, ed. Jeffrey R. Timm, pp. 171–194. Albany: State University of New York Press, 1992.

———. "Jain Questions and Answers: Who Is God and How Is He Worshiped?" in *Religions of India in Practice*, ed. Donald S. Lopez, Jr., pp. 598–608. Princeton, N.J.: Princeton University Press, 1995.

———. "The Rite of Veneration of the Jina Images," in *Religions of India in Practice*, ed. Donald S. Lopez, Jr., pp. 326–332. Princeton, N.J.: Princeton University Press, 1995.

———. "Tantra in Jainism: The Cult of Ghaṇṭākarṇ Mahāvīr, the Great Hero Bell-Ears." *Bulletin d'Études Indiennes* 15 (1997): 115–133.

———. *Jains in the World: Religious Values and Ideology in India*. New York: Oxford University Press, 2001.

———. "Bhakti in the Early Jain Tradition: Understanding Devotional Religion in South Asia." *History of Religions* 42 (2002): 59–86.

———. "Singing the Glory of Asceticism: Devotion of Asceticism in Jainism." *Journal of the American Academy of Religion* 70.4 (December 2002): 719–742.

———. "Devotional Culture in Jainism: Mānatuṅga and His *Bhaktāmara Stotra*," in *South Asian Religion and History in Culture: Essays in Honor of David Maclay Knipe*, ed. James Blumenthal, forthcoming.

Dundas, Paul. "Haribhadra on Giving." *Journal of Indian Philosophy* 30 (2002): 1–44.

———. "Some Jain Versions of the 'Act of Truth' Theme," in *Nirgrantha: Festschrift for Muni Jambūvijayajī*, ed. J. B. Jain. Ahmedabad: Sharadaben Chimanbhai Educational Research Centre, forthcoming.

Flügel, Peter. "Jaina Mahāyāna: Sīmandhar Svāmī and the Akram Vijñān Movement in Western India," in *Devotion in the South Asian Tradition*, ed. John Brockington and Anna King. Delhi: Permanent Black, forthcoming.

Granoff, Phyllis. "Worship as Commemoration: Pilgrimage, Death, and Dying in Medieval Jainism." *Bulletin d'Études Indiennes* 10 (1992): 181–202.

———. "Divine Delicacies: Monks, Images, and Miracles in the Contest between Jainism and Buddhism," in *Images, Miracles, and Authority in Asian Religious Traditions*, ed. Richard Davis, pp. 57–97. Boulder, Colo.: Westview, 1998.

———. "Other People's Rituals: Ritual Eclecticism in Early Medieval Indian Religions." *Journal of Indian Philosophy* 28 (2000): 399–424.

———. "My Rituals and My Gods: Ritual Exclusiveness in Medieval India." *Journal of Indian Philosophy* 29 (2001): 109–134.

Humphrey, Caroline. "Some Aspects of the Jain Puja: The Idea of 'God' and the Symbolism of Offerings." *Cambridge Anthropology* 9.3 (1984): 1–19.

Humphrey, Caroline, and James Laidlaw. *The Archetypal Actions of Ritual: A Theory of Ritual Illustrated by the Jain Rite of Worship*. Oxford: Clarendon Press, 1994.

Jain, Jagdish Chandra. "The Medieval Bhakti Movement: Its Influence on Jainism," in *Medieval Bhakti Movements in India*, ed. N. N. Bhattacharyya, pp. 62–73. Delhi: Munshiram Manoharlal, 1989.

Kelting, M. Whitney. *Singing to the Jinas: Jain Laywomen, Maṇḍal Singing, and the Negotiations of Jain Devotion*. New York: Oxford University Press, 2001.

Laidlaw, James. "Profit, Salvation, and Profitable Saints." *Cambridge Anthropology* 9.3 (1984): 50–70.

Mahias, M. C. *Délivrance et convivialité: Le système culinaire des Jaina*. Paris: Maison des Sciences de l'Homme, 1985.

McCormick, Thomas. "The Jaina Ascetic as Manifestation of the Sacred," in *Sacred Places, Sacred Spaces: The Geography of Pilgrimages*, ed. Robert H. Stoddard and Alan Morinis, pp. 235–256. Also, *Geoscience and Man*, vol. 34. Baton Rouge, La., Geoscience Publications, 1997.

Mishra, Madhusudan. *A Critical Study of Amrtacandra*'s Puruṣārthasiddhupayah. (Text on lay vows and conduct.) Calcutta: Punti-Pustak, 1992.

Misra, R. "The Jains in an Urban Setting." *Bulletin of the Anthropological Survey of India* 21.1 (1972): 1–67.

Orr, Leslie C. *Donors, Devotees, and Daughters of God: Temple Women in Medieval Tamilnadu*. New York: Oxford University Press, 2000.

———. "Women's Wealth and Worship: Female Patronage of Hinduism, Jainism, and Buddhism in Medieval Tamilnadu," in *Faces of the Feminine in Ancient, Medieval, and Modern India*, ed. M. Bose, pp. 124–147. New York: Oxford University Press, 2000.

Roth, Gustav. "Notes on the *Pamca-Namokkara Parama-Mangala* in Jaina Literature." *Brahmavidya* (*Adyar Library Bulletin*) 38 (1974): 1–18.

Settar, S. *Inviting Death: Historical Experiments on Sepulchral Hill*. Dharwad: Institute of Indian Art History, Karnatak University, 1986. Republished as *Inviting Death: Indian Attitude toward the Ritual Death*. Leiden: E. J. Brill, 1989.

———. *Pursuing Death: Philosophy and Practice of Voluntary Termination of Life*. Dharwad: Institute of Indian Art History, Karnatak University, 1990.

Williams, R. *Jaina Yoga: A Survey of the Mediaeval Śrāvakācāras*. (Study of texts on lay conduct.) London: Oxford University Press, 1963; reprint, Delhi: Motilal Banarsidass, 1991.

SOCIAL ORGANIZATION, INSTITUTIONS, AND MENDICANT AND LAY COMMUNITY LIFE

Agarwal, Binod C. "Diksa Ceremony in Jainism: An Analysis of Its Socio-Political Ramifications." *Eastern Anthropologist* 31 (1972): 12–31.

Babb, Lawrence A. *Alchemies of Violence: Myths of Identity and the Life of Trade in Western India*. New Delhi: Sage, forthcoming.

Balbir, Nalini. "Women in Jainism," in *Religion and Women*, ed. A. Sharma, pp. 121–138. Albany: State University of New York Press, 1994.

———. "Le baton monastique jaina: fonctions, symbolisme, controverses," in *Vividharatnakaraṇḍaka: Festgabe für Adelheid Mette*, ed. Christine Chojnacki, Jens-Uwe Hartmann, and Volker M. Tschannerl, pp. 17–56. Swistall-Odendorf: Indica et Tibetica Verlag, 2000.

———. "La question de l'ordination des enfants en milieu jaina," in *Les Ages de la Vie dans le Monde Indien*, ed. Christine Chojnacki, pp. 153–183. Lyon: Centre d'Études et de Recherches sur l'Occident Romain de l'Université de Lyon, 2001.

Banks, Marcus. "Caste, Sect, and Property: Relations in the Jain Community of Jamnagar, Gujarat." *Cambridge Anthropology* 9.3 (1984): 34–49.

———. "Defining Division: An Historical Overview of Jain Social Organization." *Modern Asian Studies* 20 (1986): 447–460.

———. "Why Move? Regional and Long Distance Migrations of Gujarati Jains," in *Migration: The Asian Experience*, ed. J. M. Brown and R. Foot, pp. 131–148. London: St. Martin's, 1994.

Bose, L. C. "Women's Wealth and Worship: Female Patronage of Hinduism, Jainism, and Buddhism," in *Faces of the Feminine in Ancient, Medieval, and Modern India*, ed. M. Bose, pp. 124–147. New York: Oxford University Press, 2000.

Brekke, Torkel. *Makers of Modern Indian Religion in the Late Nineteenth Century*. Oxford: Oxford University Press, 2002.

Caillat, Colette. *Atonements in the Ancient Ritual of the Jaina Monks*. L. D. Series no. 40. Ahmedabad: L. D. Institute of Indology, 1975.

Carrithers, Michael. "Naked Ascetics in Southern Digambar Jainism." *Man* 24.2 (1989): 219–235.

———. "Concretely Imagining the Southern Digambar Jain Community, 1899–1920." *Modern Asian Studies* 30.3 (July 1996): 523–548.

Cort, John E. "The Śvetāmbar Mūrtipūjak Jain Mendicant." *Man* (n.s.) 26 (1991): 549–569.

———. "Two Models of the Śvetāmbara Mūrtipūjak Jain Layman." *Journal of Indian Philosophy* 19 (1991): 391–420.

———. "The Gift of Food to the Wandering Cow: Lay-Mendicant Interactions among the Śvetāmbar Mūrtipūjak Jains," in *Ascetic Culture: Renunciation and*

Worldly Engagement, ed. K. Ishwaran, pp. 89–110. Leiden: E. J. Brill, 1999. Also, *Journal of Asian and African Studies* 34 (1999): 89–110.

———. "The Intellectual Formation of a Jain Monk: A Śvetāmbara Monastic Curriculum." *Journal of Indian Philosophy* 29 (2001): 327–349.

———. "How Jains Know What They Know: A Lay Jain Curriculum," in *Nirgrantha: Festschrift for Muni Jambūvijayajī*, ed. J. B. Jain. Ahmedabad: Sharadaben Chimanbhai Educational Research Centre, forthcoming.

Deo, Shantaram B. *History of Jaina Monachism from Inscriptions and Literature*. Poona: Deccan College Postgraduate and Research Institute, 1956.

Derrett, J. Dundan M. "Hemācārya's *Arhannīti*: An Original Jaina Juridical Work of the Middle Ages." *Annals of the Bhandarkar Oriental Research Institute* 57 (1976): 1–21.

Doss, M. "Jains and Entrepreneurship: Interplay of Religion and Society towards Ecomonic Progress," in *Religion, Society, and Economics: Eastern and Western Perspectives in Dialogue*. Frankfurt: Peter Lang, 2003.

Flügel, Peter. "Askse und Devotion: Das rituelle Systeme der Terapanth Svetambara Jains." Ph.D. dissertation, Johannes-Gutenberg Universität, Mainz, 1994.

———. "The Ritual Circle of the Terāpanth Śvetāmbara Jains." *Bulletin d'Études Indiennes* 13–14 (1995–1996): 117–176.

———. "The Code of Conduct of the Terāpanth Samaṇ Order." *South Asian Research* 23.1 (2003): 7–53.

———. "Demographic Trends in Jain Monasticism," in *Doctrines and Dialogues: Studies in Jain History and Culture*, ed. Peter Flügel. London: Routledge Curzon, forthcoming.

Fohr, Sherry E. "Gender and Chastity: Female Jain Renouncers." Ph.D. dissertation, University of Virginia, 2001.

Granoff, Phyllis. "Patrons, Overlords, and Artisans: Some Comments on the Intracacies of Religious Donation in Medieval Jainism." *Bulletin of the Deccan College Post-Graduate and Research Institute* 54–55 (1994–1995): 269–291.

Jain, Jagdish Chandra. *Life in Ancient India as Depicted in the Jain Canon and Commentaries: 6th century BC to 17th century AD*. New Delhi: Munshiram Manoharlal, 1984.

Jain, Muni Uttam Kamal. *Jaina Sects and Schools*. Delhi: Concept Publishing, 1975.

Jain, Ravindra K. *The Universe as Audience: Metaphor and Community among the Jains of North India*. Shimla: Indian Institute of Advanced Study, 1999.

Kelting, Whitney M. "Writing Great Laywomen: Jain Memorials and Contested Ideals." *Bulletin d'Études Indiennes* 19 (2002): 201–218.

———. "Good Wives, Family Protectors: Writing Jain Laywomen's Memorials." *Journal of the American Academy of Religion* 71.3 (September 2003): 637–657.

Laidlaw, James. *Riches and Renunciation: Religion, Economy, and Society among the Jains*. Oxford: Clarendon Press, 1995.

———. "A Free Gift Makes No Friends." *Journal of the Royal Anthropological Institute* (n.s.) 6.4 (December 2000): 617–634.

Lodrick, D. O. *Sacred Cows, Sacred Places: The Origin and Survival of Animal Homes in India*. Berkeley: University of California Press, 1981.

Munzer, Stephen R. "Heroism, Spiritual Development, and Triadic Bonds in Jain and Christian Mendicancy and Almsgiving." *Numen* 48 (2001): 47–80.

Nevaskar, B. *Capitalists without Capitalism: The Jains of India and the Quakers of the West*. Westport, Conn.: Greenwood, 1971.

Prasad, Nand Kishore. *Studies in Buddhist and Jaina Monachism*. Muzaffarpur: Research Institute of Prakrit, Jainology, and Ahimsa, 1972.

Reynell, Josephine. "Renunciation and Ostentation: A Jain Paradox." *Cambridge Anthropology* 9.3 (1984): 20–33.

———. "Honour, Nurture, and Festivity: Aspects of Female Religiosity amongst Jain Women in Jaipur." Ph.D. dissertation, University of Cambridge, 1985.

———. "Prestige, Honour and the Family: Laywomen's Religiosity amongst the Śvetāmbar Mūrtipūjak Jains in Jaipur." *Bulletin d'Études Indiennes* 5 (1987): 313–359.

Salter, Emma. "Raj Bhakta Marg: The Path of Devotion to Srimad Rajacandra, a Jain Community in the Twenty-First Century." Ph.D. dissertation, University of Cardiff, 2003.

Sangave, Vilas A. *Jaina Community: A Social Survey*, second rev. ed. Bombay: Popular Prakashan, 1980.

Sen, Amulya Chandra. *Schools and Sects in Jaina Literature*. Calcutta: Viśva Bhāratī Series no. 3, 1931.

Sen, Madhu. *A Cultural Study of the* Niśītha Cūrṇi. Amritsar: Sohanlal Jaindharma Pracharak Samiti, 1975.

Shāntā, N. *The Unknown Pilgrims: The Voice of the Sādhvis. The History, Spirituality, and Life of the Jaina Women Ascetics*, trans. Mary Rogers. Delhi: Sri Satguru Publications, 1997.

Tatia, Nathmal, and Muni Mahendra Kumar. *Aspects of Jaina Monasticism*. New Delhi: Today & Tomorrow's Printers and Publishers, 1981.

Tukol, T. K. *Sallekhanā Is Not Suicide*. L. D. Series no. 55. Ahmedabad: L. D. Institute of Indology, 1976.

Tuschen, Stefanie. "Das Bhaṭṭāraka-Amt bei den Digambara-Jainas in Karṇāṭaka." Magisterarbeit im Fachgebiet Religionswissenschaft, Philipps-Universität, Marburg, Germany, 1997.

Vallely, Anne. *Guardians of the Transcendent: An Ethnography of a Jain Ascetic Community*. Toronto: University of Toronto Press, 2002.

BIOGRAPHY, MYTHOLOGY, AND NARRATIVE LITERATURE

Jain Mahābhāratas, Rāmāyaṇas, Purāṇas, and Universal Histories

Bai, B. N. Sumitra, and Robert J. Zydenbos. "The Jaina *Mahābhārata*," in *Essays on the Mahābhārata*, ed. A. Sharma, pp. 251–273. Leiden: E. J. Brill, 1982.

Bandyopadhyay, Sankar Prasad. "A Study on the Jaina-Purāṇas." *Jain Journal* 34.2 (October 1999): 91–101.

Bloomfield, Maurice. *The Life and Stories of the Jaina Savior Pārśvanātha*. Baltimore: Johns Hopkins University Press, 1919.

Chaugule, B. A., and N. V. Vaidya, trans. Paumacariyam *of Vimalasūri*. (Trans. of chapters 1–4.) Thalakwadi, Belgaum: B. A. Chaugule and N. V. Vaidya, 1936.

Cort, John E. "An Overview of the Jaina Purāṇas," in *Purāṇa Perennis: Reciprocity and Transformation in Hindu and Jaina Texts*, ed. Wendy Doniger, pp. 185–206. Albany: State University of New York Press, 1993.

Fynes, R. C. C., trans. *The Lives of the Jain Elders* (*Sthavirāvalīcaritra* of Hemacandra). Oxford: Oxford University Press, 1998.

Jain, Hiralal, and Adinath N. Upadhye. *Mahāvīra: His Times and His Philosophy of Life*. Varaṇasi: Bhāratīya Jñānapīṭha, 1974; third ed., 1998.

Jaini, Padmanabh S., trans. "*Pāṇḍava-Purāṇa* of Vādicandra: Text and Translation." *Journal of Indian Phiosophy* 25.1 (1997): 91–127 (Cantos I and II); 25.6 (1997): 517–560 (Cantos III and IV); 27.3 (1999): 215–278 (Cantos V and VI).

Johnson, Helen M. *The Lives of Sixty-three Illustrious Persons* (translation of *Triṣaṣṭiśalākāpuruṣacaritra* of Hemacandra). 6 vols. Gaekwad's Oriental Series, vols. 51, 77, 108, 125, 139, 140. Baroda: Oriental Institute, 1931–1962.

Kashalikār, M. J. "Hemacandra's Version of the Mahābhārata." *Journal of the Oriental Institute, Baroda* 19.1–2 (1969): 234–246.

Kulkarni, V. M. "The Jaina Rāmāyaṇas and Their Source," in *The Ramayana Tradition in Asia*, ed. V. Raghavan, pp. 57–59. New Delhi: Sahitya Akademi, 1980.

———. *The Story of Rāma in Jain Literature*. Ahmedabad: Saraswati Pustak Bhandar, 1990.

Lalwani, K. C., trans. "Life of Mahāvīra" (trans. of Canto 74, vv. 14–380 of the *Mahāpurāṇa*). *Jain Journal* 7.4 (April 1973): 200–218.

Malvania, Dalsukh. "The Story of Bharata and Bāhubali." *Jain Journal* 15 (April 1981): 141–152.

Shah, Umakant P. "*Rāmāyaṇa* in Jaina Tradition," in *Asian Variations in* Rāmāyaṇa, ed. K. R. Srinivasa Iyengar, pp. 226–241. New Delhi: Sahitya Akademi, 1983.

Sikdar, J. C. "Kulakara System of Society as Depicted in the Jaina Agamas." *Jain Journal* 7.3 (January 1973): 142–150.

Strohl, G. Ralph. "The Image of the Hero in Jainism: Ṛṣabha, Bharata, and Bāhubali in the *Ādipurāṇa* of Jinasena," Ph.D. dissertation, University of Chicago Divinity School, 1984.

Upadhye, Adinath N. "Jinasena and His Works," in *Mélanges d'Indianisme à la Mémoire de Louis Renou,* pp. 727–732. Paris: Publications de l'Institut de Civilisation Indienne, 1968.

Narrative Literature and Kāvya

Babb, Lawrence A. "Time and Temples: On Social and Metrical Antiquity," in *Ethnography and Personhood: Notes from the Field,* ed. Michael W. Meister, pp. 193–222. Jaipur: Rawat Publications, 2000.

Balbir, Nalini. "The Monkey and the Weaver-Bird: Jaina Versions of a Pan-Indian Tale." *Journal of the American Oriental Society* 105 (1985): 119–134.

———. "Scènes d'alchimie dans la littérature jaina." *Journal of the European Ayurvedic Society* 1 (1990): 149–164.

———. "The Story of Solomon's Judgment Revisted," in *Tessitori and Rajasthan* (Proceedings of the International Conference Bikaner, 21–23 February 1996), ed. Donatella Dolcini and Fausto Freschi, pp. 65–99. Udine: Società Indologica Luigi Pio Tessitori, 1999.

Bender, E., ed. and trans. *The Sālibhadra-Dhanna-Carita (The Tale of the Quest for Ultimate Release by Sālibhadra and Dhanna). A Work in Old Gujarātī.* New Haven, Conn.: American Oriental Society, 1992.

Bloomfield, Maurice. "The Śālibhadra Caritra: A Story of Conversion to Jaina Monkhood." *Journal of the American Oriental Society* 43 (1923): 257–313.

Bruhn, Klaus. "Bibliography of Studies Connected with the Āvaśyaka Commentaries," in *Catalogue of the Papers of Ernst Leumann in the Institute for the Culture and History of India and Tibet, University of Hamburg,* comp. B. Plutat, pp. 119–136. Stuttgart: Franz Steiner, 1998.

Chakravarti, A. *Jaina Literature in Tamil.* Delhi: Bhāratīya Jñānapīṭha, 1974.

Chaugule, B. A., and N. V. Vaidya, trans. Samarāichcha-Kahā *of Haribhadrasūri,* trans. of chapter 6. Belgaum: B. A. Chaugule and N. V. Vaidya, 1936.

Dundas, Paul. "The Jain Monk Jinapati Sūri Gets the Better of a Nāth Yogī," in *Tantra in Practice,* ed. David. G. White, pp. 231–238. Princeton, N.J.: Princeton University Press, 2000.

Ghatage, A. M. "Narrative Literature in Jain Mahārāṣṭrī." *Journal of the Bhandarkar Oriental Research Institute* 36 (1934–1935): 26–43.

Granoff, Phyllis. "This Was My Life: Autobiographical Reflections and the Quest for Liberation in Medieval Jain Story Literature." *Annals of the Bhandarkar Oriental Research Institute* 75 (1994): 25–50.

———. "Jain Stories Inspiring Renunciation," in *Religions of India in Practice*, ed. Donald S. Lopez, Jr., pp. 412–417. Princeton, N.J.: Princeton University Press, 1995.

———. "The Jina Bleeds: Threats to the Faith in Medieval Jain Stories," in *Images, Miracles, and Authority in Asian Religious Traditions*, ed. Richard Davis, pp. 55–97. Boulder, Colo.: Westview Press, 1998.

———, ed. *The Clever Adulteress and Other Stories: A Treasury of Jain Literature*. Oakville, Ontario: Mosaic Press, 1990; reprint, Delhi: Motilal Banarsidass, 1993.

———, trans. *The Forest of Thieves and the Magic Garden: An Anthology of Medieval Jain Stories*. Delhi: Penguin Books, 1998.

Handiqui, K. K. *Yaśastilaka and Indian Culture*, second ed. Sholapur: Jaina Saṃskṛti Saṃrakshaka Sangha, 1968.

Jain, Jagdish Chandra. *The* Vasudevahiṇḍi: *An Authentic Jain Version of the* Bṛhatkathā. L. D. Series no. 59. Ahmedabad: L. D. Institute of Indology, 1977.

———. *Prakrit Narrative Literature: Origin and Growth*. New Delhi: Munshiram Manoharlal, 1981.

Jain, Prem Suman, ed. *Significance of Prakrit Narrative Literature*. Mysore: Department of Jainology and Prakrits, University of Mysore, 1986.

Jamkhedkar, A. P. Vasudevahimdi: *A Cultural Study*. Delhi: Agam, 1984.

Kulkarni, V. M., ed. *A Treasury of Jain Tales*. Ahmedabad: Sharadaben Chimanbhai Educational Centre, 1994.

Kumar, Muni Mahendra, trans. *Jaina Stories as Gleaned from Canonical Texts*, English trans. K. C. Lalwani. Delhi: Motilal Banarsidass, 1984.

Lefeber, R. "Jain Stories of Miraculous Power," in *Religions of India in Practice*, ed. Donald S. Lopez, Jr., pp. 426–433. Princeton, N.J.: Princeton University Press, 1995.

Nawab, Sarabhai Manilal. *The Collection of Kalaka Story, part 1, English Version, History, Legends, and Miniature Paintings*. Ahmedabad: Sarabhai Manilal Nawab, 1958.

Ryan, James D. "The *Cīvakacintāmaṇi* in Historical Perspective." Ph.D. dissertation, University of California, Berkeley, 1985.

Sandesara, Bhogilal J. *Literary Circle of Mahāmātya Vastupāla and Its Contribution to Sanskrit Literature*. Bombay: Bharatiya Vidya Bhavan, 1953.

Sharma, T. R. S., trans. *Janna: Tale of the Glory-Bearer, the Episode of Candaśāsana*. New Delhi: Penguin Books India, 1994.

Tawney, C. H., trans. *The* Kathākośa *or Treasury of Stories*. London: Royal Asiatic Society, 1895; reprint, New Delhi: Munshiram Manoharlal, 1975.

———. *The* Prabandhacintāmaṇi *or Wishing-stone of Narratives*. Calcutta: Asiatic Society of Bengal, 1901; reprint, Delhi: Indian Gallery, 1982.

Vijayalakshmy, R. *A Study of* Cīvakacintāmaṇi. L. D. Series no. 82. Ahmedabad: L. D. Institute of Indology, 1981.

Biography

Banārasīdāsa. *Ardhakathānaka: Half a Tale*. Translated, introduced, and annotated by Mukund Lath. Jaipur: Prakrit Bharati Academy, 1981.

Bhandari, S. M. *Shrimaj Jayachandra: A Spiritual Apostle*. Jodhpur: S. M. Bhandari, 1976.

Bhatnagar, R. P., ed. *Acharya Tulsi: Fifty Years of Selfless Dedication*. Ladnun: Jain Vishva Bharati, 1985.

Bühler, G. *The Life of Hemacandrācārya*, trans. Manilal Patel. Shantiniketan: Siṅghī Jaina Jñānapīṭha, 1936.

Granoff, Phyllis. "The Miracle of a Religious Biography without Miracles: Jain Biographies of the Pratyekabuddha Karakandu." *Journal of Indian Philosophy* 14 (1986): 390–404.

———. "The Jain Biographies of Haribhadra: An Inquiry into the Origins of the Legends." *Journal of Indian Philosophy* 16 (1988): 1–24.

———. "The Jain Biographies of Siddhasena: A Study of the Texture of Allusion and the Weaving of a Group Image." *Journal of Indian Philosophy* 17 (1989): 329–384, and 18 (1990): 109–125.

———. "Religious Biographies and Clan Histories among the Śvetāmbara Jains of North India." *East and West* 39 (1989): 195–215.

———. "The Politics of Religious Biography: The Biography of Balibhadra the Usurper." *Bulletin d'Études Indiennes* 9 (1991): 75–91.

———. "The Householder as Shaman: Jain Biographies of Temple Builders." *East and West* 42 (1992): 301–317.

———. "Biographical Writing amongst the Śvetāmbara Jains," in *According to Tradition: Hagiographical Writing in India*, ed. Rupert Snell and W. Callewaert. Wiesbaden: Otto Harrassowitz, 1994.

———. "From Detatchment to Engagement: The Construction of the Holy Man in Medieval Śvetāmbara Jain Literature," in *Constructions hagiographiques dans le monde indien*, ed. Francoise Mallison, pp. 97–121. Paris: Librairie Honoré Champion, 2001.

Granoff, Phyllis, and Koichi Shinohara. *Speaking of Monks: Religious Biography in Asia*. Oakville, Ontario: Mosaic Press, 1992.

———, eds. *Monks and Magicians: Religious Biography in Asia*. Oakville, Ontario: Mosaic Press, 1988; reprint, Delhi: Motilal Banarsidass, 1994.

———, eds. *Other Selves: Autobiography and Biography in Cross-Cultural Persepctive*. Oakville, Ontario: Mosaic Press, 1994.

Mahāprajña, Yuvācārya. *Steering the Wheel of Dhamma: A Biography of Acharya Sri Tulsi*, trans. R. K. Seth. Ladnun: Jain Vishva Bharati, 1994.

Nathmal, Muni (= Ācārya Mahāprajña). *Acharya Bhikṣu: The Man and His Philosophy*, trans. N. Sahal. Delhi: Adarsh Sahitya Sangh Prakashan, 1968.

Sharma, Jagdish P. "Hemacandra: The Life and Scholarship of a Jaina Monk." *Asian Profile* 3 (1975): 195–215.

Sunavala, A. J. *Vijaya Dharma Suri: His Life and Work*. Cambridge: Cambridge University Press, 1922.

Mythology

Cort, John E. "Medieval Jaina Goddess Traditions." *Neumen* 34 (1987): 235–255.

———. "Absences and Transformations: Ganesh in the Shvetambar Jain Tradition," in *Ganesh the Benevolent*, ed. Pratapaditya Pal, pp. 81–94. Bombay: Marg Publications, 1995.

Deleu, Jozef. "Die Mythologie des Jainismus," in *Wörterbuch der Mythologie*, vol. 1.5, *Götter und Mythen des Indischen Subkontinents*, ed. H. W. Haussig, pp. 207–284. Stuttgart: E. Klett, 1984.

Dhaky, M. A., ed. *Arhat Pārśva and Dharaṇendra Nexus*. Ahmedabad: L. D. Institute of Indology, and Delhi: Bhogilal Leherchand Institute of Indology, 1997.

Jha, S. *Aspects of Brahmanical Influence on the Jaina Mythology*. Delhi: Bharat Bharati Bhandar, 1978.

Shah, Umakant P. "Minor Jaina Deities." *Journal of the Oriental Institute, Baroda* 31.3 (March 1982): 274–290, and 31.4 (June 1982): 371–378.

Sharma, J. P. *Jaina Yakshas*. Meerut: Kusumanjali Prakashan, 1994.

Zydenbos, Robert J. "The Jain Goddess Padmavati," in *Contacts between Cultures: South Asia*, vol. 2, ed. K. I. Koppedrayer. Lewiston, N.Y.: Edwin Mellen Press, 1990.

———. "Jaina Goddesses in Kannada Literature," in *Studies in South Asian Devotional Literature: Research Papers 1988–1991*, ed. A. W. Entwistle and F. Mallison, pp. 135–145. New Delhi: Manohar, and Paris: L'École Francaise d'Extreme Orient, 1994.

ART, ARCHITECTURE, AND ICONOGRAPHY

Alphen, Jan van, ed. *Steps to Liberation: 2,500 Years of Jain Art and Religion*. Antwerp: Ethnografisch Museum, 2000.

Asher, Catherine B. "North India's Urban Landscape: The Place of the Jain Temple." *Islamic Culture* 73 (1999): 109–150.

Basu, Chandreyi. "Redefining the Nature of Cultural Regions in Early India: Mathurā and the Meaning of 'Kuṣāṇa' Art (1st–3rd Centuries A.D.)." Ph.D. dissertation, University of Pennsylvania, 2001.

Bhattacharya, B. C. *The Jaina Iconography*. Delhi: Motilal Banarsidass, 1974.

Brown, William N. *The Story of Kālaka*. Washington, D.C.: Smithsonian Institution, Freer Gallery of Art, 1933.

———. *A Descriptive and Illustrated Catalogue of Miniature Paintings of the Jaina* Kalpa-sūtra *as Executed in the Early Western Indian Style*. Washington, D.C.: Smithsonian Institution, Freer Gallery of Art, 1934.

———. *Manuscript Illustrations of the* Uttarādhyayana Sūtra. American Oriental Series, vol. 2. New Haven, Conn.: American Oriental Society, 1941.

Bruhn, Klaus. *The Jina-Images of Deogarh.* Leiden: E. J. Brill, 1969.

———. "The Grammar of Jina Iconography I." *Berliner Indologische Studien* 8 (1995): 229–283.

———. "The Grammar of Jina Iconography II." *Berliner Indologische Studien* 13/14 (2000): 273–337.

Caillat, Colette, and R. Kumar. *The Jain Cosmology*, trans. R. Norman. Basel: R. Kumar, and Bombay: Jaico Publishing House, 1981.

Coomaraswamy, Ananda K. *Jaina Art.* New Delhi: Munshiram Manoharlal, 1994.

Cort, John E. "Connoisseurs and Devotees: Lockwood de Forest and the Metropolitan Museum of Art's Jain Temple Ceiling." *Orientations* 25.3 (March 1994): 68–74.

Doshi, Saryu. *Masterpieces of Jain Painting.* Bombay: Marg Publications, 1985.

Fischer, Eberhard, and Jyotindra Jain. *Art and Rituals: 2,500 Years of Jainism in India.* New Delhi: Sterling Publishers, 1977.

Ghosh, A., ed. *Jaina Art and Architecture.* 3 vols. New Delhi: Bhāratīya Jñānapīṭha, 1974.

Ghosh, N. *Sri Sarasvati in Indian Art.* Delhi: Sri Satguru Publishers, 1984.

Jain, Jyotindra, and Eberhard Fischer. *Jaina Iconography.* 2 vols. Leiden: E. J. Brill, 1978.

Joshi, N. P. "Early Jaina Icons from Mathurā," in *Mathurā: The Cultural Heritage*, ed. Doris M. Srinivasan, pp. 332–367. New Delhi: Manohar and American Institute of Indian Studies, 1989.

Laughlin, Jack C. *Ārādhakamūrti/Adhiṣṭhāyakamūrti: Popular Piety, Politics, and the Medieval Jain Temple Portrait.* New York: Peter Lang, 2003.

Leoshko, Janice. "Depicting a Peaceful Victory." *Orientations* 25.10 (October 1994): 58–66.

Mohapatra, R. P. *Jaina Monuments of Orissa.* New Delhi: D. K. Publishers, 1984.

Motichandra (with U. P. Shah). *New Documents of Jaina Painting.* Bombay: Mahāvīra Jaina Vidyālaya, 1975.

Nagar, Shantilal. *Iconography of Jaina Deities*, 2 vols. Delhi: Shantilal Nagar, 1999.

Nagarajaiah, Hampa. *Mānastambha: Jaina Pillar of Eminence.* Bangalore: C. V. G. Publications, 2000.

———. *Indra in Jaina Iconography.* Hombuja: Sri Siddhantakirti Granthamale, 2002.

Pal, Pratapaditya, ed. *The Peaceful Liberators: Jain Art from India.* Los Angeles: Los Angeles County Museum of Art, 1994.

Pereira, José. *Monolithic Jinas: The Iconography of the Jain Temples of Ellora.* Delhi: Motilal Banarsidass, 1977.

Quintanilla, Sonya R. "Emergence of the Stone Sculptural Tradition at Mathura: Mid-Second Century B.C.–First Century A.D." Ph.D. dissertation, Harvard University, 1999.

———. "Āyāgapaṭas: Characteristics, Symbolism, and Chronology." *Artibus Asiae* 60 (2000): 79–137.

———. "Closer to Heaven than the Gods: Jain Monks in the Art of Pre-Kushan Mathura." *Marg* 52 (2001): 57–68.

Settar, S. "The Cult of Jvālāmālinī and the Earliest Images of Jvālā and Śyāma." *Artibus Asiae* 31 (1969): 309–320.

Shah, Umakant P. "Age of Differentiation of Digambara and Śvetāmbara Images and the Earliest Known Śvetāmbara Bronzes." *Bulletin of the Prince of Wales Museum of Western India* 1 (1952): 100–113.

———. *Studies in Jaina Art*. Varanasi: Jaina Cultural Research Society, 1955.

———. *Jaina-Rūpa-Maṇḍana: Volume One*. New Delhi: Abhinav Publications, 1987.

Shah, Umakant P., and Ernest Bender. "Mathurā and Jainism," in *Mathurā: The Cultural Heritage*, ed. Doris M. Srinivasan, pp. 209–213. New Delhi: Manohar and American Institute of Indian Studies, 1989.

Shah, Umakant P., and M. A. Dhaky. *Aspects of Jaina Art and Architecture*. Ahmedabad: Gujarat State Committee for the Celebration of 2,500th Anniversary of Bhagavan Mahavira Nirvana, 1975.

Sivaramamurti, C. *Panorama of Jain Art*. New Delhi: Times of India, 1983.

Thapylal, Kiran Kumar. *Jaina Paintings*. New Delhi: Wiley Eastern, 1995.

Tiwari, M. N. P. *Ambikā in Jaina Art and Literature*. New Delhi: Bhāratīya Jñānapīṭha, 1989.

———. "Studies on Jaina Art: A Brief Survey and Prospectus." *Jain Journal* 27.4 (April 1993): 210–214.

Wayman, Alex. "The Mathurā Set of Aṣṭamaṅgala (Eight Auspicious Symbols) in Early and Later Times," in *Mathurā: The Cultural Heritage*, ed. Doris M. Srinivasan, pp. 236–246. New Delhi: Manohar, and American Institute of Indian Studies, 1989.

Vyas, R. T., ed. *Studies in Jaina Art and Iconography and Allied Subjects*. Vadodara: Oriental Institute, and New Delhi: Abhinav Publications, 1995.

SACRED PLACES

Balbir, Nalini. "Recent Developments in a Jaina Tīrtha: Hastināpur (U.P.)," in *The History of Sacred Places in India as Reflected in Traditional Literature*, ed. H. Bakker, pp. 177–85. Leiden: E. J. Brill, 1990.

Carrithers, M. "Passions of Nation and Community in the Bahubali Affair." *Modern Asian Studies* 22 (1988): 815–844.

Chojnacki, Christine. "Monts sacrés et alchimie jaina au Moyen Age: L'*Ujjayantakalpa* de Jinaprabhasūri (14th century)," in *Vividharatna-karaṇḍaka: Festgabe für Adelheid Mette*, ed. Christine Chojnacki, Jens-Uwe Hartmann, and Volker M. Tschannerl, pp. 139–171. Swistall-Odendorf: Indica et Tibetica Verlag, 2000.

Clermont, Lothar. *Jainism and the Temples of Mount Abu and Ranakpur*, trans. Chitra Harshvardhan. New Delhi: Prakash Books, 1998.

Cort, John E. "Pilgrimage to Shankheshvar Pārshvanāth." *Center for the Study of World Religions Bulletin* 14 (1988): 63–72.

———. "Communities, Temples, Identities: Art Histories and Social Studies in Western India," in *Ethnography and Personhood: Notes from the Field*, ed. Michael W. Meister, pp. 101–128. Jaipur: Rawat Publications, 2000.

———. "Patronage, Authority, Proprietary Rights, and History: Communities and Pilgrimage Temples in Western India," in *Ethnography and Personhood: Notes from the Field*, ed. Michael W. Meister, pp. 165–192. Jaipur: Rawat Publications, 2000.

Dhaky, M. A., and U. S. Moorti. *The Temples in Kumbhāriyā*. New Delhi: American Institute of Indian Studies, and Ahmedabad: L. D. Institute of Indology, 2001.

Doshi, Saryu. *Homage to Shravana Belgola*. Bombay: Marg Publications, 1981.

Granoff, Phyllis. "Medieval Jain Accounts of Mt. Girnār and Mt. Śatruñjaya: Visible and Invisible Sacred Realms." *Journal of the Oriental Society, Baroda*, forthcoming.

Jayantavijayaji, Muni. *Holy Abu*, trans. U. P. Shah. Bhavnagar: Śrī Yaśovijaya Jaina Granthamālā, 1954.

Kumar, Sehdev. *A Thousand Petalled Lotus: Jain Temples of Rajasthan, Architecture and Iconography*. New Delhi: Abhinav Publications, 2001.

Nagarajaiah, Hampa. *Jina Parsva Temples in Karnataka*. Hombuja: Sri Siddhantakirti Granthamale, 1999.

Sagar, Mahopadhyaya Lalitprabh. *World Renowned Jain Pilgrimages: Reverence and Art*. Jaipur: Prakrit Bharati Academy, 2000.

Sangave, Vilas A. *The Sacred Shravanabelagola: A Socio-Religious Study*. New Delhi: Bhāratīya Jñānapīṭha, 1981.

Singh, Harihar. *Jaina Temples of Western India*. Varanasi: P. V. Research Institute, 1982.

Singhvi, L. M. *Jain Temples in India and around the World*. New Delhi: Himalayan Books, 2002.

Titze, Kurt. *Jainism: A Pictorial Guide to the Religion of Non-Violence*, second ed. Delhi: Motilal Banarsidass, 2000.

Vaid, U. Pannalal, ed. *Teerth Darshan*. English ed., 3 vols. Chennai: Shree Jain Prarthana Mandir Trust, 2002.

JAINISM BEYOND SOUTH ASIA

Banks, Marcus. "Competing to Give, Competing to Get: Gujarati Jains in Britain," in *Black and Ethnic Leaderships in Britiain: The Cultural Dimensions of Political Action*, ed. M. Anwar and P. Werbner, pp. 226–250. London: Routledge, 1991.

———. *Organizing Jainism in India and England*. Oxford: Clarendon Press, 1992.

———. "Jain Ways of Being," in *Desh Pradesh: The South Asian Experience in Britain*, ed. R. Ballard, pp. 231–250. London: Hurst, 1994.

———. "Why Move? Regional and Long Distance Migrations of Gujarati Jains," in *Migration: The Asian Experience*, ed. Judith M. Brown and Rosemay Foot, pp. 131–148. New York: St. Martin's Press, and Oxford: St. Anthony's College, 1994.

Zarwan, J. "The Social Evolution of the Jains in Kenya." *Hadith* 6 (1974) (History and Social Change in Africa, ed. B. A. Ogot): 134–144.

BIBLIOGRAPHIES AND THE STUDY OF JAINISM

Bibliographies

Banerjee, Satya Ranjan. *Chhotelal Jain's Jaina Bibliography, Edited, Rearranged, Revised, and Augmented in Collaboration with the Author*, second rev. ed. New Delhi: Vir Sewa Mandir, 1982.

Bruhn, Klaus. "Bibliography of Studies Connected with the Āvaśyaka-Commentaries," in *Catalogue of the Papers of Ernst Leumann in the Institute for the Culture and History of India and Tibet, University of Hamburg*, comp. B. Plutat, pp. 119–136. Stuttgart: Franz Steiner, 1998.

Caillat, Colette, and Nalini Balbir. "Jaina Bibliography: Books and Papers Published in French or by French Scholars from 1906 to 1981." *Sambodhi* 10 (April 1981–January 1982): 1–41.

Jain, Kapoor Chand. *Bibliograhy of Prakrit and Jaina Research*, second ed. Lhatauli, Uttar Pradesh: Shri Kailash Chand Jain Memorial Trust, 1991.

Jain, Sagarmal, and Arun Pratap Singh. *Doctoral Dissertations in Jaina and Buddhist Studies*. Varanasi: P. V. Research Institute, 1983.

Satyaprakash, ed. *Jainism: A Select Bibliography*. Gurgaon: Indian Documentation Service, 1984.

Upadhye, Adinath N. *Bibliography of the Works of Dr. A. N. Upadhye*. Sholapur: Jaina Samskrti Samrakshaka Sangha, 1977.

The Study of Jainism

Bruhn, Klaus. "Jainology in Western Publications I," in *Jain Studies in Honour of Jozef Deleu*, ed. Rudy Smet and Kenji Watanabe, pp. 13–42. Tokyo: Hon-no-tomosha, 1993.

Caillat, Colette. "Jainology in Western Publications II," in *Jain Studies in Honour of Jozef Deleu*, ed. Rudy Smet and Kenji Watanabe, pp. 43–51. Tokyo: Hon-no-tomosha, 1993.

———. "Jaina Studies in Europe." *Sambodhi* 22 (1998): 1–10.

———. "Luigi Pio Tessitori and International Cooperation in the 19th–20th Century," in *Tessitori and Rajasthan* (Proceedings of the International Conference, Bikaner, 21–23 February 1996), ed. Donatella Dolcini and Fausto Freschi, pp. 7–27. Udine: Società Indologica Luigi Pio Tessitori, 1999.

Cort, John E. "Models of and for the Study of the Jains: Methods and Theory." *The Study of Religion* 2.1 (1990): 42–71.

———. "The Jain Knowledge Warehouses: Libraries in Traditional India." *Journal of the American Oriental Society* 115 (1995): 77–87.

———. "Recent Fieldwork Studies of the Contemporary Jainas." *Religious Studies Review* 23 (1997): 103–111.

———. "Jain Studies in North America: Prospects and Obstacles." *Jain Digest* 22.3 (2003): 8–10.

Dundas, Paul. "Recent Research on Jainism." *Religious Studies Review* 23 (1997): 111–119.

Flügel, Peter. "Jainism and the Western World: Jinmuktisūri and Georg Bühler and (Other Early Encounters." *Jain Journal* 34.1 (1999): 1–11.

Folkert, Kendall W. "Jaina Studies: Japan, Europe, India." *Sambodhi* 5.1–5.2 (July–October 1976): 138–147.

———. "Jain Studies," in *Scripture and Community: Collected Essays on the Jains*, ed. John E. Cort, pp. 23–33. Atlanta: Scholars Press, 1993.

Hara, Minoru. "Jainism," in *Studies on Indian Philosophy and Literature in Japan, 1973–1983*, part II-21 in the series *Asian Studies in Japan, 1973–1983*, p. 5 and pp. 18–19.

Jaini, Padmanabh S. "The Jainas and the Western Scholar." *Sambodhi* 5.2–3 (July 1976): 121–131. Reprinted with note on subsequent scholarship in P. S. Jaini, *Collected Papers on Jaina Studies*, pp. 23–36. Delhi: Motilal Banarsidass, 2000.

Johnson, D. C. "Georg Bühler and the Western Discovery of Jain Temple Libraries." *Jain Journal* 26.4 (April 1992): 197–209.

———. "The Western Discovery of the Jain Temple Libraries." *Libraries and Cultures* 28 (1993): 189–203.

Nakamura, Ḥajime. "Bibliographical Survey of Jainism." *The Journal of Intercultural Studies* 1 (1974): 51–75.

Uno, Atsushi. "Jaina Studies in Japan." *Jain Journal* 8.2 (October 1973): 73–78. Reprinted (without revisions) in *Jain Journal* 35.4 (April 2001): 173–178.